LIBRARY OF NEW TESTAMENT STUDIES

648

formerly the Journal for the Study of the New Testament Supplement series

Editor
Chris Keith

Editorial Board
Dale C. Allison, Lynn H. Cohick, Kylie Crabbe, R. Alan Culpepper,
Craig A. Evans, Jennifer Eyl, Robert Fowler, Juan Hernández Jr.,
John S. Kloppenborg, Michael Labahn, Matthew V. Novenson,
Love L. Sechrest, Robert Wall, Catrin H. Williams, Brittany E. Wilson

Character Studies in the Gospel of Matthew

Edited by Craig Evan Anderson and
Matthew Ryan Hauge

LONDON • NEW YORK • OXFORD • NEW DELHI • SYDNEY

T&T CLARK

Bloomsbury Publishing Plc, 50 Bedford Square, London, WC1B 3DP, UK
Bloomsbury Publishing Inc, 1359 Broadway, New York, NY 10018, USA
Bloomsbury Publishing Ireland, 29 Earlsfort Terrace, Dublin 2, D02 AY28, Ireland

BLOOMSBURY, T&T CLARK and the T&T Clark logo are trademarks of
Bloomsbury Publishing Plc

First published in Great Britain 2024
Paperback edition published 2025

Copyright © Craig Evan Anderson and Matthew Ryan Hauge, 2024

Craig Evan Anderson, Matthew Ryan Hauge and contributors have asserted
their right under the Copyright, Designs and Patents Act, 1988, to be identified
as Authors and Editors of this work.

All rights reserved. No part of this publication may be: i) reproduced or transmitted
in any form, electronic or mechanical, including photocopying, recording or by means
of any information storage or retrieval system without prior permission in writing from
the publishers; or ii) used or reproduced in any way for the training, development or
operation of artificial intelligence (AI) technologies, including generative AI technologies.
The rights holders expressly reserve this publication from the text and data mining
exception as per Article 4(3) of the Digital Single Market Directive (EU) 2019/790.

Bloomsbury Publishing Plc does not have any control over, or responsibility for,
any third-party websites referred to or in this book. All internet addresses given in
this book were correct at the time of going to press. The author and publisher
regret any inconvenience caused if addresses have changed or sites have ceased
to exist, but can accept no responsibility for any such changes.

A catalogue record for this book is available from the British Library.

A catalog record for this book is available from the Library of Congress.

ISBN: HB: 978-0-5676-9948-0
PB: 978-0-5676-9952-7
ePDF: 978-0-5676-9949-7
eBook: 978-0-5676-9951-0

Series: Library of New Testament Studies, 2345678X, volume 648

Typeset by RefineCatch Limited, Bungay, Suffolk

For product safety related questions contact productsafety@bloomsbury.com.

To find out more about our authors and books visit www.bloomsbury.com
and sign up for our newsletters.

To our friends, Sean Davidson and Matthew Flentie

Contents

List of Contributors		ix
List of Abbreviations		xi
Introduction *Craig Evan Anderson and Matthew Ryan Hauge*		1
1	Joseph: Faithful Jew and Exemplar of Jesus' Teachings *Heather M. Gorman*	15
2	The Passive Protagonist: The Characterization of Mary in the Gospel of Matthew 1–2 and the *Protevangelium* of James *Lily C. Vuong*	29
3	Matthew's Herodian Kings as Gentiles *Craig Evan Anderson*	41
4	John the Baptist, Prophet from the Margins *Tucker Samson Ferda*	55
5	Word and Deed: Jesus as a Teacher in the Gospel of Matthew *Melanie A. Howard*	71
6	Jesus and the Women: The Characterization of Jesus as King in Matthew's Gospel *Catherine Sider Hamilton*	83
7	Like Father, Like Son: Characterization of God the Father in Matthew's Gospel *Michael P. Knowles*	101
8	(Re)Positioning Power through Faith: Dyadic Power Theory, the Roman Centurion, and Jesus in Matthew 8:5-13 *Justin Marc Smith*	119
9	Peter: A Failed but Not a False Disciple According to Saint Matthew *David Lertis Matson*	133
10	The Corporate Portrayal of Women in the Gospel of Matthew as Narrative Disciples *Jeffery W. Aernie*	149
11	The Characterization of the Crowds in the Gospel of Matthew *Robert Cousland*	163

12	The Gentile Other in Matthew: A Theo-Ethnic Teaching Tool for Israel about to be Transformed *Anders Runesson*	175
13	Between Straw Man and Punching Bag: "Pharisees" as a Character in the Gospel of Matthew *Eric Ottenheijm*	191
14	Roman Rulers as Characters in Matthew's Gospel: Characterization, the Tyrant Trope, and Political Critique *Adam Winn*	209

Index of References	223
Index of Subjects	235

Contributors

Jeffrey W. Aernie (PhD, University of Aberdeen) is Head of School for the School of Ministry and Theology, Alphacrucis University College, Australia.

Craig Evan Anderson (PhD, Claremont Graduate University) is an independent scholar.

Robert Cousland (PhD, University of St. Andrews) is Professor of Early Christianity and Greek Religion & Mythology, University of British Columbia, Canada.

Tucker Samson Ferda (PhD, University of Pittsburgh) is Associate Professor of New Testament, Pittsburgh Theological Seminary, USA.

Heather M. Gorman (PhD, Baylor University) is Professor of New Testament, Johnson University, USA.

Catherine Sider Hamilton (PhD, University of St. Michael's College in the University of Toronto) is Professor of New Testament and Greek, Wycliffe College at the University of Toronto, Canada.

Matthew Ryan Hauge (PhD, Claremont Graduate University) is an independent scholar.

Melanie A. Howard (PhD, Princeton Theological Seminary) is Associate Professor and Program Director of Biblical and Theological Studies, Fresno Pacific University, USA.

Michael P. Knowles (Th.D., University of Toronto) is Professor and George F. Hurlburt Chair of Preaching, McMaster Divinity College, Canada.

David Lertis Matson (PhD, Baylor University) was formerly Professor of Biblical Studies, Hope International University, USA.

Eric Ottenheijm (PhD, Catholic Theological University in Utrecht) is Associate Professor for Judaism and Biblical Studies, Utrecht University, Netherlands.

Anders Runesson (PhD, Lund University) is Dean of the Faculty of Theology and Professor of New Testament, University of Oslo, Norway.

Justin Marc Smith (PhD, University of St. Andrews) is Associate Professor and Chair of Biblical and Religious Studies, Azusa Pacific University, USA.

Lily Vuong (PhD, McMaster University) is Professor of Religious Studies, Central Washington University, USA and Senior Fellow, Center for Advanced Studies: Beyond Canon, Universität Regensburg, Germany.

Adam Winn (PhD, Fuller Theological Seminary) is Assistant Professor, University of Mary Hardin-Baylor, USA.

Abbreviations

AB	Anchor Bible
ABD	David Noel Freedman (ed.), *The Anchor Bible Dictionary* (New York: Doubleday, 1992)
ABRL	The Anchor Bible Reference Library
AcT	*Acta theologica*
AJBI	*Annual of the Japanese Biblical Institute*
AJP	*American Journal of Philology*
ANTC	Abingdon New Testament Commentaries
ATD	Das Alte Testament Deutsch
AThR	*Anglican Theological Review*
BBR	*Bulletin for Biblical Research*
BDAG	F. W. Danker, W. Bauer, W. F. Arndt, and F. W. Gingrich, *Greek–English Lexicon of the New Testament and Other Early Christian Literature*, 3d edn (Chicago: University of Chicago Press, 1999).
BECNT	Baker Exegetical Commentary on the New Testament
BETL	Bibliotheca ephemeridum theologicarum lovaniensium
Bib	*Biblica*
BibInt	*Biblical Interpretation: A Journal of Contemporary Approaches*
BR	Bible Review
BTB	Biblical Theology Bulletin
BTS	Biblisch-Theologische Studien
BZ	*Biblische Zeitschrift*
BZNW	Beihefte zur ZNW
CBQ	*Catholic Biblical Quarterly*
CSHJ	Chicago Studies in the History of Judaism
CurTM	*Currents in Theology and Mission*
DJD	Discoveries in the Judean Desert
EBC	Expositor's Bible Commentary
ECL	Early Christianity and its Literature
EGGNT	Exegetical Guide to the Greek New Testament
ExpTim	*Expository Times*
FRLANT	Forschungen zur Religion und Literatur des Alten und Neuen Testaments
GSPT	Gorgias Studies in Philosophy and Theology
HTA	Historisch-Theologische Auslegung
HTR	*Harvard Theological Review*
ICC	International Critical Commentary
Int	*Interpretation*
JAAR	*Journal of the American Academy of Religion*
JBL	*Journal of Biblical Literature*
JCP	Jewish and Christian Perspectives
JETS	*Journal of the Evangelical Theological Society*

JHLT	*Journal of Hispanic / Latino Theology*
JR	*Journal of Religion*
JSJ	*Journal for the Study of Judaism in the Persian, Hellenistic and Roman Period*
JSNT	*Journal for the Study of the New Testament*
JSNTSup	*Journal for the Study of the New Testament*, Supplement Series
JSOT	*Journal for the Study of the Old Testament*
JSOTSup	*Journal for the Study of the Old Testament*, Supplement Series
JTI	*Journal for Theological Interpretation*
LNTS	Library of New Testament Studies
MNTS	McMaster New Testament Series
NAC	New American Commentary
NCBC	New Cambridge Bible Commentary
Neot	*Neotestamentica*
NIB	*The New Interpreter's Bible*
NICNT	New International Commentary on the New Testament
NIGTC	The New International Greek Testament Commentary
NovT	*Novum Testamentum*
NovTSup	*Novum Testamentum*, Supplements
NRT	*La nouvelle revue théologique*
NTL	New Testament Library
NTS	*New Testament Studies*
OBO	Orbis biblicus et orientalis
RBL	*Review of Biblical Literature*
RBS	Resources for Biblical Study
RSV	Revised Standard Version
SBL	Society of Biblical Literature
SBL SymS	Society of Biblical Literature Symposium Series
SemeiaSt	Semeia Studies
SNTSMS	Society for New Testament Studies Monograph Series
SP	Sacra Pagina
TAPA	*Transactions of the American Philological Association*
TBT	*The Bible Today*
TDOT	G. J. Botterweck and H. Ringgren (eds.), *Theological Dictionary of the Old Testament* (Grand Rapids, MI: Eerdmans, 1974).
TENTS	Texts and Editions for New Testament Study
THNTC	Two Horizons New Testament Commentary
TS	*Theological Studies*
TTod	*Theology Today*
TynBUl	*Tyndale Bullentin*
WBC	Word Biblical Commentary
WUNT	Wissenschaftliche Untersuchungen zum Neuen Testament
WW	*Word and World*
ZECNT	Zondervan Exegetical Commentary on the New Testament
ZNT	*Zeitschrift für Neues Testament*
ZNW	*Zeitschrift für die neutestamentliche Wissenschaft*

Introduction

Craig Evan Anderson and Matthew Ryan Hauge

Four decades ago, a shift emerged in New Testament scholarship. Enthusiasm for the old manner of analyzing the gospels (particularly the synoptics), as assemblages of discrete units that had been tradition-historically passed along by generations of witnesses, rapidly evaporated in the 1980s. In its place, New Testament scholars began to engage in a newfound appreciation of the final forms of the gospels as independent literary works that operate according to literary convention. That is, regardless of their potential to shed light on the historical circumstances surrounding the ministry of Jesus of Nazareth and his disciples, the gospels are stories and as such they communicate through plot tension reflecting conflict amongst characters in a variety of settings.[1] This book addresses a subset of the story genre, namely the use of characters, within the Gospel according to Matthew.

I. The Path to New Testament Narrative Criticism

A fascination with resurrecting the past had always been especially strong in New Testament studies, but it is far from exclusive to that field. Throughout the nineteenth century and early twentieth century, literary critics embraced a similar fascination with secular literature, upholding a romantic desire to use text to access the world and mind of the author, imagined as a creative genius. However, by the late 1930s, a literary critical movement emerged among poetry scholars that sought to cherish the text itself, distinct from the historical contexts of both its authorship and readership.[2] This movement, which would come to be known as the New Criticism, espoused close

---

[1] The emergent energy for framing the gospels as stories is evident in the titles of some of the foundational works of New Testament narrative criticism. See, e.g., David Rhoads and Donald Michie, *Mark as Story: An Introduction to the Narrative of a Gospel* (Philadelphia: Fortress Press, 1982); Jack Dean Kingsbury, *Matthew as Story* (Philadelphia: Fortress Press, 1986); David R. Bauer, "The Major Characters of Matthew's Story: Their Function and Significance," *Int* 46 (1992): 357–67, which opens with the declaration, "The Gospel of Matthew is a story about Jesus."

[2] In the penetrating words of John Crowe Ransom, "Criticism, Inc.," *Virginia Quarterly Review* 13, no. 4 (1937): 586–602, "the students of the future must be permitted to study literature, and not merely about literature" (588). See also Cleanth Brooks and Robert Penn Warren, *Understanding Poetry* (New York: Henry Holt and Company, 1938).

readings of texts, appreciating texts for their own intrinsic merits, rather than merely focusing on the contexts that produced or received them.[3]

New Criticism's interest in the text itself rather than the people (writers and readers) around it reflected broader philosophical advances in the understanding of language.[4] In the 1950s and 1960s, structuralism was becoming a dominant influence, especially in French academic circles. This was a philosophical movement that regarded language not as a mere tool controlled by people, but rather as a powerful cultural system that envelops people, shaping the worldviews of its users. Although structuralism originated in the study of linguistics, it had a profound impact on an array of social sciences.[5]

The rise of New Criticism and structuralism created the foundation for a reappraisal of narrative. Wayne C. Booth's 1961 watershed, *The Rhetoric of Fiction*, dismantled unhelpful scholarly dogmata that for decades had hollowly claimed to venerate that which is "pure" or "true" in literature.[6] Booth contended that readers should regard narrative as rhetoric and, in doing so, he introduced concepts such as the "implied author" and the "unreliable narrator," which have now become staples of narrative theory. In 1972, Gérard Genette differentiated between story (*what* a narrator tells) and discourse (*how* a narrator tells) and introduced the notion of focalization, the direction of the reader's attention.[7] In 1978, both Mieke Bal and Seymour Chatman expanded, modified, and popularized these literary critical methods.[8]

By the early 1970s these advances in literary criticism began to impact the study of the Hebrew Bible. Brevard Childs contended that the historical-critical method, which had dominated biblical scholarship for decades, was not sufficiently helpful for readers of the Bible. Childs argued for a new way to read the Bible that examines it as a completed body of canonical literature.[9] Furthermore, Rolf Rendtorff built upon the form-critical work of Gerhard von Rad and Martin Noth among others to supplant the historical-critical schema of Julius Wellhausen, which had dominated Hebrew Bible scholarship for a century.[10]

---

[3] John Crowe Ransom, *The New Criticism* (Norfolk, CT: New Directions, 1941); Cleanth Brooks, *The Well Wrought Urn: Studies in the Structure of Poetry* (London: Dobson Books, 1949); Rene Wellek and Austin Warren, *Theory of Literature*, 3rd edn (1948; repr., New York: Harcourt, Brace & World, 1956).

[4] The work of Ferdinand de Saussure, *Course in General Linguistics*, trans. Wade Baskin (New York: Philosophical Library, 1959; original French 1916), was especially influential, serving as a foundational work for structuralism.

[5] For the impact of structuralism, especially in France beginning in the 1950s and 1960s, see, e.g., the works of anthropologist Claude Lévi-Strauss, literary critic Roland Barthes, psychoanalyst Jacques Lacan, philosopher Jacques Derrida, and historian of ideas Michel Foucault, among many others.

[6] Wayne C. Booth, *The Rhetoric of Fiction* (1961; repr. Chicago: University of Chicago Press, 1983).

[7] Gérard Genette, *Narrative Discourse: An Essay in Method*, trans. Jane E. Lewin (Ithaca, NY: Cornell University Press, 1980; original French 1972).

[8] Mieke Bal, *Narratology: Introduction to the Theory of Narrative*, trans. Christine Van Boheemen (Toronto: University of Toronto Press, 1985; original Dutch 1978); Seymour Chatman, *Story and Discourse: Narrative Structure in Fiction and Film* (Ithaca, NY: Cornell University Press, 1978).

[9] Brevard Childs, *Biblical Theology in Crisis* (Philadelphia: Westminster Press, 1970); *Introduction to the Old Testament as Scripture* (Philadelphia: Fortress Press, 1979).

[10] Rolf Rendtorff, *The Problem of the Process of Transmission in the Pentateuch*, trans. John J. Scullion, JSOTSup 89 (Sheffield: Journal for the Study of the Old Testament Press, 1990; original German 1977); Gerhard von Rad, "Das formgeschichtliche Problem des Hexateuch," in *Gesammelte*

A few years later, New Criticism made inroads into New Testament studies. David Rhoads and Donald Michie established the field of New Testament narrative criticism with their groundbreaking 1982 work, *Mark as Story*, which demonstrated the benefits of applying literary criticism for analyzing the Gospel of Mark.[11] That is, they illustrated the benefit of recognizing that Mark is a story and, accordingly, readers should be mindful that it narrates a sequence of events, driven by a plot, featuring numerous characters in various settings, and implementing rhetorical devices.

Immediately following the publication of *Mark as Story*, in 1983, R. Alan Culpepper applied the literary critical methods of Booth, Génette, and Chapman to the Gospel of John in his pioneering work *Anatomy of the Fourth Gospel*, which employed their prismatic refraction of the author, differentiating the real author, the implied author, and the narrator.[12] In 1986, Robert C. Tannehill published *The Narrative Unity of Luke–Acts*, which contended that Luke–Acts constituted a unified narrative driven by the plot of Jesus and his followers trying to accomplish their mission despite opposition by their opponents.[13] Tannehill's contribution was notable because it stood in contrast to recent treatments of Luke–Acts that continued to address the textual material as small, discrete units in relation to synoptic parallels, but not in relation to the broader Luke–Acts narrative.[14] In 1986, Jack Dean Kingsbury applied narrative critical reasoning to the first gospel in order to produce his foundational study, *Matthew as Story*, the title of which transparently echoes that of Rhoads and Michie. These publications were the harbingers of a new era of New Testament studies, increasingly influenced by literary criticism.

Studien zum Alten Testament (1958; repr. Munich: Kaiser Verlag, 1961), 9–86; Martin Noth, *Überlieferungsgeschichtliche Studien. Die sammelnden und bearbeitenden Geschichtswerke im Alten Testament*, 2nd edn (1943; repr. Tübingen: Max Niemeyer Verlag, 1957); Julius Wellhausen, *Prolegomena to the History of Israel*, trans. J. S. Black and Allan Menzies (1885; repr. Atlanta: Scholars Press, 1994; original German 1878, 1883) and *Die Composition des Hexateuchs und der historischen Bücher des Alten Testaments*, 3rd edn (1899; repr. Berlin: Walter de Gruyter, 1963). In addition to Rendtorff's contribution, see also Hans Heinrich Schmid, *Der sogenannte Jahwist: Beobachtungen und Fragen zur Pentateuchforschung* (Zürich: Theologischer Verlag Zürich, 1976).

[11] Rhoads and Michie, *Mark as Story*. For a work that predates *Mark as Story*, recognizing the developments in literary criticism and considering them in terms of New Testament studies, see Norman R. Petersen, *Literary Criticism for New Testament Critics* (Philadelphia: Fortress Press, 1978).

[12] R. Alan Culpepper, *Anatomy of the Fourth Gospel: A Study in Literary Design* (Minneapolis: Fortress Press, 1983).

[13] Robert C. Tannehill, *The Narrative Unity of Luke–Acts: A Literary Interpretation*, Volume 1, *The Gospel According to Luke*, Foundations and Facets: New Testament (Philadelphia: Fortress Press, 1986).

[14] See, e.g., the review of Tannehill's book by Charles H. Talbert, *Biblica* 69, no. 1 (1988): 135–8, who cites Joseph A. Fitzmeyer's two-volume Anchor Bible commentary on Luke, *The Gospel According to Luke: A New Translation with Introduction and Commentary*, 2 vols., AB 28 (New York: Doubleday, 1981, 1985), published immediately before Tannehill's book, as emblematic of the older paradigm of gospel analysis that, due to its neglect of literary criticism, was essentially outdated already at the point of publication.

II. A Few Landmarks in Character Analysis

The aspect of literary criticism that is most relevant for the purposes of this book is character analysis, which is a subset within literary criticism. The academic study of characters goes back at least as early as Aristotle's *Poetics*. For Aristotle, narrative is a manner of imitation, art imitating life. Characters are revealed through action, and serve as moral reference points against which the audience can evaluate themselves either positively or negatively.[15] Aristotle contrasts comedy (a work of satirical or bawdy humor) and tragedy (a story emphasizing the suffering of the main character) by noting that comedy presents characters for derision (i.e., worse than people actually are) whereas tragedy presents characters for emulation (i.e., better than people actually are). Most of Aristotle's attention in *Poetics* is focused upon tragedy, for which he contends that a character should embody four qualities: The character should be good in moral purpose (χρηστός), maintain propriety (ἁρμόζω), seem realistic (ὅμοιος), and remain consistent (ὁμαλός).[16]

The ancient Greek educational system, which continued during the Roman Empire, featured three levels of education. Students with the means and ability to advance to the third level studied the art of rhetorical argumentation, and the prospect of public life lay before them.[17] In the spirit of Plato's admonition to start small, these elite students were introduced to rhetoric through a series of exercises that increased in difficulty—the *progymnasmata*. Four extended Greek handbooks of *progymnasmata* from the time of the Roman Empire have survived mostly intact.[18] The earliest of these handbooks was attributed to Aelius Theon of Alexandria, a teacher of grammar and rhetoric in the first century CE and author of works on Isocrates, Demosthenes, and Xenophon. Notably, Theon is the only writer on *progymnasmata* who allows for the students to write about their own experiences although his handbook was written for teachers, not students. On the composition of character, Theon provides these pedagogical prompts for the teacher and the student: "The properties of the person are origin, nature, training, disposition, age, fortune, morality, action, speech, (manner of) death, and what followed death." A "virtuous" narration describes these properties of the character(s) clearly, concisely, and credibly.[19]

---

[15] Aristotle, *Poetics* 1–4.
[16] Aristotle, *Poetics* 15, 1454a16–25.
[17] For a more detailed treatment of the tertiary stage, see Henry Irénée Marrou, *A History of Education in Antiquity*, trans. George Lamb (New York: Sheed & Ward, 1956), 186–216; and on rhetorical education proper, see Stanley Frederick Bonner, *Education in Ancient Rome: From the Elder Cato to the Younger Pliny* (Berkeley: University of California Press, 1977), 277–327.
[18] For a helpful introduction to these handbooks, see George A. Kennedy, *Greek Rhetoric under Christian Emperors* (Princeton, NJ: Princeton University Press, 1983), 54–72; Ruth Webb, "The *Progymnasmata* as Practice," in *Education in Greek and Roman Antiquity*, ed. Yoon Lee Too (Leiden: Brill, 2001), 289–316; and Rafaella Cribiore, *Gymnastics of the Mind: Greek Education in Hellenistic and Roman Egypt* (Princeton, NJ: Princeton University Press, 2001), 221-30. For a recent English translation, see George Kennedy, *Progymnasmata: Greek Textbooks of Prose Composition and Rhetoric*, SBLWGRW 10 (Atlanta: Society of Biblical Literature, 2003), 3–172.
[19] Kennedy, *Progymnasmata*, 78–9.

Both Aristotle's *Poetics* and Theon's handbook provide insight into the type of instruction that the gospel writers may have encountered as they thought about how to present the characters within their stories. Of course, in the nearly two millennia that have transpired since the writing of the gospels, ideas concerning characters and characterization have developed dramatically, especially recently. We may look to E. M. Forster's *Aspects of the Novel*, published in 1927, as providing the first noteworthy advice on character crafting in the modern era. The book is a collection of lively lectures that esteemed novelist E. M. Forster delivered in 1927 at Trinity College, Cambridge. In his treatment of characters, Forster lays out his famous distinction between flat and round characters.[20] Flat characters embody a single idea or quality, Forster noting that "the really flat character can be expressed in one sentence."[21] To be clear, flat characters are not necessarily reflective of poor writing; for Forster, flat characters can be very helpful and effective tools when used properly. They bear advantages in that they are easy for readers to recognize and remember because they are unalterable. Moreover, Forster asserts that "Dickens' people are nearly all flat … Nearly every one can be summed up in a sentence, and yet there is this wonderful feeling of human depth."[22] On the contrary, round characters are the inverse: they are complex so that they cannot be summarized in a single sentence, and they develop throughout the course of the story. According to Forster, "the test of a round character is whether it is capable of surprising in a convincing way."[23]

One year after Forster delivered these lectures in Cambridge, Vladimir Propp published *Morfológija skázki* (*Morphology of the Folktale*), a Russian language analysis of 100 fairy tales.[24] He found, for the fairy-tale genre, that characters were entirely subservient to the plot and were essentially interchangeable. Thus, he argued that the dragon playing the role of the villain could easily be swapped out for a whirlwind, devil, falcon, or sorceress really with no consequence for the story.[25] What matters far more than the identity of the characters is the role they play in the fairy tale. Propp distilled seven roles (regardless of the particulars of the characters who filled them) that recur in fairy tales: the villain, donor, helper, princess (and her father), dispatcher, hero, and false hero.[26]

It was not until thirty years after its initial publication in Russian that Propp's *Morphology of the Folktale* was finally published in English translation in 1958. By that time, interest in literary analysis was rapidly growing in the English-speaking academic world. Booth's seminal work, *The Rhetoric of Fiction*, appeared shortly thereafter in 1961 and four years after that W. J. Harvey produced a major work in character studies,

---

[20] E. M. Forster, *Aspects of the Novel* (1927; repr. New York: First Warbler Press, 2023), 45–52.
[21] Forster, *Aspects*, 45–6.
[22] Forster, *Aspects*, 48. Amusingly, Forster refers to novel characters as "people," given that most novel characters are human and the designation of "people" reinforces the affinity between the writer and his or her subjects.
[23] Forster, *Aspects*, 52.
[24] Vladimir Propp, *Morphology of the Folktale*, trans. Laurence Scott (Austin: University of Texas Press, 1958, 1968; original Russian 1928).
[25] Propp, *Morphology*, 12–13.
[26] Propp, *Morphology*, 79–91.

his 1965 book, *Character and the Novel*. In it, Harvey contended that the reader's exposure to characters in novels should reflect the uneven degrees of exposure that people experience with one another. Harvey notes that "a face that is no more than a blur in the crowd may for a moment be focused sharply and significantly before fading away again." And furthermore, "some characters stand in a full light, others remain shadowy, still others advance and retreat in our consciousness as readers."[27] Based upon this observation, Harvey suggests that we imagine novel characters on a spectrum. At one end are the protagonists, located there due to their importance in the story. Harvey places "background characters" at the other end of the spectrum. In the middle of the spectrum are numerous intermediate characters, but for Harvey, two merit special attention: the *ficelle* and the Card. The *ficelle* is a relatively undeveloped character that is in the novel to serve a plot function to advance the story; the Card is a comically eccentric, vibrant character, who tends to be unchanging, but yet is amusing, enigmatic, and is sometimes tinged with a pathetic or occasionally even a sinister quality.[28]

In 1978, Seymour Chatman published *Story and Discourse: Narrative Structure in Fiction and Film*, the greatest contribution of which was its ability to organize, communicate, and apply the contributions of its predecessors. Chatman openly acknowledged his indebtedness to Wayne Booth, Mikhail Bakhtin, Roland Barthes, Gérard Genette, and Tzvetan Todorov in the book's preface, writing, "my purpose is not to polemicize, but to synthesize the most powerful insights—Anglo-American, Russian, and French."[29] Regarding his notion of characters, Chatman argued for an open structuralist theory, claiming that storytellers should present characters as autonomous beings and provide items of evidence around which the audience inferentially fills in the rest, thereby participating in the character construction process.[30] With this in mind, Chatman addressed characters according to three terms: totality, traits, and uniqueness. First, he asserted that a character can never be fully known in their totality. Second, he argued that characters were the embodiment of a paradigm of traits, which may transform along with the characters as they develop throughout the course of a story.[31] Third, regarding uniqueness, Chatman noted that well-written characters ought to feel even more distinct to us than some living acquaintances in our lives. When we think of classic characters from literature, "even where the traits of a character may be forgotten, our sense of their uniqueness rarely flags."[32]

These works were some of the most important available on character analysis by the 1980s, that is, the point at which New Testament scholarship began to embrace narrative criticism as a method for understanding the gospels. Of course, the gospels are neither novels, nor fairy tales, nor films. Nevertheless, the insights of these thinkers

---

[27] W. J. Harvey, *Character and the Novel* (London: Chatto & Windus, 1966), 55–6.
[28] Harvey, *Character*, 58–68.
[29] Seymour Chatman, *Story and Discourse: Narrative Structure in Fiction and Film* (Ithaca, NY: Cornell University Press, 1978), 11.
[30] Chatman, *Story and Discourse*, 119.
[31] Chatman, *Story and Discourse*, 121–3, 126–31. Of these three terms (totality, traits, and uniqueness), Chatman devotes by far the most attention to character traits.
[32] Chatman, *Story and Discourse*, 123.

and others are instructive, providing perspectives that can help inform how we examine characters in the gospels.

III. Character Analyses of the Gospels with an Eye Toward Matthew

Although there were early analyses of characters in the Gospel according to Matthew, it took a while for many New Testament scholars to integrate effectively literary critical methods.[33] Kingsbury's 1986 book, *Matthew as Story*, was a laudable attempt at recognizing the need to engage the gospels literary-critically. His work in that book was strongly influenced by Chatman's *Story and Discourse*; not only did Kingsbury cite Chatman beginning on page one, but moreover he organized the subsections of his introductory chapter according to Chatman's arrangement: first addressing the story and then the discourse of the narrative. Through Chatman's influence, Kingsbury's character analysis was largely focused on listing traits of various characters. Nevertheless, much of the work that Kingsbury displayed in the book regarding structure and genre within Matthew was anchored more firmly in form-criticism than narratology.[34]

The *Interpretation* journal devoted its Fall 1992 volume to articles on the Gospel of Matthew, the first three of which provided literary critical analyses of Matthew. In the first article, Mark Allan Powell offered an excellent introductory explanation of the merits of literary criticism for study of the gospels.[35] In the second article, Jack Dean Kingsbury gave a plot analysis of Matthew that strongly echoed the arguments of his book, *Matthew as Story*.[36] In the third article, David R. Bauer provided character analyses of the "major characters" of Matthew.[37]

In that third article, "The Major Characters of Matthew's Story: Their Function and Significance," Bauer, a former student of Kingsbury, faithfully continued the work of his teacher, both in substance and style. Bauer's article only addressed three characters, the three that he deemed to be "major" characters: Jesus, the disciples, and Israel. Following a structural outline that Bauer inherited from Kingsbury and subsequently defended, Bauer examined the Gospel of Matthew as three units: the preparation of Jesus (Mt. 1:1-4:16), the proclamation of Jesus (Mt. 4:17-16:20), and the passion of

---

[33] For early character analyses regarding the Gospel according to Matthew that were published before *Mark as Story* (1982), see, e.g., M. Sheridan, "Disciples and Discipleship in Matthew and Luke," *Biblical Theology Bulletin* 3 (1973): 235-55; Minear, "The Disciples and the Crowds in the Gospel of Matthew," *ATR*, sup. Series 3 (1974): 28-44; Kingsbury, "The Figure of Peter in Matthew's Gospel as a Theological Problem," *JBL* 98 (1979): 67-83; and Meier, "John the Baptist in Matthew's Gospel," *JBL* 99 (1980): 383-405.

[34] Kingsbury repeatedly cited Chatman's *Story and Discourse* as a major influence on his book. He also cited the contributions of Forster and Booth, but with much less attention. Notably missing are the contributions from Gérard Genette and Mieke Bal (and, to a lesser extent, W. J. Harvey).

[35] Mark Allan Powell, "Toward a Narrative-Critical Understanding of Matthew," *Int* 46, no. 4 (1992): 341-6; see also Powell's book, *What is Narrative Criticism?* (Minneapolis: Fortress Press, 1990).

[36] Jack Dean Kingsbury, "The Plot of Matthew's Story," *Int* 46, no. 4 (1992): 347-56.

[37] Bauer, "The Major Characters," 357-67.

Jesus (Mt. 16:21-28:20).³⁸ In the first section, Bauer presented various characters as "witnesses" to Jesus, revealing qualities of Jesus. In the second section, he emphasized the activities of Jesus (preaching, teaching, and healing) and traits of Jesus (authoritative, evocative, self-sacrificial, and person-of-integrity). In the third section, Bauer recounted the trial and execution of Jesus, highlighting his quiet obedience to the divine will. Bauer asserted that his second major character, "the disciples," displayed both positive and negative traits and examined them in terms of the nature of discipleship, the performance of the twelve, and the anticipated future mission amidst opposition.³⁹ Finally, Bauer divided his third major character, "Israel," into two subgroups (the crowds and the religious leaders), both demonstrating possible responses to Jesus.⁴⁰ Bauer presented the crowds as the recipients of Jesus' ministry who respond with amazement, but yet fall short by not fully recognizing the significance of Jesus. Bauer, considered the religious leaders to be anthropocentric and aligned with Satan.

Kingsbury and Bauer provided welcome and necessary early steps to advance New Testament scholarship by applying literary critical thinking to the gospels. Yet, their work really was form-critical in its nature, simply recast with a narrative-critical veneer. This reflected the challenge that scholars faced especially early on as they tried to redirect from the form-critical and theological work that they were used to doing into literary critical analysis. Since those early days, there of course have been numerous studies on the Matthean Jesus.⁴¹ The Matthean Peter, given his peculiar role in that gospel as the recipient of the keys of the kingdom of heaven and as (possibly) the foundation of the church (Mt. 16:17-19), has received much scholarly attention.⁴² Matthew's portrayal of the disciples collectively has also been the target of scholarly interest,⁴³ as have other characters.⁴⁴

---

³⁸ Bauer, "The Major Characters," 357–60; Kingsbury, *Matthew as Story*; David R. Bauer, *The Structure of Matthew's Gospel: A Study in Literary Design*, JSNTSup 31, Bible and Literature Series 15 (Sheffield: Almond Press, 1988).
³⁹ Notably, Bauer did not differentiate key disciples (e.g., Peter and Judas) from the rest.
⁴⁰ It is not clear on what grounds Bauer removed Jesus and the disciples from under the umbrella of "Israel." Jesus and his disciples were as much Israelites as the crowds or the religious leaders, and recognition of this point is important for how one interprets the Gospel of Matthew.
⁴¹ Due to Jesus' prominence in the gospels, researchers tend to focus on aspects of his character. See, e.g., Lidija Novakovic, *Messiah, Healer of the Sick: A Study of Jesus as the Son of David in the Gospel of Matthew*, WUNT 170 (Tübingen: Mohr Siebeck, 2003); John Yueh-Han Yieh, *One Teacher: Jesus' Teaching Role in Matthew's Gospel Report*, BZNW 124 (Berlin: de Gruyter, 2004); Richard Beaton, *Isaiah's Christ in Matthew's Gospel*, SNTSMS 123 (Cambridge: Cambridge University Press, 2007).
⁴² See, e.g., Arlo J. Nau, *Peter in Matthew: Discipleship, Diplomacy, and Dispraise . . . with an Assessment of Power and Privilege in the Petrine Office* (Collegeville, MN: Liturgical Press, 1992); Kari Syreeni, "Peter as Character and Symbol in the Gospel of Matthew," in *Characterization in the Gospels: Reconceiving Narrative Criticism*, ed. David Rhoads and Kari Syreeni (London: Continuum/T&T Clark International, 1999), 106–52; John R. Markley, *Peter—Apocalyptic Seer: The Influence of the Apocalypse Genre on Matthew's Portrayal of Peter*, WUNT 348 (Tübingen: Mohr Siebeck, 2013); Robert H. Gundry, *Peter: False Disciple and Apostate according to Saint Matthew* (Grand Rapids, MI: William B. Eerdmans Publishing Co., 2015).
⁴³ See, e.g., Talvikki Mattila, "Naming the Nameless: Gender and Discipleship in Matthew's Passion Narrative," in *Characterization in the Gospels: Reconceiving Narrative Criticism*, ed. David Rhoads and Kari Syreeni (London: Continuum/T&T Clark International, 1999), 153–79; Jeannine K. Brown, *The Disciples in Narrative Perspective: The Portrayal and Function of the Matthean Disciples* (Atlanta: Society of Biblical Literature, 2002).
⁴⁴ See, e.g., J. C. R. Cousland, *The Crowds in the Gospel of Matthew*, NovTSup 102 (Leiden: E. J. Brill, 2002); Brian C. Dennert, *John the Baptist and the Jewish Setting of Matthew*, WUNT 403 (Tübingen: Mohr Siebeck, 2015).

Cornelis Bennema's 2014 book, *A Theory of Character in New Testament Narrative*, provides a clear indication of how far New Testament scholarship has advanced regarding its capacity to address characters and characterization in New Testament narrative.[45] Bennema demonstrates a comprehensive grasp of the relevant literature both in his mastery of literary critical methods and in his awareness of gospel scholarship. He counters the common application to New Testament narrative of the Aristotelian notion that ancient characters were innately flat and subordinate to action, noting that, in the New Testament, "what the characters say is equally important to what they do." Bennema cites numerous examples of New Testament characters satisfying E. M. Forster's criteria for classification as round characters: they both demonstrate development and are capable of credible surprises.[46] With this in mind, Bennema proposes a theory of character that examines characters through three steps. First, appraise what the implied author would expect the implied reader to know about the cultural, political, and textual context of the narrative as they would impact one's reading of the character.[47] Second, create a character analysis according to three criteria: complexity (How many traits does this character exhibit?), development (Does the character change and/or make surprising decisions?), and inner life (Does the reader get access to the character's psychology?). Then, based on this data, classify the character along "an aggregate continuum of degree of characterization."[48] Third, evaluate the role of the character in terms of the narrator's point of view and the plot.[49]

IV. An Overview of this Volume

Due to the increasing interest in character analysis of the gospels, Christopher W. Skinner published in 2013 an edited volume of scholarly essays through Bloomsbury/T&T Clark entitled *Characters and Characterization in the Gospel of John*.[50] In 2014, Skinner and Matthew Ryan Hauge published a follow-up volume, *Character Studies and the Gospel of Mark*, also through Bloomsbury/T&T Clark.[51] In 2018, Frank Dicken and Julia Snyder published *Characters and Characterization in Luke-Acts* through Bloomsbury/T&T Clark, in what was now becoming an unofficial series for the publisher.[52] This book, *Character Studies in the Gospel of Matthew*, will consequently complete the series for Bloomsbury/T&T Clark.

---

[45] Cornelis Bennema, *A Theory of Character in New Testament Narrative* (Minneapolis: Fortress Press, 2014).
[46] Bennema, *A Theory of Character*, 10, 61, 76–8.
[47] Bennema, *A Theory of Character*, 62–72.
[48] Bennema, *A Theory of Character*, 72–90.
[49] Bennema, *A Theory of Character*, 90–103.
[50] Christopher W. Skinner, *Characters and Characterization in the Gospel of John*, LNTS 461 (London: Bloomsbury/T&T Clark, 2013).
[51] Christopher W. Skinner and Matthew Ryan Hauge, *Character Studies and the Gospel of Mark*, LNTS 483 (London: Bloomsbury/T&T Clark, 2014).
[52] Frank E. Dicken and Julia A. Snyder, *Characters and Characterization in Luke-Acts*, LNTS 548 (London: Bloomsbury/T&T Clark, 2018).

Given that this is the fourth volume in this series, we believe that our predecessors have already laid much of the groundwork for character studies in the gospels. Therefore, besides offering this brief history of the rise of New Testament character analysis, which brought us to this point, we chose to have all the following chapters focus on individual characters in the Gospel according to Matthew. As Bennema noted in his book, "the current interest in New Testament characters has, regrettably, not led to a consensus on how to study character in biblical narrative ... There is no consensus on how to analyze, classify, and evaluate characters."[53] In light of this lack of consensus, the contributors to this volume enjoyed the freedom to follow the study of their characters wherever they led.

Joseph. The first character that receives extended treatment in the Gospel of Matthew is Joseph, the son of Jacob and husband of Mary (1:16). Joseph is a righteous dreamer and, although he does not speak, he is the active agent that moves his young family from here to there in response to a divine revelation. Heather M. Gorman closely examines these brief episodes in which Joseph is featured in the infancy narrative (1:1-17, 1:18-25, and 2:13-23). Gorman contends that the character of Joseph provides the connective thread to Abraham and David that anchors the main character within the history of Israel. And if that was not enough, it is Joseph that functions as an exemplar of faithful obedience to God illustrative of the teachings of Jesus.

Mary. Joseph receives extended treatment in the infancy narrative, but the mother of Jesus does not. She is named in the genealogy, which is noteworthy, but then vanishes into the shadows. By contrast, in the Gospel of Luke, she is the recipient of direct divine communication, sings a song in response, and is consequently enshrined as an exemplar of humility and grace throughout the history of Christianity. Lily Voung reimagines the passive characterization of Mary in the Gospel of Matthew through the lens provided by the *Protoevangelium of James*. Vuong contends that Mary is not a flat character, but a passive protagonist in the spirit of *passivum divinum*—a sacred vessel of divine will.

Herod. In the infancy narrative, Mary gives birth to Jesus, and Joseph protects his family from the dangers that lie beyond their small village. It is the time of King Herod, and Craig Evan Anderson turns our attention to the first political character in the gospel. We are introduced to King Herod in 2:1 and he dies in 2:19, but his significance within the reception history of this gospel does not reflect the brevity of his literary role. Herod is clearly a villain, but his treachery has often been interpreted as reflective of the Jews within the gospel. Anderson challenges this view and instead paves the way for an anti-imperial reading of both Herod the Great and Herod Antipas in the Gospel of Matthew.

John the Baptist. In the opening chapters of our story, the young family has escaped the political threat of the local tyrant and migrated from Bethlehem to Egypt and then

---

[53] Bennema, *A Theory of Character*, 26.

to Nazareth. In 3:1, the gospel shifts from the city to the wilderness. John the Baptist is in the wild country proclaiming the imminent arrival of the "kingdom of heaven," publicly criticizing the religious elite, and baptizing pilgrims in the Jordan river. Tucker S. Ferda highlights this shifting landscape and reads this prophet on the margins as a confirmation of the salvific work of God.

Jesus as Teacher. The main character of this story speaks his first line in 3:15, declaring the need to fulfill all righteousness. The first words of a main character can be illustrative, and in this case, they are. Righteousness is the heart of the teachings of Jesus in the Gospel of Matthew, an argument which Melanie A. Howard makes in her examination of the words and deeds of Jesus. Jesus talks frequently in the gospel, delivering speeches to whomever is present. Through these speeches the Evangelist presents Jesus as a teacher who emphasizes understanding and action—the proper enactment of the "Kingdom of Heaven."

Jesus as King. Catherine Sider Hamilton continues the examination of the presentation of the character of Jesus against the backdrop of Greco-Roman βίοι. In the beginning of the gospel, King Herod, the nominal king of the Jews, poses the question, "Where is the child who has been born king of the Jews?" (2:1). This usurper, this would-be king who speaks of the "kingdom of heaven," is texturized obliquely through the whispers of the scriptures that can be found in the characters of Tamar, Rahab, Ruth, the wife of Uriah, Mary, Rachel, the Canaanite woman, and the anointing woman. In contrast to βίοι, in which a character is articulated through characteristics, Hamilton argues that the Evangelist articulates this character through multiple layers of the history of God and the people of God. Where is this king of the Jews? The king of the Jews and his kingdom is on the cross (cf. 27:37).

God. The term θεός occurs fifty-one times spread across forty-three verses in the Gospel of Matthew. But to say God is a minor character is misleading. God does and says nothing, at least not directly. In the broadest terms, "God" is a transcendent being who is involved in the comings and goings of human beings in antiquity. Michael P. Knowles approaches the character of God in this vein. God cannot be a character in the traditional literary sense of the word—God transcends characteristics. As such, Knowles focuses our attention on God as "Father"—the one who is behind the scenes and above the scenes—and Jesus as "Son"—the one who reveals the "Father" through the scenes that unfold throughout the story.

Centurion. The leader of a hundred appears for the first time in Mt. 8 and then reappears at the end of the story to assert that Jesus truly was God's son (27:54). As a representative of Rome and the Roman military, the centurion is a revelatory example of the function of power within the gospel. Justin Marc Smith reinflates this historically flattened character in his treatment of the relationship between power and faith in 8:5-13. Jesus has no Roman authority, but the centurion is tasked to maintain Roman authority. What transpires is a tug of war for control between Jesus and the centurion as the centurion slowly slides into the pit of surrender and faith in the healing power of the other.

Peter. Prominently featured as the first among the disciples, Peter holds a special role in the Gospel of Matthew. It is to Peter that Jesus entrusts the keys to the Kingdom of Heaven and upon whom Jesus seemingly declares that he will build his church (Mt. 16:18-19). Yet to many, this declaration is in fact more cryptic than it initially appears. Moreover, a major New Testament scholar has recently advanced a bold argument claiming that Matthew showcases Peter as the exemplar of false discipleship, condemned by the gospel. However, David Lertis Matson challenges this argument, contending that Matthew may present Peter as a failed disciple but not as a false disciple.

Women. The concluding fives chapters in this volume treat corporate characters, beginning with "women." Jeffrey W. Aernie lays out before us selected passages in which women appear in the gospel, including the women in the genealogy of Jesus (1:1-18), the women who are healed by Jesus (8-9), the women who engage with Jesus in unexpected ways (15 and 20), and the faithful women who are present with Jesus at the end of our story (26-8). In every episode, each woman individually and these women collectively participate in the unfolding of the identity of Jesus and the presentation of what it looks like to be his disciple.

Crowds. As Jesus walks and talks, the crowds gather around him. The crowd is a constant throughout the story, but what is its function? One popular reading of the crowds is that they function as an undifferentiated mass, part of the setting of the narrative. Those who recognize the crowd as a character are often vexed by the rapid manner that it turns on Jesus and consents to his crucifixion. One potential solution posits a two-crowd theory. However, Robert Cousland contends that there may be a more compelling way to interpret the fickleness of the crowd. What if is the crowd is us, the readers?

Gentiles. The English word "gentile" is a transliteration of the Latin *gentilis*, which generally referred to a clan or a tribe. Over time, *gentilis* would become a divisive term, separating this from that, us from them. This history must be carefully untangled from the Greek conception of the ἔθνος that is strewn throughout the Gospel of Matthew, a task which is carried out by Anders Runesson. As one might expect, the function of the gentiles in the gospel is diverse and reflexive to the narrative task, but united by a shared literary aim, the description of the "Kingdom of Heaven." And like all characters in the story, the gentiles have a part to play.

Pharisees. In the first scene in which we encounter the Pharisees, John the Baptist is in the wild, speaking of the Kingdom of Heaven, dousing people in the waters of the Jordan, and telling everyone to change their ways. John sees the Pharisees and the Sadducees approaching, denounces them as snakes, and warns them that if they do not bear fruit they will be cut down and incinerated. From the beginning to the end of the story, the Pharisees appear repeatedly as a collective of contempt and scorn. Why are the Pharisees presented this way? Eric Ottenheijm leads us through the various traps that befall the naïve reader when encountering the villain of the story.

Rome. The entirety of the Gospel of Matthew following the brief infancy narrative is geographically set in a rather small territory essentially spanning Galilee and Jerusalem. Rome is not a setting in the Gospel of Matthew, but symbols of Rome abound in the story. The beginning, middle, and end of the gospel is propelled by three figures empowered by Rome: Herod the Great, Herod Antipas, and Pontius Pilate.

Traditionally, they have been read as minor characters, but each one is pivotal to the trajectory of the plot and the impact of the story as a whole upon the reader. Adam Winn examines each character in turn and encourages us to consider Herod the Great, Herod Antipas, and Pontius Pilate as a collective response to the Roman imperial order in the first century.

1

Joseph: Faithful Jew and Exemplar of Jesus' Teachings

Heather M. Gorman

In his magisterial commentary on the infancy narratives, Raymond Brown claims, "The figure of Joseph holds the [Matthean infancy] narrative together." Matthew's infancy narrative is "the Gospel and its destiny in miniature" and "the place where the OT and the Gospel meet." Joseph, Brown contends, holds together this miniature gospel as the righteous Jew, faithful to Torah, protector of the Messiah from the Jewish authorities, and the one who brings Jesus to "Galilee of the Gentiles" (Mt. 4:13).[1] Brown's praise for the legal father of Jesus is not unwarranted, yet Matthew's characterization of Joseph deserves further exploration. Can a character with no direct speech in the narrative and who all but disappears after the second chapter of Matthew really hold the narrative together?

In this chapter, I explore Matthew's characterization of Joseph.[2] Joseph is named in three pericopes: the genealogy (1:1-17), the conception and birth of Jesus (1:18-25), and the escape to and return from Egypt (2:13-23). He is referred to but not named in 13:55, where people from Nazareth refer to Jesus as "the carpenter's son." He is absent in the other references to Jesus' family in 2:11, where the magi "saw the child with Mary his mother," and in 12:46-50, where Jesus is told that his mother and brothers want to speak to him.[3] Thus, Matthew's primary characterization of Joseph occurs in the

---

[1] Raymond E. Brown, *The Birth of the Messiah: A Commentary on the Infancy Narratives in the Gospels of Matthew and Luke*, ABRL, upd. edn (New York: Doubleday, 1993), 231–2.
[2] Kingsbury notes that the narrator of the First Gospel is reliable and "in full accord with the implied author." Resseguie and Anderson agree. As such, rarely is there a need to distinguish between the narrator and the implied author, whom, for the sake of ease, I will refer to as "Matthew." Kingsbury notes a similar accord between the narratee and implied reader in the First Gospel, whom I will simply refer to as "the reader" or occasionally "the implied reader." See Jack Dean Kingsbury, *Matthew as Story*, 2nd edn (Philadelphia: Fortress, 1988), 31, 38–9; Janice Capel Anderson, "Mary's Difference: Gender and Patriarchy in the Birth Narratives," *JR* 67 (1987): 186, n. 10; James L. Resseguie, "A Glossary of New Testament Narrative Criticism with Illustrations," *Religions* 10, no. 3 (2019): 17.
[3] It is possible that "Mary the mother of James and Joseph" in 27:56 refers to the mother of Jesus. If that reference is not a conflation between her and another Mary, Joseph is also absent at the cross when Mary is present. See Carolyn Osiek, "Mary 4," in *Women in Scripture: A Dictionary of Named and Unnamed Women in the Hebrew Bible, the Apocryphal/Deuterocanonical Books, and the New Testament*, ed. Carol L. Meyers, Toni Craven, and Ross Shepard Kraemer (Boston: Houghton Mifflin, 2000), 123.

infancy narrative (Mt. 1–2): he connects Jesus to the families of Abraham and David and to the larger story of Israel; he is a righteous Jew with a merciful application of Torah; and he is obedient to the divine will and an example of how faithful Israel should respond to its Messiah. Further, even though Joseph is not named outside of the infancy narrative, the implied reader would recall Joseph as an exemplar of many of the teachings of Jesus, particularly Mt. 5–6, 12:46-50, and 19:1-12.

I. Jesus' Connection to Abraham and David

Matthew first introduces Joseph at the end of Jesus' genealogy, where he is called "the husband of Mary, of whom Jesus was born, who is called the Messiah" (1:16). Of course, while the genealogy is Joseph's, more than that it is Jesus'—Matthew introduces it as "an account of the genealogy of Jesus the Messiah, the son of David, the son of Abraham" (1:1). This introduction ensures that the reader grasps the two most important people in the genealogy—David and Abraham. It is not without Joseph, however, that Jesus is connected to these figures.

The importance of Joseph's role as the "son of David" is underscored when the angel addresses him as "Joseph, son of David" in the first dream (1:20)—the only time a figure besides Jesus is given this title in the New Testament.[4] Joseph's hometown of Bethlehem (2:1), the location of the birth of Jesus, supports this characterization of Joseph as son of David. Resseguie explains how setting "enlarges the traits of a character," and here the reader would recognize Joseph's origins in the town of David's birth and anointing (1 Sam. 16:1-13; 17:12, 15).[5] Matthew's quotation of Mic. 5:2—"And you, Bethlehem, in the land of Judah, are by no means least among the rulers of Judah; for from you shall come a ruler who is to shepherd my people Israel" (2:6)—reminds the reader of Bethlehem's significance as the origin of a coming ruler. Because Joseph resides in Bethlehem, Jesus is born in the city of David.

Yet the genealogy leaves the readers with a question: how is Jesus the Son of David if Joseph is not his father?[6] Joseph is described as "the husband of Mary, of whom Jesus was born," *not* as "the father of Jesus," as one expects from the pattern already established in the genealogy: "A the father of B, and B the father of C . . ." In 1:16, Matthew switches from the active ἐγέννησεν to the passive ἐγεννήθη, leaving readers to assume that

---

[4] Brown, *The Birth of the Messiah*, 138.
[5] Resseguie, "Glossary," 37. They would likely also recognize that Bethlehem was the burial place of the patriarch Joseph's mother, Rachel (Gen. 36:19-20).
[6] In an oft-cited essay, Stendahl argues that Mt. 1 answers the question "who?" (*Quis*)—i.e., Jesus is the son of David and Abraham and savior of the people—while Mt. 2 answers the question "whence?" (*Unde*)—i.e., Bethlehem, Egypt, Ramah. Brown modifies Stendahl's formula to include "how?" (*Quomodo*) and "where?" (*Ubi*). Regarding "how?" Brown says, "[H]e is son of David not through physical begetting, but through an acceptance by the Davidid Joseph of a child conceived through the Holy Spirit." See Krister Stendahl, "*Quis et Unde*? An Analysis of Mt 1-2," in *Judentum, Urchristentum, Kirche: Festschrift Für Joachim Jeremias*, ed. Walther Eltester, BZNW 26 (Berlin: Töpelmann, 1964), 94–105; Brown, *The Birth of the Messiah*, 52–4.

either the passive voice implies God is the actor or wondering who Jesus' father is.⁷ Apart from one reference in 13:55, where a skeptic of Jesus' wisdom and deeds of power refers to Jesus as the "carpenter's son," Matthew never describes Joseph as the father of Jesus or Jesus as the son of Joseph. Rather, Joseph is "the husband of Mary" (τὸν ἄνδρα Μαρίας; 1:16), the one to whom "his mother Mary had been engaged" (μνηστευθείσης τῆς μητρὸς αὐτοῦ Μαρίας; 1:18), and "her husband" (ὁ ἀνὴρ αὐτῆς; 1:19). In response to the commission from the angel of the Lord, Joseph not only takes Mary as his wife but also names her son, which "constituted legal and full adoption."⁸ This naming, then, which is emphasized at the end of the pericope, brings Jesus into the Davidic line via Joseph's *legal* paternity, rather than *biological* paternity.⁹

Because of the Messianic emphasis throughout the First Gospel, David may be the more important of the two genealogical figures in Matthew's characterization of Joseph, but Erickson makes a compelling case that Matthew parallels Joseph with Abraham. While most New Testament scholarship has focused on Jesus–Isaac parallels, Erickson offers seven parallels between Joseph's and Abraham's son announcements, including the strong verbal parallel between Gen. 17:19 (ναί ἰδοὺ Σαρρα ἡ γυνή σου τέξεταί σοι υἱόν καὶ καλέσεις τὸ ὄνομα αὐτοῦ Ισαακ) and Mt. 1:21 (τέξεται δὲ υἱόν, καὶ καλέσεις τὸ ὄνομα αὐτοῦ Ἰησοῦν).¹⁰ These parallels that liken Joseph to Abraham, the one in whom "all the families of the earth shall be blessed" (Gen. 12:3), function to expound on the genealogy and prepare the reader for Matthew's forthcoming emphasis on gentile inclusion in God's kingdom.¹¹

---

[7] Warren Carter, *Matthew and the Margins: A Sociopolitical and Religious Reading*, Bible & Liberation (Maryknoll, NY: Orbis Books, 2000), 65; Charles Thomas Davis, "Fulfillment of Creation: A Study of Matthew's Genealogy," *JAAR* 41, no. 4 (1973): 530–1.
  Schaberg, who argues that 1:1-25 was about an illegitimate conception and not a miraculous virginal one, explicitly refutes the idea of a theological passive here. Rather, she says, "The verb is mysterious, 'fraught with background,' immediately raising the question, 'begotten by whom?'" Jane Schaberg, *The Illegitimacy of Jesus: A Feminist Theological Interpretation of the Infancy Narratives*, 20th anniv. edn (Sheffield: Sheffield Phoenix, 2006), 46–7. Even if one does not accept her larger thesis, her point stands that the end of the genealogy leaves the reader with questions.

[8] Brown, *The Birth of the Messiah*, 139; John Mark Jones, "Subverting the Textuality of Davidic Messianism: Matthew's Presentation of the Genealogy and the Davidic Title," *CBQ* 56 (1994): 260; Kingsbury, *Matthew as Story*, 47; John P. Meier, *A Marginal Jew: Rethinking the Historical Jesus*, 5 vols. (New York: Doubleday, 1991), 1:217.

[9] Brown argues that Matthew places the Isa. 7:14 quotation "awkwardly in the middle of the narrative," rather than at the end of the episode (like he does repeatedly in ch. 2), in order to emphasize the Davidic sonship Jesus inherited by being adopted by Joseph via the naming. He explains, "If the formula citation had been placed at the end, the Davidic emphasis would have been obscured; for the climactic line would have been: 'They will call his name Emmanuel [which means "God with us"].'" See Brown, *The Birth of the Messiah*, 144.

[10] The other parallels include (1) an appearance to the fathers in a vision or dream; (2) a command to the fathers not to be afraid; (3) the use of the verb ἀπολύομαι; (4) mothers who get pregnant miraculously; (5) a rejection of a woman followed by a reversal of that rejection; and (6) the characterization of the fathers as just or righteous. See Richard J. Erickson, "Joseph and the Birth of Isaac in Matthew 1," *BBR* 10 (2000): 45–8. For an extensive bibliography on the Jesus–Isaac parallels, especially with reference to Isaac as a type of sacrificial offering and Isaac as foreshadowing the resurrection, see Erickson, "Joseph and the Birth of Isaac in Matthew 1," 38, nn. 7–9.

[11] Erickson, "Joseph and the Birth of Isaac in Matthew 1," 38–40. The gentile inclusion is seen almost immediately in the birth narrative where gentile magi respond faithfully to Jesus (2:1-12).

Abraham is not the only Old Testament character who Matthew parallels with Joseph. Joseph's name would certainly remind the readers of his Old Testament counterpart, the patriarch Joseph from the latter portion of Genesis.[12] Davies and Allison explain how Matthew's Joseph is similar to Genesis's Joseph: "he (1) has a father named Jacob; (2) goes down to Egypt; (3) has dreams given to him about the future;[13] (4) is chaste and godly (cf. *T. Sim.* 5.1); and (5) is long-suffering and disinclined to shame others or exhibit their faults (cf. *T. Jos.* 17.1-2)."[14] Additionally, the angel's instructions to Joseph—to take the child and his mother back to their homeland because those seeking the child's life are dead (τεθνήκασιν γὰρ οἱ ζητοῦντες τὴν ψυχὴν τοῦ παιδίου; Mt. 2:20)—are reminiscent of the Lord's instructions to Moses to similarly take his wife and sons and go back to their homeland because those seeking his life are dead (τεθνήκασιν γὰρ πάντες οἱ ζητοῦντές σου τὴν ψυχήν; Exod. 4:19).[15] These parallels characterize Joseph as one in a long line of Israelites who faithfully responded to God, a characterization Matthew develops further via contrasting him with Herod, which I will discuss below.

II. Righteous and Merciful Jew

One of the few instances of direct characterization of Joseph appears in 1:19, where Matthew says that Joseph is "righteous" (δίκαιος).[16] Seeing as this characterization comes from a reliable, omniscient narrator, the reader would accept it as a trustworthy evaluation of Joseph, yet Matthew needs to explain this character trait in light of two things he has already narrated: (1) Joseph was the husband of Mary but not the biological father of her son Jesus (1:16), and (2) Joseph and Mary were engaged, "but before they lived together, she was found to be with child from the Holy Spirit" (1:18).[17]

---

[12] Meier also notes, "[T]he fact that all of Jesus' immediate family bear 'patriarchal' and 'matriarchal' names [Joseph, Mary/Miriam, James/Jacob, Joses/Joseph, Simon/Simeon, and Jude/Judah] betokens the family's participation in the reawakening of Jewish national and religious identity, an identity that looked to the idyllic past of patriarchs for definition." See Meier, *A Marginal Jew*, 1:208.

[13] Gnuse argues that because Joseph's dreams in Genesis are visual and symbolic, they are different from Joseph's dreams in Matthew, which are auditory. He claims, then, that Matthew "finds its inspiration in the Elohist dreams of the patriarchal narratives" rather than those in the Joseph novella. The prevalence of Joseph's dreams in Genesis, however, along with their common name, suggest that readers would likely associate the characters, even if their dreams did not entirely match in form. See Robert Karl Gnuse, "Dream Genre in the Matthean Infancy Narratives," *NovT* 32 (1990): 115.

[14] W. D. Davies and Dale C. Allison Jr., *A Critical and Exegetical Commentary on the Gospel according to Saint Matthew*, 3 vols., ICC (London: T&T Clark, 1988), 1:182. Cf. Carter, *Matthew and the Margins*, 64. Note, though, that Davies and Allison are cautious in accepting a Joseph typology because, in their view, 1:15 was part of Matthew's tradition and thus not originally connected to what follows. They also note connections between Joseph and Moses' father, Amram. Hagner argues that the Joseph–Joseph parallels are not convincing because Matthew's typology focuses on Jesus, but his reasoning forces a false choice. See Donald Alfred Hagner, *Matthew 1–13*, WBC 33A (Grand Rapids, MI: Zondervan, 2018), 34.

[15] Davies and Allison, *Matthew*, 1:271.

[16] On direct characterization, see Mark Allan Powell, "Literary Approaches and the Gospel of Matthew," in *Methods for Matthew*, ed. Mark Allan Powell (Cambridge: Cambridge University Press, 2009), 50.

[17] D. Francois Tolmie, *Narratology and Biblical Narratives: A Practical Guide* (San Francisco: International Scholars Publications, 1999), 42–3.

The grammar of 1:19 (Ἰωσὴφ δὲ ὁ ἀνὴρ αὐτῆς, δίκαιος ὢν καὶ μὴ θέλων αὐτὴν δειγματίσαι, ἐβουλήθη λάθρᾳ ἀπολῦσαι αὐτήν) makes this characterization somewhat challenging to understand because it is not immediately clear how the two participial clauses ("being righteous" and "not wanting to publicly disgrace her") relate. Is Joseph's righteousness (generally understood as obedience to the law) at odds with his desire to show Mary mercy (he was righteous, *but* he did not want to disgrace her)?[18] Or is Joseph's righteousness manifest in his mercy toward Mary (he was righteous *and so* did not want to disgrace her)?[19]

The Old Testament background, historical context, and narrative dynamics of the chapter suggest that Matthew's characterization of Joseph as righteous and merciful are not at odds with one another, but nor are they the same thing—they are simply different, complementary traits of Joseph. First, on Old Testament background, Deuteronomy demanded punishment for adultery (22:13-22) and, in some cases, rape (22:23-9). Since the preceding verses in the genealogy frame Joseph's story in terms of God's work with Israel, "the authorial audience knows that Israel's law is an appropriate context in which to try to understand Joseph's actions."[20] Second, on historical context, the ideal reader would know that, as Keener puts it, "Jewish, Greek, and Roman law all demanded that a man divorce his wife if she were guilty of adultery."[21] This practice stems from ancient Mediterranean concepts of honor, which viewed adultery as a grievance against the husband. In both Greek and Jewish traditions, Neyrey explains, "the aggrieved husband must put away the guilty wife if he is to avoid being the victim of 'shame' himself."[22] Shame is a clear part of Matthew's presentation of Joseph's dilemma. Scott explains, "Mary has already shamed herself since 'she was found' to be pregnant. Joseph does not wish to add to her shame by a public denunciation."[23] Finally, on narrative dynamics, regardless of the Old Testament or historical legal necessities of divorce, "the logic of the story indicates that Joseph understood the situation to obligate or at least allow him, legally and morally, to divorce Mary rather than complete the marriage with the home-taking."[24]

---

[18] Hagner explains, "Joseph's righteousness impels him to act faithfully, which by the law's standard meant that Mary should be exposed as an adulteress and suffer the punishment (death by stoning, according to Deut 22:20-21, 23-24, but probably not insisted upon in the NT era; cf. John 8:3-11)." See Hagner, *Matthew*, 18.

[19] Hagner, Carter, and Brown argue for the former; Calkins argues for the latter. Hagner, *Matthew*, 18; Carter, *Matthew and the Margins*, 68; Brown, *The Birth of the Messiah*, 127-8; Arthus Burton Calkins, "The Justice of Joseph Revisited," *Homiletic and Pastoral Review* 88, no. 9 (1988): 12. For more on the meaning of δίκαιος in Matthew, see Davies and Allison, *Matthew*, 1:202-3; Benno Przybylski, *Righteousness in Matthew and His World of Thought*, SNTSMS 41 (Cambridge: Cambridge University Press, 1980), esp. 101-3.

[20] Warren Carter, *Matthew: Storyteller, Interpreter, Evangelist*, rev. edn (Peabody, MA: Hendrickson, 2004), 76.

[21] Craig S. Keener, *The Gospel of Matthew: A Socio-Rhetorical Commentary* (Grand Rapids, MI: Eerdmans, 2009), 91. See also Markus N. A. Bockmuehl, "Matthew 5:32, 19:9 in the Light of Pre-Rabbinic Halakhah," *NTS* 35 (1989): 291-5, who argues that divorce was mandatory for adultery among many groups in Judaism.

[22] Jerome H. Neyrey, *Honor and Shame in the Gospel of Matthew* (Louisville, KY: Westminster John Knox, 1998), 200.

[23] Bernard Brandon Scott, "The Birth of the Reader," *Semeia* 52 (1990): 89-90.

[24] Schaberg, *The Illegitimacy of Jesus*, 51.

A character described as "righteous" would most certainly uphold God's law. Seeing as how Joseph is not initially privy to information that the narrator and reader have, namely that Mary was *not* actually adulterous but rather with child from the Holy Spirit (1:18), it makes sense that he would proceed with a divorce.[25] As Brawley explains, Joseph's righteousness is not deficient, but his knowledge is.[26] Even with deficient knowledge, Matthew shows that Joseph is consistent across the ideological and spatiotemporal planes: his beliefs and values (i.e., following Torah) are consistent with his actions (i.e., to divorce Mary). Joseph is also consistent across the psychological and spatial planes: his motivation (i.e., not to further disgrace Mary) is consistent with the type of action he takes (i.e., to divorce her *quietly*).[27] His plan is to abide by the law in the most merciful way possible, and thus, in Joseph, righteousness and mercy stand side by side. Righteousness and mercy are not antithetical—Joseph does not have to choose between one or the other. But neither are righteousness and mercy the same— Joseph is not righteous *because* he did not want to disgrace Mary. Rather, Matthew lets both descriptions stand together. Joseph is righteous *and* merciful, foreshadowing the overlap of these two traits later in the narrative.

Once Joseph is given the information that the narrator and reader have—that Mary is, in fact, not adulterous but rather fulfilling the prophecy of Isa. 7:14—he continues to act in both a righteous and merciful way by immediately following the angel of the Lord's instruction to take Mary as his wife and adopt Jesus as his legal son (1:20, 24). Then the irony of Joseph's righteousness shifts once more, this time between narrated knowledge and public knowledge. Scott explains:

> Only the narrator, the implied reader and Joseph know that Jesus is adopted. From the public perspective, Joseph is the real father. This disjunction between narrated reality and the public perception ... forms an important aspect of the narrator's ideological focalization. From the narrated perspective, Joseph remains righteous, but from the public perspective he must forfeit his righteousness because by claiming Mary as his wife and naming the child he is implicitly admitting that they "came together" before they were married. Thus in order to maintain his narrated ascribed righteousness he will be publicly shamed.[28]

---

[25] Some disagree with this reading, arguing that Joseph *was* privy to Mary's conception via the Holy Spirit, but I agree with Schaberg that this understanding defies the logic of the story. See Schaberg, *The Illegitimacy of Jesus*, 51, for proponents of this view and a fuller discussion of this view's inadequacies.

[26] Robert L Brawley, "Joseph in Matthew's Birth Narrative and the Irony of Good Intentions," *Cumberland Seminarian* 28 (1990): 71.

[27] In his work on characterization in Matthew, Powell summarizes Boris Uspensky's four planes of expression as follows: "(1) the ideological plane concerns values and beliefs; (2) the phraseological plane concerns speech, or thoughts if these are articulated as speech . . .; (3) the spatial and temporal planes concern actions; (4) the psychological plane concerns motives." See Mark Allan Powell, "Characterization on the Phraseological Plane in the Gospel of Matthew," in *Treasures New and Old: Recent Contributions to Matthean Studies*, ed. David R. Bauer and Mark Allan Powell, SBLSymS 1 (Atlanta: Scholars Press, 1996), 163; Boris Uspensky, *A Poetics of Composition: The Structure of the Artistic Text and Typology of a Compositional Form*, trans. Valentina Zavarin and Susan Wittig (Berkeley: University of California Press, 1973), 8.

[28] Scott, "The Birth of the Reader," 90. Though cf. Schaberg, who adds, "[H]ome-taking, the completion of marriage, *would* remove the suspicion of seduction/adultery. A Torah-observant man would

As I will explore below, this private righteousness prepares the reader for Jesus' later teachings on righteousness, which, as Joseph's character does here, go beyond just following the law to include discerning and following God's will.[29]

Matthew develops his characterization of Joseph as righteous in one further way—through his comment that Joseph "had no marital relations with her until she had borne a son" (1:25). Through this note, Matthew not only reaffirms that Joseph is not the biological father of Jesus, but also portrays him as sexually chaste, foreshadowing Jesus' teaching on sexual ethics in the kingdom of God in Chapter 19.[30]

III. Example of Obedience and Acceptance

While Matthew told the reader outright that Joseph was righteous (direct characterization), he *shows* the reader that Joseph is obedient to God (indirect characterization).[31] As Tolmie explains, "The implied reader has to consider the information provided and formulate it in terms of a trait."[32] The author can do this via the character's actions, speech, appearance, and environment. In the case of Joseph's obedience, Matthew accomplishes this almost exclusively through his actions.

These obedient actions are embedded in what Gnuse calls a "command–execution pattern."[33] Matthew's infancy narrative contains five dream reports where a character is given specific instructions of what to do, four of which include Joseph: (1) in 1:20-5, Joseph is to marry Mary; (2) in 2:12, the magi are to return to their own country; (3) in 2:13-15, Joseph is to take Mary and Jesus to Egypt; (4) in 2:19-21, Joseph is to return to Israel with Mary and Jesus; and (5) in 2:22, Joseph is to go to Galilee. Matthew follows a specific pattern in these dreams to Joseph, with the exception of 2:22, which is a truncated dream announcement without speech from the angel. Davies and Allison articulate the pattern as follows:

A. note of circumstance (1:18b-19; 2:13; 2:19)
B. appearance of the angel of the Lord in a dream (1:20a; 2:13; 2:19)
C. command of the angel to Joseph (1:20b; 2:13; 2:20a)
D. explanation of command (γάρ clause; 1:20c; 2:13; 2:20b)
E. Joseph rises (ἐγερθείς) and obediently responds (1:24-5; 2:14-15; 2:21)[34]

probably not complete the marriage with an adulteress. But home-taking *would not* remove the suspicion of rape." Either way, because of the narrator's explanation to the reader (1:18) and the angel's explanation to Joseph (1:20), the implied reader knows that neither adultery nor rape explain Mary's pregnancy or Joseph's decision to marry her. See Schaberg, *The Illegitimacy of Jesus*, 63.

[29] Davis, "Fulfillment of Creation," 531; Martin C. Spadaro, *Reading Matthew as the Climactic Fulfillment of the Hebrew Story* (Eugene, OR: Wipf & Stock, 2015), 74; Neyrey, *Honor and Shame*, 99.
[30] Allison gives primary source evidence for religious celibacy in ancient Judaism along with Greco-Roman philosophical views about sex during pregnancy being "against nature." He also connects 1:25 with 19:10-12, which I develop further below. See Dale C. Allison Jr., "Divorce, Celibacy and Joseph (Matthew 1:18-25 and 19:1-12)," *JSNT* 49 (1993): 5–10.
[31] On the distinction between telling and showing readers what characters are like, see Powell, "Literary Approaches," 50. Powell argues that the latter is more common.
[32] Tolmie, *Narratology*, 44–5.
[33] Gnuse, "Dream Genre," 105.
[34] Davies and Allison, *Matthew*, 1:196-7. Cf. Gnuse, "Dream Genre," 104–6.

Except in 2:19-21, each of the commands and executions include a notice of how these events fulfill what was spoken through a prophet or prophets (1:23; 2:15; 2:23). Even if Joseph comes across as a somewhat robotic, flat character, the larger function of this command–execution pattern and the emphasis on fulfillment nonetheless highlight Joseph's obedience to God's will.[35]

Other aspects of Matthew's characterization of Joseph also deserve attention. The use of the same words in the angel's command and Joseph's response highlights his *careful* obedience. For example:

Command (2:20): ἐγερθεὶς παράλαβε τὸ παιδίον καὶ τὴν μητέρα αὐτοῦ καὶ πορεύου εἰς γῆν Ἰσραήλ
Response (2:21): ὁ δὲ ἐγερθεὶς παρέλαβεν τὸ παιδίον καὶ τὴν μητέρα αὐτοῦ καὶ εἰσῆλθεν εἰς γῆν Ἰσραήλ

Additionally, the immediacy apparent in Joseph's response highlights his *prompt* obedience.[36] For example:

Command (2:13): ἐγερθεὶς παράλαβε τὸ παιδίον καὶ τὴν μητέρα αὐτοῦ καὶ φεῦγε εἰς Αἴγυπτον καὶ ἴσθι ἐκεῖ . . .
Response (2:14-15): ὁ δὲ ἐγερθεὶς παρέλαβεν τὸ παιδίον καὶ τὴν μητέρα αὐτοῦ <u>νυκτὸς</u> καὶ ἀνεχώρησεν εἰς Αἴγυπτον, καὶ ἦν ἐκεῖ

Davies and Allison also point out that after the announcement of Mary's pregnancy in 1:18, Joseph is the only *active* character in the family: he is the subject of the verbs; he plans to divorce Mary; he encounters angels; he does what the angels command; he takes Mary as his wife; he refrains from sexual relations with her until after her pregnancy; he names Jesus; he hears that Archelaus is ruler and is afraid; he makes his home in Nazareth.[37] Kingsbury notes that in almost all these instances Joseph is "rendering service to Jesus," not unlike minor characters do at Jesus' passion. This puts Joseph among a cast of minor characters, most of whom, Howell observes, "are exemplary figures in Matthew's story and exhibit traits that reflect the system of values that both Jesus and Matthew as narrator advocate."[38]

Part of Joseph's obedience to the divine will includes being an example of how faithful Israel should respond to its Messiah, which is a key theme in Matthew's larger plot.[39] Matthew highlights Joseph's example by contrasting him with Herod—an

---

[35] Gnuse, "Dream Genre," 105, 113.

[36] Note also a similarly prompt response after the first dream, where Matthew notes, "When Joseph awoke from sleep he did as the angel of the Lord commanded" (1:24). Carter, *Matthew and the Margins*, 72. Davies and Allison, *Matthew*, 1:261, note other meanings for Joseph's flight to Egypt by night (the *Passover Haggadah* was at night; Jesus was taken by his enemies at his passion at night, etc.), but the presence of other meanings does not diminish the one proposed here.

[37] Davies and Allison, *Matthew*, 1:259.

[38] Kingsbury, *Matthew as Story*, 27–8.

[39] The two themes Howell articulates as central to Matthew's larger plot are promise/fulfillment and acceptance/rejection. Joseph is central in advancing both of those themes in the infancy narrative. See David B. Howell, *Matthew's Inclusive Story: A Study in the Narrative Rhetoric of the First Gospel*, JSNTSup 42 (Sheffield: JSOT Press, 1990), 111–17.

example of how Israel should *not* respond to its Messiah.⁴⁰ This contrast is embedded in how Matthew structures the infancy narrative. In between Joseph's first and second dreams, Matthew places the first story of Herod and the magi (2:1-12); in between Joseph's second and third dreams, Matthew concludes the story of Herod and the magi (2:16-18). Since readers consider each episode in light of the former one, they would consider Herod and the magi in light of Joseph's dreams and then also consider Joseph's dreams in light of Herod and the magi.⁴¹

Joseph's story begins with him having the choice to either accept or reject the angel's instructions to marry Mary and name her son, thereby accepting as his son the one the reader knows is the Messiah (1:1, 17). Joseph accepts these instructions and obeys. Herod's story begins with him responding in fear to the magi's report of the Messiah. At first, readers do not know that Herod's initial response—being frightened and then secretly calling on the Wise Men to get information for him—is rejection. A more negative characterization of Herod emerges, however, when the magi are warned to avoid Herod. Their actions are trustworthy because they are characters who responded positively to Jesus and because they were warned in a dream—thus far a reliable form of divine communication in Matthew.

Joseph's second dream, in which the angel tells him to flee with his family to Egypt because "Herod is about to search for the child to destroy him" (2:13), removes any ambiguity about Herod's character. Once more, Joseph's obedience to the angel is set in stark contrast to Herod's malevolent rejection of Jesus. When Matthew switches back to Herod's story after Joseph's second dream, the contrast deepens all the more. Herod's rage at being tricked prompts him to kill the children aged two and under in Bethlehem and the surrounding areas in order to complete his destruction of the Messiah, reminding readers of Pharaoh, the great enemy of God's people, in Exodus. Despite Herod's actions fulfilling Jeremiah's prophecy (2:17-18), he does not prevail. Meanwhile Joseph, prompted by his third and fourth dreams (2:19-23), is the one who quite literally goes out of his way to protect the Messiah—from Bethlehem to Egypt back to Judea and finally to Nazareth in Galilee (2:23). This back and forth of acceptance and rejection in the infancy narrative leaves the reader wondering how the rest of Israel will respond to the Messiah as the narrative progresses and teaches them how to interpret later parts of the narrative.⁴² When new characters are introduced, they will be compared to the standard Joseph set for how Israel should respond faithfully—with acceptance and careful, swift obedience.⁴³

---

⁴⁰ On the Joseph–Herod contrast, see Howell, *Matthew's Inclusive Story*, 117–18; Davis, "Fulfillment of Creation," 534–5; Kingsbury, *Matthew as Story*, 49.

⁴¹ Mark Allan Powell, "Narrative Criticism," in *Hearing the New Testament: Strategies for Interpretation*, ed. Joel B. Green, 2nd edn (Grand Rapids, MI: Eerdmans, 2010), 245. Matthew also contrasts Herod and the magi (rejection/acceptance; Jew/gentile; plots to kill/worship), in addition to Herod and Joseph. The former does not negate the latter. See Hagner, *Matthew*, 30–1.

⁴² On the development of this acceptance/rejection plotline later in Matthew, see Frank J. Matera, "The Plot of Matthew's Gospel," *CBQ* 49 (1987): 243.

⁴³ On how authors "educate" their readers to read their narratives correctly, especially via information early in the narrative, see Howell, *Matthew's Inclusive Story*, 115.

IV. Beyond the Infancy Narrative: An Exemplar of Jesus' Teachings

Thus far I have worked through Matthew's characterization of Joseph in Mt. 1 and 2. Beyond the infancy narrative, however, Joseph is never named and only referred to once (Mt. 13:55).[44] Nonetheless, the implied reader would recognize Joseph as an exemplar of many of the teachings of Jesus.

A. Righteousness, Mercy, and Marriage: Mt. 5–6; 19:1-10

Joseph looms large in the background of Jesus' first sermon in Matthew, where Jesus shows deep concern for righteousness: those who hunger and thirst for righteousness (δικαιοσύνη) will be filled (5:6); those persecuted for righteousness' (δικαιοσύνη) sake will have the kingdom of heaven (5:10); disciples in the kingdom of heaven must have righteousness (δικαιοσύνη) that exceeds that of the scribes and Pharisees (5:20); the Father sends rain on the just (δίκαιος) and unjust (ἄδικος) (5:45); disciples are warned not to practice their righteousness (δικαιοσύνη) before others (6:1); and they are to seek first God's kingdom and righteousness (δικαιοσύνη) (6:33). In Chapter 1, Matthew characterized Joseph directly as righteous (δίκαιος) through his commitment to honoring God's law regarding adultery.[45] Of course, when Joseph discovered the divine origin of Mary's pregnancy, he proceeded with their marriage, maintaining his righteous posture by honoring the divine will. As discussed above, the reader knows this marriage supports the characterization of Joseph as righteous because they are privy to the narrator's (and eventually Joseph's) knowledge that Mary's pregnancy is through the Spirit; yet, no other human characters in the story beyond Mary and Joseph are privy to this information, and thus Joseph's righteousness is private rather than public, perhaps even producing public shame. Joseph, then, becomes a character who models what it is to not practice one's righteousness before others (6:1) and even

---

[44] In Mt. 13:54-6, the people from Nazareth ask rhetorically, "Where did this man get this wisdom and these deeds of power? Is not this the carpenter's son? Is not his mother called Mary? And are not his brothers James and Joseph and Simon and Judas? And are not all his sisters with us? Where then did this man get all this?" The point of this pericope is not particularly about Joseph, but rather about how the origins of Jesus seem to be at odds with his wisdom and teaching. For the sake of being thorough, I note here that Matthew characterizes Joseph as a carpenter; this is not a significant part of his characterization, however, seeing as it is only mentioned here and has no clear connections with the material in chs. 1–2, outside of potentially 1:25 (the primary concern of which is Mary's virginity at the birth of Jesus, not Joseph). Most scholarly insight into this text focuses on Matthew's redaction of Mk 6:3 and the historical and theological issues related to whether the siblings of Jesus were the product of sexual union by Joseph and Mary. See Meier, *A Marginal Jew*, 1:322–3; Brown, *The Birth of the Messiah*, 132, 519.

[45] Spadaro, *Reading Matthew*, 74. Howell notes the "convergence between the narrator and Jesus on the phraseological plane ... [which is] visible in a number of words, phrases and concepts used by the narrator that are also present in Jesus' speech. For example, the narrator describes Joseph as a just (δίκαιος) man (1.19), while δίκαιος is used frequently by Jesus (5.45; 9.13; 10.41; 13.17, 43, 49; 23.29, 35; 25.37, 46) and δικαιοσύνη appears as an important term in Jesus' teaching that characterizes his own actions (3.15), those of his disciples (5.6, 10, 20, 6.33), and those of John the Baptist (21.32)." See Howell, *Matthew's Inclusive Story*, 192.

be persecuted or shamed for his righteousness (5:10). Joseph's righteousness is the opposite of the scribes and Pharisees who "on the outside look righteous to others, but inside... are full of hypocrisy and lawlessness" (23:28).[46] When the readers come to the passion narrative and see how Jesus takes the shame of others on himself, they may even recognize the cruciform shape of Joseph's earlier action of taking Mary's apparent shame on himself.

Matthew's characterization of Joseph as both righteous and merciful went side by side in Chapter 1, which prepared readers to see those traits side by side again in Chapter 5: "Blessed are the merciful" (5:7) immediately follows "Blessed are those who hunger and thirst for righteousness" (5:6). Both are apt descriptions of Joseph. If readers wonder whether righteousness and mercy are antithetical, as some scholars have done, Matthew pushes back against such an antithesis.[47] Joseph is *both* righteous and merciful in the way he handled Mary's pregnancy, as are those who are blessed in the kingdom of heaven. In fact, as the story progresses, Matthew may even be redefining righteousness to include mercy.[48]

Joseph is also in the background of Jesus' teachings on divorce (5:31-2; 19:1-12), since Joseph had planned to divorce Mary upon hearing of her pregnancy (1:19). By the time readers encounter these teachings of Jesus, though, they know that Joseph did not go through with the divorce he had originally planned. Joseph's actions are consistent with Jesus' teachings that "whoever divorces his wife, except for unchastity (πορνεία), and marries another commits adultery" (19:9; cf. 5:32).[49] Since Mary was not unchaste but instead with child from the Holy Spirit (1:18), divorce would have been inappropriate.[50] More than that, though, we see that Joseph's motives—both righteousness and mercy—are present in Jesus' teachings on divorce.[51] For Jesus, merciful righteousness means that a person is not entitled to divorce "for any cause"

---

[46] The scribes and Pharisees in Matthew are representative of the religious leaders, whom Powell describes as "flat characters who function as the antagonists of Jesus in [Matthew's] story." They almost exclusively reject Jesus. Here, then, we see the continued development of the theme of acceptance or rejection of Jesus that was introduced in the infancy narrative. Privately righteous Joseph represents Jews who accept God's Messiah; outwardly righteous religious leaders are Jews who, not unlike Herod, reject God's Messiah. See Powell, "Characterization," 171–7.

[47] Carter, *Matthew and the Margins*, 68; Schaberg, *The Illegitimacy of Jesus*, 50–1.

[48] Cf. 3:15, where Jesus "fulfills all righteousness" in his baptism through his merciful identification with humanity in its weakness and sinfulness; 5:17-43, where Jesus gives several examples of mercy as ways for disciples' righteousness to exceed that of the scribes and Pharisees; 9:10-13, where Jesus prioritizes mercy to those who see themselves as righteous; 23:1-28, where the scribes and Pharisees' behavior is characterized as unrighteous, at least in part due to their lack of mercy; 26:57–27:61 (cf. 20:28), where the righteous sufferer mercifully gives up his life for others.

[49] While there is no shortage of debate over the best translation of πορνεία—incest, adultery, fornication, sexual immorality—the particular translation is not crucial here since Mt. 1 clearly absolves Mary of any sort of sexual impropriety. On the translation of μὴ ἐπὶ πορνεία, especially reading Mt. 1 and 19 together, see Allison, "Divorce, Celibacy and Joseph," 3–4.

[50] Allison explores this point in greater depth, noting that Joseph would not be characterized as "just" had his actions "so obviously contradicted a ruling of Jesus." See Allison, "Divorce, Celibacy and Joseph," 36.

[51] I do not mean to suggest that Joseph had knowledge of Jesus' teaching on divorce before his birth. My concern here is with the continuity of Matthew's characterization of Joseph and Jesus' teaching, which the reader would encounter in that order.

(κατὰ πᾶσαν αἰτίαν; 19:3), as the Pharisees propose to Jesus, but only for a breach of the marriage covenant.

At the conclusion of Jesus' teaching on divorce in Chapter 19, the disciples conclude "it is better not to marry" (19:10), to which Jesus responds by acknowledging how hard his teaching is to accept. He then concludes, "For there are eunuchs who have been so from birth, and there are eunuchs who have been made eunuchs by others, and there are eunuchs who have made themselves eunuchs for the sake of the kingdom of heaven" (19:12). Though Joseph was not a eunuch, Matthew does note in 1:25 that Joseph "had no marital relations with her until she had borne a son." Allison argues that this notice was not just designed "for the literal fulfillment of Isa. 7:14 but also to exhibit Joseph's exemplary behavior: if Jesus' father was not exactly a eunuch for the kingdom of heaven, he certainly did know when to refrain from coupling with his wife."[52]

B. Doing the Will of the Father: Mt. 12:46-50

In Mt. 12:46-50, Jesus is speaking to the crowd while his mother and brothers wait for him outside. When someone tells Jesus about his family waiting for him, he responds as follows: "'Who is my mother, and who are my brothers?' And pointing to his disciples, he said, 'Here are my mother and my brothers! For whoever does the will of my Father in heaven is my brother and sister and mother.'" Joseph is notably absent here and has been since the end of Chapter 2. While much ink has been spilled speculating why Joseph is absent historically speaking—he was dead at this point in the ministry of Jesus, he had abandoned the family, he was neutral toward Jesus' ministry and thus not useful to the evangelists—the implied readers would recall Joseph here.[53] Jesus is redefining membership in the community, not by biological descent but by doing the will of God.[54] Matthew addressed biological descent explicitly in Chapter 1, where he showed that Jesus was the Son of David, even though not biologically—*very explicitly not biologically!*—the son of Joseph, through whom Davidic descent was transferred. On top of that, Joseph is the first example in Matthew of a character doing the will of the Father in heaven, a point the reader would not miss with the repeated angels, dreams, scripture fulfillment, and immediate obedience of Joseph to these divine directives.[55] Thus, even though Joseph is not mentioned among Jesus' family waiting for him, his legacy is there as the first one in the narrative to live according to Jesus' teaching.

---

[52] Allison, "Divorce, Celibacy and Joseph," 10. This conclusion comes after a discussion of Greco-Roman and Jewish views about refraining from sex during a woman's pregnancy. From this observation about Joseph's abstinence in light of contemporary views, he concludes, "We may be reasonably confident that there were those in Matthew's original audience who would have found such meaning in our text, and hence in Joseph an example to follow."

[53] Meier, *A Marginal Jew*, 1:317; Andries G. Van Aarde, "The Carpenter's Son (Mt 13:55): Joseph and Jesus in the Gospel of Matthew and Other Texts," *Neot* 34 (2000): 186–7.

[54] Carter, *Matthew and the Margins*, 67. The reader might pick up on a similar motif in 10:40: "Whoever welcomes me welcomes the one who sent me."

[55] Scott, "The Birth of the Reader," 92.

V. Conclusion

Brown is right—Joseph *does* hold together Matthew's infancy narrative. And he is also right that Joseph does so by being a righteous Jew, faithful to Torah, protector of the Messiah from the Jewish authorities, and the one who brings Jesus into "Galilee of the Gentiles." I hope that here I have not only supported Brown's claim, but also expanded it. Beyond Brown's description, Joseph also connects Jesus to the families of Abraham and David and to the larger story of Israel; he is also a righteous Jew with a merciful application of Torah; he is also obedient to the divine will and an example of how faithful Israel should respond to its Messiah; and he is also an exemplar of Jesus' teachings, particularly those on righteousness, mercy, divorce, abstinence, and membership in God's community based on doing God's will, not biological descent. Not bad for a guy who never speaks and isn't named after Chapter 2!

2

The Passive Protagonist: The Characterization of Mary in the Gospel of Matthew 1-2 and the *Protevangelium* of James

Lily C. Vuong

I. Introduction

Of the two canonical infancy narratives, Matthew's account is often accused of painting a less than flattering depiction of Mary, since she never speaks and is seemingly eclipsed by the acts of Joseph—the angel approaches him to discuss Mary's situation (1:20-1, cf. Lk. 1:26-38) and it is Joseph who gives Jesus his name (1:20, 25, cf. Lk. 1:31). No doubt, the Gospel of Matthew offers an infancy narrative (and gospel) from an androcentric perspective and worldview, filled with patriarchal assumptions,[1] and yet feminist interpretations reveal strikingly positive portraits of Mary and women in general in Matthew's infancy story upon a closer and higher reading—one which sees God's plans and intentions fulfilled not by men but by women.[2] Comparatively, the second-century apocryphal narrative, the *Protevangelium of James* (*Protevangelium* hereafter) offers a much more expansive infancy story, one that puts Mary's character in the spotlight. We learn significant details about Mary's early life, including her parents, infancy, and childhood (1:1–7:10), and even the familiar details of Mary's marriage to Joseph (9:1-7), Annunciation (11:1-8, cf. Lk. 1:28, 42), and birth of Jesus (19:13-16, cf.

---

[1] As it has been long noted, Matthew embodies patriarchal assumptions and androcentric perspectives: the genealogy is patrilineal and Joseph is featured in the birth narrative; God is consistently addressed as Father and in other masculine titles and pronouns; Jewish leadership and characters with status and power are identified as male, etc. See, e.g., Janice Capel Anderson, "Matthew: Gender and Reading," in *Feminist Companion to Matthew*, ed. Amy-Jill Levine (Sheffield: Sheffield Academic Press, 2001), 25–51, and Julian Sheffield, "The Father in the Gospel of Matthew," in *Feminist Companion to Matthew*, ed. Amy-Jill Levine (Sheffield: Sheffield Academic Press, 2001), 52–69. For biblical and literary critical studies that attempt to recover positive images of women and to position them as the center of narratives, see, e.g., Elaine Mary Wainwright, *Towards a Feminist Critical Reading of the Gospel According to Matthew*, BZNW 60 (1991; repr. New York: De Gruyter, 2010).

[2] Dorothy Jean Weaver, "'Wherever This Good News Is Proclaimed': Women and God in the Gospel of Matthew," *Int* 64, no. 4 (2010): 390; Dorothy Jean Weaver, "Rewriting the Messianic Script," *Int* 54, no. 4 (2000): 376–85.

Lk. 2:30, 32) are given a colorful new life.³ And yet, despite being at the center of the plot, Mary is ironically passive in the narrative. She speaks only eight times throughout the entire story (*Prot. Jas.* 11:6, 11:9, 12:6, 13:8, 13:10, 15:13, 17:9, and 17:10)⁴ and her body is almost wholly controlled by other characters. What then are we to make of these two very different depictions of Mary's passivity—Matthew provides almost no information about Mary except that she is mother to Jesus, while the *Protevangelium* is all about her. In this chapter, I would like to explore the possibility of interpreting Mary's passivity in terms of the *passivum divinum* or *divine/theological passive* in Matthew and her role as God's virgin and sacred vessel/temple in the *Protevangelium*. More specifically, I read Mary's passivity in both texts not as an androcentric silencing of her character, but as mirroring the way God is communicated to the reader in Matthew 1–2 and directly linked to her characterization as sacred vessel in the *Protevangelium*.

II. Mary in the Gospel of Matthew

A. The *passivum divinum* in Matthew 1–2

Perhaps first coined by Joachim Jeremias,⁵ the *passivum divinum* or *divine/theological passive* was traditionally viewed as the impersonal passive used in the New Testament as a way to indirectly attribute the divine as the subject of an active verb. Benedict Viviano has described it as "reverent circumlocution," resulting in the revelation of the presence of God but in a concealed way.⁶ While recent scholarship has critiqued the ubiquitous and indiscriminate overuse of the term for defining all agentless passives in the New Testament,⁷ there is general consensus that when this rhetorical or stylistic technique is properly assigned, its purpose is to demonstrate and reinforce God's active involvement in history both explicitly and implicitly. While there is debate over precisely how many *passiva divina* are used in Matthew, scholars generally agree that at least fifty occurrences exist⁸ and that Jesus' Sermon on the Mount (sayings of Jesus)

---

[3] All citations and translations of the *Protevangelium of James* are from Lily C. Vuong, *The Protevangelium of James*, Westar Tools Translations Series; Early Christian Apocrypha Series 7 (Eugene, OR: Cascade Press, 2019).

[4] See Lily C. Vuong, *Gender and Purity in the Protevangelium of James* (Tübingen: Mohr Siebeck, 2013), 174–5.

[5] Joachim Jeremias, *New Testament Theology* (New York: Charles Scribner's Sons, 1971), 10–11.

[6] Benedict Thomas Viviano, "God in the Gospel According to Matthew," *Int* 64, no. 4 (2010): 349.

[7] For a survey of the history and use of the *divine passive* as well as its imprecise use in scholarship and a discussion of more common usages of the agentless passive, e.g., "to focus attention on the original transitive object ... to downgrade the importance of the original transitive subject ...," see Peter-Ben Smit with Toon Renssen, "The *passivum divinum*: The Rise and Future Fall of an Imaginary Linguistic Phenomenon," *Filologia Neotestamentaria* 27 (2014): 3–24 (23). See also Stanley E. Porter, *Idioms of the New Testament Greek* (Sheffield: JSOT Press, 1992), 65–6; Stanley E. Porter, "Commentaries on the Book of Romans," in *On the Writing of the New Testament Commentaries: Festschrift for Grant R. Osborne on the Occasion of His 70th Birthday*, ed. Eckhard J. Schnabel and Stanley E. Porter, TENTS 8 (Leiden: Brill, 2013), 365–404, who also critiques the uncritical and overuse of the term. Specific critique of the increase of the *passiva divina* in Mark has received recent attention, i.e., Beniamin Pascut, "The So-Called Passivum Divinum in Mark's Gospel," *NovT* 54 (2012): 313–33.

[8] See Jeremias, *New Testament Theology*, 10–11; Donald S. Deer, "Les constructions à sens passif dans le grec des évangiles synoptiques: Problèmes d'interprétation et de traduction" (PhD diss., Université des

contains the most concentrated usage of the device (e.g., the Beatitudes alone attest to four *passiva divina* within a span of six verses).⁹

While Matthew's infancy narrative naturally does not include the sayings of Jesus, Robbie Booth argues that the occurrences of the *passiva divina* in Matthew can be broadly grouped into six categories: Those that occur in (1) the Sermon on the Mount; (2) fulfillment formulae; (3) eschatological imagery; (4) miraculous events; (5) divine impartations; and (6) other miscellaneous examples.¹⁰ The examples of the *passiva divina* in Matthew's infancy narrative (1–2) draw specifically from the second (fulfillment formulae) and fourth (miraculous events) categories. The fulfillment formulae provide us with four examples, the first occurring at Mt. 1:22: "All this took place to fulfill what had been spoken by the Lord through the prophet." This verse employs two *passiva divina*: πληρωθῇ, "it was fulfilled," and ῥηθὲν, "it was spoken." Here the subject of the passage, "the Lord," is hidden in the passive and made only explicit by the phrase ὑπὸ κυρίου.¹¹ The Lord is identified as the fulfiller and speaker of the events immediately described, that is: "'Look, the virgin shall conceive and bear a son, and they shall name him Emmanuel,' which means, 'God is with us'" (1:23). In many ways, "Emmanuel" functions to highlight the goals of the *passiva divina*, as it is a reminder of God's authority and supreme power over all human activities and of the fulfillment of promises revealed to the prophets of the Old Testament/Hebrew Bible—God is indeed active, present, and always with humanity, even if sometimes only indirectly. The three other examples occur at Mt. 2:15, 17, and 23. God as the active agent of πληρωθῇ ("it was fulfilled") and ῥηθὲν ("it was spoken") is subtly referenced as a veiled idiom in the context of Mary and Joseph's escape to Egypt, the massacre of the infants (here Jeremiah is specifically cited as the prophet), and Joseph's dream and return from Egypt, respectively.

The *passivum divinum* is frequently used within the category of miraculous events. In the infancy story, it once again appears in the genealogy with specific reference to Mary's conception of Jesus. In the genealogy, the traditional aorist active ἐγέννησεν ("begat") pattern attested thirty-nine times is interrupted with an aorist passive ἐγεννήθη ("was conceived") in the case of Jesus' birth. Charles Quarles argues that the grammatical change attests to God's active role in the conception of Jesus by Mary, but in an indirect way.¹² Among the various criteria often applied to determine a true

---

Sciences Humaines, Strasbourg, 1973). Charles L. Quarles lists sixty-seven occurrences in *Matthew*, EGGNT (Nashville: B&H Academic, 2017). More recently, Robbie Booth has argued for an additional two occurrences in Matthew's parables of the mustard seed and leaven: "God as the Agent of Kingdom Growth: An Argument for Divine Passives in Matthew 13:32, 33," *JETS* 62, no. 4 (2019): 705–19.

⁹ Booth's study provides a useful breakdown of the divine passive's use and frequency by comparing total word counts, passives, and divine passives for the whole gospel and selected chapters; Booth, "God as the Agent of Kingdom Growth," 707, n. 7.

¹⁰ Booth, "God as Agent of Kingdom Growth," 706–9.

¹¹ Viviano, "God in the Gospel According to Matthew," 349.

¹² Quarles, *Matthew*, 16. While more reluctant to assign the divine passive as the motivation behind many passives, Peter-Ben Smit identifies the passive involved in the birth of Jesus as a divine passive: "Something About Mary? Remarks about the Five Women in the Matthean Genealogy," *NTS* 56 (2010): 197–8, esp. n. 23. He notes, along with Moises Mayordomo-Marin, *Den Anfang hören. Lesorientierte Evangelienexegese am Beispiel von Mattäus 1–2*, FRLANT 180 (Göttingen: Vandenhoeck & Ruprecht, 1998), 238, that the syntax of Mt. 1:16 removes Joseph from the actual

passivum divinum, the use of passive verbs for actions viewed as unfit to directly attribute to God seems to be at play here in the conception of Jesus in the genealogy.[13] The use of the *passivum divinum* in Matthew's genealogy reflects the author's goal to present God as unequivocally present and yet at the same time elusive, mysterious, and hidden. As mentioned above, the reference to Jesus as Emmanuel or "God is with us" reflects a major theme in the gospel as a whole and is underscored by the reference to God's presence at Mt. 1:22 and then again in the final chapter at 28:20: "I [Jesus] am with you always." The theme of the Emmanuel passage builds on the idea of God as savior, fulfiller of promises, hearer of prayers, forgiver of sins, and deliverer of all by building upon LXX Isa. 7:14.[14] Matthew carefully draws the connection between God and Jesus by way of the virginal conception, placed on the body of Mary in her role as virgin mother. Mary plays an invaluable role in Matthew's overall goals, but his presentation of her is passive and veiled, and her depiction as virgin mother is, at best, mysterious. I suggest that Mary's passive presence represents not a devaluing of her position but rather a complement to the *passiva divina* since God has claimed Mary's body to do his works. In other words, Mary is described in language similar to that used for referencing God because she is directly connected to him and functions as an extension of his will. The presentation of Mary as passive protagonist is further exemplified in Matthew's genealogy scene and her role as Jesus' mother in the infancy narrative where she is both discretely revealed and concealed.

B. A Feminist-literary Reading of Mary as Revealed and Concealed in Matthew's Genealogy and the Infancy Narrative

Scholarship has long noted and commented on Matthew's unique genealogy. According to Mt. 1:17, this tightly structured patrilineal genealogy consists of forty-two men neatly divided into three groups of fourteen generations "from Abraham to David," "from David to the Deportation to Babylon," and "from the Deportation to Babylon to Messiah,"[15] but is interrupted by the insertion of five women: Tamar, Rahab, Ruth, the Wife of Uriah (Bathsheba),[16] and Mary. Traditional interpretations of these women speculate on what the first four Old Testament women have in common, bracketing Mary the mother of Jesus.[17] Many such interpretations attempt to make sense of the

---

genealogy of Jesus, making the divine passive a reasonable assumption. More importantly, the grammatical switch may well have been spotted by a first-century reader who would have interpreted the passive tense as indicative of divine intervention.

[13] Smit with Rennsen, *passivum divinum*, 15.
[14] Jeremias, *New Testament Theology*, 10–11.
[15] Although Mt. 1:17 notes three groups of fourteen generations, the third group only has thirteen generations.
[16] Traditional interpretation has often assumed that Matthew's reference to Uriah is an explicit reference to Bathsheba. Jeffrey Aernie's chapter in this volume offers a critique of this interpretation and notes that she is likely the daughter of an Israelite (Eliam in 2 Sam. 11:3; Ammiel in 2 Chron. 3:5), thus problematizing the interpretation that the women are connected because they are gentiles. This view, of course, is also problematic, since Mary is clearly not a gentile. As Jason B. Hood argues, it seems more plausible that Matthew specifically names Uriah, along with Tamar, Rahab, and Ruth, to develop the positive position of gentiles within Jesus' genealogy: *The Messiah, His Brothers, and the Nations: Matthew 1:1-17*, LNTS 441 (London: T&T Clark, 2011).
[17] Smit, "Something About Mary?" 191–207, critiques this approach.

androcentric genealogy by viewing the four women as sinners who involved themselves in suspicious sexual activities, proposing that their inclusion was to underscore Jesus' role as a liberator of people from their sins.[18] Other popular interpretations proffer the idea these women were foreigners and their inclusion signaled Jesus' role as a savior not only for the Jews but also the gentiles, since he too had foreign blood.[19] Interestingly, both approaches depend on interpreting the women in contrast to Mary, since she was not actually involved in a sexual scandal and is clearly Jewish. A much more fruitful method, in my opinion, is to examine the correspondences rather than the contrasts of these four women to Mary. By focusing on what they share, one finds a steady build-up to a climax that culminates with the story of Mary, in which she highlights the role already played by these predecessors.[20] In other words, the four women, as Peter-Ben Smit and others have noted, prepare and vindicate the awkward and problematic circumstances surrounding Jesus' birth.[21] Even though Mary does not speak or act, her position is clearly the focus and climax of the genealogy. The text reinforces this idea in two ways: first, Matthew interrupts the tightly formulaic structure of men's names in the genealogy to include women; and second, by his naming Mary in particular, the lineage between father (i.e., Joseph) and son (i.e., Jesus) breaks—Joseph is not described as Jesus' father but rather as "the husband of Mary, of whom Jesus was born, which is called the Messiah" (1:16).[22] What's more, Matthew allots a full-blown narrative immediately following the genealogy to explain this specific reference to Mary and her role as virgin mother. This narrative makes clear that Mary's pregnancy is not the result of unfaithfulness; that the child "conceived in her is from the Holy Spirit" (1:20) and divinely ordained to "save his people from their sins" (1:21c); that Mary's child still continues to be of the messianic line via Joseph's naming of the child Jesus (1:25) and his adoption as his son; and finally, that this is all God's work.

But what precisely is God's work here? At the core, God's ultimate plan is to "save" his people and remind them that he is ever-present via the birth of his son Jesus who is called Emmanuel. God must work within Mary's womb to bring this goal to fruition. While Mary is still primarily the object of other people's actions, Dorothy Jean Weaver notes that her act of "'bearing' the son (1:21) is the crucial 'God event' in the story."[23] More specifically, it is Mary's womb and thus her role as mother (and not wife, daughter,

---

[18] For a survey and critique of these interpretations, Hood's *Messiah, His Brothers, and the Nations* is helpful.

[19] See note 15 above. Additionally, see William D. Davies and Dale C. Allison, *A Critical and Exegetical Commentary on the Gospel according to Saint Matthew*, 3 vols., ICC (London: T&T Clark, 1988), 1:170–2, and Marshall D. Johnson, *The Purpose of the Biblical Genealogies with Special Reference to the Setting of the Genealogies of Jesus*, SNTSMS 8 (Cambridge: Cambridge University Press, 1969), 154–9. Cf. Mayordomo-Marin, *Den Anfang hören*, 248–50; John Nolland, "The Four (Five) Women and other Annotations in Matthew's Genealogy," NTS 43 (1997): 539; and Aernie's chapter in this volume for studies critical of grouping the women together.

[20] Interpreting the five women in light of their shared correspondences need not exclude nor negate the importance of viewing their specific inclusion individually or from recognizing their unique and diverse backgrounds and experiences; see Aernie's chapter in this volume.

[21] Smit, "Something About Mary," 198–201.

[22] Raymond E. Brown, *The Birth of the Messiah: A Commentary on the Infancy Narratives in Matthew and Luke*, ABRL, upd. edn (New York: Doubleday, 1993).

[23] Weaver, "Wherever This Good News Is Proclaimed," 390–401.

or sister) that puts her at the center of the drama and thus inseparable from her son. After his birth, Jesus is the object of five actions, all of which involve his mother. For instance, it is *the child with Mary his mother* (2:11) whom the magi first encounter on their arrival; it is *the child and his mother* (2:13) whom an angel instructs Joseph to protect from Herod's wrath by fleeing to Egypt; it is *the child and his mother* who travel to Egypt by night (2:14); it is *the child and his mother* (2:20) who appear in an angelic dream to Joseph with the instructions to return to Israel; and it is *the child and his mother* who make their way to Israel.[24] Mary's womb and role as mother are indispensable to God's plan and function as the focus and underlying core of the narrative despite the fact that men play the leading roles. While Matthew may articulate what King Herod, the magi, and Joseph think, say, and do, Mary and her child feature as the topic of their thinking, saying, and doing. As Mary stands closer to God than any other human (except Jesus) by way of her divine motherhood, Matthew's depiction of Mary as a passive protagonist may well reflect God's presence as the *passivum divinum* in the infancy narrative.

III. Mary and the *Protevangelium of James*

In many ways, the *Protevangelium of James*' Mary stands in complete contrast to Matthew's Mary—it is a text that, in no subtle way, focuses its attention on her. She is wholly the protagonist and all plots lead back to her. Even the subplots involving her parents or the priesthood are designed to illustrate better why she was chosen to carry out God's ultimate plan.[25] Yet, amidst all this attention *on* Mary, much of what we have is talk *of* Mary—her role as protagonist is non-traditional. To be sure, she is constantly blessed and praised not only by Gabriel at the Annunciation (*Prot. Jas.* 11:2 ff.), but also by her parents (6:2-7), townspeople (6:8), the temple priests (7:7), the high priest (6:9), Elizabeth (12:15), and so on, yet by the end of the narrative, we are hardly any closer to understanding *her* perspective. Mary is passive and silent—on only eight occasions are we privy to her direct voice,[26] and they are all brief and in direct response to another character's question. The course of Mary's life is wholly directed by others: various people guard her purity from defilement (e.g., parents, temple priests, Joseph, etc.) and her virtuous status is assessed and determined by other characters. What are we to make of Mary's passive characterization? While gender politics are always a consideration, the attribution to gender stereotypes cannot properly explain Mary's submissive nature, given that the author chose to write a text devoted wholly to Mary, one that consistently presents other women as having agency and speech. Anna (2:5, 9; 3:1-8), Judith (2:2-4, 6), Elizabeth (12:5; 22:5-7), and the two midwives (19–20) are all depicted as having control over their actions and voices. At times, the women are shown to have even more agency and voice then their male counterparts, as Anna is

---

[24] Weaver, "Wherever This Good News Is Proclaimed," 396.
[25] Vuong, *Protevangelium of James*, 81–7.
[26] That is, at *Prot. Jas.* 11:6, 11:9, 12:5, 13:8, 13:10, 15:13, 17:9, and 17:10, most of which involve Mary declaring her innocence in response to accusations about her virginal status.

clearly portrayed as the primary caregiver and decision-maker throughout Mary's infancy, childhood, and early womanhood (5:5-6:5; 7:1-3), and the midwives are active in their determination to question men who claim the extraordinary nature of the virgin birth (19).[27]

The key to understanding Mary's passivity may be found in her designation as the "Virgin of the Lord."[28] While Matthew only uses παρθένος one time throughout his gospel to describe Mary, and only indirectly via the prophesy (1:23), Mary is primarily addressed via her designation as a virgin and more specifically, as the "Lord's Virgin," nine times in the *Protevangelium* (9:1, 10:1, 13:1 [x2], 15:2 [x2], 16:1, 19:3 [x2]). Additionally, whereas Matthew's reference to παρθένος clearly refers only to her sexual status, the *Protevangelium*'s presentation of Mary's purity unmistakably extends to include not only her sexual status but other forms of purity (e.g., ritual, menstrual, genealogical, carnal, etc., as I have argued elsewhere).[29] In the *Protevangelium*, Mary is not simply sexually pure, but made holy—her body has been set aside for God's use alone. This idea is reinforced not only by her exceptional upbringing which prevented her from encountering anything "profane" (κοινός) or "impure" (ἀκάθαρτος; 6:4), or her constant confinement in sanctified places, but also by the proof of her status as *semper virgo*.[30] The climax of Matthew's designation of her as a virgin is wholly in terms of her virginal conception. By contrast, the *Protevangelium*'s climatic miracle of virginity is the virginal birth—Mary's body remains intact and undefiled despite giving birth to a child.[31] In other words, God has set aside Mary's ever-pure body to fulfill his ultimate plan for humanity. With Mary's designation as the "Lord's Virgin," she embodies what Meredith Hollman has argued to be an unparalleled receptivity to God;[32] there is no being who stands closer to God, and as such it is her body through which God works to bring about the incarnation of the Λόγος. Perhaps, not unlike the biblical prophets who functioned as vehicles through which the divine message flows,[33]

---

[27] Meredith Elliott Hollman, "Temple Virgin and Virgin Temple," in *Jesus and Mary Reimagined in Early Christian Literature*, ed. Vernon K. Robbins and Jonathan M. Potter, Writings from the Greco-Roman World Supplements 6 (Atlanta: SBL Press, 2015), 113. Lest we forget, the *Protevangelium* is "the only narrative in Christian tradition that recounts the birth of a female protagonist"; Mary Foskett, *A Virgin Conceived* (Bloomington: Indiana University Press, 2002), 141.

[28] Once Mary is given this designation, her status as pure is transportable and no longer confined to the temple space where she once lived under the protection of the temple priests; see Vuong, *Gender and Purity*, 161-90.

[29] Vuong, *Gender and Purity*, chs 2-4.

[30] Mary's virginity is questioned three times throughout the narrative, and proof is ascertained in two separate physical tests to confirm her virginity. The first test, involving a drink, is administered by the high priest who confirms Mary's (and Joseph's) innocence (16); the second test is a gynecological examination of Mary's post-partum body by a midwife who achieves confirmation not from Mary's body ironically (i.e., an intact hymen), but via God's intervention and punishment of the midwife who examines Mary in the first place (19-20).

[31] Hollman, "Temple Virgin and Virgin Temple," 104.

[32] Hollman, "Temple Virgin and Virgin Temple," 114-15.

[33] For an introduction to the role of the prophet, see Joseph Blenkinsopp, *Sage, Priest, Prophet: Religious and Intellectual Leadership in Ancient Israel*, 1st edn, Library of Ancient Israel (Louisville, KY: Westminster John Knox Press, 1995), and Mark W. Hamilton, "Prophecy and Prophets in Ancient Israel: Proceedings of the Oxford Old Testament Seminar," *Reviews in Religion and Theology* 18, no. 2 (2011): 205-7.

Mary's body too is under God's control, but it is used to convey much more than a simple message—it is used to bring forth the divine will of God's incarnation.

However, the difference between how God makes use of Mary and the biblical prophets may offer some insights into Mary's passivity. Mary rarely speaks in the narrative because her contribution to salvation history is not limited to simply relaying divine words, but actually embodying the divine. In her designation as the "Lord's Virgin," Mary's body transforms into a sacred vessel for God's use alone. Mary is passive because her role in salvation history centers on the passive occupation of her womb. As God's sacred vessel and physical locale for the incarnation, Mary becomes a sort of temple or sanctuary since she, like the Jerusalem temple, houses the divine.[34] This is achieved not simply by virtue of her motherhood of the Messiah at the moment God claims her womb, but is consistently built up in the descriptions of her childhood and upbringing, as noted above.

While the *Protevangelium* depicts Mary as a temple or sanctuary a number of different ways throughout, this image perhaps connects most intimately to the manner in which her parents present her at the Jerusalem temple as a pure gift to God. When Mary's mother Anna explicitly promises to offer her daughter as a "gift" (δῶρον) to the Lord and to have her "serve him all the days of [her] life" (καὶ ἔσται λειτουργῶν αὐτῷ πάσας τὰς ἡμέρας τῆς ζωῆς αὐτοῦ; 4:2),[35] her words recall other prominent biblical figures who are dedicated to "serving God." 1 Samuel 1–2 immediately comes to mind as a story that shares uncanny parallels,[36] as does the story of Samson and possibly even John the Baptist.[37] Like Anna, Samuel's mother, Hannah, also makes a promise to give

---

[34] In the *Armenian Gospel of the Infancy* 5.9, Mary is explicitly described as a "holy and undefiled temple and a dwelling place for [God the Word]"; Abraham Terian (ed. and trans.), *The Armenian Gospel of the Infancy with Three Early Versions of the Protevangelium of James* (Oxford: Oxford University Press, 2008), 25. Eric M. Vanden Eykel also notes that the image of Mary and the temple are conflated in the Greek Orthodox *Festal Menaion*, trans. Mother Mary and Kallistos Ware (London: Faber and Faber, 1969), hereafter cited as *FM*. There Mary is unmistakably characterized as a temple: she is called "the heavenly tabernacle" (*FM* 184), "a sacred vessel" (*FM* 186), "the living Ark of God" (*FM* 190), and "the Holy of Holies" (*FM* 192). Moreover, Mary's presence in the temple is articulated in terms of preparing for the reception of God: "Today the living Temple of the great King enters the temple to be prepared as a divine dwelling place for Him" (*FM* 184). Eric M. Vanden Eykel, *"But Their Faces Were All Looking Up": Author and Reader in the* Protevangelium of James (New York: T&T Clark, 2016), 66–7.

[35] I have argued elsewhere that Anna's and Joachim's presentation of Mary to the temple and their specific characterization of her as a gift to God is described in language reminiscent of a temple sacrifice. Vuong, *Gender and Purity*, 94–9.

[36] The motif of miraculous births by barren women in biblical narratives has been discussed at varying lengths in a number of studies: W. S. Vorster, "Protevangelium of James," *ABD*, 3:631; W. S. Vorster, "The Protevangelium of James and Intertextuality," in *Text and Testimony: Essays on New Testament and Apocryphal Literature in Honour of A.F.J. Klijn*, ed. T. Baarda et al. (Kampen, Netherlands: J. H. Kok, 1988), 272; J. K. Elliott (ed.), *The Apocryphal New Testament: A Collection of Apocryphal Christian Literature in an English Translation based on M. R. James* (Oxford: Clarendon, 1993), 51; Ronald F. Hock, *The Infancy Gospels of James and Thomas* (Santa Rosa, CA: Polebridge, 1995), 10; Paul Foster, "The Protevangelium of James," *ExpTim* 118, no. 12 (2007): 573–82, esp. 576; Paul Foster, "The Protevangelium of James," in *The Non-Canonical Gospels*, ed. Paul Foster (London: T&T Clark, 2008), 113–16; Bart D. Ehrman and Zlatko Pleše, *The Apocryphal Gospels: Texts and Translations* (Oxford: Oxford University Press, 2011), 35.

[37] Elliott, *Apocryphal New Testament*, 51; Vuong, *Protevangelium of James*, 50; and Valerie Abrahamsen, "Human and Divine: The Marys in Early Christian Tradition," in *A Feminist Companion to Mariology*,

up her child to serve God "all the days of his life" (cf. 1 Sam. 1:28: כָּל־הַיָּמִים֙ אֲשֶׁ֣ר הָיָ֔ה) upon finding out that as an infertile woman, she too has finally conceived. Even the description of Anna's dedication of Mary to the Lord and her highly controlled living conditions before the dedication recall the Nazirite vow (Num. 6:1-21) that is often associated with Samuel and others who have been dedicated for lifetime temple service. And yet, make no mistake, Mary's dedication differs significantly from those of her biblical predecessors. The common concern that Mary's ministering in the temple is problematic because she is neither male or of the priestly line (Lev. 16:1-4) becomes irrelevant in this case because she does not actually minister.[38] Unlike Samuel, who is depicted assisting Eli the priest with his duties as a functionary of the temple (e.g., 1 Sam. 2:11, 18, 35; 3:1, etc.), Mary does not partake in caring for the temple, nor does she engage in any cultic activities or priestly duties. Instead of ministering to the Lord, as is explicitly said of Samuel's activities after his parents leave the temple, Mary is administered to and treated as a temple sacrifice or sacred object.[39] The text says that she was loved by the priest and cared for like a dove, and even fed by the hand of an angel (8:1-2). The careful monitoring of Mary's pure body as a result of Anna's determination to prevent her daughter from contracting anything impure (e.g., waiting the prescribed number of days to nurse [5:9], never walking on the common ground [6:1-5], raising her in a home-made sanctuary [6:4-5], etc.) functions as a precursor to her role as sacred object and temple upon her arrival at the Jerusalem temple to live. When the priests receive Mary, they kiss her and bestow a blessing that reveals that it is through her that God will "reveal his redemption" (7:2), before placing her on the third step of the altar of the Lord. God's response of "casting his grace upon her" becomes evident as Mary dances on the altar of the Lord in the holy of holies. While her parents describe Mary as a perfect, unblemished gift offered to the Lord, she is, as Eric Vanden Eykel rightly notes, a different type of sacrifice: she does not die, but rather dances on the holy steps, reflective of her role as an integral, living part of God's plan for Israel's redemption and salvation.[40] Mary's first self-directed physical act in the *Protevangelium* is that of an embodied self, celebrating God as a pure vessel worthy of his gift. Hollman has argued that Mary's dancing "stands out as the apex of Mary's life. She exercises agency over her own body and dances before the Lord, as though accepting her place as 'the Lord's Virgin' in the temple."[41] While Mary is not given this designation until after she leaves the temple, there is no doubt that she belongs to the Lord, which explains why the priests treat her as an object for them to serve rather than as an assistant to them as temple caretakers.

While scholars often interpret Mary's stay at the temple as the climax of her exceptionally pure life and thus continued justification as God's choice for the

---

ed. Amy-Jill Levine with Maria Mayo Robbins (Cleveland: Pilgrim, 2005), 171, all note this possible parallel.

[38] Vanden Eykel contends that Mary's presence in the temple serves to express her purity and provide protection from defilement: *"But Their Faces Were All Looking Up"*, 68-9.

[39] Vanden Eykel, *"But Their Faces Were All Looking Up"*, 68-9; Hollman, "Temple Virgin and Virgin Temple," 110.

[40] Vanden Eykel, *"But Their Faces Were All Looking Up"*, 90-9, esp. 98-9.

[41] Hollman, "Temple Virgin and Virgin Temple," 111.

incarnation, her time in the temple is liminal and functions only as a stopover in the *Protevangelium*. However, the temporary nature of Mary's residency at the temple does not undermine her role as a symbolic temple or sanctuary. In fact, her departure from the temple precinct and ultimate "marriage" to Joseph continue to underscore the ways in which she functions as a temple, albeit now a movable one (i.e., tabernacle).[42] Her designation as the Lord's Virgin ensures that divinity not only follows wherever she goes but can also dwell in her womb. The *Protevangelium*'s presentation of Mary in this way, even after she leaves the temple and enters into Joseph's protection, is reinforced by the manner in which Joseph receives Mary. After the high priest enters the holy of holies to pray about what to do with Mary (since she has reached an age that poses a potential risk to the temple), he is instructed to assemble all the widowers of Israel in order to locate by lot Mary's new protector (8:7-9). Similar to the manner in which the legitimate priestly line is determined to care for the Tent of Testimony in Num. 17:1-11 (NSRV; 17:16-26 in the Masoretic Texts), Joseph is chosen to care for Mary, the symbolic temple, by way of divine selection.[43] Just as Aaron's budding rod indicates God's will, the dove that sprouts from Joseph's rod and lands on his head similarly indicates God's choice (9:5-6).

Perhaps what most concretely encourages the reading of Mary as a movable temple are the events following Joseph's selection as her guardian. Upon receiving Mary as the Virgin of the Lord, the *Protevangelium* tells us that Joseph immediately leaves to build houses, leaving Mary alone to fend for herself—a striking contrast to the extreme protection she received as a child from her parents and then from the priests during her stay at the temple. Indeed, Mary's designation as the "Virgin of the Lord," only first given to her in the context of her temple departure, functions now as her post-temple identity for the rest of the narrative, in that her status as pure is articulated primarily in terms of her sexual status as a virgin (cf. earlier, Mary's purity is primarily expressed via her ritual purity). The most striking example the *Protevangelium* presents occurs when Mary gives birth in a cave in the wilderness (20:13-18), only to face doubting witnesses to her claim to be a virgin mother with the title of "Virgin of the Lord." The climactic truth is revealed when God defends her virginal status and in the process magnifies her unparalleled closeness to the divine through a miraculous revelation. Just as the glory of God resides in a cloud that rests on a tabernacle or temple to signify God's presence in Exod. 13:21-22; 14:19, 24; 16:10; 19:16-18; 33:9-10; and Num. 16:42 (NSRV; 17:7 in the Masoretic Texts), the cloud that overshadows the cave where Mary gives birth reinforces in the *Protevangelium* the idea that God is wholly present at the birth of his child. Indeed, Joseph and the midwife are only able to enter the cave (a profane space now made holy) after the cloud contracts and a bright light is brought forth.

---

[42] Hollman argues that Mary in *Prot. Jas.* 7:1–8:1 shares structural similarity with the way sacred space relocates in the OT/Hebrew Bible (e.g., the Ark of the Covenant as described at Exod. 39–40, 1 Chron. 15–16, and 2 Chron. 5–7), drawing closer the connection between Mary and temple/tabernacle: "Temple Virgin and Virgin Temple," 115–27.

[43] The Tent of Testimony, which contained the Ark of the Covenant, served as a portable shrine. It would eventually be replaced by the Jerusalem temple, which served as the permanent home for the Ark.

The *Protevangelium*'s representation of Mary as the Lord's Virgin, temple sacrifice, symbolic temple, and moving tabernacle offers insights into her passive characterization in a narrative in which, ironically, she is the protagonist. In these roles, Mary is necessarily passive because she functions wholly to serve God and because God has chosen her body to carry out his most important work—the incarnation of the divine presence. As such, Mary holds an intimate receptivity to God, unparalleled by any other in human history. Mary is passive because God is wholly active. The description of the birth scene aptly reflects this relationship. Even in the birth of her own child, Mary is passive and shows no signs of laboring or marks of pain and distress;[44] rather, the child simply appears nursing in his mother's arms. The only active agent during the birth scene is the contraction (ὑπεστέλλετο) of the dark cloud that brings forth a bright light. The scene is climatic and poignant: Mary's contractions of childbirth are absent because God (via the cloud and bright light) actively contracts and labors for her in bringing about the birth of his son.

IV. Some Concluding Thoughts

As Janice Capel Anderson, Amy-Jill Levine, and others have articulated, the goals of feminist biblical and literary criticism are often threefold: "to highlight androcentrism in canonical texts and their interpretation, to recover positive attitudes toward women in the texts along with revisions of previous androcentric exegesis, and to displace male bias as the center of analysis with female experience."[45] It is an attempt to return voice and agency to those whose speech and acts are controlled or directed by others. In the Gospel of Matthew and the *Protevangelium of James*, Mary's obedience, submissiveness, and passivity are regularly interpreted in the light of androcentric stereotypes. As "passive agent," however, Mary stands as an oxymoron; and as such, her passivity requires a deeper and more nuanced interpretation. A feminist literary reading of Mt. 1-2 reveals Mary as a passive protagonist who features at the center of the plot, but who is disclosed to us only discretely and in a manner that shares a closeness with the *passivum divinum*. In her unparalleled role as the mother of the Messiah, Mary remains the focus of the leading male characters in Matthew's infancy narrative, even though the narrative never shares her thoughts, voice, or actions. She is second only to God in the divine plan to bring about salvation, and thus reflects a presence akin to God in

---

[44] For other examples of the painless birth motif, see Ode 19 of the Odes of Solomon and the Ascension of Isaiah. There has been some debate as to whether Mary's painless birth in the *Protevangelium* reflects docetic beliefs, but a general consensus holds that while Mary's experience of birth was miraculous, it remained still a physical birth in the *Protevangelium*. See Joseph C. Plumpe, "Some Little-Known Early Witnesses to Mary's Virginitas in Par-tu," *TS* 9, no. 4 (1948): 567-77. See also Jennifer A. Glancy, *Corporal Knowledge: Early Christian Bodies* (Oxford: Oxford University Press, 2010), 96-9. Glancy interprets Mary's physical but painless birth in light of ancient Mediterranean gender roles and expectations and argues that Mary gives birth "like a man" in order to demonstrate self-mastery and control.

[45] Anderson, "Matthew: Gender and Reading," 25.

Matthew. Despite being a text that is wholly about Mary, the *Protevangelium* also presents her as a passive protagonist. However, rather than being concealed, Mary functions as "passive-agent" in her unique role as the Lord's Virgin. As God's sacred vehicle who holds unparalleled closeness to him, Mary embodies and functions as an extension of God's greatest will; as such, Mary is necessarily and significantly passive because the only response required of her is the word "yes."

3

Matthew's Herodian Kings as Gentiles

Craig Evan Anderson

Among the four New Testament gospels, the Gospel according to Matthew is unquestionably the most focused on Jewish ethnic identity.[1] Scholars have often formulated this issue according to a Jew versus gentile binary.[2] One of the most salient narrative arcs in Matthew is the emergent inclusion of non-Jews within the target audience of Jesus' disciples: early in the gospel, Jesus instructs his disciples to avoid preaching to gentiles; by the end of the gospel, Jesus commands his disciples to spread their message to all people, gentiles included.[3] Despite this trajectory, the gospel hints at its inevitable openness to gentiles right from its outset, as it surprisingly features gentiles in Jesus' introductory genealogy.[4]

Mindful of this, interpreters have often read the encounter between Herod the Great and the magi in Mt. 2:1-6 as an overture juxtaposing Jew and gentile, laying a groundwork for a thematic contrast throughout the gospel.[5] Within this reading, the pericope flips the expected script by portraying the gentiles positively and the Jews negatively: the murderously paranoid Jewish leader, King Herod and his court harshly represent the Jews; the wise, gracious, and generous magi sympathetically represent the

---

[1] J. Andrew Overman, *Matthew's Gospel and Formative Judaism: The Social World of the Matthean Community* (Minneapolis: Fortress Press, 1990), esp. 2–5; Ulrich Luz, *The Theology of the Gospel of Matthew*, NTT (Cambridge: Cambridge University Press, 1995), 11–17; M. Eugene Boring, "The Gospel of Matthew: Introduction, Commentary, and Reflections," *NIB* 8 (Nashville, TN: Abingdon, 1995), 97.
[2] See, e.g., J. C. Fenton, *Saint Matthew* (Harmondsworth, UK: Penguin Books, 1963), 44; Douglas R. A. Hare, *Matthew*, IBC (Louisville, KY: John Knox Press, 1993), 13–15.
[3] See Donald A. Hagner, *Matthew 1–13*, WBC 33A (Dallas: Word Books, 1993), lxvi.
[4] Hare, *Matthew*, 6; Luz, *Theology of Matthew*, 26.
[5] Consider the startlingly simplistic ethnic interpretation of Fenton, *Saint Matthew*, 44, who writes of Mt. 2, "[I]n this chapter, Matthew introduces the major theme of his Gospel; the Jews have rejected the offer of salvation, but the Gentiles will accept it. Herod, his son Archelaus, and the people of Jerusalem are the representatives of the Jews; and the wise men (Magi) from the East are the representatives of the Gentiles. The Gentiles will be brought into the place which the Jews had forfeited by their unbelief." Less alarming, but still problematic, is the explanation of Hare, *Matthew*, 15, that "the opening passage of Matthew 2 sharply contrasts the acceptance of the new king by Gentile strangers with the violent rejection of him by the Jewish ruler … this undoubtedly symbolized the future rejection of Jesus by his own people and the acceptance of the gospel by Gentiles." In response to Hare, we must ask, Who are Jesus' "own people" and why would one identify Herod's court with them?

gentiles. Accordingly, through these contrasting portrayals of Jew and gentile early in the story, the narrator tips his hand, offering the hearer/reader a glimpse regarding what to expect and where the story is headed. In this chapter, I intend to show that such a reading simplifies and exaggerates ethnic differentiation in the Gospel of Matthew and, more importantly, it fails to notice the gospel's political messaging.

I. Herod the Great as a Gentile in Matthew 2

The glaring problem with the ethnic reading that contrasts a Jewish Herod against gentile magi is the observation that Mt. 2 presents Herod as a gentile. Biologically, Herod was hardly Jewish; his father, Antipater, was Idumean and his mother, Cypros, was a Nabatean Arab.[6] However, much more importantly, Matthew 2 portrays Herod through the narrative framework of Pharaoh of the Book of Exodus, someone who serves as the epitome of the gentile oppressor in the Old Testament – Pharaoh enslaves and murders Hebrews in an ethnic cleansing.[7] Thus, if the evangelist wanted to open his story with a Jew versus gentile contrast, why would he represent Jews by means of a man who is barely a half-Jew, modeled upon a notorious gentile?

If the evangelist wanted to present Herod as a Jewish representative, why not model him upon King Solomon? This would be the low hanging fruit, as both Solomon and Herod were the two famous builders of the Jerusalem temple. This would not hinder a villainous portrayal of Herod, as Solomon abandoned the God of Israel to worship the gods of his foreign wives (1 Kgs 11:1-8). Like Solomon, Herod the Great had numerous political wives and accommodated non-Jewish religious practices.[8] Moreover, the evangelist could still include the massacre and the escape to Egypt through the framework of Solomon's story. First Kings 11:14-22 recounts the story of Hadad the Edomite who escaped a massacre wrought by David and Joab in which they murdered every male in Edom. Hadad fled to Egypt and found refuge in the royal house of Pharaoh until he was ready to return. The fact that Hadad is an Edomite (i.e., Idumean) would make the irony of casting Herod as Solomon especially sharp.

Of course, we can instantly dismiss the proposal of modeling Herod upon Solomon because the Gospel according to Matthew clearly wants to present David (and therefore consequently Solomon) positively. This is evident from the opening verse, which announces "Jesus the Christ, son of David." Jesus' identification as "son of David" is woven throughout the gospel, playing an especially prominent role in Matthew in

---

[6] Joseph. *Ant.* 14.403; Joseph. *War* 1.181; Luz, *Theology of Matthew*, 27, refers to Herod the Great as Jerusalem's "semi-heathen king."
[7] See, e.g., Raymond E. Brown, *The Birth of the Messiah: A Commentary on the Infancy Narratives in the Gospels of Matthew and Luke*, ABRL (1977; new upd. edn., New York: Doubleday, 1993), 107–16.
[8] Although Herod nominally adhered to Jewish religious practice, as was politically necessary to govern Israel peaceably, he was also an enthusiastic supporter of Greco-Roman culture, much of which conflicted with Jewish religious sensibilities. See, e.g., Joseph. *Ant.* 15.267–91.

contrast with the other New Testament gospels.[9] As a matter of fact, the visit of magi to Jesus subtly echoes the Queen of Sheba visiting Solomon – a parallel that reinforces the bond between Jesus and Solomon.[10]

In addition to connecting Jesus to Jewish royalty through David (and Solomon), the manner of the genealogy and the label of Emmanuel as "God with us" illuminate Jesus' intimate link with Jewish history.[11] Moreover, the gospel affirms the authority of Mosaic law (Mt. 5:17-18; 23:1-3). As such, Matthew presents Jewish heritage positively, both historically and culturally.[12] In this light, reading the detestable, Idumean, Pharaoh-based character of Herod the Great as a Matthean representative of Jewish ethnicity makes little sense.

Consequently, the encounter between the magi and Herod does not present a gentile versus Jewish contrast. Rather it serves as a gentile versus gentile contrast. In this way it remains faithful to one of the sources that influenced the Matthean birth narrative: the story of Balaam's oracles (Num. 22–24).[13] In that story, (gentile) King Balak of Moab feels threatened by the Israelites approaching through the wilderness, and he therefore tries to enlist (gentile) diviner Balaam to curse them. However, Balaam the diviner can only utter oracles celebrating the prosperous future of the Israelites, most notably foreseeing that "a star shall come out of Jacob." Thus, just like the Balak–Balaam story, the Herod–magi story is about two gentile parties discussing the inevitable future hope for Israel, symbolized by a star.

II. Matthew's Gospel in the Aftermath of the Temple Destruction of 70 CE

Scholars have exhaustively debated the geographic and chronological setting for the composition of Matthew. Most agree that the Gospel according to Matthew was completed probably in Syria (most likely in Antioch) at the end of the first century CE.[14]

---

[9] Whereas John features only one reference to Jesus as a descendant of David (Jn 7:42), and Mark and Luke employ the title "Son of David" four times (Mk 10:47-8// Lk. 18:38-9; Mk 12:35, 37// Lk. 20:41, 44), Matthew features it as many as ten times. Matthew incorporates all four instances in Mark (Mt. 20:30-1// Mk 10:47-8; 22:42, 45// Mk 12:35, 37) plus six other instances (Mt. 1:1; 9:27; 12:23; 15:22; 21:9, 15). See Jack Dean Kingsbury, "The Title 'Son of David' in Matthew's Gospel," *JBL* 95, no. 4 (1976): 591-602.

[10] Cf. Brown, *The Birth of the Messiah*, 193; John Nolland, "The Sources for Matthew 2:1-12," *CBQ* 60, no. 2 (1998): 290.

[11] For the thematic importance of "God with us" within the Gospel of Matthew and its link to salvation history, see Jack Dean Kingsbury, *Matthew as Story*, 2nd edn (Philadelphia: Fortress, 1988), 40-2.

[12] Kingsbury, *Matthew as Story*, 149–51; Hagner, *Matthew 1–13*, lxiv; Catherine Sider Hamilton, "'His Blood Be upon Us': Innocent Blood and the Death of Jesus in Matthew," *CBQ* 70, no. 1 (2008): 82–100 (esp. 99–100).

[13] Brown, *Birth of the Messiah*, 193–6; Boring, "The Gospel of Matthew," 142.

[14] See, e.g., Georg Strecker, *Der Weg der Gerechtigkeit: Untersuchung zur Theologie des Matthäus* (Göttingen: Vandenhoeck & Ruprecht, 1962), 35–7; Raymond E. Brown and John P. Meier, *Antioch and Rome: New Testament Cradles of Catholic Christianity* (New York: Paulist Press, 1983), 1–86 (esp. 45–72); Kingsbury, *Matthew as Story*, 148, 152; Boring, "The Gospel of Matthew," 105–6. For a more extensive exploration, see also the excellent review of scholarship concerning the date and provenance of the Gospel of Matthew in W. D. Davies and Dale C. Allison Jr., *A Critical and Exegetical*

For my purposes here, the location of writing is not terribly important, but the timing is. Throughout this chapter I affirm and build upon the mainstream scholarly opinion that Mark was written in *c.* 70–75 CE in response to the Jewish Revolt (66–70 CE) and the Roman destruction of the Jerusalem temple in 70 CE; Mark then served as a source for Matthew, which was subsequently written in *c.* 85–90 CE.[15]

However, agreeing to date Mark to *c.* 70–75 CE is not necessarily affirming a claim that Mark was a finished book in *c.* 75 CE. Matthew D. C. Larsen has recently made a compelling case that we should view Mark as *hypomnēmata* (Greek) or *commentarii* (Latin), fluid notes around which one could create a finished book.[16] Larsen contends that the tremendous degree of overlap between Mark and Matthew indicates that Matthew is in fact simply a more complete version of Mark.[17] In this light, I affirm that a version of Mark circulated by *c.* 75 CE, but it was a fluid text – a concept that will be significant later in this chapter.

The year 70 CE was catastrophic for the Jews, creating a seismic shift in Jewish history. The Jews bottled up in Jerusalem suffered through the horrors of a siege, the destruction of their temple, massive quantities of war dead, the enslavement of large segments of the population, and the revocation of any semblance of political self-governance thereafter. The crushing defeat overwhelmed the Jews with problems. There were demographic problems, as Jewish refugees fled the land and Roman soldiers and administrators took control of it. There were political problems, as Rome denied Jerusalem any autonomy thereafter, keeping it tightly restrained under military occupation by the Roman Tenth Legion. But the most existentially worrisome problems were religious: the Jerusalem temple, now gone, had served as the epicenter of Jewish religious practice; its destruction signaled that its god had abandoned the Jewish people, or worse, had failed.

The destruction of the Jerusalem temple redistributed the power balance of Jewish factions. Power ended for those who enjoyed authority before 70 CE: the revolutionary Jewish factions had been killed or enslaved by Rome; the temple-centered Sadducees disappeared. At the same time, peripheral factions gained clout. The popular, yet marginal Pharisees were not as impacted as others by the destruction of the temple, because their religious practice already was not reliant on the temple.[18] The case was even more extreme for Jewish Christians for whom the temple destruction both validated their prophetic critiques of the Jerusalem-based Jewish leadership and affirmed their apocalyptic notions of Jesus' cosmic significance, given that the temple fell within a generation of Jesus' execution.[19] Although no faithful Jew could look

---

Commentary on the Gospel according to Saint Matthew, 3 vols., ICC (London: Bloomsbury/T&T Clark, 1988, 1991, 1997), 1:127–46.

[15] Scholarship addressing the synoptic problem is massive and peripheral to the focus of this chapter. For a comprehensive and persuasive argument in favor of Mark as a source for Matthew, see Davies and Allison, *Matthew*, 1:97-126; see also Dennis R. MacDonald, *Two Shipwrecked Gospels: The Logoi of Jesus and Papias's Exposition of Logia about the Lord* (Atlanta: Society of Biblical Literature, 2012).

[16] Matthew D. C. Larsen, *Gospels before the Book* (New York: Oxford University Press, 2018).

[17] Larsen, *Gospels before the Book*, 4, 100–14.

[18] Overman, *Matthew's Gospel and Formative Judaism*, 35–8.

[19] See, e.g., Mt. 24:1-35 (esp. 24:1-2); Mt. 27:50-2.

favorably upon gentile political domination of Israel, Jewish Christians at least had a way to explain it theologically to their satisfaction.

The Gospel of Matthew is reluctant to attack Rome directly; doing so could be dangerous. The gospel's attempt to distance Rome from any explicit accusation of guilt for the execution of Jesus is especially evident in Pontius Pilate's handling of Jesus' fate: Pilate's wife warns him that a troubling dream showed her that Jesus was innocent (Mt. 27:19); Pilate subtly attempts to dissuade the Jerusalem crowd from choosing to crucify Jesus, questioning why they want to crucify him (Mt. 27:23); Pilate publicly washes his hands of the matter and declares his own innocence of the execution to which the crowd agrees (Mt. 27:24-5).

According to Matthew, what is at stake in the crucifixion of Jesus is the entire fate of Israel. The immediate outcome of Jesus' crucifixion is an apocalyptic foreshadowing of Rome's destruction of Jerusalem forty years later in 70 CE: the temple curtain tears top to bottom (thereby polluting and invalidating the temple), the earth shakes, rocks split, and dead people wake (Mt. 27:51-2). It is the Jerusalem crowd, riled up by "the chief priests and the elders" (οἱ ἀρχιερεῖς καὶ οἱ πρεσβύτεροι) in Mt. 27:20, who Matthew holds responsible for the death of Jesus and therefore, consequently, the destruction of Jerusalem. This is especially clear when "the people as a whole answered, 'His blood be on us and on our children'" (καὶ ἀποκριθεὶς πᾶς ὁ λαὸς εἶπεν, Τό αἷμα αὐτοῦ ἐφ' ἡμᾶς καὶ ἐπὶ τὰ τέκνα ἡμῶν), thereby incurring a blood debt that the gospel writer knows those people and their children will pay forty years later.[20]

However, the fact that the evangelist explicitly faults failed Jewish leadership and not Rome for the death of Jesus, and consequently the destruction of Jerusalem, does not mean that the gospel refrains from criticizing Roman authority. It simply critiques Rome through inuendo. It is along this line that we may ask: What is the value of Matthew's disparaging portrayals of King Herod the Great and Herod Antipas decades after they held power?

III. Reading Two Herod Episodes in Three Temporal Settings

The characterization of the Herodian kings in Matthew hinges upon two episodes. The first is the aforementioned episode of Herod the Great meeting with the magi and subsequently ordering the massacre of Jewish male children (Mt. 2:1-18); the second is the flashback story relating the circumstances that lead to Herod Antipas ordering the death of John the Baptist (Mt. 14:1-12).[21]

---

[20] Many interpreters, especially in the past, have read Mt. 27:25 as a perpetual ethnic condemnation of Jews. For example, Lillian C. Freudmann, *Antisemitism in the New Testament* (Lanham, MD: University Press of America, 1994), 277, writes, "Not only had Jews acquired complete and sole blame for Jesus' death, but their descendants were doomed for all time as deicides." Furthermore, she claims through her reading of Mt. 27:25 that "Matthew ascribed perpetual guilt to Jews." However, these statements were already becoming outdated at their point of publication. Beginning especially in the 1990s, most scholars started to reject this ethnically anachronistic and historically unmoored reading, favoring a generationally limited judgment. This is clearest when one reads Mt. 27:25 as an *ex eventu* rationalization for the destruction of the Jerusalem temple in 70 CE. For a brief list of scholarship on the issue, see Hamilton, "His Blood Be upon Us," 82–100 (esp. 83, n. 2).

[21] In addition to the two episodes centering upon Herod the Great (Mt. 2:1-18) and Herod Antipas (Mt. 14:1-12), the "Herodians," a pro-Herodian Jewish political faction, appear in league with the

Both episodes function similarly, communicating on multiple levels. The most convenient way to organize analysis of this is temporally; both episodes communicate according to three temporal settings: the distant past, the recent past, and the present. Regarding the distant past, both employ the time-worn conventions of folklore; they reverberate with the echoes of familiar narrative elements retold with countless variations. Regarding the recent past, both bear a semblance of credibility, as the narrative portrayals of Herod the Great and Herod Antipas comport with known characteristics of their historical antecedents. Regarding the present, both episodes comment meaningfully upon the current political situation of Matthew's audience at the end of the first century CE. This third temporal setting will be the focus of my argument in this chapter.

A. The Distant Past: A Folkloric Reading

First, both episodes function on a timeless, folkloric level. Matthew 2:1-18 rather transparently overlays the birth of Jesus upon the story of Moses. As we have already seen, it does this by portraying King Herod modeled after two gentile villains in the Moses story: the Pharaoh who nearly killed the infant Moses and the paranoid King Balak of Moab who worked with a diviner to try to thwart Moses and Israel. The birth story of Moses itself participates in the well-worn trope of the hero as endangered infant. We find this in the Legend of Sargon, the birth of Cyrus, and the births of Romulus and Remus, to name just a few.[22]

Similarly, Matthew 14:1-12 is riddled with echoes of popular old tales, especially drawing from the Hebrew Bible (and Apocrypha). The idea of a prophet (John the Baptist) speaking against the marriage of a king (Herod Antipas) and queen (Herodias) reflects Elijah's critique of the marriage of Ahab and Jezebel (1 Kgs 17–21). The incident of a rash vow (Herod Antipas' vow) leading to the death of an innocent victim (John the Baptist) recalls Jephthah murdering his daughter (Judg. 11:29-40). The notion of a woman (Herodias) exploiting a king's vow (Herod Antipas' vow) amidst a banquet mirrors Esther's clever manipulation of Ahasuerus (Est. 7).[23] The image of a woman (Herodias' daughter) seducing a leader (Herod Antipas) in the context of a banquet that leads to the display of a beheaded opponent (John the Baptist) echoes Judith's destruction of Holofernes (Jdt. 12:10–13:16).[24]

Pharisees in Mt. 22:15-22. See E. Mary Smallwood, *The Jews Under Roman Rule: From Pompey to Diocletian, A Study in Political Relations* (1976; repr. Atlanta: SBL, 2015), 163–4.

[22] See, e.g., Luz, *Matthew*, 25.

[23] The king's willingness to grant the female petitioner (Esther/ Herodias' daughter) "half of my kingdom" (notice the verbatim construction in Est. 7:2 [LXX] and Mk 6:23: ἡμίσους τῆς βασιλείας μου) especially solidifies the connection to the Book of Esther in Mark's version of this scene, which Matthew subsequently appropriated, although Matthew omits this phrase.

[24] Pheme Perkins, "The Gospel of Mark: Introduction, Commentary, and Reflections," in *The New Interpreter's Bible*, Vol. 8 (Nashville, TN: Abingdon Press, 1995), 598, draws attention to these examples.

These two episodes (Mt. 2:1-18 and 14:1-12) work in tandem as dark satire pairing comic incompetence with ghoulish violence. In both cases, the kings' ineptitude is laughable.[25] Herod the Great is so ill-informed regarding a potential political threat from his own territory that he must learn about it from foreign astrologers;[26] Herod Antipas impulsively and irresponsibly offers to grant a near-boundless wish because he gets excited by his niece's dancing. Yet, despite the pitiable buffoonery of these two Herodian kings, one cannot laugh at them because these episodes feature scenes of chilling violence that stifle any potential for humor. Although the murder of countless innocent boys is obviously the more tragic of the two, the grim picture of John's decapitated head on a platter nevertheless creates a grisly image that haunts the gospel's audience. Together these two episodes utilize folkloric tropes to lampoon the cruel excesses of unchecked power.

B. The Recent Past: A Historically Plausible Reading

Second, the circumstances, characterizations, and actions of the Herodian kings in both episodes basically cohere with what we know about their historical antecedents as narrated by Josephus. Matthew 2 portrays Herod the Great as a paranoid leader, anxiously trying to stay informed about any potential rival to his throne. He is casually murderous, willing to shed innocent blood to advance his personal goals. As scholars often recognize, this characterization readily comports with Josephus' biography of Herod the Great embedded within his *Jewish War* and *Antiquities*, despite the absence of any mention of a Bethlehemite infant massacre in Josephus' works.[27] According to Josephus, Herod established political clout by marrying into the Hasmonean dynasty. Once his reign was secured, he murdered the Hasmoneans to eliminate lingering political threats. His Hasmonean victims include his wife, Mariamne, as well as his two sons through her, Alexander and Aristobulus. He also murdered Mariamne's brother, mother, and grandfather. Moreover, Herod's victims were not restricted to the Hasmoneans. He ordered the execution of his firstborn son, Antipater II. Also, he arranged for a mass execution upon his death to coerce public mourning to align with his death. Even though Josephus does not record any mass slaughter of infants during

---

[25] Although it may appear erroneous to label Herod Antipas a "king" given his designation as a "tetrarch," Mt. 14:1-12 uses both titles interchangeably. It applies "tetrarch" (τετραάρχης) to Herod Antipas in Mt. 14:1 and refers to him as "king" (βασιλεὺς) in Mt. 14:9. See also on this point, Harold W. Hoehner, *Herod Antipas: A Contemporary of Jesus Christ* (1972; repr. Grand Rapids, MI: Academie Books, 1980), 149-51; Donald A. Hagner, *Matthew 14–28*, WBC 33B (Grand Rapids, MI: Zondervan, 1995), 410; Davies and Allison, *Matthew*, 2:463.

[26] Nolland, "Sources," 286, writes, "In the present narrative we have the unlikely picture of Herod, so well provided with informers, depending exclusively on the return of the Magi for his information. This is likely to be the result of source mergers." Although source merger may have been involved in this, it alone cannot account for the resultant picture of Herod's ineptitude. The final redactor chose to leave Herod dependent upon the magi for information and this is best explained as satire.

[27] See, e.g., Brown, *Birth of the Messiah*, 225–8.

Herod's last years, scholars readily concede that such an action would certainly fit the profile, consistent with what Josephus tells us about Herod the Great.[28]

Similarly, Matthew 14 notes that Herod Antipas had scandalously married Herodias, the former wife of his brother, Philip, and Antipas ordered the beheading of John the Baptist in response to John's public critique of the marriage. Once again, Josephus provides an account of Herod Antipas that features details quite consistent with this episode in Matthew 14. According to Josephus, Herod Antipas did in fact marry Herodias, who had been formerly married to Antipas' brother, Philip.[29] Moreover, Josephus notes that Antipas ordered the execution of John the Baptist, albeit for a slightly different reason than the one that Matthew cites.[30] Although Matthew provides a more detailed account of the events surrounding the execution and a similar but different motive for the execution, the two versions nevertheless agree in terms of the basic facts.

C. The Present: Political Critique

Third, both episodes address the present. Thus far, we have seen how these two episodes apply timeless folkloric tropes as they narrate plausible anecdotes that conform to known characteristics of their historical antecedents. Yet, to the gospel's original audience in the last quarter of the first century CE, what is the value of critiquing Herod the Great, who had died nearly a century earlier? Similarly, why critique Herod Antipas given that Caligula had removed Herod Antipas from power and sent him into exile in 39 CE, roughly fifty years before the writing of the Gospel of Matthew?

The great theological crisis at the end of the first century CE to which all Jewish sects (including Christians) had to respond was Rome's destruction of the Jerusalem temple in 70 CE. Notably, when war first broke out between the Jews and Romans four years earlier (66 CE), the Herodian leadership in Israel, King Herod Agrippa II and his sister, Berenice, sided with the Romans. In 69 CE, when Titus marched his legions on Jerusalem, he and Berenice developed a sexual relationship. In such, we have a Herodian princess sleeping with the man who destroyed the Jerusalem temple. Thus, we can say the Herodians were both figuratively and literally in bed with the Flavians. Berenice aggressively lobbied for Vespasian to become emperor amidst the political uncertainties

---

[28] Cf. Peter Richardson, *Herod: King of the Jews and Friend of the Romans* (Columbia: University of South Carolina Press, 1996), 297, claims, regarding the infant massacre in Mt. 2, that "there is little in the story that carries historical conviction" due to the differences between the infancy narratives of Matthew and Luke and the absence of the account in Josephus' writings. Nevertheless, Richardson notes that the gift-bearing visitation of foreign dignitaries (such as the magi) is well attested around the time of Herod the Great, citing Tigranes the Younger of Armenia in 66 BCE, Queen Helena of Adiabene in the 40s CE, and the dignitaries who celebrated Herod's completion of Caesarea Maritima.

[29] The exact identities of the people involved is confusing as there seem to be multiple sons of Herod the Great named both "Herod" and "Philip." It appears that Herodias divorced her husband, Herod Philip, in favor of Herod Antipas the Tetrarch of Galilee, whereas Salome, the daughter of Herodias and Herod Philip, married Philip the Tetrarch of Trachonitis. Joseph. *Ant.* 18.136–7; Lk. 3:1; Davies and Allison, *Matthew*, 2:469–70.

[30] Joseph. *Ant.* 18.118–19.

of 69 CE. When Titus eventually became emperor a decade later in 79 CE, Berenice traveled to Rome to join Titus, hoping to marry him. However, the Roman people rejected her as another Cleopatra VII.

Beginning with the deferential loyalty that Antipater I, father of Herod the Great, showed to Rome in the mid-first century BCE, the Herodians had been consistently faithful to Rome. Then, amidst the dark times for Israel during which Roman legions were killing and enslaving the Israelite population and destroying its one temple, the Herodians doubled down on their loyalty to Rome, with Berenice supporting Vespasian and trying to marry Titus. Even if there was no actual marriage, the Herodians were effectively wed to the Romans in the minds of most Jews in the last quarter of the first century CE.

Consequently, the two Herodian episodes in the Gospel of Matthew resonate with subversive implications for the Flavian ruling family, particularly toward Emperor Domitian (r. 81–96 CE), the son of Vespasian and brother of Titus, who ruled at the time during which the evangelist wrote the Gospel of Matthew. Of course, it would be dangerous for the gospel to flagrantly mock Roman leadership. This demonstrates why the folkloric and historic levels of reading the two Herodian episodes are essential. They provide plausible deniability. If ever questioned about the episodes, the author and original audience of the Gospel of Matthew could easily point out their folkloric commonalities with other stories and the historical credibility of their portrayals of Herodian kings. Nevertheless, it would be very clear to the community who produced this gospel during Domitian's reign that the two Herodian episodes are poking subtle jabs at Emperor Domitian.

One of the questions pertaining to Matthew 2 is: Why do star-following astrologers serve as the human emissaries announcing Jesus' birth? The narrative requires the "star" to direct the magi to a particular house.[31] Dale C. Allison Jr. argues that the "star" (ἀστέρα) is in fact an angel.[32] But then, why does not the narrative simply refer to the light as an angel (ἄγγελος), especially given the prominence of angels in Matthew 1–2?

One answer to this brings us back to Balaam's prophecy of a star in Numbers 24. But beyond this, stars and astrologers had great significance in the late first-century-CE Roman Empire.[33] When Emperor Claudius was assassinated by eating a poisoned mushroom, one of the main portents marking his demise was the appearance of a star (ἀστήρ) that lingered for a long time (Cass. Dio 60.35.1). Similarly, a star (ἀστήρ)

---

[31] For a defense of the believability of a guiding star for a first-century-CE audience, see Brown, *Birth of the Messiah*, 170–1; Dale C. Allison Jr., *Studies in Matthew: Interpretation Past and Present* (Grand Rapids, MI: Baker Academic, 2005), 17–28.

[32] Allison, *Studies in Matthew*, 28–9.

[33] Frederick H. Cramer, *Astrology in Roman Law and Politics* (Philadelphia: American Philosophical Society, 1954). For the Eastern orientation of astrology, see, e.g., Jörg Rüpke, *Pantheon: A New History of Roman Religion*, trans. David M. B. Richardson (Princeton, NJ: Princeton University Press, 2018), 303, who writes, "Astrology, the 'Chaldean discipline,' became popular from the second century BC onward. Backed by the prestige that was accorded anything ancient and Oriental, the discipline was in fact a symbiosis of Greek mathematics and Babylonian astronomic writings, refined by its practitioners on an on-going basis." See also F. Rochberg-Halton, "Elements of the Babylonian Contribution to Hellenistic Astrology," *Journal of the American Oriental Society* 108, no. 1 (1988): 51–62.

appeared again at the death of Vespasian (Cass. Dio 66.17.2). The Romans recognized the predictive abilities of astrologers, such as that exemplified by the astrologer (ἀστρολόγος) who foresaw that Nero would rule and kill his mother by observing the movement of the stars (ἀστέρων) (Cass. Dio 61.2.1). Consequently, imperial elites recognized that the ability of astrologers to interpret the stars potentially threatened royal power. While securing power during the reign of Claudius, Agrippina banished astrologers from Italy and punished their associates (Cass. Dio 60.33.3b). Similarly, Vespasian banished astrologers from Rome, even though he himself consulted them (Cass. Dio 66.9.2).[34]

Of all first-century Roman emperors, Domitian seems to have been the most worried about astrologers predicting his replacement.[35] When Domitian was just a young boy, Chaldean astrologers had predicted the time of his death (Suet., *Dom.* 14.1). He was a deeply paranoid ruler who tried to compensate for his inadequacies with bravado, bluster, and cruelty (Cass. Dio 67.14.4). He casually executed people, especially those whom he perceived as threats, including killing a man for consulting astrologers (Cass. Dio 67.12.2). Domitian learned the birthdays and even birth hours (relevant to astrological prediction) of noble men that he regarded as potential claimants to his throne in the case of his assassination and he had many of these noble men executed. Domitian was suspicious of Nerva because astrologers predicted that he would rule, and consequently plotted to kill Nerva. However, an astrologer who secretly favored Nerva protected him from Domitian by lying to Domitian, saying that Nerva was not a threat because he would die within days (Cass. Dio 67.15.6). In the end, Domitian was of course right to be worried – there was a conspiracy against him that was ultimately successful (Suet., *Dom.* 16–17).[36] According to Suetonius (*Dom.* 16.1), on the day before he was assassinated, Domitian affirmed to his companions, *fore ut sequenti die luna se in Aquario cruentaret factumque aliquod existeret, de quo loquerentur homines per terrarum orbem* ("that on the next day the moon would bleed in Aquarius and something would happen that people would discuss all over the world"). Sure enough, the astrological prediction proved to be correct: on September 18, 96 CE, seemingly late

---

[34] For a nuanced analysis of the banishment of astronomers, see Pauline Ripat, "Expelling Misconceptions: Astrologers at Rome," *Classical Philology* 106, no. 2 (2011): 115–54. See also Tamsyn Barton, *Ancient Astrology*, Sciences of Antiquity (1994; repr. London: Routledge, 2001), 44–8.

[35] Barton, *Ancient Astrology*, 48–9. As some scholars have noted, Domitian's supposed astrological paranoia may be a propagandistic component of the historians recording his reign. For example, Andrew W. Collins, "The Palace Revolution: The Assassination of Domitian and the Accession of Nerva," *Phoenix* 63, no. 1 (2009): 73–106, writes, "Suetonius' account of Domitian's murder (Suet., *Dom.* 14–17) contains an extraordinary set of fourteen stories involving, omens, astrology, prophecy, and epiphany, which all relate to, or foreshadow, the fall of the emperor ... It has long been argued that many of these stories are *post factum* propaganda when Domitian's killing was understood as divine fate" (76). Nevertheless, even if we concede to the likely supposition that these elements are propagandistic, Suetonius wrote only twenty-five years after Domitian's death and his description of Domitian's actions, even if fictitious, would still be plausible to his readership. Thus, despite the reality of whether or not Domitian was fascinated with astrology, there was nevertheless a popular impression that he was and that is all that would be necessary for the readership of Matthew to link Herod the Great in Mt. 2 to Emperor Domitian.

[36] J. D. Grainger, *Nerva and the Roman Succession Crisis A.D. 96–99* (London: Routledge, 2003), 1–6.

in the 10 am hour just as the moon was positioned in Aquarius, conspirators murdered Domitian, and Nerva replaced him as emperor.[37]

Similarly, the account in Mt. 14:1-12 that relates the circumstances in which Herod Antipas executes John the Baptist bears strong ties to Domitian. According to Mt. 14:1-12, Herod Antipas had arrested John because John had publicly criticized Antipas' marriage to Herodias, wife of Antipas' brother, Philip (Mt. 14:3-4). Antipas was reluctant to arrest John out of fear of the crowd (Mt. 14:5). However, after his niece/daughter-in-law danced for him on his birthday, he made an oath to grant her a far-reaching wish, presumably in the impulsive heat of his sexual arousal for her. Herodias capitalized on the open-ended nature of the oath and used her daughter to attain John the Baptist's head on a platter.

Elements of this story hearken back to Agrippina's manipulation of Emperor Claudius. Agrippina was both the niece and wife of Claudius and, as such, she functioned similarly to the mother–daughter dyad of Mt. 14:1-12 (Cass. Dio 60.31.8). Once she became his wife, Agrippina gained control over Claudius. She eliminated rivals including a woman named Lollia Paulina, whose decapitated head Agrippina had requested for inspection, verifying her victim's identity by the peculiarities of the teeth (Cass. Dio 60.32.4). Similarly, Agrippina's son, Emperor Nero, ordered the execution of a rival, Rubellius Plautus, and afterward inspected his decapitated head, noting what a big nose Plautus had (Cass. Dio 62.14.1).

Like Herod Antipas, Domitian had a controversial marriage. Domitian had taken Domitia, the wife of Lucius Lamia Aelianus, away from her husband and married her. After Domitian became emperor, he divorced Domitia on a charge of adultery and then lived with his niece, Julia, as a wife.[38] Later he reconciled with Domitia by popular demand, but he nevertheless continued his sexual relationship with his niece (Cass. Dio 67.3.2). Like Herod Antipas, Domitian faced public criticism for his divorce by the younger Helvidius Priscus, whose farce on Paris and Oenone seemed implicitly to indict Emperor Domitian (Suet., *Dom.* 10.4).

Given the tight correspondence between the Herod Antipas episode in Mt. 14:1-12 and Mk 6:17-29, one may question how these episodes could critique Emperor Domitian, given that he began his reign in 81 CE and, earlier, I stated support for dating a version of Mark to 70-75 CE. However, bearing in mind Larsen's arguments for the textual fluidity of Mark, it is easy to notice that Mk 6:17-29 juts out from its context as a separable flashback intruding upon the narrative timeline.[39] It is an anecdotal

---

[37] For a fascinating examination of astronomical models determining the positioning of the moon on the day of Domitian's death as a means to elucidate Suet., *Dom.* 16, see Pierre Brind'Amour, "Problèmes astrologiques et astonomiques soulevés par le récit de la mort de Domitien chez Suétone," *Phoenix* 35 (1981): 338–44.

[38] As Richard Alston, *Aspects of Roman History, AD 14–117* (London: Routledge, 1998), 179, notes, "Domitian's niece, Julia Augusta, was associated with Domitian's reign, appearing on coins from as early as c. 80–1 in association with Venus and being included in sacrifices for the safety of the emperor."

[39] Larsen, *Gospels before the Book*; Rudolf Bultmann, *The History of the Synoptic Tradition*, trans. John Marsh (1931; rev. edn New York: Harper & Row, 1968), 301, writes of Mk 6:14-29, "This is a legend exhibiting no Christian characteristics. We cannot know from what tradition Mark has taken it. But since it could hardly have had a place in the Christian tradition from the very beginning, it would

expansion hanging merely upon the brief note in Mk 6:16, which mentions that Herod Antipas had John the Baptist beheaded.[40] Luke 9 serves as a witness to the fact that this episode is unnecessary to the surrounding narrative.[41] Consequently, this Herod Antipas episode (Mt. 14:1-12; Mk 6:17-29) seems to be an addition to Mark, perhaps added to Mark around *c.* 83 CE, when the buzz surrounding Domitian's marriage was at its height.[42] This Herod Antipas episode is notably absent from the gospels of Luke and John.[43] These two gospels were both most likely written in the early second century CE, perhaps twenty years or so after the death of Domitian; consequently, critiquing long-dead Domitian would not be relevant or helpful to the message of Luke or John.

IV. Conclusion

In summary, the Gospel of Matthew uses the two episodes featuring Herodian kings as darkly satiric caricatures of the gentile oppressors – the Roman Empire. The episodes communicate according to timeless folkloric tropes and simultaneously bear the semblance of historical credibility as they depict the Herodian kings in a manner that is basically consistent with what people knew about them. However, they also glisten with subtle critique of Roman political authority, especially that of Emperor Domitian. These episodes depict the Herodian kings as Domitian, who was unnerved by astrologers, paranoid of being replaced, the subject of public scorn for his marital practices, infatuated with his niece, and cruelly violent.

---

seem probable that Mark took it over from Hellenistic Jewish tradition." Similarly, Boring, "The Gospel of Matthew," 319, notices the peculiarity of this episode, writing of Mt. 14:1-12, "Matthew here takes over the bizarre story of Mark 6:14-29 ... the only story in either Gospel not directly concerned with Jesus."

[40] M. Eugene Boring, *Mark: A Commentary*, NTL (Louisville, KY: Westminster John Knox Press, 2006), 178-9, notes that the martyrdom of John the Baptist anticipates the subsequent martyrdoms of Jesus and then of the disciples. In Mark, the word παραδίδωμι ("hand over") links the arrests of John the Baptist (Mk 1:14) and Jesus (Mk 3:19; 9:31; 10:33; 14:10-11, 18, 21, 41-4; 15:1, 10, 15), and anticipates the arrest of the disciples (Mk 13:9-13). Yet Boring acknowledges of Mk 6:17-29, that "formally, the story is unrelated to the martyr tradition ... John is intercalated into the Jesus story, not vice versa." Similarly, Davies and Allison, *Matthew*, 2:464, 475–6, acknowledge that even though Matthew has truncated Mark's version of the story, nevertheless, in Matthew's version, "the parallelism between John and Jesus has been somewhat enhanced" (464). Thus, though Mark 6:17-29 bears evidence of originating from an independent source, the authors of both Mark and Matthew utilized the material to participate in a martyrdom theme.

[41] Luke uses this material minimally, excising almost all of it and informing his reader of the fate of John the Baptist with two brief reports: Lk. 3:19-20 and 9:7-9.

[42] Perkins, "The Gospel of Mark," 598, notes that, regarding Mk. 6:17-29, "Mark's account ... appears to be a legendary development based on earlier stories of prophets and the wicked rulers." Davies and Allison, *Matthew*, 2:464, remark, "As for the story in Mk 6:17-29, which is not a story about Jesus at all, its history can only be guessed. Our own suspicion is that a pre-Markan and perhaps non-Christian story-teller combined an account of John the Baptist's martyrdom with popular traditions about Antipas' court and then glossed the whole with OT motifs." I agree with most of this assessment; however, the "pre-Markan" concept seems to envision a temporal fixity to the composition of the Gospel of Mark that may be unwarranted. Once again on this, see Larsen, *Gospels before the Book*.

[43] John merely includes a brief note regarding the beheading of John the Baptist in 9:9.

Recognizing that the two Herod episodes function as anti-imperial satire, critiquing Rome at the end of the first century CE, explains many of the features in the episodes that are historically problematic. Perhaps the Jewish sons that Herod the Great massacres (Mt. 2:16) and for whom Rachel weeps (Mt. 2:17-18) are the Jewish soldiers slaughtered by Rome in 66–70 CE, the "sons of Bethlehem" defending King David's Jerusalem. Davies and Allison ask of Mt. 14:1-12// Mk 6:17-29, "Would a Herodian princess have performed a sensuous dance before strangers? And how could Herod, who was under the Roman thumb, have promised anybody half of his kingdom?"[44] No, a Herodian princess would probably not sensuously dance before a court of strangers, but the image offers fine mockery of an emperor infatuated with his niece. Moreover, no, Herod Antipas did not have the authority to grant a near boundless wish, but Emperor Domitian did. Furthermore, perhaps the seemingly mistaken designation of Herod Antipas as a "king" (βασιλεὺς) in Mt. 14:9 and Mk 6:14, 25, 27, when everyone knows that Herod Antipas was no king, functions as a wink to the reader who knows, during Domitian's reign, who the "king" really is.

---

[44] Davies and Allison, *Matthew*, 2:465.

4

John the Baptist, Prophet from the Margins

Tucker Samson Ferda

The apostle Paul has been called the "the protean apostle" because, like Proteus of Homer's *Odyssey*, he changes in the hands that hold him.[1] John the Baptist has had a similar fate, and this has happened already in the New Testament. All four New Testament gospels reconfigure the character of John in the light of their overarching narrative aims. This reconfiguration appears particularly intentional in the Gospel of Matthew, who positions John's ministry in such a way that his preaching and baptizing activity anticipate the eschatological redemption of Israel and stand in parallel to the teaching of Jesus who comes "after" (ὀπίσω) him. I will argue here that Matthew's artful characterization of John depends upon and seeks to reinforce the narrative's larger concerns regarding salvation history and Christology. Moreover, I will contend that through the character of John, Matthew stresses that God's purposes for Israel in this moment were operative on the margins of society, away from the centers of worldly power and authority, and visible only to those with eyes to see and ears to hear.

I. Salvation History, Christology, and Matthew's Creative Reshaping of John

The characterization of John in Matthew is constrained, to some degree, by Matthew's sources, especially Mark.[2] Mark had already (i) connected John to Isa. 40, (ii) stressed his call for repentance, (iii) initiated Jesus' public ministry with the baptism of John, and (iv) returned later to describe John's death as a crucial transition point in the ministry of Jesus. As Matthew's narrative maintains all these features, his characterization of John has a distinctly "Markan" imprint.[3]

---

[1] Wayne A. Meeks, "The Christian Proteus," in *The Writings of St. Paul*, ed. Wayne A. Meeks (New York: Norton, 1972), 435–44.
[2] On Markan priority and Matthew's use of Mark (as I assume throughout this chapter), see W. D. Davies and Dale C. Allison Jr., *A Critical and Exegetical Commentary on the Gospel according to Saint Matthew*, 3 vols., ICC (Edinburgh: T&T Clark, 1988–97), 1:97–126.
[3] Also noted by Mark Goodacre, "Mark, Elijah, the Baptist and Matthew: The Success of the First Intertextual Reading of Mark," in *The Gospel of Matthew*, vol. 2 of *Biblical Interpretation in Early Christian Gospels*, ed. Thomas R. Hatina, LNTS 310 (New York and London: T&T Clark, 2008), 73–84.

But that is just the beginning. With these narrative threads in Mark—along with what Matthew has found in the double tradition—Matthew creatively refashions the character of John within a new and larger theological tapestry.[4] Just as Matthew physically expands Mark's Gospel in terms of content, so too John the Baptist's character is expanded, both materially and theologically, as shaped by Matthew's understanding of salvation history and Christology. We focus first on salvation history.

While Mark's Gospel begins with John "in the wilderness" (1:4), Matthew sets that wilderness ministry into a larger context. Matthew's opening genealogy sets out a particular understanding of salvation history and even captures some of the narrative's key theological claims in miniature.[5] Here Jesus, the Messiah, stands alongside Abraham and David (1:1); these three figures structure and periodize significant epochs in Israel's history (1:17). Readers expect that the ministry of Jesus connects to the well-known promises made to Abraham and David concerning blessing the nations (Gen. 12) and the messianic restoration of David's throne (2 Sam. 7), respectively.[6] Moreover, as Jesus appears "fourteen generations" after the Babylonian exile (1:17), the narrative anticipates that his work will bring about the undoing of that low point in a dramatic new-exodus event.[7] It is hardly a coincidence that immediately after the genealogy we find Joseph instructed to name the child "Jesus" because "he will save his people from their sins" (1:21).[8] This statement should not be lifted from its immediate context to signify an abstract "salvation" from abstract, individual, "sins." The "sins" in question are of "his people" (τὸν λαὸν αὐτοῦ), collectively,[9] and the traditional linkage between exile and the sins of Israel (e.g. Deut. 28:15, 63-8; 2 Chron. 36:14-21; Jer. 32:23-35; Ezek. 36:16-21; Bar. 1:15-3:8; *1 En.* 89:73-5) implies a connection to the genealogy. Thus, the genealogy, and its aftermath, place Jesus within the larger story of Israel and shape his mission as a climactic solution to a pre-existing salvation-historical plight.[10]

---

[4] I believe much of this material came from Q, but that is not essential to defend for this chapter. For a discussion of John the Baptist in Q, see Wendy J. Cotter, "'Yes, I Tell You, and More Than a Prophet': the Function of John in Q," in *Conflict and Invention: Literary, Rhetorical, and Social Studies on the Sayings Gospel Q*, ed. John S. Kloppenborg (Valley Forge, PA: Trinity Press International, 1995), 117-38. Two of the most influential redaction-critical studies include Wolfgang Trilling, "Die Täufertradition bei Matthaus," *BZ* 3 (1959): 271-89, and Gerd Häfner, *Der verheißen Vorläufer* (Stuttgart: Katholisches Bibelwerk, 1994).

[5] Cf. Krister Stendahl, "Quis et Unde? An Analysis of Mt 1-2," in *Judentum Urchristentum Kirche: Festschrift für Joachim Jeremias*, ed. Walther Eltester (Berlin: Töpelmann, 1960), 94-105.

[6] I use "reader" throughout the chapter due to convention and this volume's focus on narrative criticism, but that does not preclude the reality of oral/aural contact with Matthew among its original recipients. On this question, see Holly E. Hearon, "Storytelling in Oral and Written Media Contexts of the Ancient Mediterranean World," in *Jesus, the Voice, and the Text: Beyond the Oral and the Written Gospel*, ed. Tom Thatcher (Waco, TX: Baylor University Press, 2008), 89-110.

[7] Cf. Nicholas G. Piotrowski, *Matthew's David at the End of Exile: A Socio-Rhetorical Study of Scriptural Quotations*, NovTSup 170 (Leiden and Boston: Brill, 2016). Here I follow and interpret Matthew's claim that there are "fourteen generations" from the exile to "the Christ" (1:17), while noting that the actual number in the genealogy as given is thirteen. For discussion of this much-debated issue, see H. Daniel Zacharias, *Matthew's Presentation of the Son of David: Davidic Tradition and Typology in the Gospel of Matthew* (London: Bloomsbury/T&T Clark, 2017), 40-7.

[8] All translations are my own unless otherwise indicated.

[9] On this passage, see Tucker S. Ferda, "The Soldiers' Inscription and the Angel's Word: The Significance of 'Jesus' in Matthew's *Titulus*," *NovT* 55 (2013): 221-31.

[10] For a rich discussion, see Richard B. Hays, *Echoes of Scripture in the Gospels* (Waco, TX: Baylor University Press, 2016), 109-13.

Matthew's subsequent narrative assumes this salvation-historical viewpoint, which is important for Matthew's initial characterization of John the Baptist.[11] Before Chapter 3 of Matthew, readers find that "the Christ" (1:17) who appears fourteen generations "from the exile" is in the process of recapitulating key moments in Israel's first exodus: he suffers oppression under a new Pharaoh, Herod the Great, and yet is protected (2:1-14); he spends time in Egypt (2:14-15); and he is called "out" as God's "son," just as Israel was (2:15). John the Baptist emerges in the thick of this larger recapitulation (3:1ff.), as Jesus' immersion in the waters of baptism (3:13-17), his "testing" "in the wilderness" immediately after (4:1-11), and then his going "up the mountain" after that to give authoritative teaching (5:1), evoke the Red Sea, the wilderness wandering and testing, and the Sinai revelation, respectively.[12] In all of this, there is a twist, however. When Jesus recapitulates, he does not stumble. So the rerunning of Israel's history in the person of Israel's Messiah is a task of "fulfilling all righteousness" (3:15) and of calling others to join him in that (cf., e.g., 5:20, 48).[13] Matthew's John is obviously a participant in this salvation-historical task, as his baptism is necessary for Jesus "to fulfill all righteousness,"[14] yet he also demands higher righteousness of others in his call for repentance and bearing fruit (3:8-10).[15] One might even say that the character of John and his warning not to trust in Abrahamic ancestry functions in Matthew as a kind of commentary on Matthew's genealogy and the story of salvation history implied therein, as the genealogy itself teaches that Abrahamic ancestry does not guarantee covenantal blessing. The list of names moves through memories of sin and idolatry, and ultimately to exile (1:11-12).

There is more to say on these matters if we look closely at John's first appearance in the narrative. Mark begins with a composite citation of scripture (Isa. 40:3; Exod. 23:20; Mal. 3:1) before focusing on John's activity of baptizing (1:2-4), leaving it to the reader to infer a connection between the action and the scripture. But Matthew, after mentioning the holy family settling in Nazareth in fulfillment of scripture (2:23)—likely the sprouting of Isa. 11's "branch" (נצר)[16]—transitions to John in this way (3:1-3):

> 1 In those days, John the Baptist appeared preaching in the wilderness of Judea saying, 2 "Repent, for the Kingdom of Heaven has drawn near!" 3 This is the one spoken of by Isaiah the prophet, saying, "the voice of one crying in the wilderness: prepare the way of the Lord. Make straight his paths."

---

[11] On John in salvation history in Matthew, see Josef Ernst, *Johannes der Täufer: Interpretation—Geschichte—Wirkungsgeschichte* (Berlin: de Gruyter, 1989), 182–5.
[12] See Dale C. Allison Jr., *The New Moses: A Matthean Typology* (Minneapolis: Fortress, 1993), 137–91.
[13] The use of πληρόω here likely indicates the "filling up" something—just as in 23:32, though here the inverse of righteousness: "fill up the measure of your ancestors (ὑμεῖς πληρώσατε τὸ μέτρον τῶν πατέρων ὑμῶν)."
[14] Cf. "it is fitting *for us*" (πρέπον ἐστὶν ἡμῖν; 3:15).
[15] Note also 21:32: "John came to you in the way of righteousness (ἐν ὁδῷ δικαιοσύνης) ..."
[16] See Robert H. Gundry, "Topographical Christology in Matthew's Narrative of Jesus' Birth and Infancy," in *"To Recover What Has Been Lost": Essays on Eschatology, Intertextuality, and Reception History in Honor of Dale C. Allison Jr.*, ed. Tucker S. Ferda, Daniel Frayer-Griggs, and Nathan C. Johnson, NovTSup 183 (Leiden and Boston: Brill, 2021), 195–213 (209).

Having alluded to Isaiah with Jesus' "Nazarene" roots (2:23), Matthew returns immediately to Isaiah for the appearance of John (3:1), also removing Mark's lines from Exod. 23:20 and Mal. 3:1 and specifying with a characteristic fulfillment citation that John is Isaiah's "voice of one crying out in the wilderness." In addition to Matthew's specificity, the connection to Isa. 40 takes on added depth in the light of the narrative thus far, since this Isaianic oracle of "comfort" to the exiles that their sins are forgiven and that the return of Israel's God is imminent parallels the drama constructed in Matthew's own narrative about Jesus, "Emmanuel, God with us" (1:23), who has come to save "his people from their sins" (1:21). Interestingly, it is precisely here that Matthew places on the lips of John the first appearance of the phrase "the kingdom of heaven" in the narrative. Matthew thereby links the near-arrival of the kingdom with the near-arrival of Israel's God in Isa. 40's wilderness announcement, maintaining Mark's eschatological understanding of "the kingdom of God" while also deepening its connection to a particular climactic stage in salvation history.[17]

As Matthew identifies John with Isaiah 40's "voice," it is fitting that the First Evangelist emphasizes the oracular character of John's ministry. This also constitutes a slight divergence from Mark. Mark introduces John "baptizing in the wilderness and proclaiming a baptism" (βαπτίζων ἐν τῇ ἐρήμῳ καὶ κηρύσσων βάπτισμα; 1:4), whereas in Matthew "John the Baptist" (Ἰωάννης ὁ βαπτιστής) appears "proclaiming in the wilderness of Judea" (κηρύσσων ἐν τῇ ἐρήμῳ τῆς Ἰουδαίας; 3:1). What Mark presents as John's primary action—baptizing (βαπτίζων)—becomes in Matthew a title (ὁ βαπτιστής), leaving room for his primary activity—proclaiming (κηρύσσων)—to modify the prepositional phrase "in the wilderness" (ἐν τῇ ἐρήμῳ). The firmer linkage between the location of John "in the wilderness" and his proclaiming—surely under the influence of Isa. 40's "voice of one crying out in the wilderness"—coheres with Matthew's portrait of John as a whole here: a reshuffling of the order of items in Mark means that John's baptizing activity is not mentioned by Matthew until a full six verses into Chapter 3, whereas in Mark the "baptizing" is front and center.

Matthew has also emphasized the oracular character of John by adding new, non-Markan material to the account. The upshot is that Matthew's John is more loquacious and speaks at a higher decibel. Whereas Mark's John speaks minimally and only with reference to the "stronger one" who comes "after" him (Mk 1:7-8), Matthew's John fills out the summary statement "repent, for the kingdom of Heaven has drawn near" with a befitting proclamation of his own. John's ascetic life in the desert now matches a new, fiery intensity: he predicts imminent judgment as well as issues an earnest call for repentance and bearing good fruit (3:7-10). John's words in the narrative are at this point the longest and most substantive "speech" of any character, and his jarring if not abrasive opening, "brood of vipers!" (3:7), functions to highlight the serious and momentous nature of this time of decision in Israel's history.[18] Moreover, Matthew

---

[17] On the importance of Isaiah for Matthew as a whole, see Richard Beaton, "Isaiah in Matthew's Gospel," in *Isaiah in the New Testament*, ed. Steve Moyise and Maarten J. J. Menken (London: T&T Clark, 2005), 63–78.

[18] John's opening monologue begins with "you brood of vipers!" (v. 7) and ends with "unquenchable fire" (v. 12). What Sirach contains about Elijah (48:1) would apply just as well to Matthew's John: "a prophet like fire (ὡς πῦρ) . . . his word like a lamp burns" (ὡς λαμπὰς ἐκαίετο).

supplements John's predictions of the coming "stronger one" in Mark with a more fulsome—and fearsome—description of his mission:

Mk 1:7-8	Mt. 3:11-12
7 One stronger than me comes behind me, the thongs of whose sandals I am not worthy to stoop down to untie. 8 I baptized you with water, but he will baptize you with the Holy Spirit (ἐν πνεύματι ἁγίῳ).	11 I baptize you with water for repentance, but the one who comes behind me is stronger than me, whose sandals I am not worthy to carry. He will baptize you with the Holy Spirit and fire (πνεύματι ἁγίῳ καὶ πυρί). 12 His winnowing fork is in his hand and he will clear his threshing floor and he will gather (συνάξει) the wheat into the storehouse but the chaff he will consume (κατακαύσει) with unquenchable fire (πυρὶ ἀσβέστῳ).

In Mark there is no explicit mention of judgment, only the future baptismal activity of the Church. Matthew's John, however, predicts both restoration and judgment, a "baptism with the Holy Spirit and fire."[19] It is clear that the material Matthew adds in v. 12 elaborates on the twofold effects of this "baptism with the Holy Spirit and fire": some will be gathered (from συνάγω), some will be consumed (from κατακαίω).[20] The character of John thus functions to cast a light on the future of salvation history, revealing a Deuteronomic-like "two-ways" (Deut. 30:15-20). He raises the stakes.

As important as John is in the salvation history of Israel, Matthew's narrative is even more concerned to use John's character to build up and magnify the activity of Jesus. We might even say that Matthew's characterization of John is contingent on Matthew's Christology. The structural arrangement of Matthew's narrative shows that John's appearances function to transition between various stages of Jesus' own career.[21] In the first place, the initial baptizing activity of John anticipates Jesus' own public ministry. Matthew constructs a near identical parallel between them:

	John	Jesus
geographical location	"in the wilderness of Judea" (Mt. 3:1)	"in Capernaum, in the territory of Zebulun and Naphtali" (Mt. 4:13)
fulfillment of scripture	The "voice in the wilderness" from Isa. 40:3 (Mt. 3:3)	The "light in the darkness" from Isa. 9:1-2 (LXX 8:23–9:1) (Mt. 4:15-16)
summary proclamation	μετανοεῖτε· ἤγγικεν γὰρ ἡ βασιλεία τῶν οὐρανῶν (Mt. 3:1)	μετανοεῖτε· ἤγγικεν γὰρ ἡ βασιλεία τῶν οὐρανῶν (Mt. 4:17)

[19] See Rudolf Bultmann, *History of the Synoptic Tradition*, trans. John Marsh, rev. edn (Peabody, MA: Hendrickson, 1963), 246–7. Matthew also probably anticipates the future baptismal activity of the Church in John's prediction of the coming one's "baptism with spirit and fire," as the gospel ends with Jesus' command to "baptize" "in my name" (28:19). The prediction about the coming one's baptism is fulfilled through his disciples, as Jesus promises "I will be with you (μεθ' ὑμῶν) all the days" (28:20). See Poul Nepper-Christensen, "Die Taufe im Matthäusevangelium," *NTS* 31 (1985): 189–207.

[20] It is not clear if the inclusion of "with fire" in John's "he will baptize you with the Holy Spirit and fire" describes the one and the same baptism of the holy one—which affects recipients differently—or if John here speaks of two tasks: baptizing some with the Holy Spirit (as in Mark), and baptizing others with a destroying fire. For a great discussion, see Daniel Frayer-Griggs, *Saved Through Fire: The Fiery Ordeal in New Testament Eschatology* (Eugene, OR: Pickwick, 2016), 135–44.

[21] Cf. James L. Jones, "References to John the Baptist in the Gospel according to Mathew," *AThR* 41 (1959): 298–302. See also Jack Dean Kingsbury, *Matthew: Structure, Christology, Kingdom* (Philadelphia: Fortress, 1975), 13–17.

John and Jesus' opening acts are mirror images of each other. We get the sense that John and Jesus, while forerunner and Messiah, respectively, are also co-agents of the same, Isaianic-inspired mission of announcing the coming kingdom and calling for repentance in the light of that.[22] The character of John functions to "prepare the way" for Jesus in this particular manner.[23] Additional parallels between their teachings, specifically as they pertain to the importance of obedience and "bearing fruit," only reinforce this impression.[24]

John largely exits the narrative for Jesus' early preaching and healing activity in Galilee,[25] but Matthew returns to the Baptist for a series of teachings from Jesus about John specifically (often known as the "Baptist block," 11:2-30). This material appears strategically placed immediately after Jesus' sending of the Twelve to expand his mission (where they, too, now "proclaim" [from κηρύσσειν] that ἤγγικεν ἡ βασιλεία τῶν οὐρανῶν; 10:7), and immediately before a series of controversy stories which culminate in the rejection of Jesus at Nazareth (12:1–13:58). John thus appears at a transitional point in Jesus' own ministry where he begins to face growing opposition and rejection. Of course, in this precise respect John has already "prepared the way" for Jesus, as he himself opposed the Pharisees and Sadducees (3:7), was "handed over" (4:12), and is now "in prison" (11:2). It is fitting, then, that Jesus characterizes John here as a common man, the antithesis of Herod Antipas with his fine robes (11:8), one whose lifestyle was ridiculed and his call for repentance rejected by "this generation" (11:18).[26] "From the days of John the Baptist until now," Jesus declares, "the kingdom of heaven has suffered violence" (11:12). What was true of John is true of Jesus, and will become truer still in what transpires.

---

[22] It appears that Matthew has Isaiah in mind throughout the entire sequence. The rewording of Mark's description of the spirit's descent at Jesus' baptism likely intends to pick up Isa. 11:2's "the spirit of God will rest upon him" (note Isa. 11 was just invoked for Jesus' Nazarene roots: 2:23). Cf. Mt. 3:16's πνεῦμα θεοῦ . . . ἐπ᾽ αὐτόν and Isa. 11:2's ἐπ᾽ αὐτὸν πνεῦμα τοῦ θεοῦ. For a broader discussion, see James D. G. Dunn, "John the Baptist's Use of Scripture," in *The Gospels and the Scriptures of Israel*, ed. Craig A. Evans and W. Richard Stegner, JSNTSup 104 (Sheffield: Sheffield Academic Press, 1994), 42–54.

[23] Paul Foster, "The Eschatology of the Gospel of Matthew," in *"To Recover What Has Been Lost": Essays on Eschatology, Intertextuality, and Reception History in Honor of Dale C. Allison Jr.*, ed. Tucker S. Ferda, Daniel Frayer-Griggs, and Nathan C. Johnson, NovTSup 183 (Leiden and Boston: Brill, 2021), 77–103 (84): "the eschatological tone of his [Jesus'] own preaching and purpose is set by John the Baptist."

[24] Mt. 3:10 and 7:19 are identical. Another particularly striking connection is that between Jesus' claim in the parable of the two sons (which is about John the Baptist), that one son ἐποίησεν τὸ θέλημα τοῦ πατρός (21:31), and Jesus' teaching in 7:21 that ὁ ποιῶν τὸ θέλημα τοῦ πατρός μου will enter the kingdom of heaven. It may also be that Jesus' claim that "there is none greater born of women than John the Baptist . . . yet the least in the kingdom is greater than he" (11:11) uses John's own devaluation of physical descent (e.g., "born of women") to teach about the values of the kingdom, vis-à-vis John himself! On parallels in general, see Edgar Krentz, "None Greater Among Those Born of Women: John the Baptist in the Gospel of Matthew," *CurTM* 10 (1983): 333–8; Brian C. Dennert, *John the Baptist and the Jewish Setting of Matthew*, WUNT 2/403 (Tubingen: Mohr Siebeck, 2015), 175–8.

[25] With one exception: the question about fasting (Mt. 9:14-15).

[26] It is also fitting that Matthew has added to the Baptist block Jesus' own woe over Galilean cities, where he laments the fact that his call for repentance—a clear echo of John—was rejected, and his miracles unheeded. It is likely that Matthew has moved this passage to the Baptist block precisely because of its putative connection to John's message. See Tucker S. Ferda, *Jesus, the Gospels, and the Galilean Crisis*, LNTS 601 (London: Bloomsbury/T&T Clark, 2019), 223–5.

After Jesus' rejection at Nazareth (Mt. 13:54-8), we see the darkening clouds gather, as Matthew returns to John a third time for a rather extensive description of his unjust death (14:1-12).[27] This passage appears near the end of Jesus' Galilean ministry and helps transition the narrative to his journey to Jerusalem and death on the Passover. As John dies at the hands of the political elite, the story anticipates Jesus' own fate. Jesus comes "after" (ὀπίσω) John (Mt. 3:11) not merely in terms of the tone and content of his message, nor even in opposition and rejection, but in his very death.[28]

Though the character of John dies midway through the narrative, his memory and legacy persist. The spotlight falls on John one final time (explicitly at least) after Jesus' triumphal entry and temple action. Jesus recalls John to defend his "authority" (21:23-7), asking his interlocutors if John's "baptism" (τὸ βάπτισμα τὸ Ἰωάννου) was "from heaven" (ἐξ οὐρανοῦ) or "from mortals" (ἐξ ἀνθρώπων)? The question is particularly fraught at this point in the narrative precisely because John is dead. Jesus, opposed by the temple elite, asks his interlocutors to reflect on the question of the divine legitimation of an executed prophet. As the narrative so far has woven their ministries closely together, to conclude that John's baptism was indeed "from heaven"—which Matthew certainly assumes is the case—then Jesus' "authority" is also divinely sanctioned. Opposing Jesus, like opposing John, is opposing the will of God.[29] Matthew adds to Mark a further parable about "two sons" which stresses the point that John came "in the way of righteousness," and that opposition to him (and to Jesus, by implication) is actually opposition to the kingdom (21:28-32). The very next parable about the wicked tenants makes a similar point (21:33-44). While it does not mention John by name, he is clearly included among the "servants" sent by the owner of the vineyard and killed by the tenants.[30] That story ends, too, with a promise of vindication (21:40-3). Thus, Matthew has characterized John in such a way in this curtain call to theologize his unjust death and use it to make a larger point about the accomplishment of God's purposes despite opposition.

Were we to summarize how John's fourfold appearance in Matthew functions in the narrative as a whole, we could say that John emerges when and because the evangelist wants to talk about Jesus. Moreover, in terms of the characterization of John, we conclude that John has been remade somewhat into the image of Jesus in Matthew. Salient characteristics of Matthew's Jesus—focus on his teaching, his rejection, his

---

[27] On placement, see Lamar Cope, "The Death of John the Baptist in the Gospel of Matthew, or, The Case of the Confusing Conjunction," *CBQ* 38 (1976): 515–19.

[28] Cf. Janice Capel Anderson, *Matthew's Narrative Web: Over, and Over, and Over Again*, JSNTSup 91 (Sheffield: Sheffield Academic Press, 1994), 172: "*John is the foreshadower as well as the forerunner of Jesus*" (italics in original).

[29] The speech of Gamaliel in Acts, which adopts very similar language, confirms the interpretation advanced here: "I tell you, keep away from these men and leave them alone; because if this plan or this undertaking is from men (ἐξ ἀνθρώπων), it will fail, but if it is from God (ἐκ θεοῦ), you will not be able to destroy them. In that case you may even be found fighting against God!" (Acts 5:38-9).

[30] The language of the parable itself evokes John's preaching (3:10), as the servants come seeking the "fruits" (τοὺς καρπούς) of the vineyard (21:34). The NRSV unfortunately disguises this connection by taking καρπός in the parable as "produce."

death in alignment with scripture—now find their antecedent in John, a teaching and speaking prophet,[31] who was rejected, and, too, "handed over" to death.[32]

There is another crucial way in which Matthew's Christology has shaped the characterization of John the Baptist. To borrow language from the Fourth Gospel, we might say that Matthew's John "decreases" so that Jesus may "increase" (Jn 3:30). This is somewhat paradoxical since John gets more stage time in Matthew than in any of the other gospels. But we can identify a Christological constriction of John's role in numerous scenes, starting again with John's initial proclamation in the desert. Readers have learned by this point that Jesus' very name communicates his task to "save his people from their sins" (1:21). This mission requires a reconfiguration of John's work, since Mark had contended that John announced a "baptism of repentance for the forgiveness of sins" (βάπτισμα μετανοίας εἰς ἄφεσιν ἁμαρτιῶν; 1:4). Matthew conspicuously severs the connection between John's baptism and the forgiveness of sins: John's baptism becomes merely a "baptism for repentance" (εἰς μετάνοιαν). It is Jesus' work, for Matthew, that is connected to the "forgiveness of sins," as the precise phrase εἰς ἄφεσιν ἁμαρτιῶν reappears at the Last Supper with reference to Jesus' sacrificial death ("this is my blood of the covenant which is poured out for many for the forgiveness of sins"; 26:28).[33] John and his baptismal rite are merely preparation— again "prepare" the way from Isa. 40—for the real work of redemption brought about by the Messiah.[34] Here Matthew leans into the characterization of John noted earlier: he is a prophet calling for repentance and renewed covenant faithfulness in a climactic moment in Israel's history.

Matthew also greatly humanizes John the Baptist by investing his character with a psychological depth and complexity lacking in Mark. This has the result of building up the superiority of Jesus and making John into a model of discipleship.[35] Matthew maintains John's declaration in Mark that he is "not worthy" to take care of Jesus' sandals (Mk 1:7),[36] and further adds to it. Now, before Jesus is baptized, John expressly declares his inferiority to Jesus by stating that Jesus should be the one baptizing him (Mt. 3:14). The character John thus recognizes rightly who Jesus is—something that never happens in Mark explicitly—and rightly upholds Jesus' higher dignity by deferring to him.[37] This kind of obsequiousness finds its closest parallels in later

---

[31] It is interesting to compare Mark and Matthew on this front. Mark's "active" Jesus is preceded by an active John (who speaks very little), while Matthew's "teacher" is preceded by a teaching John.

[32] On the connection between Isa. 53 and παραδίδωμι, see Joel Marcus, *Mark 1-8*, AB 27 (New Haven, CT: Yale University Press, 2000), 171.

[33] Cf. Davies and Allison, *Matthew*, 1:300, 305–6.

[34] It is likely that the general de-emphasizing of John's baptism in Matthew is related to Matthew's Christology, as the gospel ends with *Jesus'* command that his disciples baptize in the light of the accomplishments of his own mission ("all authority in heaven and on earth have been given to me"; 28:18).

[35] John as a model of discipleship is stressed by Lisa M. Bowens in her excellent essay, "The Role of John the Baptist in the Gospel of Matthew," *WW* 30 (2010): 311–18, esp. at 315: "The author consistently subordinates John in order to demonstrate the discipleship aspect of John's character."

[36] Traditionally the work of a slave; cf. Davies and Allison, *Matthew*, 1:315.

[37] Cf. Julius Wellhausen, *Evangelienkommentare* (repr. Berlin: de Gruyter, 1987), 183.

encounters in which figures come to Jesus seeking various forms of respite, and show their deference by falling down, petitioning, or otherwise demonstrating their respect (8:2; 8:8; 9:18; 9:27-8; 15:25; etc.).[38] Thus, John's disposition in the baptismal narrative is a kind of model for the posture of faithful discipleship in Matthew that combines right knowledge with right action.

Given this early congruence between knowledge and action, it is all the more shocking that the next we hear of John is that he has had something of a crisis of faith. Matthew begins the "Baptist block" with John's own doubts, voiced by his disciples: "are you the coming one, or shall we wait for another?" (11:3). Matthew leaves no reason to read John's inquiry as anything other than sincere.[39] The character of John has thus developed and changed in the narrative, as we know was possible given extant characterization techniques.[40] In any case, the motive behind John's question is not immediately clear. It must relate to the nature of Jesus' messianic mission, as the question is prompted by "hearing" about "the works of the Christ" (τὰ ἔργα τοῦ Χριστοῦ; 11:2)—that is, activities narrated from chapters 4–10. And we can probably go further still. While much of Jesus' early activity in these chapters repeats themes from John's own proclamation, as already noted, there is some *novum* here. Due to Matthew's reorganization of his sources, much of the material in chapters 4–10 is authoritative teaching (chs. 5–7) and miracle stories, specifically stories of physical healing and restoration (chs. 8–9). The latter, while not opposed to the teaching of John in any way, also stand out as somewhat unanticipated by John's proclamation as Matthew has presented it. It is likely, then, that John inquires because the "works" of "the coming one" are not exactly what he expected.[41] In view of this, Jesus' response is multilayered. Jesus invites the proper "seeing" and "hearing" of precisely what had likely prompted John's question (his miracle-working activity), while also narrating that activity with stock phrases from Isaiah.[42] As Matthew has stressed Isaiah's connection to the work of both characters, Jesus' response confirms John's Isaianic-inspired ministry at the same time that he defends his own.

In other ways, too, Matthew brings John and Jesus together more closely: they share much of the same teaching about repentance, judgment, and good deeds; they are both inspired by the scriptures; and they are unified in mission. And yet these connections function to highlight the "more than" features of Jesus' own activity.[43] The sober

---

[38] Interestingly, none of the Twelve disciples do this, even though, they, too, will rightly recognize Jesus' identity.

[39] In the history of interpretation, many have balked at the idea that John the Baptist may have entertained this question seriously, suggesting that John feigned doubt to instruct his disciples. See discussion in Jacques Dupont, "L'ambassade de Jean-Baptiste (Matthieu 11,2-6; Luc 7,18-23)," *NRT* 83 (1961): 805–21.

[40] For an important recent attempt to nuance and complexify the view that ancient literary characters were static and one-dimensional, see Cornelis Bennema, *A Theory of Character in New Testament Narrative* (Minneapolis: Fortress, 2014). Cf. Bowens, "Role," 313–14.

[41] In confirmation of this, one should note the common reactions of *surprise* to Jesus' activity (8:27; 9:33; etc.), and the raising of *questions* (8:27; 9:11, 14, 33; etc.).

[42] See M. Eugene Boring, "The Gospel of Matthew: Introduction, Commentary, and Reflections," *NIB* 8 (Nashville, TN: Abingdon, 1995), 266–8.

[43] On the "two-sided riddle"—so-named—of tighter parallelism *and* heightened inferiority, see John Meier, "John the Baptist in Matthew's Gospel," *JBL* 99 (1980): 383–405 (386).

ascetism of the John who fasts contrasts with the joyful table-fellowship of the Jesus who feasts (11:18-9), making the latter stand out, even while they are about the same divine mandate. In Jesus, the time of the wedding and the bridegroom is here, so now is not the time for fasting (9:14-15). The character of John is thus the closest parallel to Jesus in the narrative, yet also, paradoxically, a sometimes foil.

Despite the clouding of John's Christological acuity in Mt. 11:2-6, Jesus in no way changes his positive evaluation of the Baptist. John remains not just a "prophet" but "more than a prophet," indeed "the greatest born of women" (11:9-11). John is Elijah, the "messenger" of Exodus 23:23, the "messenger of the covenant" of Malachi 3:1 (11:10, 14). In this we see the character of John, even in his doubt, highlight an important feature of Jesus' own teaching: the prioritization of obedience to the will of God over other possible boundary markers.[44] Jesus himself had concluded the Sermon on the Mount with a warning for those who say "Lord, Lord," but do not do the will of God (7:24-7). John, whose current predicament in prison is the direct consequence of his coming "in the way of righteousness" (21:32) and not wavering from it, garners praise from Jesus, even if John's question would suggest he is somewhat on the fence in joining the chorus of "Lord, Lord." Herein the questioning and struggling John continues to be a model of discipleship for Matthew's readers.[45]

II. Prophet from the Margins: Hiddenness and Opposition

While Matthew distinguishes John from Jesus, the evangelist also emphasizes that they share a certain marginal position vis-à-vis the religious and political powers.[46] Matthew's Gospel as a whole has a larger point to make here about the way in which the plan of God is carried out in this fourteenth generation "from the exile": it is not from the center, but from the margins, that God's plan is accomplished, and the proper recognition of God's agency in seemingly unexpected places requires eyes to see and ears to hear.

Matthew's infancy narrative develops the theme, carried into and through the portrayal of John's public ministry. The opening chapters of Matthew present a startling disjuncture between claims of massive salvation-historical significance on the one hand, and inconspicuous realities on the other. The genealogy claims that Jesus belongs with the likes of Abraham and David as an epoch-shaping figure in Israel's history, and yet we find in the narrative a refugee child, born to unaccomplished parents, fleeing persecution at the hands of Herod the Great. In all of this, Matthew makes clear with the use of scripture that there is more going on below the surface of things. Jesus is the

---

[44] For a great discussion, see Nathan Eubank, "Damned Disciples: The Permeability of the Boundary between Insiders and Outsiders in Matthew and Paul," in *Perceiving the Other in Ancient Judaism and Early Christianity*, ed. Michal Bar Asher Siegal et al. (Tübingen: Mohr Siebeck, 2017), 33–47.

[45] Cf. the great line from Bowens, "Role," 316: "Disciples follow Jesus even when they do not always understand what he is doing or where he is leading them."

[46] For a wider discussion, see Warren Carter, *Matthew and the Margins: A Sociopolitical and Religious Reading*, Bible and Liberation Series (Maryknoll, NY: Orbis, 2000).

true "king of the Jews," not Herod; the star at his birth fulfills the messianic oracle of Balaam, yet the scribes do not recognize it; the settling in no-name Nazareth signals Jesus' messianic identity as Isaiah's "shoot" from the stump of Jesse.

Similarly on the margins, John the Baptist first appears not in Jerusalem or any polis but in the wilderness.[47] We learn nothing of his background and pedigree.[48] We see merely a loner who does not practice piety before an audience (6:1), who does not worry about food or clothing (3:4; cf. 6:25-33), who does not store up treasures on earth (6:19-21). His first words are a bold and abrasive rebuke of religious leaders: "You brood of vipers!" (3:7). He exits the main stage as quickly as he entered, "handed over" (4:12) to the political elite, later executed as a pawn in a birthday-party game (14:1-12). But as with Jesus, so with John: there is more to the story. This man at the margins is actually at the center of God's purposes for Israel and the nations. Matthew makes this plain with both explicit and implicit use of scripture. John is the one Isaiah predicted would come; John's clothing signals that he is the long-awaited Elijah who is to come "before the great and manifest day of the Lord" (LXX Mal. 3:22).[49]

It is important to note here that Matthew, like Mark, does not expressly signal at this point in the narrative (3:1-17) that John is Elijah. Rather, he allows the implication of John's clothing and location by the Jordan to rest below the surface of the narrative.[50] There is, in this sense, a hiddenness to the identity of John produced by an artful reticence in narration. The form of dramatic irony only reinforces the content: the ideal reader of Matthew knows who John truly is, while many of the characters in the narrative do not. This characterization technique supports Matthew's larger purpose of narrating seemingly marginal events in Rome's empire—not least the crucifixion of a would-be king—within the larger plan of God.

In many ways, the focus of Jesus' own teaching about John in the "Baptist block" is precisely the nature of his hidden identity. Jesus begins by raising the question, "What did you go out into the wilderness to observe?" (11:7). That is, who is John, really? Jesus then provides a number of pointed identity claims, all of which cohere with the evaluative perspective of the narrative but which are also not obvious to many of the characters in the story.[51] Jesus highlights the contrast between John and Herod Antipas in terms of their social positions and lifestyles, and stresses that *John* is "the greatest born of women" (11:11). Here John highlights the alternative value system of the kingdom of heaven (cf. 5:1-12). In addition, John is identified with the ἄγγελος from Exodus (23:20), the messenger of the covenant from Malachi (3:1), and, Jesus now says explicitly, "Elijah who is to come" (11:14).[52] In such astounding claims we see that the

---

[47] On the symbolism of wilderness, see Donald Senior, *The Landscape of the Gospels* (New York: Paulist, 2020), 26-7.
[48] This contrasts markedly with Luke, where we first meet John, via his well-established priestly father, in the temple in Jerusalem (1:5-25).
[49] Contra Ernst, *Johannes der Täufer*, 26, who denies any connection to Elijah here.
[50] In 2 Kgs 1:9, Elijah is described as a man who "wore a garment of haircloth, with a girdle of leather about his loins" (RSV).
[51] Matthew then has Jesus end this little reflection on John's identity with the refrain, "let the one who has ears, hear" (11:15), which confirms the interpretation advanced here.
[52] Matthew's Jesus will later repeat this claim upon descending to the mount of transfiguration—"I tell you that Elijah has already come" (17:11)—with the inclusion of another crucial detail, *not* present in Mark, "and they did not recognize him" (οὐκ ἐπέγνωσαν αὐτὸν; 17:12).

disclosure of the identity of John also unveils the lateness of the eschatological hour. If Elijah is here, then the truth of John's own prediction is assured: the kingdom of heaven "has drawn near" (ἤγγικεν; 3:2), and the axe is indeed "now" (ἤδη) "at the root of the trees" (3:10). The need for Jesus to teach about the identity of John, and to rebuke some of his contemporaries for being "unable to interpret the signs of the times" (16:3), is one and the same.

Of course, like the characterization of John elsewhere in the narrative, the hiddenness motif ultimately serves Matthew's Christology, and that is ironically apparent in the Baptist block itself. Jesus' teaching about the identity of John begins with a response to the Baptist's failure to recognize the true identity of Jesus: "[A]re you the coming one, or should we wait for another?" (11:3). Just as Jesus points to scripture to clarify who John truly is, asking his hearers, "what did you go out to the wilderness to see (θεάσασθαι)?" (11:7), so too he tells John's disciples to report "what you hear and see" (ἃ ἀκούετε καὶ βλέπετε) (11:4), summarizing his own activity with unmistakable echoes of scripture.[53] It is fitting that Matthew ends the Baptist block with the Johannine thunderbolt: "At that time Jesus said, I praise you, Father, Lord of heaven and earth, because you hid (ἔκρυψας) these things from the wise and the intelligent and revealed them to infants" (11:25). Matthew's "at that time" is the occasion of speaking to the crowds about John the Baptist, so the "these things" (ταῦτα) which have been hidden includes not only John's identity (11:7-15), but the identity of Jesus disclosed to John (11:1-6). The "wise and the intelligent" do not receive, but "the infants" do. One of the main points of the Baptist block comes into precise focus here: God is not working at the center where some expected, but God is indeed working all the same among "the infants," the desert ascetic, the "glutton and drunkard" (11:19), and just as the scriptures foretold. John the Baptist himself must be reminded of this at the beginning of the scene—a striking characterization technique which humbles the character of John at the same time that it demonstrates the truth of his own proclamation about the centrality of Jesus in salvation history. Jesus holds the truth of John's own proclamation at a time when he cannot.

If God's working on the margins through Jesus and John means that God's ways are "hidden" to many, it also means that God's ways are opposed by many. Indeed, the inability to perceive the truth in Matthew does not lead to passive disengagement, but active, even violent, opposition. By Matthew's framing, however, this opposition actually serves to confirm the truth of what John and Jesus are about, because the evangelist characterizes both as "prophets" (e.g., 11:9, 13; 13:57).[54] "Prophets" in Matthew are consistently portrayed as marginal figures, persecuted and rejected, but nonetheless at the center of God's will. Jesus teaches in the Sermon on the Mount, "Blessed are you when they revile you and persecute you and say all kinds of evil against you on account of me. Rejoice and be glad, because your reward is great in heaven, for thusly they persecuted the prophets who were before you" (τοὺς προφήτας τοὺς πρὸ ὑμῶν; 5:11-12). Jesus returns to the idea later when excoriating the "scribes and Pharisees":

---

[53] It may not be coincidence that the first item in Jesus' list is "the blind see" (11:5).
[54] Cf. Trilling, "Täufertradition," 274–5, 282–6.

You build the tombs of the prophets and decorate the monuments of the righteous ones, and you say, "If we were living in the times of our fathers, we would not have fellowshipped with them in shedding the blood of the prophets." Therefore, you testify against yourselves that you are the sons of those who murdered the prophets, and you will fill up the measure of your fathers. Snakes, brood of vipers! How will you flee from the judgment of Gehenna?

Mt. 23:29-33

It is not a coincidence that the prophet Jesus, nearing his own unjust death, speaks here in the style and idiom of John the Baptist, the prophet, who went before Jesus and too was murdered. In the final line—"You brood of vipers! How will you flee from the judgment of Gehenna?" (Mt. 23:33)—the connection is unmistakable:

John: γεννήματα ἐχιδνῶν, τίς ὑπέδειξεν ὑμῖν φυγεῖν ἀπὸ τῆς μελλούσης ὀργῆς;
Jesus: γεννήματα ἐχιδνῶν, πῶς φύγητε ἀπὸ τῆς κρίσεως τῆς γεέννης;

Without even mentioning John's name, Matthew links the characters of Jesus and John together via a shared prophetic legacy in Israel's past and via a shared prophetic vocation in the present. The parable of the wicked tenants a few chapters earlier (21:33-46) made the same point. There John (who has been the topic of conversation since the "Question of Authority," 21:23ff.) is certainly included among the list of rejected "servants"—the prophets of Israel—preparing for Jesus, the unique "son," who shares the same fate.[55] The parable of the wedding feast (22:1-14), which Matthew has decided to place in immediate sequence, continues the same line: many slaves are sent to invite all to the wedding, and they are "seized ... mistreated ... and killed" (22:6). Both parables make clear whose side God is on, despite the rejection. From the perspective of the narrative, any one character's reaction to John or Jesus says more about that character than it does about John or Jesus.

The characterization of John in Matthew as a rejected and persecuted prophet is thoroughgoing and quite distinctive in comparison to the other gospels. It dominates the opening act, as Matthew frames John's initial proclamation as a prophetic denouncement of the religious and political leaders[56] (whereas in Luke the same mini-sermon is given to "the crowds" otherwise interested in John's baptism; 3:7).[57] Later, in the Baptist block, Jesus teaches that "from the days of John the Baptist until now" the

---

[55] It should be stressed that, in Matthew's presentation, the common people overwhelmingly side with John; it is the leaders who oppose him. The popularity of John is stressed at the outset of his ministry (e.g., "the people of Jerusalem and all Judea were going out to him"; 1:5) and confirmed at the end (e.g., the "chief priests and elders" [11:23] "fear the crowd" that "regards John as a prophet"; 11:26). This, too, parallels Jesus. Matthew later explains that it is the "chief priests and elders" who persuade the "the crowds" to ask for Barabbas rather than Jesus (27:20). For further discussion, see Warren Carter, "The Crowds in Matthew's Gospel," *CBQ* 55 (1993): 54-67.

[56] It may be that, in Matthew, the "Pharisees and Sadducees" come not to be baptized, but to observe (and perhaps critique) his baptism, as they come ἐπὶ τὸ βάπτισμα αὐτοῦ (3:7). It is much clearer in Luke that the crowds come "in order to be baptized by him" (βαπτισθῆναι ὑπ᾿ αὐτοῦ; 3:7).

[57] Yet the scope of the projected audience appears to widen as the monologue continues, which also confirms Walter Wink, *John the Baptist in the Gospel Tradition* (Cambridge: Cambridge University

"kingdom" (which John himself proclaimed in 3:2) has "suffered violence" and "violent ones take it by force" (11:12). The prophetic identity of John unlocks this enigmatic saying: as John is a "prophet" (11:9), he suffers the violent opposition expected for prophets, an opposition which serves to characterize the ministry of Jesus too (ἕως ἄρτι). Jesus makes the same point later when descending the mount of transfiguration: "Elijah is indeed coming first and will restore all things; but I tell you that Elijah has already come, and they did not recognize him, but they did to him whatever they pleased. So also the Son of man is about to suffer at their hands" (17:11-12).[58] Again we see here the differentiation between John and Jesus—"Elijah" and "Son of man," respectively—and also a shared prophetic mission and shared prophetic fate.[59]

John the Baptist's death at the hands of Herod Antipas also contributes to this prophetic characterization.[60] The John, Herod, and Herodias triangle echo Elijah, Ahab, and Jezebel, which makes good sense because we otherwise know that John is "Elijah who is to come" (11:14). This intertextuality changes the readers' encounter with John's death: for while it seems the marginal man from the desert is easily discarded, readers know how the old story ends. Readers know that the prophet John, like Elijah before him, is on the side of the God of Israel.

As the characterization of John elsewhere serves as a model of discipleship for Matthew's readers (as noted above), the same is probably true for this prophetic typology. Matthew places the Baptist block immediately after Jesus' sending of the Twelve, and his instructions have also been greatly expanded by Matthew with clear predictions of violent opposition (10:16-23). As commentators note, it is very likely that this mission charge addresses rather transparently later realities in the Christian mission.[61] So Jesus' prediction of such opposition, juxtaposed to the lauded memory of John "the prophet," again holds John up as a model in the midst of such circumstances. The same is true of Mt. 23, discussed above, where Jesus, still speaking in the idiom of John, declares, "Therefore I send you prophets, sages, and scribes, some of whom you will kill and crucify, and some of whom you will flog in your synagogues and pursue from town to town, so that upon you may come all the righteous blood shed on earth, from the blood of righteous Abel to the blood of Zechariah son of Barachiah" (23:34-5).

Press, 1968), 34, n. 1, that Matthew's "Pharisees and Sadducees" is redactional. There is no reason to think the prediction of the coming one (3:11-12) is delivered only to the Pharisees and Sadducees. A similar thing happens in the Sermon on the Mount, which begins with Jesus addressing his disciples (5:2) and ends with the astonishment of the crowds (7:28).

[58] Matthew has modified Mark on the basis of scripture: (i) Matthew removes Mark's mention that John died "just as it is written about him" (9:13), surely because he knows there is no such prediction; (ii) he deepens the connections to Malachi, changing Mark's present tense "he restores" (ἀποκαθιστάνει) to the future tense "he will restore" (ἀποκαταστήσει), just as in LXX Mal. 3:23 (cf. Sir. 48:10).

[59] When people reportedly believe that Jesus may be "John the Baptist, Elijah, Jeremiah, or one of the prophets" (16:14), this is not the whole truth—as Peter next makes clear—but also not entirely off base.

[60] As well as the motif of opposition: whereas Mark blames the death on Herodias, indicating that Herod was sympathetic to John (Mk 6:20), Matthew stresses that Herod "wanted to kill" John (14:5). See Meier, "John," 399.

[61] See, e.g., Davies and Allison, *Matthew*, 2:160-4.

Here Jesus looks back to the prophets of old and to the legacy of John, and then looks forward to the post-crucifixion period, linking all past, present, and future together under the same prophetic banner.

III. Conclusion

John the Baptist in Matthew is a complex character with a clear narrative role: he is an eschatological prophet on the cusp of a great new exodus event, preparing Isaiah's "the way of the Lord" with both his words and his deeds.[62] John is more prominent in Matthew than in the other gospels, but this is because Matthew has decided to reshape John in the mold of Jesus and thereby maximize the Christological potential of his character. Like Jesus, John announces the kingdom, calls for repentance, is "handed over" and violently opposed, resides on the margins of society, and yet stands at the center of God's purposes for Israel and the nations. At the same time, Matthew humbles John and makes him a model of discipleship.

If we step back to look at the whole, we see in the character of John, Matthew working through one of the central theological crises of early Christianity and the core narratological dilemma for the evangelists as a whole: to show how the suffering and death of the Messiah on a Roman cross is not only the will of God but paradoxically confirms the truth of God and the nature of God's kingdom. To "prepare the way" for this, Matthew requires his readers to adopt a certain epistemological posture to grasp truly the identity of the man in the wilderness; readers of Matthew must be able to read below the surface of things. The form of the narrative itself reinforces this content. As at Golgotha, so "in the wilderness": "let the one who has ears to hear, hear!"

---

[62] Contra Wink, *John the Baptist*, 41: Matthew's John is "more comprehensive than Mark's," but "less profound."

5

Word and Deed: Jesus as a Teacher in the Gospel of Matthew

Melanie A. Howard

I. Introduction

"Those who can, do. Those who can't, teach." This unfortunate, yet well-known, aphorism offers a pithy derision of teaching as a practice. It suggests a fundamental dichotomy that prioritizes action over instruction. Such a sentiment, though, could hardly be more foreign to Matthew's understanding of the task of teaching as it is embodied in Jesus.

The Gospel of Matthew presents Jesus as a teacher. Even the most cursory examination of the gospel would yield this conclusion, and indeed, much scholarly ink has already been spilled in exploring Jesus' role as a teacher in Matthew.[1] Given the limited scope of this exploration, I do not presume to offer a comprehensive accounting of the many facets of Matthew's characterization of Jesus as a teacher. Rather, I hope merely to demonstrate one aspect of Matthew's character development of Jesus: Jesus' presentation as a teacher who emphasizes the importance of both cognitive understanding of his teaching *as well as* the enactment of ethical actions that support the vision of the Kingdom of Heaven as it appears throughout the gospel.[2] In this

---

[1] Cf., e.g., Laurie Brink, "Matthew's Portrait of Jesus as Teacher," *TBT* 49, no. 1 (Jan. 2011): 17–23; Samuel Byrskog, "Jesus as Messianic Teacher in the Gospel According to Matthew: Tradition History and/or Narrative Christology," in *The New Testament as Reception*, ed. Mogens Müller and Henrik Tronier (London: Sheffield Academic Press, 2002), 83–100; Samuel Byrskog, *Jesus the Only Teacher: Didactic Authority and Transmission in Ancient Israel, Ancient Judaism and the Matthean Community* (Stockholm: Almqvist & Wiksell International, 1994); Troy M. Troftgruben, "Lessons for Teaching from the Teacher: Matthew's Jesus on Teaching and Learning Today," *CurTM* 40, no. 6 (Dec. 2013): 387–98; John Yueh-Han Yieh, *One Teacher: Jesus' Teaching Role in Matthew's Gospel Report* (Berlin: de Gruyter, 2004).

[2] The phrase "Kingdom of Heaven" appears multiple times throughout the Gospel of Matthew: in 3:2; 4:17; 5:3, 10, 19-20; 7:21; 8:11; 10:7; 11:11-12; 13:11, 24, 31, 33, 44, 45, 47, 52; 16:19; 18:1, 3-4, 23; 19:12, 14, 23; 20:1; 22:2; 23:13; 25:1. In addition to this, sometimes the gospel prefers the term "Kingdom" alone (4:23; 6:10; 8:12; 9:35; 13:19, 38, 41; 24:14; 25:34) or an unspecified kingdom that seems to be attributed to Jesus (16:28; 20:21). In a few less-common instances, the gospel uses "Kingdom of God" (6:33 [depending on how the textual evidence is read here]; 12:28; 19:24; 21:31, 43) or a kingdom attributed to the "Father" (13:43; 26:29). An exploration of how this Kingdom functions within the

characterization, Jesus emerges among the gospel's characters as the only character who rightly embodies the role of "teacher."

To make this argument, I begin by situating Matthew's characterization of Jesus within the historical context of ancient teaching practices to highlight the ways in which this characterization fits within the perspective of the gospel's early implied audiences. With that context provided, I then turn to examine Matthew's presentation of Jesus as a teacher who upholds the expectation that cognitive understanding and ethical action must be combined.[3] This observation is then supported by an examination of the audience of Jesus' teaching and through exploring Matthew's characterization of Jesus as a "New Moses," in contrast to other religious teachers.

II. Ancient Teaching Practices

Although Matthew is creating a narrative and characterizing Jesus in a particular way, seeing how this presentation emerges naturally from the setting of first-century pedagogy makes this narrative more comprehensible. In examining these first-century precedents for teaching, it is helpful to attend both to Greco-Roman pedagogical practices as well as to the religious education that would have permeated the world of Second Temple Judaism.[4]

In a significant study of ancient educational practices, Raffaella Cribiore paints a picture of the unstable world of ancient education. Cribiore observes that "schools," as such, did not exist apart from the teachers who taught there, and given this, an individual teacher's decision to relocate could effectively eliminate educational opportunities in a given locale.[5] This situation also invested teachers, especially itinerant καθηγηταί, with a degree of control over their pupils. As Cribiore observes, "Since competition was limited to a degree, a teacher of secondary education was in the position of controlling his clients. Naturally, the consequences were particularly disastrous in the country, where a departing καθηγητής was likely to leave a student in the lurch."[6]

---

gospel is beyond the scope of the chapter, but broadly speaking, this Kingdom seems to be characterized by its immediacy, its proximity to miracles of healing, its availability to marginalized populations, its high esteem for righteousness, its great worth, its potential for growth, and its unusual valuation of social status.

[3] I use the phrase "cognitive understanding" here (and throughout this chapter) to differentiate between information that might be verified by a test of one's memory (e.g., I know that two plus two equals four) versus knowledge that must be demonstrated by action (e.g., I know how to ride a bicycle). Likewise, I specify *ethical* action to differentiate between those actions that might be identified as morally neutral (e.g., brushing one's teeth) versus those that have ethical import (e.g., choosing to purchase fair trade goods).

[4] While Second Temple Judaism was, of course, enmeshed within the larger Greco-Roman world, I am treating these as separate educational systems with some traits that were unique to each even as overlap would have also existed between these systems.

[5] Raffaella Cribiore, *Gymnastics of the Mind: Greek Education in Hellenistic and Roman Egypt* (Princeton, NJ: Princeton University Press, 2001), 18.

[6] Cribiore, *Gymnastics of the Mind*, 54. For other explorations of the ways in which literacy and power dynamics intermingled, see Alan K. Bowman and Greg Woolf (eds.), *Literacy and Power in the Ancient World* (Cambridge: Cambridge University Press, 2009).

As an example of the power that such καθηγηταί could hold in this regard, Cribiore quotes at length from a letter from a mother to her son in which she laments the sudden departure of her son's καθηγητής and the need for her son to secure an alternative instructor.[7] Although the letter itself does not identify the reason for the instructor's departure, Cribiore speculates that it might have been due to the instructor's desire to pursue more profitable opportunities.[8] Similarly, Cribiore also points to another letter from one Neilos to his father Theon that laments the poor selection of καθηγηταί in the area and their steep rates.[9] In short, Cribiore suggests that the geographical instability of teachers could contribute to tension between teachers and students as a result of teachers' power over their students' educational prospects.

Such a tension may be in the background of Jesus' own denunciation of the scribes and Pharisees wielding power over others, as will be further explored below.[10] Indeed, issues of power between the educator and the student may have been in play within Jewish educational settings as well. Martin Goodman suggests that reverence for religious texts may well have granted a degree of power to the educated scribes who produced such texts.[11] Thus, within both Greco-Roman and Jewish settings, some educational practices could be linked to social power.

While much more could be said about teaching *practices*, one might also consider the *content* of teaching. Throughout a full course of study, students of Greco-Roman educational systems might encounter any number of disciplines: grammar, rhetoric, gymnastics, mathematics, and philosophy, among others. This liberal arts education would ideally have the effect of training students to be well-rounded and productive citizens (cf. Aristotle, *Politics* 8.1337a).

While Jesus' teaching in Matthew also seems geared at producing a certain type of "citizen" for the Kingdom of Heaven, such a robust curriculum is beyond the scope of his instruction. Thus, it is important to consider how the content of Jesus' teachings may align specifically with Jewish religious education. However, this is not to suggest a sharp dichotomy between Greco-Roman and Jewish backgrounds to the Gospel of Matthew when it comes to a picture of education. Indeed, as Tyler Stewart has suggested, at least in the case of the *Letter of Aristeas* and 2 Maccabees, one can detect resonances between Hellenistic and Jewish education.[12] Thus, despite the differences

---

[7] Cribiore, *Gymnastics of the Mind*, 48, citing *P. Oxy.* VI.930.
[8] Cribiore, *Gymnastics of the Mind*, 48.
[9] Cribiore, *Gymnastics of the Mind*, 57–8, citing *P.Oxy.* XVIII.2190.
[10] Given that a full exploration of Greco-Roman educational practices is beyond the scope of this chapter, one might consult any number of other sources that address the topic in much greater detail: Martin Lowther Clarke, *Higher Education in the Ancient World* (London: Routledge, 2012); Werner Jaeger, *Paideia: The Ideals of Greek Culture*, trans. Gilbert Highet, 3 vols. (New York: Oxford University Press, 1965–86); Bernard Legras, *Éducation et culture dans le monde grec (VIIe-Ier siècle av. J.-C.)* (Paris: Sedes, 1998); Teresa Morgan, *Literate Education in the Hellenistic and Roman Worlds* (Cambridge: Cambridge University Press, 1998); Lee Too (ed.), *Education in Greek and Roman Antiquity* (Leiden: Brill, 2001).
[11] Martin D. Goodman, "Texts, Scribes and Power in Roman Judaea," in *Literacy and Power in the Ancient World*, ed. Alan K. Bowman and Greg Woolf (Cambridge: Cambridge University Press, 2009), 99–108.
[12] Tyler A. Stewart, "Jewish *Paideia*: Greek Education in the Letter of Aristeas and 2 Maccabees," *JSJ* 48 (2017): 182–202.

between Greco-Roman and Jewish education, both systems might be understood as holding similar values (e.g., the formation of students and the transmission of knowledge), even as the specific content within those systems might differ.

To understand Matthew's portrayal of Jesus as a teacher within this Jewish educational system, it may be helpful to consider the emphases that emerge within the content of Rabbinic Jewish teaching. Although the documents from the Rabbinic period post-date Jesus' teaching practice, William H. U. Anderson suggests they can be usefully read alongside New Testament texts since "some of the data can definitely be dated before the Common Era and is reflected in various pieces of literature from that period."[13] Thus, several Rabbinic period texts may help to fill out a picture of the religious education that may be in the background of Matthew's Gospel.

In seeking to understand the content of the Matthean Jesus' teaching, Rabbinic texts can offer a helpful point of comparison. One theme that emerges within these texts is the importance of coupling study with action. So, for example, *m. 'Avot* 1:15 attributes to Shammai the exhortation to make the study of Torah a fixed practice and to speak little but do much. Similarly, *m. 'Avot* 4:5 attributes to Rabbi Ishmael the instruction, "He who learns in order to teach, it is granted to him to study and to teach. But he who learns in order to practice, it is granted to him to learn and to teach and to practice." This focus on both learning and action is one that will emerge within the Matthean Jesus' teaching and become a point of contention between him and the scribes and Pharisees, as will be explored further below.

The Gospel of Matthew is, of course, a literary creation of its author, and as such, it can be explored along narrative-critical lines (as the remainder of this chapter will do). However, insofar as it is a literary creation arising from a particular time and place within the historical timeline, it is helpful to know something of the larger historical and cultural milieux from which it arises. As this brief exploration has illustrated, the gospel's presentation of Jesus as a teacher is even more understandable when viewed within this context.

III. Jesus as Teacher in Matthew

A. Word and Deed in Jesus' Teaching Ministry

While Matthew will develop his characterization of Jesus as a teacher through the depiction of Jesus' choice of students, his comparison to Moses, and his contrast with other teachers, one of the gospel's most prominent emphases in its depiction of Jesus as a teacher is the necessity for teaching to result in both correct cognitive understanding and ethical action. This emphasis is apparent both in the Sermon on the Mount as well as in the parable of the sheep and the goats in 25:31-46. Thus, it is to these two parts of the gospel we now turn.

---

[13] William H. U. Anderson, "Jewish Education Around the Time of the New Testament (100 bce-100 ce)," *Journal of Beliefs and Values* 18, no. 2 (1997): 217.

The emphasis on comprehension coupled with proper action emerges most clearly within the Sermon on the Mount and Jesus' connection between his own teaching and the Mosaic law (5:17-20). In this section of instruction devoted to highlighting the ongoing relevance and importance of the law, Jesus emphasizes this point by explaining that whoever performs these commandments and teaches others to do so as well will be called great in the Kingdom of Heaven (5:19b). This statement is programmatic for understanding the role of teaching, and specifically Jesus' portrayal as a teacher, in the Gospel of Matthew. That is, Jesus here articulates the way in which teaching itself can lead to being called great in the Kingdom of Heaven. Notably, the formula that he provides for achieving this designation includes not *only* the teaching itself but *also* the proper performance of "the least of the commandments" (τῶν ἐντολῶν τούτων τῶν ἐλαχίστων; 5:19a). In other words, proper teaching must be deeply entwined with proper practice.

The importance of ethical action accompanying cognitive understanding appears at the end of the Sermon on the Mount as well. In 7:24-7, Jesus offers a brief parable to illustrate the outcome that he desires for his audience.[14] In this parable of two men building houses, one with a rock foundation and one with a foundation of sand, Jesus contrasts the wisdom of those who hear his words and "do them" (ποιεῖ αὐτούς; 7:24) with the folly of those who hear his words but fail to act upon them (7:26).

While the Matthean Jesus' focus on teaching producing action is introduced in his first teaching block in the Sermon on the Mount (chs. 5–7), this emphasis persists through the narrative's final section devoted to Jesus' teaching in Chapter 25. The emphatic eschatological thrust of Chapter 25 marks it as distinct from other blocks of Jesus' teaching in Matthew to this point in the narrative. However, in the pericope of 25:31-46, the Matthean Jesus returns to the key point that had been undergirding his teachings throughout the gospel: that learning must be accompanied by action for the sake of the "least of these" (25:45). That is, in the text that unfolds, Jesus' teaching emphasizes not the acquisition of intellectual knowledge or assent to theological principles as the basis for achieving "eternal life" (25:46), but rather the proper performance of acts of care for "the least of these" (25:40, 45). In other words, the ethical actions toward which Jesus' teachings in the gospel point are actions taken for

---

[14] To be sure, Jesus himself does not explicitly identify this speech as a "parable." Nonetheless, insofar as this text presents a story with an attention-grabbing plotline, it seems to fit well within the larger parable genre. Providing a precise definition of parable is beyond the scope of this chapter. However, one might consider that in his foundational work on parables, even C. H. Dodd gave a rather ambiguous definition to this art form, defining a parable as "a metaphor or simile drawn from nature or common life, arresting the hearer by its vividness or strangeness, and leaving the mind in sufficient doubt about its precise application to tease it into active thought"; *The Parables of the Kingdom* (New York: Scribner's Sons, 1961), 5. For a more thorough treatment of this topic, see Klyne Snodgrass, *Stories with Intent: A Comprehensive Guide to the Parables of Jesus* (Grand Rapids, MI: Eerdmans, 2008), 22-4. By Snodgrass's count, Matthew introduces ten additional unique parables beyond those found in Mark and Luke. While Luke includes more unique parables (eighteen, by Snodgrass's count), Matthew's reliance on parables as a teaching method is certainly not insignificant. Charles Hedrick also provides helpful categories for considering the types of parables within the Synoptic Gospels; *Many Things in Parables: Jesus and His Modern Critics* (Louisville, KY: Westminster John Knox, 2004), 2.

the sake of those who are suffering, marginalized, or otherwise oppressed. Such actions demonstrate the values of the Kingdom of Heaven that have pervaded Jesus' teachings and ministry throughout the gospel.

Here, then, Matthew creates a narrative link between the Sermon on the Mount's instructions to teach and do even the "least of the commandments" (5:19) and the eschatological discourse's instructions to pursue proper action in relation to those individuals who are identified as the "least." Aside from the scriptural quotation in Matthew 2:6, these are the only places where Matthew uses the term "least" (ἐλάχιστος). In this way, the gospel connects the importance of knowledge and action, even in the smallest matters.

The *inclusio* formed by these first and last major teaching blocks in Matthew highlights the gospel's presentation of Jesus as a teacher who is concerned with the connection between cognitive understanding and ethical action. However, this emphasis also appears subtly elsewhere in the gospel between these two bookends. Without offering an exhaustive or comprehensive explanation of these examples, a few may be identified briefly:

- Mt. 12:33—In this short aphorism about the fruit of trees, Jesus suggests that knowledge about a tree can be gained from observing its performance of fruit-bearing.
- Mt. 13:23—Jesus' explanation of the parable of the sower interprets the seed that fell on good ground as individuals who not only "understand" (συνιείς) the word but also "bear fruit and take action" (καρποφορεῖ καὶ ποιεῖ).
- Mt. 19:16-26—When the rich young man asks Jesus about what action he should take (τί . . . ποιήσω; 19:16), Jesus responds first by ensuring that the young man has attained cognitive understanding of the commandments (19:17-19) before also offering instruction for ethical action (19:21).
- Mt. 24:43-4—In the context of Jesus' eschatological discourse, he offers the example of a homeowner whose *knowledge* of an intruder prompts his *action* of staying awake to sabotage the intruder's plans.
- Mt. 25:13—As a conclusion to the parable of the bridesmaids, Jesus points to the necessity of action (Γρηγορεῖτε; "keep awake") because of a corresponding lack of knowledge (οὐκ οἴδατε; "you do not know").

While each of these examples could be explored in far more depth, they nonetheless offer a sampling of the ways in which attention to both cognitive understanding and ethical action permeate Jesus' teaching throughout the gospel.

In short, from the first major teaching block in the gospel to its last, Matthew presents Jesus as a teacher who is emphasizing the importance of not only intellectual assent to the theoretical principles that he expounds, but also action that demonstrates this understanding. In other words, Matthew's presentation of Jesus as a teacher highlights the gospel's claim that Jesus' teaching, unlike that of the hypocritical scribes and Pharisees (cf. 23:3), combines proper words with proper deeds. This emphasis is borne out in the gospel in several other ways: through Jesus' particular choice of students; through a comparison between Jesus and Moses; and through a contrast between Jesus and other teachers. To each of these topics we now turn.

B. Jesus' Students

One of the ways in which Matthew presents Jesus as a teacher who emphasizes both cognitive understanding of his teaching as well as ethical action is through the students to whom Jesus is depicted as directing much of his teaching. That is, Jesus aims his instruction at those who are most likely not only to attain an intellectual grasp of his teaching but also demonstrate changed behavior as a result.

Given Matthew's portrayal of Jesus as a teacher who values both orthodoxy and orthopraxy in his teaching, it is notable who Jesus leaves *out* of his lessons. As Jack Dean Kingsbury notes, "Jesus presents none of his great speeches to the religious leaders, for there is never a time in Matthew's story when their ears are not deaf to his teaching."[15] That is, the Matthean Jesus' choice not to waste the pearls of his wisdom on these leaders (cf. 7:6) may well be due to his recognition that not only will they not hear his words, but they will also not enact them. As such, the narrative might suggest that they emerge as even more unwise than the foolish ones who at least hear Jesus' words but fail to act upon them (cf. 7:26).

While Jesus does not offer teaching to the religious leaders who will fail to perceive and act upon his message, he is far more generous in sharing his wisdom with those who have already demonstrated their willingness to act at his word based on their decision to take up a life of discipleship. As John Yieh observes, "Jesus defines himself as the teacher and indeed the only teacher of *his disciples and followers*, not of outsiders."[16] Yieh's point here is reinforced as Jesus explicitly instructs the crowds and his disciples (23:1) not to call anyone other than him "teacher" (23:10).

Yet, beyond simply presenting obedient characters in the narrative itself as Jesus' primary students, Matthew also seems to hint that the students of Jesus' teaching may reside beyond the narrative alone. As Kingsbury observes, this supposition might be confirmed by the times throughout the narrative when the Matthean Jesus appears to "talk past" the actual characters in the story, such as in his instructions related to discipline within a church community that would not yet have existed at the time in which the narrative sets Jesus' pronouncement (18:15-20). Kingsbury asks, "If in his great speeches Jesus periodically speaks past his story-audience of crowds or disciples, whom in addition to the latter is he addressing in these instances? From a literary-critical standpoint, he is addressing the implied reader(s)."[17] That is, in Matthew's portrayal of Jesus as a teacher of both word and deed, the narrator seems to assume that the implied audience will, like the disciples in the narrative itself, be able both to comprehend and to act upon Jesus' instruction.

C. Jesus as a New Moses

As Matthew presents Jesus as a teacher in both word and deed, the gospel establishes Jesus' teaching authority by casting him in a role that evokes the great teacher of the law

---

[15] Jack Dean Kingsbury, *Matthew as Story* (Philadelphia: Fortress, 1988), 107.
[16] Yieh, *One Teacher*, 75.
[17] Kingsbury, *Matthew as Story*, 109. Kingsbury identifies these "great speeches" as "the Sermon on the Mount (chaps. 5–7); the missionary discourse (9:35–10:42); the discourse in parables (13:1-52); the ecclesiological discourse (17:24–18:35); and the eschatological discourse (chaps. 24–25)" (105).

in the Hebrew Bible: Moses. In an examination that explores the verbal links between Matthew's narrative and Septuagint descriptions of Moses' actions, John Yieh suggests that Matthew includes several verbal parallels especially at the beginning of the Sermon on the Mount (chs. 5–7) (including "going up on the mountain" [ἀνέβη εἰς τὸ ὄρος, 5:1; cf. ἀναβαίνοντός μου εἰς τὸ ὄρος, Deut. 9:9 LXX], "sitting down" [καθίσαντος, 5:1; cf. וַיֵּשֶׁב, Deut. 9:9 MT] to teach, and "going down the mountain" [Καταβάντος δὲ αὐτοῦ ἀπὸ τοῦ ὄρους, 8:1; cf. κατέβαινεν Μωυσῆς ἐκ τοῦ ὄρους, Exod. 34:29 LXX]). These parallels, Yieh suggests, would have evoked for early audiences of the gospel similar language that described Moses' own actions.[18] While these verbal links create a connection between Matthew's Jesus and Moses, Yieh also suggests that "Jesus is like Moses in his role as law-giver, but he is greater than Moses insofar as he ordains the law, not simply passes it on."[19] That is, for as authoritative as Moses was, Yieh understands Matthew as suggesting that Jesus may be even more so, evidenced especially in the so-called "Antitheses" of 5:21-48 as well as in Jesus' pronouncement about the ongoing validity of the Mosaic law (5:17-20). That is, Matthew positions Jesus not just as any interpreter of the Mosaic law but as one who is in the authoritative position to offer an endorsement of the law.

Beyond just the verbal links that Matthew creates to connect Jesus with Moses, the Matthean Jesus also conjures reminiscences of Moses through the content of his instruction, especially in Matthew 8:1-4 and 19:1-12, as well as to a lesser extent in 23:2-3. We turn now to explore briefly each of these texts.

The link between Jesus' teaching practice and healing ministry has already been demonstrated elsewhere.[20] Nonetheless, I wish to highlight briefly one of the ways in which this connection emerges in relation to Matthew's portrayal of Jesus as a teacher in the line of Moses. In Matthew 8:2, a man with leprosy approaches Jesus seeking to be made clean. After granting the man's request (8:3), Jesus provides instructions that the man should "show himself to the priest and offer the gift that Moses commanded" (8:4). Following on the heels of Jesus' programmatic statement about the importance of the Mosaic law (5:17-20), this instruction to the erstwhile leper suggests that the Matthean Jesus is acknowledging the important legacy and ongoing relevance of the Mosaic law for his own ministry.

The connection between Jesus and Moses is also apparent in the controversy over divorce in Matthew 19:3-12. When Pharisees come to test Jesus in relation to his views on divorce (19:3), Jesus begins by pointing to the early chapters of Genesis as the relevant material for deciding the issue (19:4-6). When his interlocutors persist in asking about what Moses commanded (19:7), Jesus counters that the issue was not Moses' *command*, but rather his *allowance* due to the hard-heartedness of people (19:8). In this episode, then, the Pharisees emerge as poor interpreters of the Mosaic law. In contrast, Matthew paints a picture of Jesus as the true interpreter of Moses who is better equipped to understand the laws set down by his ancestor in the faith.

---

[18] Yieh, *One Teacher*, 19–21. Dale Allison, on whose work Yieh draws, also highlights this language of "going up" and "sitting down" as points of connection between the description of Moses and Jesus; Dale Allison, "Jesus and Moses (Mt 5:1-2)," *ExpTim* 98, no. 7 (Apr. 1987): 203–5.

[19] Yieh, *One Teacher*, 21.

[20] Byrskog, "Jesus as Messianic Teacher," 91.

Finally, the connection that Matthew makes between Jesus and Moses also emerges in the contrast that becomes evident between Jesus and other so-called teachers of the law. In Matthew 23:2, Jesus acknowledges that the scribes and Pharisees "sit on Moses's seat." That is, for all intents and purposes, they *should* be the clear heirs to the teaching authority invested in Moses throughout the Hebrew Bible. However, while Jesus affirms doing what they *say* (ὅσα ἐὰν εἴπωσιν ὑμῖν ποιήσατε, 23:3a), he offers clear instruction to avoid imitating them in their action (κατὰ δὲ τὰ ἔργα αὐτῶν μὴ ποιεῖτε, 23:3b). Thus, while the scribes and Pharisees can lay claim to their identity as the didactic heirs of Moses, they utterly fail to live up to the legacy of their predecessor in their inability to produce the correct ethical actions to accompany their teaching. Hence, only Jesus emerges in Matthew as the true heir of Moses.

In short, in Matthew's presentation of Jesus as a teacher, Jesus' authority is deeply entwined with that of the great teacher, Moses. Though Matthew's characterization of Jesus as a teacher who emphasizes instruction in both word and deed may not be as explicit in this aspect of the gospel's presentation of Jesus, it may nonetheless be implied in the presentation of Jesus as one whose teaching authority is in line with that of Moses'. Furthermore, Matthew's emphasis on Jesus as a teacher of both information and ethical action aligns well with the background of Rabbinic teaching. Even if the link between Jesus and Moses does not explicitly point to the significance of both word and deed, the background of Rabbinic teaching that upholds the importance of both the study of Moses' law and its practice could suggest that this link is stronger than what it may first appear.

D. Jesus in Contrast to Other Teachers

The connection between Jesus and Moses explored above already hints at the contrast that Matthew is developing between Jesus and other so-called teachers within the gospel. Where the scribes and Pharisees *should* be fulfilling the role of teacher by virtue of their position and authority, it is Jesus, not these other teachers, who is described in the gospel as teaching with authority (7:28-9). Furthermore, as identified above, it is Jesus, not these others, who emerges as the true heir of Moses' teaching authority.

The diatribe against the scribes and Pharisees in Matthew 23 sets up a stark contrast between the image of Jesus as a teacher as it has emerged up to this point in the narrative and the supposed "teachers" of the law. These "teachers," Jesus avers, mislead their students (23:13), offer harmful instruction (23:15), misunderstand the fundamental nature of what they teach (23:16-22), ignore matters of justice (23:23-4), and concern themselves with how others perceive them (23:25-8).

While there are several issues with the leadership and teaching of the scribes and Pharisees, the heart of these issues is the fundamental hypocrisy that the Matthean Jesus identifies in these leaders. That is, they "speak but they do not act" (23:3). Within Matthew's presentation of what it means to be a qualified teacher, this fundamental failure to practice what one preaches is evidence of one's failure as a teacher.

Beyond differentiating Jesus' identity as a teacher on the basis of right ethical action (as opposed to the hypocrisy of the scribes and Pharisees), Matthew also uses this discourse against the scribes and Pharisees to highlight Jesus as the *only* legitimate teacher within the gospel. That is, where Jesus claims that the other so-called teachers enjoy being addressed by the title "Rabbi," he instructs the crowds and his disciples not to use such titles among themselves since they have only one teacher (23:8, 10) who holds authority over his students (cf. 10:24).[21] Thus, Matthew highlights Jesus' own legitimate role as a teacher over against the alleged didactic authority of other characters in the narrative.

In many ways, the Matthean Jesus' critiques of other teachers can be further understood when viewed against the ancient teaching practices of καθηγηταί. As Cribiore has observed, these itinerant teachers would have been able to exercise a great deal of control and power over their students because of their ability to move away from a given locale and leave their students behind.[22] It is notable, then, that in several cases where Jesus uses the illeism "Teacher" for himself (10:24-5; 26:18), he chooses the language of διδάσκαλος rather than καθηγητής. However, in the context of his denunciation of the scribes and Pharisees in Chapter 23, Jesus instructs the crowds and his disciples (23:1) that they are not to be called καθηγητής since they have only one καθηγητής: the Messiah (23:10). Although the text does not indicate that the scribes and Pharisees were pursuing the title καθηγητής themselves, in the narrative context of a denunciation of their teaching practices, one might infer that Jesus understood them to be doing so.

This inference might also be substantiated by the Matthean Jesus' claim that the scribes and Pharisees seek to be addressed publicly as "Rabbi" (23:7). Although one might wonder whether Jesus' denunciation of the scribes and Pharisees in Chapter 23 is hyperbolic based on the reference to swallowing camels (23:24) and the encouragement to murder prophets (23:31-2), instructions from the Babylonian Talmud on the proper address of a teacher would seem to substantiate this part of Jesus' claim. In *b. Sanhedrin 100a*, Rav Nahman is attributed with the insight that addressing a teacher by name rather than by the title "Rabbi" could be grounds for punishment.[23] By indicating

---

[21] Although a different lexeme appears in 23:8 (διδάσκαλος) compared to 23:10 (καθηγητὴς), I agree with Benedict Viviano in detecting at least a subtle *inclusio* structure in 23:8-10 in which the text moves from an implicit identification of Christological teaching authority in 23:8 to an explicit identification of theological paternal authority in 23:9 and then to an explicit identification of Christological teaching authority in 23:10; Benedict Viviano, "Social World and Community Leadership: The Case of Matthew 23.1-12, 34," *JSNT* 39 (1990): 8-9. Thus, while the language itself is admittedly not identical, I take Matthew's use of διδάσκαλος and καθηγητής as more or less synonymous terms that help to hold together the chiastic structure. While J. Duncan M. Derrett points to one position that might take the διδάσκαλος of 23:8 to refer to God based on an understanding of this passage's possible connections to Isa. 54:13 and Jer. 31:33-4, such a position fails to take into account the ways in which Matthew elsewhere (10:24-5; 26:18) shows no reticence in seeming to apply the title διδάσκαλος to Jesus; J. Duncan M. Derrett, "Mt 23,10 a Midrash on Is 54,13 and Jer 31,33-34," *Bib* 62, no. 3 (1981): 377. I am more convinced by Philip Esler's position that, "For Matthew καθηγητής was a teacher of higher dignity than an ordinary διδάσκαλος"; Philip Esler, "Intergroup Conflict and Matthew 23: Towards Responsible Historical Interpretation of a Challenging Text," *BTB* 45, no.1 (2015): 49. In other words, while the dissimilar vocabulary here suggests that Matthew understands *some* distinction between a διδάσκαλος and a καθηγητής, it seems more likely that this is a difference in *degree*, not a difference in *kind*.

[22] Cribiore, *Gymnastics of the Mind*, 54.

[23] Cf. Étan Levine's discussion of this text: "Ancient Jewish Education: A Composite Picture," *American Benedictine Review* 21, no. 2 (1970): 242.

that his followers are *not* to pursue such titles (23:10), the Matthean Jesus emerges in contrast to the teaching practices of the scribes and Pharisees as they are described within the gospel.[24]

IV. Jesus as Teacher for the Implied Audience

To this point, we have primarily explored the ways in which the gospel presents Jesus as a teacher who emphasizes the importance of word and deed. However, in several ways, the narrative also points beyond itself to illustrate how its implied audience is meant to take up the implicit imperative to continue this work.

The gesture to the gospel's implied audience is arguably most visible at its close. The gospel's conclusion with the commissioning of the disciples (28:16-20) suggests that even as the narrative reaches its ending point, Jesus' teaching mission is not cast aside. Rather, Jesus modifies the grammatical imperative to make more disciples (28:19) with three participles to indicate the means by which this discipleship should be accomplished: by going, by baptizing, and by teaching (διδάσκοντες; 28:20). This suggests that for the Matthean Jesus, the task of teaching is meant to extend even beyond his own earthly ministry.

Where Jesus had initially instructed his audience in the importance of teaching and doing even the least of Moses' commandments (τῶν ἐντολῶν; 5:19), now he commissions his disciples to teach what *he* has commanded (ἐνετειλάμην; 28:20). Thus, the comparison between Jesus and Moses is brought full circle. Where Matthew initially portrays Jesus as the true heir to Moses' teaching authority, here, at the gospel's conclusion, the evangelist turns to the disciples (and by extension, to the gospel's implied audience) to entrust *them* with the task of interpreting a great teacher's commandments. Even here, though, as Jeannine Brown observes, "for Matthew, the disciples and the church do not possess authority; it belongs to Jesus alone (28:18). Their access to that authority is through his presence with his people (1:23; 18:20; 28:20)."[25] Thus, even to the end, Jesus remains the "one teacher" (23:8, 10) within the gospel.

Matthew's characterization of Jesus as a teacher not only plays an important role in understanding the gospel's narrative but also illuminates expectations about the implied audience of the gospel. That is, Matthew presents Jesus as a teacher who fits well with some expectations of ancient Rabbinic educators who would promote both study and action in their teaching and learning.[26] However, Matthew also characterizes Jesus as an instructor who nonetheless challenges some ancient norms. As Anderson puts it, Jesus "was an educator of the classical mode of his day. The content of

---

[24] One must be careful to note here that Jesus' criticism still falls within a larger Jewish paradigm. That is, Jesus' critique of the practices of the scribes and Pharisees is an intra-Jewish critique and should not be understood in an anti-Jewish or supersessionist way. For a more detailed discussion of the nature of the conflict described in Mt. 23, see Esler, "Intergroup Conflict and Matthew 23," 38–59.

[25] Jeannine K. Brown, "Matthew's 'Least of These' Theology and Subversion of 'Us/Other'," in *Matthew: Texts @ Contexts*, ed. Nicole Wilkinson Duran and James P. Grimshaw (Minneapolis: Fortress, 2013), 295.

[26] Cf. *m. 'Abot* 1:15; 4:5.

Jesus' doctrine may have been radically different—the pedagogical conventions he used were not."²⁷

As Anderson notes, despite Jesus' use of traditional teaching methods, the content of Jesus' teaching in the gospel pushes back against traditions of the established social order, including its value of status, wealth, and other markers of earthly treasure that pale in comparison with heavenly treasures (cf. 6:19-21; 19:21). Jesus' challenge to prevailing social ideologies may reflect the narrative's concern to address the situation of the gospel's implied audience. As Samuel Byrskog observes:

> The author of Matthew and the group around him needed to establish their own identity and withdrew therefore from the contemporary attempts to legitimize the authority of the Jewish teachers by means of a didactic title; they refused to use the same title for themselves and for Jesus, instead confessing Jesus as by every measure a unique teacher and instructor.²⁸

In other words, Jesus' instruction to his audience *within* the narrative to refuse the title "teacher" for themselves (23:10) might also be understood as a gesture to the gospel's implied audience *beyond* the narrative. As that implied audience wrestles with the imperative of Jesus' emphasis on proper word and deed, they are to be reminded that they are all on an equal footing in the shadow and pursuit of the gospel's protagonist.

V. Conclusion

Throughout the gospel, Matthew presents Jesus as a teacher who emphasizes the importance of pairing instruction with action. As he embodies his own teaching in this regard, Jesus takes ethical action for the "least of these" that is consistent with the content of the material that he teaches throughout the gospel.

From the earliest block of Jesus' sustained teaching (chs. 5–7) to the last (25:31-46), the gospel depicts Jesus as a teacher who emphasizes not only proper cognitive understanding, but also appropriate ethical action. The narrative uses several means to characterize Jesus as this teacher of both word and deed. First, it depicts him as choosing an audience that is capable of taking the sort of action that his teaching would seem to demand. Beyond that, the narrative also constructs a parallel between Jesus and Moses that has the effect of demonstrating Jesus' pedagogical authority in contrast to other alleged "teachers." In sum, the Gospel of Matthew presents Jesus as a teacher both in word and deed.

---

[27] Anderson, "Jewish Education," 221.
[28] Byrskog, "Jesus as Messianic Teacher," 99.

6

Jesus and the Women: The Characterization of Jesus as King in Matthew's Gospel

Catherine Sider Hamilton

I. Introduction

In striking contrast to Mark, Jesus in Matthew is Son of David, anointed king, from the gospel's beginning. "The book of the genesis of Jesus Christ, *son of David*, son of Abraham," the gospel begins. The title "Christ" (χριστός), "anointed one," in conjunction with "Son of David" adds emphasis to the characterization of Jesus as kingly.[1] In the next chapter, the magi call Jesus "King of the Jews." Indeed, as Matthew 2 demonstrates, the character of Jesus as king is already in the birth narrative a key problem that drives the plot: how shall Jesus King of the Jews reign when Herod King in Jerusalem seeks to kill him?[2] In this chapter I explore the character of Jesus in Matthew's birth narrative under the rubric of kingship. I begin this exploration with the scriptures within which Matthew's narrative of Jesus unfolds and in particular with the women of the genealogy and Rachel, whose weeping brings the narrative of the birth of Jesus to a close. I begin with these women and their scriptural stories because it is my contention that this is where Matthew's narrative begins in its characterization of Jesus. Jesus emerges as a character in the First Gospel not frontally, through the description of his personal traits, but obliquely and against a background, the background of the history of God's people and God's promises told in Israel's scriptures. To discover the character of Jesus

---

[1] See J. D. Kingsbury, *Matthew as Story*, 2nd rev. edn (Philadelphia: Fortress, 1988), 45–6, for Son of David and Christ as (distinct) titles. Kingsbury (*Matthew as Story*, 46) notes that χριστός in Matthew has a number of meanings—it describes Jesus not only as Son of David (and so "King") but also "Son of God" (16:16; 26:63, 68) or "Coming One" (11:2-3, references as in Kingsbury). In Israel's scriptures, χριστός, "anointed one," may describe king or prophet or priest. In Mt. 1:1, in conjunction with the term Son of David, its royal sense is close at hand, and Matthew's Gospel continues, as we will see, by drawing attention to the Davidic, royal, character of Jesus the Christ. For the purposes of this chapter, I focus on the royal sense of "Christ" brought to the fore at the gospel's beginning, not to exclude other senses of the word but in order to explore this sense.

[2] On the centrality of kingship as an attribute of Jesus in Matthew, see especially B. M. Nolan, *The Royal Son of God: The Christology of Matthew 1-2 in the Setting of the Gospel*, OBO 23 (Göttingen: Vandenhoeck and Ruprecht, 1979) and D. J. Weaver, "Power and Powerlessness: Matthew's Use of Irony in the Portrayal of Political Leaders," in *SBL 1992 Seminar Papers*, ed. E. H. Lovering Jr. (Atlanta: Scholars, 1992), 456–60.

as king in Matthew's Gospel, it is necessary to seek him against the background of this history as Matthew delivers it to us in genealogical names and quotations of scripture. In order to see what Matthew is doing in his characterization of Jesus as king it is helpful to set the gospel briefly against the background of other contemporary treatments of character. Thus, I will proceed in two steps, beginning with a brief comparison of Matthew's opening presentation of Jesus to the presentation of characters in several roughly contemporary Greco-Roman βίοι. I will then move to a study of Jesus as king through the lens of the women, from Tamar to Rachel, who frame the birth of Jesus.

II. Matthew's Jesus and Characterization in Greco-Roman βίοι (*Lives*)

The first and early second century saw a flourishing interest in the lives (βίοι) of famous people, from Philo's *Life of Moses* to Tacitus' *Agricola*, Plutarch's *Parallel Lives*, and Suetonius' *Lives of the Caesars*.[3] Josephus too, writing history rather than *Lives*, nevertheless describes characters within the history. Richard Burridge has argued extensively that the gospels belong within the βίος genre; these *Lives* provide therefore a useful background against which to read Matthew's characterization of Jesus. The excerpts offered here, however, suggest a conclusion more cautious than Burridge's: if there are commonalities between the βίος and Matthew's Gospel in the presentation of character, there is also a striking difference, evident even in this small sample. The difference, I propose, illuminates Matthew's characterization of Jesus.

How do the Greco-Roman *Lives* treat character?[4] The following are a few examples, illustrative rather than exhaustive. Josephus introduces Abraham with a character description: "He was remarkably clever, both in understanding all things and persuading his hearers, and in his conjectures, he was not mistaken."[5] Plutarch, on the Gracchi, is similarly descriptive: "In face and look and demeanour Tiberius was humble and calm, while Gaius was high-strung and impetuous."[6] Suetonius says of Augustus, "He was exceedingly handsome and utterly charming in all the stages of his life, even though he did not care about any kind of finery." A paragraph of description follows.[7] Even the

---

[3] For an extensive analysis of the βίος genre, see Richard Burridge, *What Are the Gospels? A Comparison with Graeco-Roman Biography*, 2nd edn (Grand Rapids, MI: Eerdmans, 2004); cf. the 25th anniversary edition published by Baylor University Press, 2018. That the gospels are a form of ancient βίος is now the consensus view. Some, however, are cautious. For a critique of Burridge's method and conclusions, see Adela Yarbro Collins, "Genre and the Gospels," *JR* 75, no. 2 (1995): 239–46 (review article) and Loveday Alexander, "What is a gospel?" in *The Cambridge Companion to the Gospels*, ed. Stephen C. Barton (Cambridge: Cambridge University Press, 2006), 13–33.

[4] For a fuller discussion of character in the βίος, see Burridge, *What Are the Gospels*, 117, 139–40, 144, 199, 205.

[5] Joseph. *Ant.* 1.7.1. Compare Josephus on Herod (*War* 1.21.13): "He had the same strength in body that he had in mind ... He once brought down 40 wild beasts in one day." Translations of ancient texts are my own unless otherwise indicated.

[6] Plut. *Ti. Gracch.* 1.2.

[7] Suet. *Aug.* 79.1.

often-terse Tacitus offers comment on character. Of Antonius Primus, he says, "Success revealed in that sort of character greed and arrogance and other hidden evils."[8] And he introduces Agricola with a description of his virtues, even as a boy:

> He was shielded from the snares of sinners not merely by his own good and upright nature but because from the outset of his childhood the home and the guide of his studies was Massilia, a blend and happy combination of Greek refinement and provincial simplicity ... [His love of philosophy was driven by a] soaring and ambitious temper;... he achieved the rarest of feats: he was a student, yet preserved a sense of proportion.[9]

In these examples from Josephus, Tacitus, Plutarch, and Suetonius, Greco-Roman biography and historiography at the time of Matthew's Gospel overtly describes and analyzes character.[10]

The portrayal of Jesus in Matthew's Gospel is striking by contrast. Jesus is introduced three times in the first two chapters of the gospel. Each time the introduction is spare: "The book of the genesis of Jesus Christ, son of David, son of Abraham" (Mt. 1:1); "Now the birth of Jesus Christ was this way" (Mt. 1:18); "When Jesus was born in Bethlehem of Judaea in the days of Herod the king, behold magi from the East came to Jerusalem" (Mt. 2:1). We do know something about Jesus as a character. Jesus is given titles ("Christ" [1.1] and "King of the Jews" [2.2]), an ancestry, names (Jesus and Emmanuel) and birth by the Holy Spirit. But what we know is different in kind from what we know about Abraham or Agricola, Pericles or Alcibiades. Plutarch says of the birth of Pericles, "In other respects the form of his body was perfect, but his head was elongated and out of proportion. Hence the statues of him, almost all of them, are covered with helmets."[11] And of Alcibiades, Plutarch says, "Of Alcibiades' beauty it is perhaps not necessary to say anything, except that as a child and as a youth and as a man, in every season and age of his life, his beauty blossomed and made him always lovely and pleasant" (Plut., *Alc.* 1.1). Pericles has a big head; Alcibiades is gorgeous; Tacitus' Agricola is good, straightforward, and well-educated, brought up by his fond mother to be cultivated and virtuous.[12] In the birth narrative and throughout Matthew's history of Jesus, by

---

[8] Tac. *Hist.* 3.49, trans. Pitcher. Cited in L.V. Pitcher, "Characterization in Ancient Historiography," in *A Companion to Greek and Roman Historiography*, ed. John Marincola, Blackwell Companions to the Ancient World, 2 vols. (Oxford: Blackwell, 2007), 102–17 (116). Again, Tacitus on Tiberius when Tiberius is asked to succeed Augustus: "He discoursed variously on the greatness of the empire and his own want of confidence. [Excerpts follow.] There was more in such a speech of dignity than of good faith. In any case Tiberius' speech, whether by nature or by habit, was always hesitating and obscure, even when he was not trying to conceal anything" (Tac. *Ann.* 1.11). In addition to this kind of analysis linked to anecdote, there is a great deal of direct description, as we have seen. Physical appearance, intelligence and education, skills, passions, virtues and vices—all are detailed.

[9] Tac. *Agr.* 4.2–3. Oddly enough, Burridge (*What Are the Gospels?* 170) says of the *Agricola*, "Direct analysis of Agricola's character comes only in the concluding chapters praising him (Agr. 44-46)"— yet here is direct analysis at the beginning, as well.

[10] As, indeed, Burridge notes, yet discounts (*What Are the Gospels*, esp. 139, 140, 170). I continue to explore characterization in Greco-Roman *Lives* below.

[11] Plut. *Per.* 3.2.

[12] Cf. Tac. *Agr.* 4; 44–6.

contrast, we are told nothing about Jesus' physical appearance, his fortune, his education, his intelligence, his disposition, his "manner of life."[13] How old is he when he comes from Galilee to John the Baptist? We do not know. Where is he located, precisely, on the social scale? We do not know. What are his personal interests and proclivities? Is he handsome or ugly? What kind of upbringing did he have? Is he gentle and composed, like Tiberius Gracchus, or high-strung like Gaius? Again, we do not know.

The lacunae are all the more striking given ancient conventions of composition. Theon's *Progymnasmata* notes the centrality of character (πρόσωπον, person) to a narrative and lists the properties of character. The list includes (in addition to origin, death and what follows death) nature, training, disposition, age, fortune, and morality.[14] Cicero, Matthew Hauge notes, offers a similar list.[15] Thus Tacitus introduces Poppaea: "This woman had everything but a good soul. For her mother, the most beautiful woman of her day, had given her distinction and beauty alike. Her wealth was equal to the splendour of her birth. Her conversation was pleasant and she was not silly. She seemed modest. But her life was depraved" (*Ann.* 13.45).[16] Nature, training, disposition, fortune, morality all appear in this short description. But Matthew's narrator says of Jesus, "Then Jesus came from Galilee to the Jordan to be baptized by John."

In ancient biography, character is portrayed through words and deeds. "Thus the character of Cato is portrayed through anecdotes, sayings and stories," Burridge states.[17] So in their eschewing of direct character description, he concludes, the gospels are like ancient biography. Yet in Greco-Roman biography, anecdote often leads into or supplements direct character analysis. Plutarch says, "By nature, Alexander was a great gift-giver, and he gave still more as his wealth grew ... I will recall a few instances" (*Alex.* 39.1). Several anecdotes illustrating Alexander's generosity follow. This Plutarch does again and again in each of the *Lives*. Philo says of Moses (with delightful circumlocution):

> With temperance and self-control he bound [his adolescent desires] as if with reins ... *For* to his stomach he never gave anything beyond the necessary tributes which nature has appointed, and as for the pleasures of the organs below the stomach, except for the begetting of lawful children he paid them no heed at all.[18]

---

[13] Cf. Tac. *Agr.* 1:1: Tacitus tells the reader that "the deeds and ways of famous men" (*clarorum virorum facta moresque*) have been a subject of interest from ancient times to now; so he will tell the acts and mores of Agricola.

[14] See Matthew Ryan Hauge, "The Creation of Person in Ancient Narrative and the Gospel of Mark," in *Character Studies and the Gospel of Mark*, ed. Christopher W. Skinner and Matthew Ryan Hauge, LNTS 483 (London: Bloomsbury, 2014), 57–77, esp. 62; George A. Kennedy, *Progymnasmata: Greek Textbooks of Prose Composition and Rhetoric*, SBLWGRW 10 (Atlanta: Society of Biblical Literature, 2003). I am indebted in this paragraph to Hauge's helpful summary.

[15] Cic. *Inv. rhet.* 1.25.36. Cited in Hauge, "The Creation of Person," 62–3. That Theon and Cicero agree "is not surprising," Hauge adds (63), "given the static nature of the educational curriculum in antiquity."

[16] Tac. *Ann.* 13.45. For my rendering of the last sentence, see Tacitus, *The Annals of Imperial Rome*, trans. Michael Grant (Baltimore, MD: Penguin, 1956), 296.

[17] Burridge, *What Are the Gospels*, 171. Cf. Plut. *Alex.* 1.2 and Patricia Cox, *Biography in Late Antiquity: A Quest for the Holy Man*, American Council of Learned Societies (Berkeley: University of California Press, 1983), xiii, cited in Burridge, 137: "Anecdotes are the major vehicles of biographical characterizations."

[18] Philo, *Vit. Mos.* 1.6.25, 28-9. *LCL* 289, p. 288, 290.

As in Plutarch, anecdote serves analysis.[19] Burridge offers a description of characterization in the ancient βίος: "a mixture of literary units, notably anecdotes, stories, speeches and sayings ... displays the subject's character indirectly, through words and deeds *rather than by direct analysis*."[20] But this is not entirely correct. On the contrary, in the examples from Greco-Roman βίοι above, indirect portrayal illustrates or leads into direct analysis. And that analysis paints a detailed picture of τὸ πρόσωπον, the person in inner and outer traits. Matthew, by comparison with the Greco-Roman βίοι, is spare, and eschews analysis.

This is not to say that there is no characterization of Jesus in Matthew; indeed there is. When John the Baptist says to Jesus at the Jordan, "I need to be baptized by you, and do you come to me?" (Mt. 3:14), we know immediately that Jesus' authority in the matter of repentance and forgiveness of sins exceeds that of John. Pilate's wife says to Pilate, "Have nothing to do with that innocent man [τῷ δικαίῳ ἐκείνῳ], for I have suffered greatly today in a dream because of him" (27:19), and we know that Jesus is innocent and, indeed, righteous, and this by divine verdict.[21] What Elizabeth Struthers Malbon argues for Mark's Gospel is true in Matthew's Gospel too: "characters are known by what they say and by what they do, and by what others (the narrator and other characters) say and do to, about, or in relation to them."[22] I am not arguing that there is no characterization of Jesus in Matthew; I am arguing rather that the characterization of Jesus in Matthew is different in kind to the characterization of Moses in Philo, Abraham in Josephus, Alexander in Plutarch, *divus Augustus* in Suetonius. To notice the difference is to be able to ask what, exactly, Matthew's Gospel is doing in the portrayal of Jesus.

III. A Character "Fraught with Background": Scripture and the Characterization of Jesus in Matthew

Terry Donaldson notes that the narrative study of Christology in the New Testament is appropriate because "the gospel proclamation at the heart of the New Testament is in its essence a narrative," a story in which Jesus of Nazareth is the main character, and which "in turn, functions as the surprising climax to a larger story having to do with God's dealings with the world through the covenant people Israel."[23] The gospel narratives—and Jesus as a character within them—are part of a larger narrative. This is,

---

[19] Cf. Plut. *Cic.* 25.1; Josephus on Herod, *War* 1.21.13; Tacitus on Tiberius, *Ann.* 1.11.
[20] Burridge, *What Are the Gospels*, 140 (italics added).
[21] On the meaning of δίκαιος in Matthew and the Hebrew Scriptures—in particular its multi-valence, encompassing both innocence and righteousness in the context of judicial bloodshed—see Catherine Sider Hamilton, *The Death of Jesus in Matthew: Innocent Blood and the End of Exile* (Cambridge: Cambridge University Press, 2017), 32–44 et passim.
[22] Elizabeth Struthers Malbon, *Mark's Jesus: Characterization as Narrative Christology* (Waco, TX: Baylor, 2009), 14, 17. Cf. Kingsbury, *Matthew as Story*, 10–11.
[23] Terence L. Donaldson, "The Vindicated Son: A Narrative Approach to Matthean Christology," in *Contours of Christology in the New Testament*, ed. Richard N. Longenecker (Grand Rapids, MI: Eerdmans, 2005), 100–21 (104).

I suggest, a crucial insight for the study of Jesus as a character in Matthew's Gospel. Jesus as a character in Matthew stands in relation not just to the gospel story but to Israel's history; Jesus is a character "fraught with background."

This is Erich Auerbach's term.[24] Comparing Homer's Odysseus to Abraham he says, "Homer ... knows no background."[25] Nothing in the characterization of Odysseus is unexpressed; his nature and origin, all things about him, are "visible and palpable in all their parts."[26] One thinks of Plutarch's Alcibiades, lovely and pleasant and blossoming with beauty.[27] What is to be seen about Alcibiades, as about Odysseus, is immediately present, on the surface of the narrative. The story of Abraham in Genesis, by contrast, "extends into depths." Abraham is explained "not only by what is happening to him at the moment, nor yet only by his character (as Achilles' actions by his courage and pride, and Odysseus' by his versatility and foresightedness)"—or Philo's Abraham by his sagacity and Tacitus' Poppaea by her depravity—"but by his previous history."[28]

The same thing, I propose, is true for Matthew's Jesus. As in Genesis, direct characterization is restrained, even inadequate by Greco-Roman standards. To pay attention to the difference between Matthew's Jesus and Plutarch's Pericles is to ask how Matthew characterizes Jesus, and what role Auerbach's "background" might play.

Background, in fact, makes itself felt in the gospel's opening line: "Jesus the Christ, the son of David, the son of Abraham." Matthew is, like Plutarch or Tacitus, giving an ancestry, which he then details in the genealogy.[29] But at the same time, Mt. 1:1 locates Jesus in relation to two iconic figures and moments in *Israel's* narrative, David and Abraham, the father of the people Israel and the father of the kingdom promised to David.[30] From the very first line, Jesus does not stand alone; he is not, like Plutarch's Pericles or Tacitus' Agricola, the eponymous hero of a story that is centrally his own. Rather, he stands against the background of the history of Israel.

"To read the Gospel of Matthew well is to read it with the Jewish story line ... rumbling in the mind," Patrick Schreiner writes.[31] This is hardly a new observation, but

---

[24] Erich Auerbach, *Mimesis: The Representation of Reality in Western Literature*, trans. Willard R. Trask (Princeton, NJ: Princeton University Press, 1953), 12. Cf. David Rhoads, Joanna Dewey, and Donald Michie, *Mark as Story: An Introduction to the Narrative of a Gospel*, 3rd edn (Minneapolis: Fortress, 2012), 101: in his portrayal of character, "Mark was influenced by the narratives of the Hebrew Bible."

[25] Auerbach, *Mimesis*, 4.

[26] Auerbach, *Mimesis*, 6, 13.

[27] Plut. *Alc.* 1.1. Cf. Philo's Moses, temperate and self-controlled, or Tacitus' Poppaea, beautiful, wealthy, distinguished, pleasant in conversation...and depraved.

[28] Auerbach, *Mimesis*, 12.

[29] Cf. for instance Plut., *Ant.* 1.1, *Per.* 3.2, *Ti. Gracch.* 1.1.

[30] Cf. 2 Sam. 7: 12-16. The commentators note the way in which the genealogy serves to locate Jesus as a character in relation to Israel: R. T. France, *The Gospel of Matthew*, NICNT (Grand Rapids, MI: Eerdmans, 2007), 35, notes that "'Son of Abraham' locates David and his successor within the fuller history of the chosen people"; John Nolland, *The Gospel of Matthew: A Commentary on the Greek Text*, NIGTC (Grand Rapids, MI: Eerdmans, 2005), 71 says of γένεσις (1:1), "This first use of γένεσις is concerned with the origins of Jesus in relation to the larger shape of the history of God's people." Cf. Davies and Allison's discussion of 1:1 against its scriptural background: W. D. Davies and Dale C. Allison Jr., *A Critical and Exegetical Commentary on the Gospel according to Saint Matthew*, 3 vols., ICC (London: T&T Clark, 1988/2004), 1:149–60.

[31] Patrick Schreiner, *Matthew, Disciple and Scribe: The First Gospel and Its Portrait of Jesus* (Grand Rapids, MI: Baker Academic, 2019), 7. Cf., of course, Richard Hays, *Echoes of Scripture in the Gospels*

in a reading of Jesus as a character in Matthew it takes on new significance. What does it mean to read this text for an understanding of Jesus as character when this text overtly locates itself in relation to other texts—the Hebrew scriptures—and another history, Israel's history?

In what follows I will explore a reading of Jesus as a character in Matthew through the lens of Israel's history as it is presented to the reader in the women of Matthew's birth narrative. I will then pursue connections, themselves suggested by the narrative, with two other women in Matthew's Gospel to discover a presentation of Jesus, through the lens of the women and history of Israel, in the character of king.

IV. The Women of the Genealogy and Jesus as King

Matthew's genealogy is far more than a list of names: as in Mt. 1:1, the narration in its choice of facts has evaluative power.[32] Jesus is Son of David, Son of Abraham … and, anomalously, son of five women. Jewish genealogies include women only rarely; hence these women, four women of Israel's scriptures and Mary, catch the reader's eye.[33] From a narrative point of view, though the narrator offers in the genealogy no direct description of Jesus, in the selection of these unexpected women, "the effect is still a rigorous control over the reader's own range of judgement."[34] If Jesus in the gospel's opening line is located firmly within the history of Israel, what do these women of Israel's history tell us about him?

A. Tamar and the Lion of Judah

Tamar, and not Sarah, is the first woman named, although Sarah might have been the more obvious choice in this genealogy of the "son of Abraham." Why, then, Tamar?[35] Tamar comes into the genealogy at the time of Judah. Judah, as the informed reader knows,[36] is the

---

(Waco, TX: Baylor University Press, 2016). Kingsbury, in *Matthew As Story*, says of Jesus as a character in Matthew, "He is the Son of Abraham … because it is in him that the entire history of Israel, which had its beginning in Abraham, attains its goal (1:17)" (47).

[32] Cf. Wayne C. Booth, *The Rhetoric of Fiction*, rev. edn (Chicago: University of Chicago Press, 1983), 177: "Most seeming facts carry … a heavy load of evaluation. They order in some way the importance of the parts; they work on the beliefs of the reader." Booth is talking about fiction, but the comment is true of narrative generally.

[33] Cf. the commentaries, esp. Davies and Allison, *Matthew*, 1:170: "Matthew's citation of four [Old Testament] women must signal some special interest."

[34] Booth, *Rhetoric of Fiction*, 184.

[35] On the women of the genealogy and their function in Matthew's Gospel more broadly, see my article, "From Tamar and Mary to Perpetua: Women and the Word in Matthew," in *Paul and Matthew among Jews and Gentiles: Essays in Honour of Terence L. Donaldson*, ed. Ronald Charles, LNTS 628 (London: Bloomsbury/T&T Clark, 2021), 131–45.

[36] On the question of communication between narrator and intended audience in the use of scriptural allusions, see R. T. France, "The Formula Quotations of Matthew 2 and the Problem of Communication," *NTS* 27, no. 2 (1981): 233–51. On the "informed reader" (or hearer) in Matthew, see Dale Allison, "Anticipating the Passion: The Literary Reach of Matt 26:47–27:56," *CBQ* 56 (1994): 701–14, here 702–3: "I define informed hearers as those who (1) were familiar with the LXX and (2) heard and reheard Matthew … That my informed reader or hearer is also the implied reader I

Lion of Israel (Gen. 49:9), "preeminent ancestor of the Davidic dynasty."[37] To Judah the promise of a throne is made:

> Judah is a lion's whelp …
> The scepter shall not depart from Judah,
> Nor the ruler's staff from between his feet.
>
> Gen. 49:9-10 NRSV

By naming Tamar and no other woman before her, the narrator draws attention to Judah and in him to the dynastic hope of Israel.

Tamar is herself crucial to this hope. Judah, in Genesis 38, has no heir. His eldest son is married to Tamar and dies childless; his second son is married to Tamar and dies childless; Judah refuses to fulfill his levirate obligation and marry his third and only remaining son to Tamar their widow. Jacob's prophecy, the scepter in the line of Judah, is at risk: shall it be spoken? Tamar (sent away from her husbands' home) disguises herself and conceives a son—twin sons—by Judah. Tamar thus makes possible the continuation of the line of Judah so that the dynastic promise might be uttered. To name her here is to awaken the memory of the promise of a throne in the line of Judah and God's extraordinary provision, in this woman's faithfulness to the levirate law, for the promise's utterance. Tamar's name places the emphasis in the genealogy right at its beginning on kingship.

B. Rahab and the Promises of Israel's God

Rahab is unusual not only as a woman in a patrilineal genealogy but as the wife of Salman. Rahab is the wife of Salman nowhere else in the Bible or Second Temple or rabbinic literature; she is Matthew's insertion.[38] Here, too, the facts have evaluative force. Who is Rahab? She is the one who shelters the Israelite spies so that God's promise to Abraham of land and a people might be fulfilled.[39] To name Rahab is to draw attention to the promise to Abraham.

---

believe to be the case." The informed reader/hearer knows the scriptural stories. Cf. Luz's discussion of the reader's role in intertextuality in Ulrich Luz, "Intertexts in the Gospel of Matthew," *HTR* 97, no. 2 (2004): 119–37, esp. 121-3. See also Booth, *Rhetoric of Fiction*, 177: "As a rhetorician, an author finds that some of the beliefs on which a full appreciation of his work depends come ready-made, fully accepted by the postulated reader as he comes to the book."

[37] John Paul Heil, "The Narrative Roles of the Women in Matthew's Genealogy," *Bib* 72, no. 4 (1991): 538–45 (539).

[38] Commentators often object that "OT chronology separates Rahab and Salman by almost two-hundred years" (Davies and Allison, *Matthew*, 1:173). This is true, counting backwards from David. Yet as Richard Bauckham points out, the chronology works counting *forward*. Nahshon, Salman's father, is leader of the tribes of Israel in the wilderness. It is thus perfectly logical that his son Salman should be married to Rahab at the time of the conquest. See Richard Bauckham, "Tamar's Ancestry and Rahab's Marriage: Two Problems in the Matthean Genealogy," *NovT* 37, no. 4 (1995): 313–29, esp. 326.

[39] "And I will give to you and to your offspring after you the land where you are now an alien, all the land of Canaan" (Gen. 17:8). Cf. Josh. 2:9: "I know that the Lord has given you this land."

But there is more in Rahab's story. Rahab protects the spies in express disobedience to the king of Jericho: "Then the king of Jericho sent orders to Rahab, 'Bring out the men who have come to you.'... But the woman took the two men and hid them" (Josh. 2:3-4, NRSV). Just at this point, the narrative recalls Exodus and the Israelite resistance to the king of Egypt. "But the woman took the two men and hid them," Josh. 2:4 reads in English translation. But "them" is inaccurate; in the Hebrew, she hides "him": ותצפנו ('and-she-hid-him').[40] The singular suffix "him" is odd, following as it does upon "the two men." Tikva Frymer-Kensky notes the singular suffix and proposes an echo of Exodus. In Exod. 2:2 Moses' mother hides "him" (ותצפנהו, 'and-she-hid-him'); the same Hebrew verb is used with an alternate form of the singular suffix.[41] In Josh. 2:10, Rahab recalls the crossing of the Red Sea and Israel's defeat of Sihon and Og, kings beyond the Jordan; in 2:9 she echoes the song of Moses in Exod. 15:15-16.[42] The echo of Exodus in Joshua 2 is deliberate. In these echoes, Rahab frames the spies' visit not only in terms of the fulfillment of God's promises to Abraham, but in terms of the sovereignty of God. "She hid *him*": the king of Jericho is foiled by the faith of the prostitute just as the king of Egypt was foiled by the faithfulness of Moses' mother. The spies are saved on Rahab's roof from the king's men just as Israel was saved from the armies of Pharaoh at the Red Sea. Israel will conquer Jericho and her king, just as Israel defeated "the kings of the Amorites that were beyond the Jordan" (Josh. 2:10). Who is king? That is the question Joshua 2 asks, and Rahab answers it unequivocally: "The Lord your God is indeed God in heaven above and on earth below" (Josh. 2:11). This she says even as her king seeks the Israelites to kill them.

In Matthew 2, Herod king of the Jews seeks to kill Jesus, "the one born king of the Jews" (Mt. 2:2)—and the reader of the genealogy is not surprised. The narrative has prepared the ground for just such a conflict over kingship in the anomalous inclusion of Rahab in the genealogy. If Tamar's name tells us that Jesus "the Christ, the son of David" inherits a throne in the line of Judah, Rahab's name declares—out of the mouth of a gentile and a prostitute—the sovereignty of God and the resistance to God's sovereignty by the kings of the earth.

C. Ruth and David the King

With the next woman in the genealogy the focus on kingship continues. Ruth is the great-grandmother of "David the king." Like Rahab she, though a gentile, allies herself with Israel and with Israel's God ("your people shall be my people, and your God my God"; Ruth 1:16). Like Tamar she asks Boaz to honor the levirate obligations of the next-of-kin (Ruth 3:9-10). That there is more than one family's heritage at issue in Ruth's faithfulness and the birth of a "son" to Naomi becomes clear in the book's happy end: the witnesses to the wedding of Ruth and Boaz say, "May the Lord make the

---

[40] ותקח האשה את־שני האנשם ותצפנו (Josh. 2:4). The pronoun "him," singular, is given in the verb's suffix.
[41] Tikva Frymer-Kensky, "Rahab," in *Women in Scripture: A Dictionary of Named and Unnamed Women in the Hebrew Bible, the Apocryphal, Deuterocanonical Books, and the New Testament*, ed. Carol Meyers, Toni Craven, and Ross S. Kraemer (Grand Rapids, MI: Eerdmans, 2000), 140–1 (141).
[42] Frymer-Kensky, "Rahab," 141.

woman who is coming into your house like Rachel and Leah, who together built up *the house of Israel*" (Ruth 4:11, italics added).

> May you produce children in Ephrathah and bestow a name in Bethlehem; and, through the children that the Lord will give you by this young woman, may your house be like the house of Perez, whom Tamar bore to Judah.
>
> Ruth 4:11-12

The brief genealogy that concludes the Book of Ruth begins from Perez, son of Judah. Ruth carries forward the dynastic promise to Judah. The narrator, stepping in at the book's end, makes the point clear: "They named him Obed; he became the father of Jesse, the father of David" (Ruth 4:17). "David" is the book's last word. In naming Ruth, Matthew's narrator once again draws attention to a woman whose faithfulness to Israel's God brings to fruition the promise to Judah of a throne. This is the story of Jesus, son of David the king.

D. David the King and the Wife of Uriah: Innocent Blood

The four Old Testament women named in Matthew's genealogy are all mentioned within four verses, beginning with Judah and ending with David the king. Their names call up kingship, the promise to the son of Abraham of a throne. This genealogy is already commentary: by reference to these women of Israel's history it describes Jesus first and foremost in the character of king.[43]

Immediately, however, the narrator problematizes the promise. The gospel narrator names one more woman in the Davidic sequence: "David was the father of Solomon by the wife of Uriah" (2:6). If Matthew's women are anomalous in a Jewish genealogy, this woman is anomalous in Matthew's genealogy: she alone has no name. Commentators note that the absence of "Bathsheba" draws attention to Uriah. Since Uriah is a Hittite, this recalls the promise of a blessing to the gentiles in Abraham.[44] Yet the phrase "wife of Uriah" in association with David is not redolent of blessing, least of all for Uriah, for David takes Uriah's wife and has Uriah killed. In calling her "wife of Uriah," the narrator again selects facts carefully. For the phrase "wife of Uriah" occurs not in 1 Chronicles (which Matthew is in part following here, and in which she is called Bathsheba) but in

---

[43] For further explication of the ways in which the Matthean narrative deliberately calls up the women's stories in their names, see especially E. Anne Clements, *Mothers on the Margins: The Significance of the Women in Matthew's Genealogy* (Eugene, OR: Pickwick, 2014). See also Elaine Wainwright, *Towards a Feminist Critical Reading of the Gospel according to Matthew* (Berlin: de Gruyter, 1991); John Paul Heil, "The Narrative Roles of the Women in Matthew's Genealogy," *Bib* 72, no. 4 (1991): 538–45; Wim J. C. Weren, "The Five Women in Matthew's Genealogy," *CBQ* 59 (1997): 288–305.

[44] See the commentaries: France, *Matthew*, 37; Craig Keener, *The Gospel of Matthew: A Socio-Rhetorical Commentary*, 2nd edn (Grand Rapids, MI: Eerdmans, 2009), 80; Jeannine K. Brown and Kyle Roberts, *Matthew*, Two Horizons NT Commentary (Grand Rapids, MI: Eerdmans, 2018), 25. Davies and Allison, *Matthew*, 1:174, make the point but add, "'wife of Uriah' could also evoke the sin of David, who had Uriah killed."

2 Samuel 11–12, the story of David's adultery and bloodshed. In that story of David's sin, Bathsheba is called "wife of Uriah" four times.[45]

In naming her "the wife of Uriah," the narrator offers commentary on Jesus as king. Jesus, the genealogy has established, is to be described first of all as son of Tamar and Ruth, anointed one in the line of David and Judah. Yet the kingship he inherits is problematic. For in David's taking Uriah's wife and shedding Uriah's innocent blood a shadow falls over the house of Judah, as Nathan intimates:

> Why have you despised the word of the Lord, to do what is evil in his sight? You have struck down Uriah the Hittite with the sword, and have taken his wife to be your wife, and have killed him with the sword of the Ammonites. Now therefore the sword shall never depart from your house.
>
> 2 Sam. 12:9-10, NRSV

Jesus the Christ, the son of David, inherits a throne that is both promised by God and shadowed by the spilling of innocent blood.[46]

In the continuation of the genealogy, the narrator marks the kingship's decline: the generations of the kings of the house of Judah lead into "the deportation to Babylon" (1:11). This comment is not in 1 Chronicles 3. With it, the narrator closely links kingdom and exile. The time of the house of Judah is now the time leading into the Babylonian exile. Indeed, the narrative creates a frame around the genealogy's first 10 verses (1:2-11) that further links the kingdom-promise to exile. Twice the narrator adds "and his brothers" to the genealogy: at the name of Judah ("Judah and his brothers," 1:2) and at the name of Jechoniah ("Jechoniah and his brothers," 1:11). Judah is the one to whom the promise of a scepter is given. Jechoniah is the king under whom the sons of Judah go down into exile. As a descriptor of Jechoniah, the phrase "and his brothers" makes little sense. Jechoniah, it seems, has no brothers.[47] But as a narrative device, it makes a crucial historical and theological point: the repetition of "and his brothers" (which at 1:2 designates the twelve tribes of Israel) draws the whole house of Israel into this history, as it also draws together these two moments, Judah's and Jechoniah's, the promise of kingship and the loss of it.[48] Here in the deportation, for Jechoniah "and his brothers," the whole house of Israel, is the end to which the promise of a scepter spoken to Judah has come.

---

[45] For a detailed reading of "wife of Uriah" against the background of 2 Samuel and David's bloodshed, see my discussion in *The Death of Jesus in Matthew: Innocent Blood and the End of Exile* (Cambridge: Cambridge University Press, 2017), 195–202.

[46] So also Francis Watson, *The Fourfold Gospel: A Theological Reading of the New Testament Portraits of Jesus* (Grand Rapids, MI: Baker Academic, 2016), 36–7. I do not think, however (as I hope this chapter indicates), that his further conclusion—that "the same shadow" of sin (chiefly adultery) hangs over the other Old Testament women in the genealogy—is supported by the evidence either in the women's own stories or in their reception-history.

[47] Or perhaps one brother, Zedekiah (1 Chron. 3:16, but see Nolland, *Matthew*, 81—it is more likely that 1 Chron identifies Zedekiah as Jechoniah's uncle). In either case, "brothers" does not apply, strictly speaking.

[48] Jeannine Brown and Kyle Roberts, *Matthew*, 27, also note the echo of 1:2 in 1:11, though they read it as a reference in both cases to exile. "Referencing the twelve patriarchs [at 1:2] could remind Matthew's reader of the time away from the land promised to their descendants—the time in Egyptian 'exile.'" This seems a stretch. More obvious is the reference to the twelve tribes, and so to the whole house of Israel. With "and his brothers" at 1:11, the history of the house of Israel comes full circle, from the promise of a throne to the loss of it.

In the Old Testament women he names, then—all four of them in four verses between Judah and David the king—the narrator first focuses the reader's eye on Jesus' kingship, and then problematizes that kingship. With the repeated phrase "and his brothers," the narrator suspends kingship between promise and exile. In the summary comments at 1:11-12 and 1:17, the narrator explicitly divides the history of Israel into the time before and after exile. This is the history into which Jesus comes as king. How shall the promise of kingship, the promise to the house of Judah, the promise carried forward so remarkably through the actions of Tamar and Rahab and Ruth be fulfilled? How shall the promise of a scepter be fulfilled in the wake of David and "the wife of Uriah," in the wake of innocent blood and in the time "after the deportation," when no one, any longer, is called king? What does it mean in this context to be Son of David, ὁ λεγόμενος Χριστός (1:16), the one called Christ?

Jesus is under-described with regard to character traits in Matthew's opening presentation (and, I would argue, in the gospel as a whole). With regard to "his people" (Mt. 1:21), by contrast, he is richly defined. The genealogy locates him in relation to the whole house of Israel, Judah and Tamar, Rahab, Ruth, David and the wife of Uriah, Jechoniah and his brothers. In the narrator's presentation of facts and occasional comments, the genealogy presents this history as the history of promise and exile, kingdom and deportation, the time before and after Babylon. It is the king and the kingdom promise that is at issue, a promise made in the time of Judah "and his brothers," realized in David the king, but also problematized in David and the wife of Uriah and Uriah's innocent blood; lost in the time of Jechoniah "and his brothers." The genealogy locates Jesus in relation to this history precisely as Χριστός, Son of David, anointed king (1:1; 1:16). Jesus appears in the gospel's first words in the character of king, but it is a kingship fraught with background. Jesus as king is known in Matthew's gospel not first of all in his *acta moresque*, the deeds and manner of life of the man himself, but in the women who preceded him, in Tamar and Ruth and the wife of Uriah, in Judah and his brothers, in David the king. Who Jesus is as "king" in this narrative is a question inseparable from the history into which he comes and inseparable from the scriptures that tell that history. To return for a moment to Auerbach, Jesus Christ, son of David, son of Abraham is explained, like Abraham, "not only by what is happening to him at the moment, nor yet only by his character ... but by his previous history"—what God has promised and has already accomplished in a history that is, Matthew's narrator makes clear, not just "his," Jesus', but that of his people Israel.[49]

In the careful selection of facts, then, the narrator presents Jesus in the genealogy as the Christ-King of Israel's hope. The narrator sets his kingship within a narrative framed (in Judah and Tamar, in Rahab and Ruth) by promise of a throne and, in David and the wife of Uriah, in Jechoniah and the deportation, by its loss. Jesus is thus delineated as a character in Matthew's beginning only in relation to Israel's history and hope, and not at all in terms of the kind of traits that describe the individual in the ancient *bios*—looks, temperament, talents, passions, generosity, discipline (or the lack of it), wealth, education. In the stories summoned up by their names we know more

---

[49] Auerbach, *Mimesis*, 12.

about Ruth and Rahab, Tamar and the wife of Uriah, than we do about Jesus. Yet precisely their stories, the scriptural history to which the narrator summons the reader, richly delineate the term "Son of David." The character of Jesus as king is fraught with background, and the anomalous women and the narrator's voice-over serve to unveil it. The two final women named in the birth narrative, Mary and Rachel, speak to either pole—promise and exile—of the narrative of kingship unveiled in the genealogy.

E. Mary

In Mary, the patrilineal genealogy finds its surprising climax: Mary ἐξ ἧς ἐγεννήθη Ἰησοῦς ὁ λεγόμενος Χριστός ("from whom was born Jesus called the Christ"; 1:16). In the end, the son to whom the long sequence of men leads is not the son of these men, but of the woman Mary. Mary's child, as the narrator reveals, is not by Joseph but by the Holy Spirit (1:18). And this birth by a virgin, the narrator tells us, has a background in the promises of God. The narrator comments: "This whole thing happened so that the word spoken by the Lord through the prophet might be fulfilled" (1:22). What is that word?

> *Behold a virgin shall conceive and bear a son, And they shall call his name Emmanuel,* which is translated "God with us."
>
> 1:23

Behold a virgin shall conceive: Matthew's narrative locates the child within the scriptural history and in this way reveals who he is. He is the one promised to the kingdom of Judah precisely in the time when the kingdom promise was threatened. To Ahaz King of Judah, whose heart is shaking like a tree before the wind at the news of the armies of Israel and Aram marching against him, Isaiah says, "Hear then, O house of David! ... The Lord himself will give you a sign. Look, the young woman is with child and shall bear a son and shall name him Immanuel," and before the child is two years old, Israel, before whose two kings you are in dread, will be undone (Isa. 7: 13-16, NRSV).[50] The birth of Immanuel promises deliverance to Judah's king and kingdom. The prophecy was applied to Hezekiah, a Davidic king-deliverer; the reader may thus hear in it specifically the promise of a king for Israel in its time of need.[51]

In its narrative context, however, the promise of deliverance for the kingdom is shadowed. The birth of Immanuel marks, in Isa. 7:16, the end of the current threat to the throne and house of Judah. But the very next verse points to subjugation and exile in "the king of Assyria" (Isa. 7:17). These two themes, a kingdom for Judah and the exile

---

[50] For Matthew's "virgin" (παρθένος, following LXX Isa. 7:14) as an interpretation of the Hebrew עלמה (which may mean "young woman" more broadly), see the commentaries, esp. Davies and Allison, *Matthew*, 1:213-14; France, *Matthew*, 55–6; Nolland, *Matthew*, 101.

[51] For Jewish traditions connecting Isa. 7:14 to Hezekiah, see Davies and Allison, *Matthew*, 1.213. They cite Justin, *Dial.* 43; *Exod. Rab.* on 12:29; *Num. Rab.* on 7:48. Nolland, *Matthew*, 101, observes that if the child in Isa. 7:14 is interpreted as Ahaz's son and heir, a messianic interpretation suggests itself. France, *Matthew*, 57, argues that Isaiah's thought moves in a messianic direction from 7:14 to Isa. 9 and 11.

that threatens it, help to structure Matthew's opening narrative as well. Matthew 1:23 thus draws attention to the scriptural history just at the point where it shares the birth narrative's joint theme of kingdom and exile.[52]

F. Rachel's Weeping

It is perhaps not surprising, then, that the narrative of the birth of Jesus son of David comes to an end in the weeping of Rachel.

A voice was heard in Ramah,
Weeping and loud lamentation,
Rachel weeping for her children
And she would not be comforted,
For they are no more.

Mt. 2:18

This is a quotation of Jer. 31:15. In Jeremiah, Rachel weeps at Ramah as her "children," the people Israel, go into Babylon in exile. Matthew's narrator introduces this quotation at the end of the story of Herod and the magi and the exile of the child Jesus in Egypt (2:1-15). Like the genealogy, this whole episode stands under the sign of kingship. As the narrator names Jesus "Christ," "son of David" in Mt. 1:1, so at their arrival in Jerusalem the magi call him "King of the Jews" (Mt. 2:2). If "Christ," "Son of David" is Israel's word, hailing Jesus from within Israel as Israel's king, "King of the Jews" is the gentiles' word, acknowledging him king in Israel and indeed beyond Israel, as the magi's obeisance indicates (2:2).[53] The magi's visit, like the genealogy, thus explicates the character of Jesus as king.

Again, it is not in the description of Jesus himself that the narrator characterizes him as king, but in the history of Israel that unfolds around him, now and in the scriptural past. Themes adumbrated in the women of the genealogy here appear again. As the naming of Tamar focuses the genealogy on the promise to Judah (Ἰούδας,1:2), so the magi seek the king "of the Jews" (τῶν Ἰουδαίων, 2:2). The echo serves, as a literary device, to bring this child "born king of the Jews" together with the promise of a scepter to Judah. Theologically, it announces a typological reading of history. Jacob's words to Judah and Isaiah's words to Ahaz find a fulfilment in the words of the magi at the birth of Jesus. Jesus is the long-awaited king.

The words of the magi that follow further explicate the character of Jesus' kingship. "For we have seen his star *in the East*, and we have come to kneel before him" (2:2). The promise to Judah ends with the obeisance of the peoples: "the scepter shall not depart

---

[52] For more detailed discussion of Mt. 1:23 against its background in Isa. 7:14, see my "Quartet for the End of Time: The Fourfold Gospel, History, and Matthew's Birth Narrative," in *Writing the Gospel: A Dialogue with Francis Watson*, ed. Catherine Sider Hamilton with Joel Willitts, LNTS 606 (London: Bloomsbury/T&T Clark, 2019), 145–65.

[53] The literature discussing the breadth of meaning of προσκυνέω here and elsewhere in Matthew's gospel is large. The point for our purposes is that, whether or not προσκυνέω has the sense of "worship" here, it indicates Jesus' kingship.

from Judah ... until ... the obedience of the peoples [עמים MT, ἐθνῶν LXX] is his" (Gen. 49:10). When magi from the East kneel before Jesus, the promise to Judah is realized. When they appeal to the star, they call up another promise, and—again—the obeisance of the nations to Israel's king. "A star shall come out of Jacob, and a scepter shall rise out of Israel," Balaam says (Num. 24:17); Israel "shall devour the nations [גוים MT, ἔθνη LXX]" (24:8). Balaam, echoing Gen. 49:9-10, takes up the promise of a scepter to Judah and applies it explicitly to Israel's sovereignty over the gentile nations.[54] The obeisance of the magi before the child called "King of the Jews" recalls the dominion promised to Judah, promised again by Balaam, and carried forward in Tamar and Ruth, Rahab and the wife of Uriah, a dominion here, in the kneeling magi, encompassing even the nations. The magi, echoing (unwittingly) Balaam's prophecy, interpret for the reader who Jesus is as king. Jesus as king in Mt. 2:2 is the one in whom the promises to Judah are fulfilled in both aspects: there is a Judaean king in Israel, and his sovereignty is known among the nations.

Yet the proclamation here at Jesus' birth of Israel's long-awaited scepter, the king before whom even the nations bow, ends in the weeping of Rachel. Why should the birth of the King of the Jews lead to the tears of a mother of Israel? As in the phrase "the wife of Uriah" (Mt. 1:6), here too the narrator problematizes the promise: "When King Herod heard this, he was shaken [ἐταράχθη], and all Jerusalem with him" (2:3). In this comment the narrator points to a hostility to God's promises on the part of the kings of the earth already adumbrated in the mention of Rahab. In the days of Rahab, the king of Jericho seeks to kill the men of Israel; in the days of Moses, the king of Egypt seeks to kill the Hebrew boy.[55] So now Herod, king in Jerusalem, seeks the Christ-child's life. If the birth narrative arrives triumphantly at the child born "King of the Jews," yet immediately the shadow rises. The throne in Herod's hands is again the seat of bloodshed.

> Then Herod seeing that he had been duped by the magi was very angry, and he sent and killed all the children in Bethlehem and all the country round about who were two years old and under, according to the time which he had ascertained from the magi.
>
> Mt. 2:16

The narrator comments:

> Then was fulfilled the word spoken through Jeremiah the prophet saying,
> "A voice was heard in Ramah,

---

[54] Num. 24:17: "A scepter shall rise out of Israel"; cf. Gen. 49:10: "The scepter shall not depart from Judah"; Num. 24:9: "He crouched, he lay down like a lion, like a lioness: who will rouse him up?"; cf. Gen. 49:9: "He crouches down, he stretches out like a lion, like a lioness—who dares rouse him up?"

[55] For the echoes of the Moses story in Matthew 2, see Raymond E. Brown, *The Birth of the Messiah: A Commentary on the Infancy Narratives in the Gospels of Matthew and Luke*, ABRL, upd. edn (New York: Doubleday, 1993), 180, 194, 214–16, and the commentaries.

weeping and loud lamentation,
Rachel weeping for her children."

Mt. 2:17-18

The comment draws together Herod's bloodshed and the ancient exile. It draws together, too, the genealogy and the birth of Jesus. As David's bloodshed leads in the genealogy into "the deportation to Babylon," so Herod's slaughter leads into an echo of exile, the mothers of Bethlehem weeping for the loss of Israel's children as Rachel wept at Ramah.[56] "King" in Matthew's Gospel is a name fraught with background, and the background already at the beginning of Jesus' life encompasses promise and loss, a king for God's people and another king's bloodshed, the faithfulness of Tamar and the weeping of Rachel.

To follow the narrator through the genealogy and birth narrative in the wake of the women he names and the scriptures to which he draws attention is to find the character of "Jesus the Christ, Son of David, son of Abraham" explicated against the history and hope of Israel. It is a history permeated by the promise of a king and a kingdom. It is a kingship shadowed by sin: the blood of Uriah, the blood of Bethlehem's children, the blood of the innocent unjustly shed. If it begins with Tamar's trick and in her the realization of the promise to Judah, it ends in Rachel's weeping and the echo of exile.

Into this history Jesus comes as "Christ" and "king of the Jews." The rest of the gospel—and so too Jesus' character as king—is in large part the outworking of the conflict thus created. How shall God's promised king reign from the throne stained by blood? How shall the scepter and its universal sway be true for the people who are, even in Jerusalem, in exile? What can it mean for Jesus to be Christ, son of David, King of the Jews, in the time "after the deportation"?

To trace fully this conflict and so the character of Jesus as king in Matthew is the work of a much longer piece. Here I offer two pointers toward its outworking, in two further women.

V. Jesus as King: the Canaanite Woman and the Woman Who Anoints

A. The Canaanite Woman

"Son of David!" the Canaanite woman cries after Jesus. "Have mercy on me, Lord, son of David" (Mt. 15:22). Together with the blind men at Mt. 9:27 and 20:30, she is one of

---

[56] I am puzzled by R. T. France's puzzlement here ("Why does Matthew feel that this text—Jer. 31:15 // Mt. 2:18—is appropriate here?" *Matthew*, 86). Given the problem of exile raised in the genealogy precisely in connection to David the king, Jer. 31:15 is perfectly fitting. Rachel's weeping at the exile closes the circle between David the king, his bloodshed and the people's exile, and Herod the king, his bloodshed and an exile that is, the quotation suggests, ongoing. This is the time "after the deportation to Babylon," when the king in Jerusalem is not "the King of the Jews," and the blood of Israel's children is shed not by the Babylonians but by her own king. Rachel weeps *now* in Bethlehem, in the place of the promise of a throne for God's people. Exile is no longer out there, but here, at the heart of the promise.

only a few supplicants who approach Jesus with the royal title on their lips. In her cry, the promise to Judah highlighted by the women of the genealogy is brought to the forefront—as it is also brought forward by the blind men and the crowds at Jesus' entry into Jerusalem (Mt. 21:9; cf. 21:15). But she is a gentile. When she names Jesus king in the line of David, the promise to Judah sounds in all its fullness: here is the king who wields the scepter not only in Jerusalem but over the peoples. Indeed, the Canaanite woman, alone among the supplicants who call Jesus "son of David," kneels before him: ἡ δὲ ἐλθοῦσα προσεκύνει αὐτῷ (Mt. 15:25). Her action echoes the words of the magi: καὶ ἤλθομεν προσκυνῆσαι αὐτῷ (Mt. 2:2). In the Canaanite woman's homage as in the magi's, Jacob's promise to Judah is being realized. In her πίστις (15:28)—as in Ruth's trust or Rahab's declaration of the lordship of Israel's God—Jesus is publicly hailed by the nations as sovereign. In healing her daughter, Jesus accepts her homage and names himself king not only in Jerusalem but among the nations. Like the magi (and Rahab and Ruth), the Canaanite woman thus serves to reveal further the character of Jesus as it has been bruited in the birth narrative: this is the king in the line of Judah, heir of the promise of a sovereignty that encompasses the nations.

B. The Anointing Woman

In the birth narrative, however, this kingship in the line of Judah is problematic. David the king sheds innocent blood and exile envelops the land. Herod the king slaughters the children at the birth of the King of the Jews and Rachel's weeping is heard now in Bethlehem as it was heard in Jeremiah in the time of the exile. If the Canaanite woman's obeisance speaks to the promise of a throne, the anointing woman speaks to the nature of that throne.

Just before Jesus has supper at the house of Simon the leper, the chief priests and elders of the people gather together against Jesus to kill him (26:3-6). At supper, a woman comes to Jesus bearing an alabaster jar of costly myrrh. She pours it over his head (26:7). The narrator notes that it is Jesus' head over which she pours the oil; in John, it is Jesus' feet. In this detail, the narrator guides the implied reader: in pouring the oil over Jesus' head, the woman anoints Jesus as king. The opening words of the gospel come to fruition: Jesus is χριστός, Son of David, the one who is anointed king.

To the narrator's interpretation of the woman's action, however, Jesus adds another interpretation. The disciples are outraged at the expense. In rebuking them, Jesus says, "she has poured this myrrh over my body to prepare me for burial."[57] Jesus' comment crucially tempers the comment of the narrator. The narrator, like the anointing woman and the Canaanite woman, has seen correctly that Jesus appears in the character of king. Jesus accepts the tribute. He does not stop the anointing woman; he allows her to

---

[57] See Malbon, *Mark's Jesus* and "History, Theology, Story: Re-Contextualizing Mark's 'Messianic Secret' as in *Character Studies and the Gospel of Mark*, 35-56, for the distinction in Mark between what the narrator says about Jesus and what Jesus says about himself (hence also the distinction between narrator and implied author) in the characterization of Jesus. Here there is in Matthew a similar instance of conflicting readings that together illuminate Jesus' character more fully than would be possible without the narrator/implied author distinction.

offer her gift to him as king here at the end of the story, as the magi offered their gifts to the child born King of the Jews at its beginning. But he then defines both her anointing and his kingship. He is the king who reigns from the tomb.

In this way—by juxtaposing the voices of the narrator and the character Jesus—the implied author achieves a nuanced interpretation of Jesus in the character of king. Both kingdom and tomb are true. It is not quite, as Terry Donaldson has said, that "Jesus chooses the path of humble, obedient sonship" over the path of royal sovereignty.[58] Rather, Jesus finds (and defines) the path of royal sovereignty *in* the humiliating death of the cross. In the anointing woman's homage, and the narrator's and Jesus' variant interpretations of it, the reader sees who Jesus is: king and crucified one. "Christ"—anointed one, Son of David, King of the Jews—is a name that is fully spoken in the place of the cross.

VI. Conclusion

"King" is in Matthew's Gospel a conflicted title. The kingship recalled in the genealogy and wielded by Herod includes both scepter and sin in its history, both sovereignty and bloodshed pointing to exile. The gospel narrator adopts the term nonetheless in his characterization of Jesus, even highlights it, calling Jesus from the beginning "anointed one" and "son of David." Against the background of Israel's history, through the women of the genealogy, the magi and the weeping of Rachel, and then in the meeting with the Canaanite and the anointing woman, Jesus' character as king unfolds. Jesus' character as king is, thus, profoundly linked to the history of his people. As a character he does not stand alone. He does not stand out, like Pericles or Antony, in his handsomeness or his passion or his generosity or his father's politics. Rather he stands within a larger narrative of God's promises and God's people. Where Greco-Roman biography focuses on the individual in his or her greatness (or depravity), detailing virtues (or vices) physical, intellectual, moral, Matthew describes Jesus not by telling us how he looks or how he was brought up or what kind of temperament he has, but by placing him within the scriptures and the history of the people Israel. The story of his character as king is the story of the promises that are theirs, in Judah and Tamar, in Ruth and Rahab and David the king. It is the story also of the desolation that is theirs, in David and the wife of Uriah and Uriah's blood, in Herod's slaughter and the weeping of Rachel. It is this whole story that is encompassed in the character of Jesus as king in Matthew's Gospel. The promise to Judah, carried forward so tenaciously by Tamar, finds its outworking in this king who does not silence the weeping of Rachel but makes her cry his own. *This is Jesus, the King of the Jews* (27:37): the titulus brings the narrative full circle. Where is the one born King of the Jews (2:2)? He is to be found here, on the cross.

---

[58] Donaldson, "The Vindicated Son," 118–20 (118).

7

Like Father, Like Son: Characterization of God the Father in Matthew's Gospel

Michael P. Knowles

However suitable it may seem from the perspective of critical scholarship, there is a certain irony to discussing God as a literary "character" in the Gospel of Matthew, insofar as the author—by most accounts an observant Jew—would likely have considered such an idea distasteful, if not offensive.[1] For the writer as for his intended audience, God is neither a literary convention nor the product of artistic depiction. In principle mysterious and holy, God cannot be characterized or accounted for in the same manner as human agents: "After all, most dimensions associated with character—physical appearance, social status, personal history, local habitation—do not apply to [God] at all. They are meant to be conspicuous by their absence, which impresses on the reader ... the qualitative difference that separates God from humans *and* pagan gods."[2] What Meir Sternberg proposes in principle, the evangelist demonstrates in practice: as elsewhere in biblical narrative, divine attributes are not communicated in an orderly fashion but indirectly or "piecemeal ... in a distributed, often oblique and tortuous unfolding of features."[3]

Matthew's properly theological convictions—which is to say, his convictions regarding the character and characteristics of God—are for the most part assumed rather than asserted. The God of this gospel is intrinsically "good" (19:17), the "living God" (16:16; 26:63), giver of all life and thus "God ... of the living" (22:32). In keeping with Jewish tradition, the "God of Abraham ... Isaac ... and Jacob" is all powerful (3:9; 12:28; 19:26; 22:29), sustainer of the natural order (6:26-30), the "Lord of heaven and earth" (11:25). Whether the words of scripture are understood as coming directly "from the mouth of God" (so Mt. 4:4, citing LXX Deut. 8:3) or through the mouths of prophets (1:22; 2:15), Israel's God is thereby revealed as worthy of all honor (4:7), worship (4:10),

---

[1] Here, "Matthew" must refer to the implied author of the text, insofar as the text is our only means of access to its originator.
[2] Meir Sternberg, *The Poetics of Biblical Narrative: Ideological Literature and the Drama of Reading* (Bloomington: Indiana University Press, 1985), 323. In this context, "readers" must be understood to indicate Matthew's audience in general, "hearers" included.
[3] Sternberg, *Poetics of Biblical Narrative*, 323; further, Marianne Meye Thompson, "'God's Voice You Have Never Heard, God's Form You Have Never Seen': The Characterization of God in the Gospel of John," *Semeia* 63 (1993): 185-7.

obedience (6:24; 15:3; 22:21, 37), and imitation (5:48), especially in the form of "deeds of loving kindness" (25:31-46). With respect to active divine agency, Warren Carter has shown that Matthew's opening genealogy, his appeal to dreams, angelic intervention, and the Holy Spirit, as well as his frequent recourse to fulfilment citations, all serve to demonstrate God's providential control over the history of Israel and the advent of the Messiah. More specifically, the naming of Jesus (etymologically, "YHWH saves"—"for he will save his people from their sins"; 1:21)—and Matthew's citation of "Emmanuel," "which means, 'God is with us'" (1:23, from Isa. 7:14) both identify Jesus as the one through whom God's character and providential sovereignty are now manifest. By such means, "God, unnamed but assumed throughout, emerges as the main character" in the unfolding of salvation history and therefore also as the controlling perspective in Matthew's narrative.[4]

Thus, in contrast to widespread consensus among his contemporaries that the people of God remain in spiritual exile, Matthew is persuaded that God's saving rule is newly manifest in Jesus of Nazareth (so 3:2; 4:17).[5] In contrast, second, to uncertainty regarding the activity of God's Spirit in the current life of Israel, Matthew perceives the Spirit of prophecy and holiness to rest on Jesus so fully (3:16; 12:28) that he represents the divine presence itself (1:23; 18:20; 28:20).[6] As yet a third distinctive feature in his portrait of the Messiah, Matthew turns familiar devotional language concerning God as "Father" to more focused narrative and theological ends. In this gospel, the identity of God as "Father" is closely linked, on the one hand, to Jesus' identity as the anointed "Son" and messianic heir and, on the other, to the exclusive demands of Christian discipleship.[7]

I. Human "Fathers" and Christian Discipleship

In this gospel, all forty-four references to God as "Father" occur on the lips of Jesus (see Table 7.1: God as Πατήρ in Matthew's Gospel).[8] Conversely, references to human fathers are predominantly negative, appear for the most part in narrative material, and typically represent all that disciples must leave behind on account of allegiance to the Messiah. For instance, James and John quit their father Zebedee "immediately" upon hearing Jesus' call to follow him (4:21-2). Another, unnamed disciple seeks leave to discharge his familial obligations, saying, "Lord, first let me go and bury my father"

---

[4] Warren Carter, *Matthew: Storyteller, Interpreter, Evangelist*, rev. edn (Peabody, MA: Hendrickson, 2004), 107-13 (107-8).
[5] See further N. T. Wright, *The New Testament and the People of God*, Christian Origins and the Question of God 1 (Minneapolis: Fortress, 1992), 268-71.
[6] On the Spirit of God in Second Temple Judaism, see David E. Aune, *Prophecy in Early Christianity and the Ancient Mediterranean World* (Grand Rapids, MI: Eerdmans, 1983), 103-6.
[7] Robert Mowery, "God, Lord, and Father: The Theology of the Gospel of Matthew," *BR* 33 (1988): 24-36, notes that whereas θεός serves most frequently in this gospel as a general term for God and κύριος appears predominantly in scriptural citations, the designation πατήρ is unique to Jesus, employed only when he is speaking "to God, to his disciples, or to audiences composed of his disciples and the crowds" (27).
[8] The text of Matthew is cited from Michael W. Holmes (ed.), *The Greek New Testament: SBL Edition* (Lexham, MD: Society of Biblical Literature, 2011-13), with critical apparatus cited from *Novum*

Like Father, Like Son

Table 7.1 God as Πατήρ in Matthew's Gospel

#	Ref					
1.	5:16		τὸν	πατέρα	ὑμῶν	τὸν ἐν τοῖς οὐρανοῖς
2.	5:45		τοῦ	πατρὸς	ὑμῶν	τοῦ ἐν οὐρανοῖς
3.	5:48		ὁ	πατὴρ	ὑμῶν	ὁ οὐράνιος
4.	6:1	παρὰ	τῷ	πατρὶ	ὑμῶν	τῷ ἐν τοῖς οὐρανοῖς
5.	6:4		ὁ	πατήρ	σου	ὁ βλέπων ἐν τῷ κρυπτῷ
6.	6:6a		τῷ	πατρί	σου	τῷ ἐν τῷ κρυπτῷ
7.	6:6b	καὶ	ὁ	πατήρ	σου	ὁ βλέπων ἐν τῷ κρυπτῷ
8.	6:8		ὁ	πατὴρ	ὑμῶν	
9.	**6:9**			**Πάτερ**	ἡμῶν	ὁ ἐν τοῖς οὐρανοῖς
10.	6:14		ὁ	πατὴρ	ὑμῶν	ὁ οὐράνιος
11.	6:15		ὁ	πατὴρ	ὑμῶν	
12.	6:18a			τῷ πατρί		σου τῷ ἐν τῷ κρυφαίῳ
13.	6:18b	καὶ	ὁ	πατήρ	σου	ὁ βλέπων ἐν τῷ κρυφαίῳ
14.	6:26	καὶ	ὁ	πατὴρ	ὑμῶν	ὁ οὐράνιος
15.	6:32		ὁ	πατὴρ	ὑμῶν	ὁ οὐράνιος
16.	7:11		ὁ	πατὴρ	ὑμῶν	ὁ ἐν τοῖς οὐρανοῖς
17.	7:21	τὸ θέλημα	τοῦ	πατρός	μου	τοῦ ἐν τοῖς οὐρανοῖς
18.	10:20	τὸ πνεῦμα	τοῦ	πατρὸς	ὑμῶν	
19.	10:29	ἄνευ	τοῦ	πατρὸς	ὑμῶν	
20.	10:32	ἔμπροσθεν	τοῦ	πατρός	μου	τοῦ ἐν [τοῖς] οὐρανοῖς
21.	10:33	ἔμπροσθεν	τοῦ	πατρός	μου	τοῦ ἐν [τοῖς] οὐρανοῖς
22.	**11:25**			**πάτερ**		κύριε τοῦ οὐρανου καὶ τῆς γῆς
23.	11:26	ναὶ	ὁ	πατήρ		
24.	11:27a	ὑπὸ	τοῦ	πατρός	μου	
25.	11:27b		ὁ	πατήρ		
26.	11:27c		τὸν	πατέρα		
27.	12:50	τὸ θέλημα	τοῦ	πατρός	μου	τοῦ ἐν οὐρανοῖς
28.	13:43		τοῦ	πατρὸς	αὐτῶν	
29.	15:13		ὁ	πατὴρ	μου	ὁ οὐράνιος
30.	16:17		ὁ	πατήρ	μου	ὁ ἐν τοῖς οὐρανοῖς
31.	16:27		τοῦ	πατρὸς	αὐτοῦ	
32.	18:10		τοῦ	πατρός	μου	τοῦ ἐν οὐρανοῖς
33.	18:14	ἔμπροσθεν	τοῦ	πατρὸς	[ὑμῶν]	τοῦ ἐν οὐρανοῖς
34.	18:19	παρὰ	τοῦ	πατρός	μου	τοῦ ἐν οὐρανοῖς
35.	18:35		ὁ	πατήρ	μου	ὁ οὐράνιος
36.	20:23	ὑπὸ	τοῦ	πατρός	μου	
37.	23:9	ὑμῶν	ὁ	πατὴρ		ὁ οὐράνιος
38.	24:36		ὁ	πατὴρ		μόνος
39.	25:34		τοῦ	πατρός	μου	
40.	26:29		τοῦ	πατρός	μου	
41.	**26:39**			**πάτερ**	μου	
42.	**26:42**			**πάτερ**	μου	[γενηθήτω τὸ θέλημά σου]
43.	26:53		τὸν	πατέρα	μου	
44.	28:19	εἰς τὸ ὄνομα	τοῦ	πατρὸς		[καὶ τοῦ υἱοῦ καὶ τοῦ ἁγίου πνεύματος]

(8:21). Since decedents are normally interred on the day of death, the man is, in effect, requesting that he might postpone obedience to Jesus' summons in deference to his living father. Yet Jesus' response is uncompromising to the point of harshness: "Follow me, and let the dead bury their own dead" (8:22). Less easily recognized is the fact that Jesus' invitation to a wealthy young man to become a disciple, trading his many possessions for "treasure in heaven," involves forsaking his father and mother also, since this is one of the commandments that he claims to observe (19:16-22; cf. 19:29).

The call of the Messiah supersedes all social bonds and obligations, without exception. On the one hand, Jesus quotes Exod. 20:12 and 21:17 as commandments from the very mouth of God: "For God said, 'Honor your father and your mother,' and, 'Whoever speaks evil of father or mother must surely die'" (Mt. 15:4). Yet, he declares:

> I have come to set a man against his father, and a daughter against her mother, and a daughter-in-law against her mother-in-law; and one's foes [ἐχθροί] will be members of one's own household. Whoever loves father or mother more than me is not worthy of me; and whoever loves son or daughter more than me is not worthy of me.
>
> Mt. 10:35-7

Indeed, Jesus predicts that the antipathy he advocates will be reciprocated by those whom faithful disciples must forsake: "Brother will betray brother to death, and a father his child, and children will rise against parents and have them put to death" (10:21). Although without indicating which members of his immediate or extended family (the sense of οἰκιακοί in 10:36) may have become a "foe," Jesus all but repudiates his own kin in a passage that—pointedly—makes no mention of a human father:

> While he was still speaking to the crowds, his mother and his brothers were standing outside, wanting to speak to him. Someone told him, "Look, your mother and your brothers are standing outside, wanting to speak to you." But to the one who had told him this, Jesus replied, "Who is my mother, and who are my brothers?" And pointing to his disciples, he said, "Here are my mother and my brothers! For whoever does the will of my Father in heaven is my brother and sister and mother."
>
> Mt. 12:46-50[9]

Testamentum Graece 28th Revised Edition, ed. Barbara and Kurt Aland et al. (Stuttgart: Deutsche Bibelgesellschaft, 2012) and verified with reference to the University of Münster Institute for New Testament Textual Research New Testament Transcripts Prototype (http://nttranscripts.uni-muenster.de). Word frequencies have been checked against the earlier work of Robert Morgenthaler, *Statistik des neutestamentlichen Wortschatzes*, 3rd edn (Zürich: Gotthelf, 1982). Ulrich Luz, *Matthew: A Commentary*, trans. James E. Crouch, ed. Helmut Koester, Hermeneia (Minneapolis: Fortress, 2001), 1:35, counts forty-five Matthean references to "πατήρ about God," without, however, providing verse references. The noun appears sixty-three times in Matthew (Morgenthaler, sixty-four); the remaining nineteen instances are at 2:22; 3:9; 4:21, 22; 8:21; 10:21, 35, 37; 15:4 [*bis*], 5, 6; 19:5, 19, 29; 21:31; 23:9a, 30, 32.

[9] For the textual status of 12:47, see Bruce M. Metzger, *A Textual Commentary on the Greek New Testament*, 2nd edn (Stuttgart: Deutsche Bibelgesellschaft, 1994), 26–7.

Whatever the reaction of his immediate family may have been, Jesus faces incomprehension and outright rejection from the townsfolk who have known him since childhood. Here the evangelist's choice of vocabulary implies a contrast between the response of his πατρίς ("patrimony, hometown") and the intimacy Jesus enjoys with his heavenly Father:

> He came to his hometown [πατρίδα] and began to teach the people in their synagogue, so that they were astounded and said, "Where did this man get this wisdom and these deeds of power? Is not this *the carpenter's son*? Is not his mother called Mary? And are not his brothers James and Joseph and Simon and Judas? And are not all his sisters with us? Where then did this man get all this?" And they took offense at him. But Jesus said to them, "Prophets are not without honor except in their own country [πατρίδι] and in their own house [οἰκίᾳ]."
>
> Mt. 13:54-7

It is striking that this passage contains the only mention of Joseph (albeit unnamed, in contrast to Mary and four male siblings) outside the infancy narratives. Even in that context, however, the role of Joseph is already overshadowed by a fulfilment citation of Hos. 11:1 that attributes Jesus' paternity, rather, to God: "This was to fulfill what had been spoken by the Lord through the prophet, 'Out of Egypt I have called *my son*'" (2:15).

The Greek term πατήρ can also have the extended sense of "ancestor, progenitor," as is equally the case with the Hebrew אב (e.g., Deut. 26:5). In Jesus' diatribe against the Pharisees, this more figurative usage has a no less pejorative tone:

> You say, "If we had lived in the days of our ancestors [τῶν πατέρων ἡμῶν], we would not have taken part with them in shedding the blood of the prophets." Thus you testify against yourselves that you are descendants [υἱοί] of those who murdered the prophets. Fill up, then, the measure of your ancestors [τῶν πατέρων ἡμῶν]. You snakes, you brood of vipers! How can you escape being sentenced to hell?
>
> Mt. 23:30-3[10]

In sum, whether with regard to Jesus himself, those whom Jesus calls to follow him, or his theological opponents, Matthew's Gospel portrays human fathers and family loyalties in almost wholly negative terms.

---

[10] Claiming that such polemic represents a universal anti-Judaism, Burnett incorrectly assumes that for Matthew the scribes and Pharisees are representative of Judaism as a whole, attributing to him (by implication) the view of Jn 8:44 that "the Devil is their father": Fred W. Burnett, "Exposing the Anti-Jewish Ideology of Matthew's Implied Author: The Characterization of God as Father," *Semeia* 59 (1992): 164–5.

II. "Your Father": God and the Disciples

Since characterization of God as "Father" is not uncommon within the Judaisms of his day, such usage on Jesus' part cannot be considered innovative in principle.[11] But what is notable is that all references to God as "Father" in Matthew's Gospel come from Jesus, in keeping with his claim at 11:27 to be the sole source and arbiter of divine knowledge. In this way, Matthew as author and editor encodes within his text Jesus' exclusive right to delineate the character of God.[12]

Of the first nineteen references between 5:16 and 10:29, all but two speak of "*your* Father" (i.e., ὁ πατήρ σου/ὑμῶν). Conversely, of the remaining twenty-five from 10:32 to 28:19, only one (τοῦ πατρὸς ὑμῶν at 18:14) has a second-person pronoun: ὁ πατήρ μου appears fifteen times and ὁ πατήρ αὐτοῦ twice, while the other seven are without personal pronouns. In other words, the first ten chapters of Matthew for the most part refer to God as "your Father," while throughout the last eighteen chapters Jesus speaks of God most frequently in the first person as "my Father." The tone of the earlier references is predominantly one of affirmation for disciples: "Your Father," Jesus assures them, "knows what you need before you ask him" (6:8); "Look at the birds of the air," he continues, "They neither sow nor reap nor gather into barns, and yet your heavenly Father feeds them. Are you not of more value than they?" (6:26). Such, indeed, is God's perfect knowledge that it extends even to the death of the lowliest creature: "Are not two sparrows sold for a penny? Yet not one of them will fall to the ground apart from your Father" (Mt. 10:29).[13] Their heavenly Father's provision is set in contrast to that of human fathers, whom Jesus characterizes as "evil" in principle:

---

[11] References to God as "Father" are relatively frequent throughout Hebrew scripture (and are predominantly corporate in focus: e.g., Deut. 32:6; Isa. 63:16; Mal. 2:10, etc.), as well as in contemporary apocalyptic and devotional literature. Similar language is evident in the Dead Sea Scrolls and other intertestamental literature with regard to Israel, the elect community, and the elect individual alike, on which see Torleif Elgvin, "The Mystery to Come: Early Essene Theology of Revelation," in *Qumran Between the Old and New Testaments*, ed. Frederick H. Cryer and Thomas L. Thompson, JSOTSup 290 (Sheffield: Sheffield Academic, 1998), 122–3 and nn. 23–6. References of God as "Father" also appear in synagogal prayers (notably the Shemoneh Esreh) and the Mishnah, e.g., *m. Kil.* 9.8; *m. Roš Haš.* 3.8; *m. Yoma* 8.9; *m. Soṭah* 9.15; *m. 'Abot* 5.20. See further Helmer Ringgren, 'אב,' *TDOT* 1: 16–19.

[12] According to Burnett, "Jesus' father language in Matthew is so exclusive not just in that there are no 'your father' references in relation to Jesus' opponents, but also in that his 'my father/your father' language portrays the Jewish leaders as 'anti-sons' or negative witnesses to sonship and, consequently, to salvation"; Burnett, "Anti-Jewish Ideology," 165–6, *et passim*. This fails to account for the nature (and polarizing rhetoric) of internecine polemic within Second Temple Judaism, especially in light of traditions of Deuteronomistic prophetic critique. Given Matthew's unqualified endorsement of Israelite history (1:2-17) and Torah (5:17-20), such language as likely reflects proximity as displacement. See, e.g., Anders Runesson, "Rethinking Early Jewish-Christian Relations: Matthean Community History as Pharisaic Intragroup Conflict," *JBL* 127, no. 1 (2008): 95–132.

[13] Since the Jerusalem Talmud records a similar saying from the second-century Palestinian Rabbi Simeon bar Yohai ("Without heaven, even a bird does not perish, all the more so a human being"; *y. Šebu.* 39b), such adages appear to be proverbial. Text cited from Jacob Neusner, *The Jerusalem Talmud: A Translation and Commentary* (Peabody, MA: Hendrickson, 2008).

What man of you, if his son asks him for bread, will give him a stone? Or if he asks for a fish, will give him a serpent? If you then, *who are evil*, know how to give good gifts to your children, how much more will your Father who is in heaven give good things to those who ask him!

Mt. 7:9-11, RSV

Corresponding to the acuity of divine perception and the fulness of heavenly provision is the disciples' own sense of God's holiness and judicial authority, which rightly inspire holy fear (10:28, 30). Yet such is the confidence they are to have in their Father's mercy that Jesus concludes with reassurance: "So do not be afraid; you are of more value than many sparrows" (10:31).

What distinguishes them from gentiles is not only their sense of being divine "sons" but also the intentional reliance on the Father that should result from such an awareness (6:32). "Your Father," Jesus tells the disciples, both sees and rewards every act of piety performed in secret—prayer, fasting, and almsgiving alike (6:4, 6, 18).[14] Conversely, acts of piety performed in order to gain the approbation of others forfeit any heavenly recompense (6:1). Given what Jesus says in 10:17-20, this contrast is not intended to preclude fearless confession of faith in him as Messiah, but rather to draw disciples into direct trust and interaction with God as their own heavenly Father. Nor does Jesus mean that disciples must shield their piety altogether from the sight of their community. Rather, he intends their devotion to have the same effect on others as does his on them: "You are the light of the world ... let your light shine before others, so that they may see your good works and give glory to your Father in heaven" (5:14, 16). That is, the Messiah and his disciples alike turn the attention of onlookers toward God.

According to Jesus, filial piety on the part of his followers entails not only full reliance but also direct imitation of their heavenly Father:

I say to you, Love your enemies and pray for those who persecute you, so that you may be [sons] of your Father in heaven [υἱοὶ τοῦ πατρός ὑμῶν τοῦ ἐν οὐρανοῖς]; for he makes his sun rise on the evil and on the good, and sends rain on the righteous and on the unrighteous ... Be perfect, therefore, as your heavenly Father is perfect.

Mt. 5:44-5, 48

Furthermore, imitation calls for reciprocity, such that failure to extend mercy to others entails forfeiture of mercy for oneself: "If you forgive others their trespasses," Jesus tells them, "Your heavenly Father will also forgive you; but if you do not forgive others, neither will your Father forgive your trespasses" (6:14-15). Thus, the divine filiation of which Jesus speaks in this gospel is not a matter of trust alone, but also of concrete action. Nor, therefore, is verbal profession alone a sufficient measure of piety or obedience: "Not everyone who says to me, 'Lord, Lord,' will enter the kingdom of heaven, but only the one who does the will of my Father in heaven" (7:21).

---

[14] Fittingly, Jesus' five references to the Father who abides "in secret" and sees what is done "in secret" (6:4, 6 [*bis*], 18 [*bis*]) are the only ones in this gospel addressed to disciples in the singular (i.e., ὁ πατήρ σου).

Of course, Jesus has more than this to say about God in the first ten chapters of Matthew. Nonetheless, the specific passages reviewed thus far delineate a theological outlook and devotional orientation that he evidently considered normative both for himself and for his followers. To the extent that subsequent readers of the gospel hear themselves addressed—even indirectly—by Jesus' references to "Your Father," Matthew's narrative inculcates a particular disposition on their part toward God, so as to evoke in them the same sense of filial identity, reliance, and practical obedience that characterize Jesus' more immediate hearers within the text.

III. "My Father": The God of Jesus

The evangelist's recasting of Q material offers a clue to the significant shift of vocabulary that occurs from 10:32-3 onward. Conscious of rising opposition to his ministry, Jesus both warns and encourages his disciples of what is at stake in faithful confession: "Everyone therefore who acknowledges me before others, I also will acknowledge before my Father in heaven; but whoever denies me before others, I also will deny before my Father in heaven."[15] Whereas, prior to this point, Jesus' references to God have focused primarily on the kindness and generosity of "*your* Father," Matthew now directs attention toward the filial piety of the Messiah himself. Allegiance to the Messiah begins to overlap more explicitly with allegiance to the God of Israel.

As noted earlier, Jesus' designation of God as "my Father" is not the only form of divine address within the latter two-thirds of the gospel. The explanation of the wheat and the weeds concludes with an assurance that "the righteous will shine like the sun in the kingdom of *their* Father" (13:43); Jesus promises that "the Son of Man is to come with his angels in the glory of *his* Father" (16:27), and warns his followers to "call no one your father on earth, for *your* one Father is in heaven [εἷς γάρ ἐστιν ὑμῶν ὁ πατὴρ ὁ οὐράνιος]" (23:9).[16] Nor, more generally, do the theological references in this material characterize the God of Israel in a distinctive manner. As elsewhere in Matthew (and Judaism generally), God is said to govern human history (24:36), reveal truth (16:17), answer prayer (18:19; 26:53), demand mercy (18:35), order the destiny of the saints (20:23; 25:34), and pronounce final judgment (15:14). Even the concept of angels who both behold God and watch over minor saints (so 18:10) has numerous parallels in contemporary Jewish literature.[17]

Taken together, the sixteen Matthean references to ὁ πατήρ μου are distinctive not for their depiction of God *per se*, but for what they intend to say about the identity and spirituality of Jesus: characterization serves as an expression of Christology. Not only

---

[15] The parallel passage in Lk. 12:8-9 refers rather to being acknowledged or denied "before the angels of God." This explanation assumes the two-source theory of synoptic relationships.

[16] Author's translation; cf. 18:14, ἔμπροσθεν τοῦ πατρὸς ὑμῶν (so ℵ D¹ K L W Δ ƒ¹ etc.; μου B N Γ Θ 078 ƒ¹³ cop Origen, etc.). See further Metzger, *Textual Commentary*, 36. Here and throughout, citation of textual witnesses is representative rather than comprehensive.

[17] So W. D. Davies and Dale C. Allison, *A Critical and Exegetical Commentary on the Gospel according to Saint Matthew*, 3 vols., ICC (London: T&T Clark, 1991), 2:770-2; Luz, *Matthew* 2:441-3.

does Jesus' language shift from ὁ πατήρ σου/ὑμῶν in the earlier chapters to ὁ πατήρ μου thereafter, his use of the latter expression also develops in the course of the narrative, incrementally unfolding his self-understanding as Messiah. The first of these references, at the conclusion of the Sermon on the Mount (7:21), deflects attention away from acclamation of Jesus as "Lord" and toward the supreme importance of obedience to God alone, which seems remarkable when compared to the centrality of such confession, for example, in Pauline theology (so Rom. 10:9; 1 Cor. 12:3; 2 Cor. 4:5, etc.). As we have seen, the next two position Jesus as patron and intermediary between the disciples and God, the one whose recognition or denial determines recognition or denial by the Father (10:32-3). Next, Mt. 11:27 underscores this role more emphatically: "All things have been handed over to me by my Father," says Jesus; "No one knows the Son except the Father, and no one knows the Father except the Son and anyone to whom the Son chooses to reveal him." The evangelist's choice of verbs here is significant: ἐπιγινώσκειν implies "personal, concentrated experiential knowledge."[18] Although Jesus' apprehension of other matters may be incomplete (the timing of the eschaton, for instance, according to 24:36), the language of 11:27 indicates singular intimacy and comprehension. Indeed, Jesus claims not only that his knowledge of God is definitive, but also that he is the divine plenipotentiary, whose powers include the right to serve as intermediary and disclose the identity of God to his followers in turn.[19]

This pivotal affirmation governs interpretation of the ensuing reference in 12:50: "Whoever does the will of my Father in heaven is my brother and sister and mother." Viewed in isolation, this statement might simply reiterate the intent of 7:21 (with its emphasis on fulfilling "the will of my Father in heaven"), while again repudiating the customary bonds of home and hearth. But in its present context, it must mean more specifically that whoever does the will of the Father *as revealed by the messianic Son* not only shares fictive kinship with him but also, by implication, is thereby enfranchised into the filial relationship of which he speaks. After all, to be a sibling—even by adoption—is to share common parentage (as indicated more directly in 23:9: "Call no one your father on earth, for you have one Father—the one in heaven").

Similarly, Jesus' refutation of his opponents—"Every plant that my heavenly Father has not planted will be uprooted" (15:13)—is, on the face of it, another appeal to the power of divine judgment. But in light of the unfolding exposition of Jesus' own filial status, it also implies vindication of his identity as the messianic Son, precisely because God is his Father. This is even more clearly the case with Jesus' response to Peter's confession at Caesarea Philippi: "Blessed are you, Simon son of Jonah! For flesh and blood has not revealed this to you, but *my* Father in heaven" (16:17). Just, therefore, as the Son reveals the Father (11:27), so the Father reveals the Son, a premise especially evident at Jesus' baptism and transfiguration. On both occasions, God enters directly into Matthew's narrative in the form of a voice from heaven which declares, Οὗτός

---

[18] Davies and Allison, *Matthew*, 2:281.
[19] As with the designation of God as "Father," reference to righteous individuals as "sons of God" is not without precedent in Judaism (on which see R. T. France, *Matthew: Evangelist and Teacher* [Downers Grove, IL: InterVarsity, 1998], 292–8); nonetheless, Matthew's characterization of Jesus implies a unique degree of identification and filial authority.

ἐστιν ὁ υἱός μου ὁ ἀγαπητὸς ἐν ᾧ εὐδόκησα (3:17; 17:5). The significance of these dramatic irruptions cannot be underestimated, for they characterize the Father as unequivocally as the Father characterizes the Son: not only does the God of heaven speak aloud for human apprehension, but "When God speaks, he speaks of Jesus."[20]

It is worth pausing to consider the implications for Matthew's readership of this rising crescendo of messianic affirmations. Their cumulative effect is to suggest that such claims are not validated on the basis of Matthean rhetoric or as a result of careful reading alone, but rather in direct relation to the God of whom Jesus testifies. At least for readers concerned with theology and allegiance to God, Matthew poses the challenge of openness to the Father's revelation of Jesus as the messianic Son. The same will be true even of otherwise straightforward assertions: "Take care that you do not despise one of these little ones; for, *I tell you*, in heaven their angels continually see the face of my Father in heaven" (18:10); "Truly *I tell you*, if two of you agree on earth about anything you ask, it will be done for you by my Father in heaven" (18:19); "So my heavenly Father will also do to every one of you, if you do not forgive your brother or sister from your heart" (18:35). In each passage, reference to ὁ πατήρ μου indicates that the authority of such statements is rooted in Jesus' claim to divine sonship, implying a direct correlation of Jesus' intentions with the supreme will of God. More explicit still is Jesus' description of his kingly reign as ordained and ordered by God (20:23: "to sit at my right hand and at my left ... is for those for whom it has been prepared by my Father"), as a result of which the identity of the monarch in the parable of the sheep and goats becomes at once transparent: "Then the king will say to those at his right hand, 'Come, you that are blessed by my Father, inherit the kingdom prepared for you from the foundation of the world'" (25:34).[21] Then, finally, filial dependence and devotion find their fullest expression in the cluster of vocatives with which Jesus addresses the One whose will he is committed to fulfill:

> He threw himself on the ground and prayed, "My Father [Πάτερ μου], if it is possible, let this cup pass from me; yet not what I want but what you want."
>
> 26:39

> Again he went away for the second time and prayed, "My Father [Πάτερ μου], if this cannot pass unless I drink it, your will be done."
>
> 26:42

> And about three o'clock Jesus cried with a loud voice, "Eli, Eli, lema sabachthani?" that is, "My God, my God [Θεέ μου θεέ μου], why have you forsaken me?"
>
> 27:46

---

[20] Francois J. Viljoen, "The Matthean Characterisation of Jesus by God the Father," *HTS Teologiese Studies/Theological Studies* 75, no. 3 (2019): 7 (*et passim*).

[21] Although Jesus subsequently refers to "my Father's kingdom" (26:29)—not, that is, exclusively his own.

Here, the directness of Jesus' address to God corresponds in devotional terms to the theological intimacy implied by his intensifying use of the expression ὁ πατήρ μου throughout this gospel.

Thus, within the theology of Matthew's Gospel the characterization of God cannot be considered apart from the identity of Jesus himself: the concept of God as "Father" corresponds to that of Jesus as "Son" (and vice versa). Nonetheless, the clarity with which Matthew depicts Jesus is inversely proportionate to his largely indirect characterization of God. In terms of the four categories of narrative perspective proposed by Boris Uspensky,[22] the ultimate source of this gospel's ideological point of view breaks into the spatial-temporal plane in the form of divine speech (the phraseological plane) just twice. Instead, Matthew accords priority on all three levels to Jesus, who both articulates and embodies the definitive expression of God's will "on earth as it is in heaven." Even so, the most definitive expression of this gospel's—and God's—point of view is on the psychological plane, with Jesus addressing God directly as θεέ μου and especially πάτερ μου.

IV. Structural Symbolism in the Service of Characterization and Theology

Attending more closely to instances of vocative address reveals another, less obvious series of literary strategies by which the evangelist highlights the spirituality of the Messiah in characterizing God as his "Father." The term Πατήρ with reference to God occurs seventeen times within the Sermon on the Mount, with these titles arranged in five chiastic sets that are internally differentiated by the qualifying clauses that Matthew employs in each case (see Table 7.2: Πατήρ in the Sermon on the Mount). Although not every parallel is exact, they are sufficiently consistent as to be unmistakable.[23] Here, variations in terminology for God as "Father" have both a structural and a thematic function: the resulting chiasm highlights Jesus' vocative address to God in the Lord's Prayer.

Discerning chiastic patterns in New Testament texts remains a controverted interpretative method, given the uncertainty both of appropriate criteria for verification and of its heuristic value in the context of oral recitation.[24] Luz's word of caution is salutary: "We should speak of chiastic ring compositions only where the parallels occur within clearly recognizable textual units."[25] The evidentiary value of matching vocabulary will generally correspond to the thematic and theological prominence of

---

[22] Boris Uspensky, *A Poetics of Composition: The Structure of the Artistic Text and Typology of a Compositional Form*, trans. Valentina Zavarin and Susan Wittig (Berkeley: University of California Press, 1973).

[23] This pattern was also briefly noted in Michael P. Knowles, "Reading Matthew: The Gospel as Oral Performance," in *Reading the Gospels Today*, ed. Stanley E. Porter, MNTS 8 (Grand Rapids, MI: Eerdmans, 2004), 64–5.

[24] See the careful discussion of methodology by Ian H. Thomson, *Chiasmus in the Pauline Letters*, JSNTSup 111 (Sheffield: Sheffield Academic, 1995), 13–45.

[25] Luz, *Matthew*, 1:7, n. 35.

Table 7.2 Πατήρ in the Sermon on the Mount

1.	5:16	A¹	τὸν πατέρα ὑμῶν τὸν ἐν τοῖς οὐρανοῖς
2.	5:45	A²	τοῦ πατρὸς ὑμῶν τοῦ ἐν οὐρανοῖς
3.	5:48	B¹	ὁ πατὴρ ὑμῶν ὁ οὐράνιος
4.	6:1	B²	τῷ πατρὶ ὑμῶν τῷ ἐν τοῖς οὐρανοῖς
5.	6:4	C¹	ὁ πατήρ σου ὁ βλέπων ἐν τῷ κρυπτῷ
6.	6:6a	C²	τῷ πατρί σου τῷ ἐν τῷ κρυπτῷ
7.	6:6b	C³	ὁ πατήρ σου ὁ βλέπων ἐν τῷ κρυπτῷ
8.	6:8	D	ὁ πατὴρ ὑμῶν
9.	6:9	E¹	Πάτερ ἡμῶν ὁ ἐν τοῖς οὐρανοῖς· ἁγιασθήτω τὸ ὄνομά σου
10.	6:14	E²′	ὁ πατὴρ ὑμῶν ὁ οὐράνιος
11.	6:15	D′	ὁ πατὴρ ὑμῶν
12.	6:18a	C¹′	τῷ πατρί σου τῷ ἐν τῷ κρυφαίῳ
13.	6:18b	C³′	ὁ πατήρ σου ὁ βλέπων ἐν τῷ κρυφαίῳ
14.	6:26	B¹′	ὁ πατὴρ ὑμῶν ὁ οὐράνιος
15.	6:32	B²′	ὁ πατὴρ ὑμῶν ὁ οὐράνιος
16.	7:11	A¹′	ὁ πατὴρ ὑμῶν ὁ ἐν τοῖς οὐρανοῖς
17.	7:21	A²′	τοῦ πατρός μου τοῦ ἐν τοῖς οὐρανοῖς

such language within the larger work, even as proposed structural parallels will prove persuasive to the degree that their individual components demonstrate conscious redactional intent. In the present instance, names and titles for God are, by definition, theologically significant (especially so in the mouth of Jesus), while Matthew's redactional activity is easily demonstrated by comparison with Mark and Luke.

Set 1

A¹ Mt. 5:16 [M]   A¹′ Mt. 7:11 [≠ Lk. 11:13]
    τὸν πατέρα ὑμῶν τὸν ἐν τοῖς οὐρανοῖς   ὁ πατὴρ ὑμῶν ὁ ἐν τοῖς οὐρανοῖς

Here the phrasing of the parallel elements is identical, although the grammatical function of the respective adjectival clauses requires a different case for each. The first is without Synoptic parallel; the second differs from the wording (itself textually uncertain) of the otherwise similar Lk. 11:13.

A² Mt. 5:45 [≠ Lk. 6:35]   A²′ Mt. 7:21 [≠ Lk. 6:46]
    τοῦ πατρὸς ὑμῶν τοῦ ἐν οὐρανοῖς   τοῦ πατρός μου τοῦ ἐν τοῖς οὐρανοῖς[26]

In this pair of phrases only the person and number of the possessive pronouns differ, in addition to which Mt. 7:21 includes the definite article. Both descriptors are redactionally distinct: in place of Matthew's υἱοὶ τοῦ πατρὸς ὑμῶν, and so on, Lk. 6:35 reads υἱοὶ ὑψίστου, while Lk. 6:46 makes no reference to the "Father." All four readings in this set are thus uniquely Matthean.

[26] Omit τοῖς K L W f¹³.

Set 2

B¹ Mt. 5:48 [+ Lk. 6:36]
    ὁ πατὴρ ὑμῶν ὁ οὐράνιος²⁷

B¹′ Mt. 6:26 [≠ Lk. 12:24]
     ὁ πατὴρ ὑμῶν ὁ οὐράνιος

Here the correspondence is exact. In Mt. 5:48 the adjectival attributive ὁ οὐράνιος has been added to the Q text evidenced at Lk. 6:36, while the parallel to Mt. 6:26 at Lk. 12:24 reads simply, ὁ θεός.

B² Mt. 6:1 [M]
    τῷ πατρὶ ὑμῶν τῷ ἐν τοῖς οὐρανοῖς²⁸

B²′ Mt. 6:32 [+ Lk. 12:30]
     ὁ πατὴρ ὑμῶν ὁ οὐράνιος²⁹

By contrast, these phrases are clearly dissimilar: apart from the question of case, the respective attributive clauses employ different, albeit cognate terms. Matthew 6:1 is without Synoptic parallel, whereas in 6:32 the evangelist has added ὁ οὐράνιος to the Q text represented by Lk. 12:30 (ὑμῶν δὲ ὁ πατήρ).

Set 3

C¹ Mt. 6:4 [M]
    ὁ πατήρ σου ὁ βλέπων ἐν τῷ κρυπτῷ
    ἀποδώσει σοι

C² Mt. 6:6a [M]
    τῷ πατρί σου τῷ ἐν τῷ κρυπτῷ

C³ Mt. 6:6b [M]
    ὁ πατήρ σου ὁ βλέπων ἐν τῷ κρυπτῷ
    ἀποδώσει σοι

C¹′ Mt. 6:18a [M]
     τῷ πατρί σου τῷ ἐν τῷ κρυφαίῳ³⁰

C³′ Mt. 6:18b [M]
     ὁ πατήρ σου ὁ βλέπων ἐν τῷ
     κρυφαίῳ ἀποδώσει σοι

The correspondence between the components of this series is more complex, since both "halves" of the chiasm constitute matched sets of their own. The initial set (C¹–C³) is itself chiastic:

6:4   ὁ πατήρ σου ὁ βλέπων ἐν τῷ κρυπτῷ
6:6a   τῷ πατρί σου τῷ ἐν τῷ κρυπτῷ
6:6b ὁ πατήρ σου ὁ βλέπων ἐν τῷ κρυπτῷ

The key difference between this language and that of its double counterpart in 6:18 (C¹′–C³′) lies with the evangelist's choice of (synonymous) adjectives: κρυφαῖος in place of the earlier κρυπτός, as is clear in the otherwise close correspondence between C¹/C³ and C³′. Apart from the change of adjectives, juxtaposing all five components of this set reveals an exact alternation of phrasing:

---

²⁷ ἐν τοῖς οὐρανοῖς (D*) K Δ Θ Tertullian.
²⁸ Omit τοῖς ℵ* D Z f¹.
²⁹ Omit ὁ οὐράνιος ℵ cop^bo Clement of Alexandria (not cited in NA28).
³⁰ Omit second article: ℵ*; for κρυφαίῳ read κρυφία D*; κρυπτῷ K L W Γ Δ Θ f¹³ (as at 6:18b).

6:4	ὁ πατήρ σου ὁ βλέπων ἐν τῷ κρυπτῷ ἀποδώσει σοι
6:6a	τῷ πατρί σου τῷ ἐν τῷ κρυπτῷ
6:6b	ὁ πατήρ σου ὁ βλέπων ἐν τῷ κρυπτῷ ἀποδώσει σοι
6:18a	τῷ πατρί σου τῷ ἐν τῷ κρυφαίῳ
6:18b	ὁ πατήρ σου ὁ βλέπων ἐν τῷ κρυφαίῳ ἀποδώσει σοι

Set 4
D   Mt. 6:8 [M]   D´   Mt. 6:15 [M]
     ὁ πατὴρ ὑμῶν[31]   ὁ πατὴρ ὑμῶν[32]

As with the previous series, these components appear in material that is without Synoptic parallel.

Set 5
E   Mt. 6:9 [+ Lk. 11:2]   E´   Mt. 6:14 [≠ Mk 11:25]
     Πάτερ ἡμῶν ὁ ἐν τοῖς οὐρανοῖς[33]   ὁ πατὴρ ὑμῶν ὁ οὐράνιος[34]

The first of these phrases includes a vocative, a feature not replicated in 6:14 because the latter does not represent direct address, while the variation between the modifying clause ὁ ἐν τοῖς οὐρανοῖς and the adjectival attributive ὁ οὐράνιος also distinguished the components in series A and B, respectively. Of all the texts examined thus far, only Mt. 6:14 reflects Markan precedent. Other than the vocative, ὁ πατὴρ ὑμῶν ὁ ἐν τοῖς οὐρανοῖς in Mk 11:25 is identical to Mt. 6:9, yet here Matthew chooses to break the sequence of chiastic parallels that has obtained to this point. This divergence means that all seventeen formulations of πατήρ as a title for God in the Sermon on the Mount are shaped by the hand of the evangelist.

That the parallels in this chiastic series occur sequentially among the corresponding elements of each set (A¹ : A¹´ followed by A² : A²´, etc.) yet inversely within the chiasm as a whole (A–B–C–D–E–E´–D´–C´–B´–A´) can hardly be accidental. Moreover, parallel elements occur in contexts that otherwise lack linguistic or thematic similarity: they appear as a redactional overlay that operates independently of the flow of the narrative.

As with any chiasm, this structural device serves to highlight the central set (E : E´), or, more broadly, the Lord's Prayer that is framed by this pair of elements. Indeed, employing an uneven number of components in the third set (C has three elements, whereas C´ has only two) structures the chiasm in such a way that eight instances of πατήρ precede the opening petition of the Lord's Prayer while eight follow it (see Table 7.3: Vocative uses of Πατήρ in Matthew, column α). Together, structural and thematic features confirm Luz's observation that the Sermon on the Mount is fashioned around

---

[31] ὁ θεός ὁ πατὴρ ὑμῶν: ℵ¹ B cop^(sa.mae); ὁ πατὴρ ὑμῶν ὁ οὐράνιος 892^c syr^h; txt ℵ* D K L W Z Δ Θ *f*¹³ etc. (cf. Metzger, *Textual Commentary*, 12–13).
[32] ὑμῖν: ℵ; cf. D.
[33] Omit article: ℵ*; τῷ οὐρανῷ cop^(mae); Didache.
[34] ἐν τοῖς οὐρανοῖς Θ it.

6:9-13: "The Lord's Prayer is its central text."[35] More precisely, by accentuating the opening words of this paradigmatic prayer, Matthew brings together the piety of Jesus, the Messiah's own characterization of God as "Father," and the intended spirituality of Jesus' disciples in a single, unique phrase: "Πάτερ ἡμῶν."[36]

Beyond the initial seventeen references to God as "Father" in the Sermon on the Mount, there are a further twenty-seven instances of πατήρ as a divine title in the remainder of Matthew's Gospel, for a total of forty-four (see Table 7.3, column γ). Just as the concentric pattern in the Sermon on the Mount centers on Jesus' direct address to the Father (demarcated by the vocative), so the twenty-second (again structurally central) occurrence in the entire collection is likewise vocative, with Jesus again praying to the Father (see Table 7.3, column δ):

> I thank you, Father [πάτερ], Lord of heaven and earth, because you have hidden these things from the wise and the intelligent and have revealed them to infants; yes, Father [πατήρ], for such was your gracious will.
>
> 11:25-6

The vocative at 11:25 appears all the more striking in comparison to the nominative immediately following. In addition, the title κύριε τοῦ οὐρανοῦ καὶ τῆς γῆς (unique in this gospel) recalls the earlier petition that God's will be accomplished "on earth as in heaven" (6:10), suggesting a thematic link between the two prayers. Finally, just as the initial series of seventeen ended with language recalling the Lord's Prayer (7:21), so this

Table 7.3 Vocative uses of Πατήρ in Matthew

				Instances of πατήρ			
				α	β	γ	δ
1–8	Sermon on the Mount	5:16–6:8		8	21	17	22
9		6:9	Πάτερ ἡμῶν	1			
10–17		6:14–7:21		8			
18–21		10:20–33		4	21	27	22
22		11:25	πάτερ κύριε	1			
23–40		11:26–26:29		18			
41		26:39	πάτερ μου	2			
42		26:42	πάτερ μου				
43–4		26:53–28:19		2			
				44			

---

[35] Luz, *Matthew*, 1:172; cf. 1:7–8.

[36] Although Paul not infrequently refers to God as ὁ πατὴρ ἡμῶν (especially in letter openings), nowhere else in the New Testament does the vocative πάτερ address God with the first-person plural pronoun.

second series concludes with a reference to τὸ ὄνομα τοῦ πατρός (28:19; cf. 6:9, ἁγιασθήτω τὸ ὄνομά σου). Buttressed in each instance by echoes of the Lord's Prayer, Jesus' vocative address to God as "Father" thus appears at the structural and theological center both of seventeen such references in the Sermon on the Mount and of the entire collection of forty-four.[37]

In this way, cryptic redactional markers highlight theological values that are of paramount concern to the evangelist, if not also his immediate circle. Here combined with numerical patterning, chiasm creates structural cohesion in the service of narrative and theological intentionality: to quote Jacob Milgrom, "By the use of repeated words and inner chiasms, and, above all, by the choice of the center or fulcrum around which the inversion is structured, the ideological thrust of each author is revealed. In a word, structure is theology."[38] There is no way of knowing whether Matthew's original audience (literate or not) would have been alert to such strategies, and therefore what rhetorical function they are intended to serve. Nonetheless, close examination brings to light core theological convictions concerning God, Jesus, and his disciples that the evangelist has encoded within the structure of his narrative.

V. Conclusion: Characterization and Discipleship

In the classic, theological sense, the divine character is not subject to debate: the God of Israel is unchangeably holy, perfect, and just. Characterization, in the literary sense, may therefore turn to more particular ends. Nowhere in this gospel is this more clearly so than in the evangelist's depiction of God as "Father" in relation to Jesus as "Son." As announced in the opening verse, Jesus is "the son of David, the son of Abraham," designations that imply continuity of commission and divine favor with the progenitors of the Jewish faith. More audaciously, the citation of Hos. 11:1 in Mt. 2:15 identifies Jesus as representative of the nation a whole, the "son" called out of bondage in Egypt as a sign of adoption by God. Superseding ancestry and religious heritage alike as sources of messianic identity, the voice of heaven makes a still more definitive claim: "This is my Son, the Beloved, with whom I am well pleased" (3:17; 17:5). Since they occur solely on the lips of Jesus, references in Matthew's Gospel to God as "Father" represent the Messiah's response to divine endorsement. In relation to those around him, Jesus is the one who makes the Father known (11:27), inviting his disciples into fellowship with the one he calls "your Father," ὁ πατὴρ ὑμῶν. As the gospel narrative unfolds, Jesus refers more frequently to "my Father," ὁ πατήρ μου, thereby emphasizing his own sense of filial intimacy with God. Even more definitive, highlighted by means of structural and numerical devices, are four uses of the vocative by which Jesus and his disciples alike address God directly, either as πάτερ μου or πάτερ ἡμῶν.

---

[37] The final two vocatives in 26:39 and 26:42 are likewise symmetrically positioned relative to 11:25 and the beginning of the collection (see Table 3, col. β).

[38] Jacob Milgrom, *Leviticus 23–27: A New Translation with Introduction and Commentary*, AB 3B (New York: Doubleday, 2001), 2129–30.

In this way, Matthean literary characterization serves not only theology, or Christology in particular, but the spirituality of discipleship also. By emphasizing the piety of the Messiah, together with Jesus' inclusion of his followers in filial allegiance to God, Matthew underscores the breadth of this invitation, so that in recognition of Jesus' identity as the true "Son of God" (14:33; 16:16; 27:54), the prospect of divine adoption and devotion to the Father extends to Matthew's audience also.[39] At this juncture, the process of reception (whether for hearers or readers) leads beyond the text itself.[40] With or without a conscious attempt at proselytizing, texts—especially religious texts—solicit assent from their audiences, both real and implied. Yet for a text that presumes to speak of God, the veracity of its presentation cannot be determined on the basis of the narrative alone. Here the strategies and categories of critical scholarship begin to collapse, as the text points beyond the work of its author, however artful, and toward the transcendent subject of which it speaks. In such a situation, textual appropriation becomes a profoundly existential undertaking, one that challenges readers, for example, with the limitations of the text and therefore with the limitations of reading also. Reading, in these circumstances, is less a question of literary theory than of operative theology itself. At least, that is what the author of Matthew's Gospel appears to have had in view.

---

[39] Further indicated by explicit reference to disciples as υἱοὶ θεοῦ (5:9) and υἱοὶ τοῦ πατρός (5:45); cf. 7:9-11; 13:38; 17:25-6. As Thompson ("God's Voice You Have Never Heard," 200) observes concerning the characterization of God in John's Gospel, "the story functions not so much by giving information about God, although much about God is assumed or implied in the text, as by drawing the reader into the narrative so that the reader will understand God from the point of view of the narrator and Jesus, the principal character."

[40] For discussion of oral and literary modes of reception for Matthew's text, see Knowles, "Reading Matthew," *passim*.

8

(Re)Positioning Power through Faith: Dyadic Power Theory, the Roman Centurion, and Jesus in Matthew 8:5-13

Justin Marc Smith

I. Introduction

As Jennings and Liew have observed, "In the history of modern Matthean scholarship, interpretations of Matt 8:5-13 have generally been straightforward. The Roman centurion demonstrates his 'great faith' with his 'impressive' analogy of Jesus' identity and authority; as a result, the centurion receives from Jesus a healing for his beloved 'servant.'"[1] The recognition of the centurion's faith fits within the larger presentation of the gentiles as generally being demonstrative of faith in Matthew's Gospel.[2] Narrative critics have typically folded the characters in Matthew into the rather broad categories of Jesus, the disciples, the Pharisees and the crowds (with some differentiation).[3] Janice

---

[1] Theodore W. Jennings Jr. and Tat-Song Benny Liew, "Mistaken Identities but Model Faith: Rereading The Centurion, The Chap, and The Christ in Matthew 8:5-13," *JBL* 123, no. 3 (2004): 467-94 (467). See their significant footnote on pages 467-8 (n. 1) detailing the history of the treatment of the subject of the centurion.

[2] John A. Barnet, *Not the Righteous but Sinners: M.M. Bakhtin's Theory of Aesthetics and the Problem of Reader-Character Interaction in Matthew's Gospel*, LNTS 246 (London: T&T Clark, 2003). See Luke Macnamara, "Characterisation in the Gospels and Acts: A Review of Recent Studies," *Proceedings of the Irish Biblical Association* 41-2 (2020): 44-59. By gentile I am referring to anyone who would not identify or be identified as being part of Israel. Simply put, gentiles would be "non-Jews." See Kelly R. Iverson, "Gentiles," in *The Dictionary of Jesus and the Gospels*, ed. J. B. Greed, J. K. Brown, and N. Perrin (Downers Grove, IL: IVP Academic, 2013), 302-9; 302 and esp. 304-5 for discussion on gentiles in Matthew. Faith in this context is defined as "a bond of trust, inspired by what [individuals] first and subsequently heard and saw Jesus say and do." James D. G. Dunn, *Christianity in The Making*, Vol. 1: *Jesus Remembered* (Grand Rapids, MI: Eerdmans, 2003), 132. This would function well in this context as the centurion is presented as one who is aware of Jesus' ability to heal prior to encountering him.

[3] Barnet, *Not the Righteous but Sinners*, 2-3. See Janice Capel Anderson, "Matthew: Gender and Reading," *Semeia* 28 (1983): 3-27 (10-11). See Jack Dean Kingsbury, *Matthew as Story*, 2nd edn (Philadelphia: Fortress Press, 1988), 10; Paul S. Minear, *Matthew: The Teacher's Gospel* (New York: Pilgrim Press, 1982), 10-11; and David R. Bauer, "The Major Characters of Matthew's Story: Their Function and Significance," *Int* 46 (1992): 357-67.

Capel Anderson's five-fold grouping includes a separate treatment of the gentiles.[4] The advantage here is the recognition of the diverse presentations of gentiles in Matthew. I would argue here that in the case of the centurion, there has been a tendency by modern critics to "flatten" him as a character.[5] As a way to investigate the traits of characters in the gospels that appear infrequently or have short interactions in the narrative, interdisciplinary approaches continue to be of use.[6]

The characterization of the centurion will be assessed using historical, literary, and psychological approaches. Rüggemeier and Shively have argued the following concerning a well-defined interdisciplinary approach to characterization:

> While historical and literary approaches provide us with necessary cultural, linguistic, textual, and rhetorical tools for describing characters, what we need is an accompanying cognitive model to explain the complex mental and emotional processing involved in characterization.[7]

While this chapter will not attempt to address the specific interdisciplinary approach that Rüggemeier and Shively propose, I *will* attempt to draw together historical, literary, and psychological approaches in a way that might prove to be fruitful going forward as we continue to consider how characters and characterization might be engaged in a

---

[4] Anderson, "Matthew," 10–11. Barnet's folding of the gentiles into the larger category of crowds with a recognition of gentiles as supplicants may not accurately portray the diversity found within the larger group of "gentiles" in Matthew's gospel: Barnet, *Not the Righteous but Sinners*, 3–4. For some initial discussion of character/characterization, see Fred W. Burnett, "Characterization and Reader Construction of Characters in the Gospels," *Semeia* 63 (1993): 1–28.

[5] Jeannine K. Brown, *The Gospels as Stories: A Narrative Approach to Matthew, Mark, Luke, and John* (Grand Rapids, MI: Baker, 2020), 68–71. Here Brown offers a helpful discussion of ancient and modern characterization. I recognize that the terms "flat" and "round" to describe characters has generally been abandoned by narrative critics with a preference for seeing characters on a spectrum, with characters as more or less dynamic. However, there can still be a tendency to flatten characters even if that language is being employed less. See Michael R. Whittenton, *Configuring Nicodemus: An Interdisciplinary Approach to Complex Characterization*, LNTS 549 (London: T&T Clark, 2019), 40–4. His discussion of character development in the ancient world would be of special interest to those who would argue that characters in Greco-Roman literature were essentially static. This would affect the potential to see development in the centurion in Mt. 8:5-13.

[6] There has been some helpful work done on interdisciplinary approaches to the gospels recently (particularly using cognitive approaches). See Whittenton, *Configuring Nicodemus*, 11–54; Elizabeth E. Shively, "Becoming a Disciple without Seeing Jesus: Narrative as a Way of Knowing in Mark's Gospel," in *Let the Reader Understand: Studies in Honor of Elizabeth Struthers Malbon*, ed. E. K. Broadhead (New York: T&T Clark, 2018), 35–50; Jan Rüggemeier and Elizabeth E. Shively, "Introduction: Towards a Cognitive Theory of New Testament Characters: Methodology, Problems, and Desiderata," *BibInt* 29, no. 4–5 (2021): 403–29; Jan Rüggemeier, *Poetik der markinischen Christologie. Eine kognitiv-narratologische Exegese*, WUNT II 458 (Tübingen: Mohr Siebeck, 2017); Michael R. Whitenton, *Hearing Kyriotic Sonship: A Cognitive and Rhetorical Approach to the Characterization of Mark's Jesus*, Biblical Interpretation Series 148 (Leiden: Brill, 2016). See also Michal Beth Dinkler, "Building Character on the Road to Emmaus: Lukan Characterization in Contemporary Literary Perspective," *JBL* 136, no. 3 (2017): 687–706, esp. 687–706; "New Testament Rhetorical Narratology: An Invitation toward Integration," *BibInt* 24, no. 2 (2016): 203–28; Michal Beth Dinkler, "A New Formalist Approach to Narrative Christology: Returning to the Structure of the Synoptic Gospels," *HTS Teologiese Studies/ Theological Studies* 73 (2017): 1–11.

[7] Rüggemeier and Shively "Introduction," 410–11.

more dynamic way. The outcome here is not innovative: the centurion *is* demonstrative of faith. However, that conclusion becomes clear not through tropes or flattened characterizations alone, but through examining the interpersonal power dynamics (and developments) between Jesus and the centurion as presented in this Matthean pericope.

II. Dyadic Power Theory

Bertrand Russel has argued that "the fundamental concept in social science is Power, in the same way that Energy is the fundamental concept in physics."[8] Power is of special significance in personal relationships and inter-personal interactions because of the interdependence that stems from the way that individuals need others "to attain their goals" and how "this dependence creates power."[9] In assessing how power is used (and abused) in relationships, Norah Dunbar has proposed an updated version of power theory that reworks versions of the theory of power first put forth by Rollins and Bahr, which she terms: Dyadic Power Theory (DPT).[10] Central to DPT is the definition of power. The definition of power as it is employed in this chapter is "the capacity to produce intended effects, and in particular the ability to influence the behavior of another person."[11] Power is further broken down into three domains: "power bases," "power processes," and "power outcomes."[12] Power bases refer to the kinds of resources that are often used as the basis of control in relationships.[13] Power processes detail "the

---

[8] Bertrand Russel, *Power: A New Social Analysis* (New York: Norton, 1938), 10. See Norah E. Dunbar, "Dyadic Power Theory: Constructing a Communication-Based Theory of Relational Power," *Journal of Family Communication* 4, no. 3 (2004): 235-48 (235). This quotation is faithful to the capitalization in the original text.

[9] Dunbar, "Dyadic Power Theory," 235-6. See Linda D. Molm, "The Conversion of Power Imbalance to Power Use," *Social Psychology Quarterly* 51, no. 2 (1988): 108-22.

[10] Dunbar, "Dyadic Power Theory," 235-6. See Boyd C. Rollins and Stephen J. Bahr, "A Theory of Power in Relationships in Marriage," *Journal of Marriage and the Family* 38 (1976): 619-27. Much of the foundation for DPT comes from research into the power dynamics of marriages and family relationships. However, many of the conclusions reached and propositions offered by DPT work well to describe power interactions in even casual relationships and interactions. Dunbar, Lane and Abra note how DPT functions in the interactions of strangers and the results fit with the overall understanding of how power works according to DPT. See Norah E. Dunbar, Brianna Lane, and Gordon Abra, "Power in Close Relationships: A Dyadic Power Theory Perspective," in *Communicating Interpersonal Conflict in Close Relationships: Contexts, Challenges, and Opportunities*, ed. Jennifer A. Samp (New York: Routledge, 2017), 75-92; esp. 81-2.

[11] Dunbar, "Dyadic Power Theory," 235-6. Dunbar notes that some necessary distinguishing elements of power (manifest power, latent power, and invisible power) have been put forth by Aafke Komter, "Hidden Power in Marriage," *Gender and Society* 3, no. 2 (1989): 187-216. It might be of interest to consider how these elements of power might be at play in the interaction between Jesus and the centurion in Mt. 8:5-13. Here, manifest power is most readily seen ("visible outcomes of power") but latent and invisible power might be at play as well: Dunbar, "Dynamic Power Theory," 236.

[12] Dunbar, "Dynamic Power Theory," 237. See Bernadette Gray-Little and Nancy Burks, "Power and Manifestation in Marriage: A Review and Critique," *Psychological Bulletin* 93 (1983), 513-38.

[13] This would include "reward power and coercive power, which represents a person's right to reward and punish; legitimate power, derived from holding a high-status position sanctioned by society; referent power, held when others admire and emulate a person; and expert power, which is derived from having knowledge in a needed field": Dunbar, "Dynamic Power Theory," 237. See John R. P.

specific strategies used to exert power in interactions such as decision making, problem solving, and conflict management."[14] The third and final domain, power outcomes, "refers to the resulting influence on others' thoughts, beliefs, and actions and includes the results of decision making in terms of who makes the decision or who 'wins.'"[15] All of the aforementioned dynamics of power come into play within DPT.[16] Dunbar builds out DPT on a number of theoretical definitions:

> *Power* is the ability or potential to influence or control the behavior of another person. Consistent with previous theorizing about power, this is considered to be a perception of one's own capacity relative to an interaction partner, not an absolute.[17] *Control attempts* are attempts by one person to change the behavior of another ... Individuals may use any behavior as a means of attempting control including dominance ... stonewalling or withdrawal ... or non-negotiation ... *Counter-control attempts* are responses to control attempts from an individual's interaction partner.[18] *Control* has occurred when actual compliance follows a control attempt. *Authority* refers to norms regarding who "ought to" control different situations in a relationship. These are culturally accepted norms, based partially on status, to which interaction partners adhere. *Resources* are anything that one partner makes available to the other, helping the latter satisfy needs or

---

French and Bertram Raven, "The Bases of Social Power," in *Studies in Social Power*, ed. D. Cartwright (Ann Arbor, MI: Institute for Social Research, 1959), 150–67. French and Raven are responsible for the seminal work on power bases. Of interest here would be Jesus in relationship to the centurion in terms of power bases. Both Jesus and the centurion would seem to operate from different power bases: the centurion from the base of legitimate power (as described here) and Jesus (and possibly the centurion) from the base of referent power (if we imagine that Jesus was one who was admired and emulated), and Jesus alone from the base of expert power (derived from the knowledge of healing). Subsequently, informational power and credibility power have been added to the list above by some theorists: Dunbar, "Dynamic Power Theory," 237.

[14] These strategies can include "dominance behaviors" that include physical behaviors as well as various psychological behaviors ("stonewalling," "withdrawal," or "non-negotiation": Dunbar, "Dynamic Power Theory," 237.

[15] Dunbar, "Dynamic Power Theory," 237. See Ronald E. Cromwell and David H. Olsen, "Power in Families," in *Power in Families*, ed. Ronald E. Cromwell and David H. Olsen (Beverly Hills, CA: Sage, 1975), 3–11. If we were to conceive of who "wins" in the interaction between Jesus and the centurion, we might envision a win–win situation. The centurion wins by having his servant healed and Jesus wins through reorienting the interaction away from power and towards faith.

[16] See Dunbar, "Dynamic Power Theory," 238, for a discussion on where DPT intersects with other theories of power in close relationships.

[17] The power for the centurion stemming from his power bases would be contrasted with the lack of power to heal and the need for Jesus to intervene.

[18] Dunbar notes that "partner" typically has romantic connotations, but this not need be the case as this can apply to any number of relationships including casual ones: Dunbar, "Dynamic Power Theory," 239. It could be the case that the centurion's seeking healing from Jesus (Mt. 8:5-6) can be seen as a control attempt (based on the definitions provided through DPT); Jesus' initial response in Mt. 5:7, if understood as a question (Ἐγὼ ἐλθὼν θεραπεύσω αὐτόν—Am I to come and heal him?), could be seen as a counter-control attempt and a pushback on the centurion's request/control attempt. See W. D. Davies and Dale C. Allison Jr., *A Critical and Exegetical Commentary on the Gospel According to Saint Matthew*, 3 vols., ICC (Edinburgh: T&T Clark, 1988–97), 2:21-2; Anthony Saldarini, *Matthew's Christian-Jewish Community*, CSHJ (Chicago: University of Chicago Press, 1994), 72, n. 16; and Donald Senior, "Between Two Worlds: Jewish Christians and Gentiles in Matthew's Gospel," *CBQ* 61, no.1 (1999): 1–23; esp. 17, n. 36.

attain goals. Finally, the term relative is used to refer to power differences between partners in relation to each other.[19]

Combined with these definitions, Dunbar builds DPT on a number of assumptions related to power dynamics. The most relevant assumptions here would be that; 1) "the resources, authority, and power of the individual are less important than the perception of relative differences;" 2) "that power and control are relevant constructs in relationships primarily, but not exclusively, when conflict arises"; and 3) "that people are rational, goal-oriented individuals who form their own perceptions about their position in the relationship and then use those perceptions to plan out strategies and carry out those strategies for influencing others."[20] One of the chief benefits of DPT is precisely the ability to address power dynamics in the absence of overt conflict. It is unclear from the context of the pericope (Mt. 8:5-13) if there is inherent personal conflict between Jesus and the centurion, apart from the larger Roman–Jewish conflicts of the period, and we need not presume such a conflict between the two. Instead, we may notice how power is being negotiated and renegotiated in their interaction, while acknowledging the possibility of positive outcomes for both.

The final element of DPT as presented by Dunbar is a series of propositions:

P1. Increases in relative authority are related to increases in relative resources.

P2. Increases in relative resources produce increases in relative power.

P3. Increases in relative authority produce increases in relative power.

P4. The relation between perceived relative power and control attempts is curvilinear such that partners who perceive their relative power as extremely high or low will make fewer control attempts, although partners who perceive their relative power as equal or nearly equal will make more control attempts.

P5. An increase in the number of control attempts will produce a greater probability of an increase in the amount of control.

P6. As a partner's perception of his (her) own power relative to that of his (her) partner increases, his (her) counter-control attempts will increase.

P7. Counter-control attempts have a negative effect on control for the initiation of the original control attempt.

P8. The relation between perceived relative power and satisfaction in curvilinear such that partners who perceive their relative power as extremely high or low will report lower levels of satisfaction compared to partners who perceive the relative power differences as small or moderate.[21]

---

[19] Dunbar, "Dynamic Power Theory," 238-9. Italics are original to Dunbar.
[20] Dunbar, "Dynamic Power Theory," 239-40.
[21] Dunbar, "Dynamic Power Theory," 240-2. See Dunbar, Lane, and Abra, "Power in Close Relationships," 86-8, where four more propositions (P9-P12) are added to this model. One proposition, proposition 9, would be of most interest here: "P9: Control/counter-control attempts will be more frequent in high-high dyads than low-low dyads": Dunbar, Lane, and Abra, "Power in Close Relationships," 86. Here we would expect Jesus and the centurion, both operating from bases of relative power, to have multiple control and counter-control attempts.

Some important observations emerge here as it relates to DPT and specifically as it is related to the interactions between Jesus and the centurion in Mt. 8:5-13. P4 draws out the concept that interactors who understand their power to be relatively balanced will seek to make more control attempts. This may help shape our reading of Jesus and the centurion as it relates to the back-and-forth of their interaction. P5-P7 are notable as they relate to both the number of attempts on the part of the centurion as well as the effect that Jesus' question regarding coming to the centurion's home may have had on the centurion himself. The application of DPT in this specific instance may produce both a deeper appreciation of the power dynamics at play in this narrative and a deeper appreciation of the potential for reorienting those dynamics away from power and towards faith.

III. The Roman Centurion in Matthew 8:5-13

As previously mentioned, there has been no shortage of literature on characters and characterization in the gospels broadly and on characters in Matthew specifically. Drawing from the work of Hylan, Powell, and Malbon, Brown puts forth the following list of the ways that authors portray their characters: 1) "what a character says"; 2) "what a character does"; 3) "what other characters say in relation to that character"; 4) "what other characters do in relations to that character"; 5) the narrator's (implied author's) more direct characterization"; 6) "social realities outside the narrative relevant to the character, construed by readers"; and 7) "other potentially relevant points of comparison or illumination: settings, plot, themes."[22] Brown's approach here is especially advantageous as it relates to assessing the power dynamics of the interaction between Jesus and the centurion in Mt. 8:5-13. The interactions between Jesus and the centurion, in many ways, revolve around the actions of the two combined with their words (control attempts and counter-control attempts). What these characters do and say in this context are shaped by the contours of DPT and provide a framework through which to interpret both the characters and their interaction. Further, Brown offers a helpful corrective that we as modern readers should exercise restraint in seeking to "psychologize biblical characters."[23] Even though I am employing theory from psychology I will endeavor to avoid trips into the mind of either Jesus or the centurion. My purpose here is not to try to draw out the inner motivations of the

---

[22] Brown, *The Gospels as Stories*, 72–3. See Susan E. Hylan, "The Disciples: The 'Now' and the 'Not Yet' of Belief in Jesus," in *Character Studies in The Fourth Gospel: Narrative Approaches to Seventy Figures in John*, ed. Steven A. Hunt, D. Francois Tolmie, and Ruben Zimmerman (Grand Rapids, MI: Eerdmans, 2016), 214-27; esp. 217–23; Mark Allan Powell, "Characterization and the Phraseological Plane of the Gospel of Matthew," in *Treasures Old and New*, ed. David R. Bauer and Mark Allan Powell, SBLSymS 1 (Atlanta: SBL Press, 1996), 161–77; and Elizabeth Struthers Malbon, *Characterization as Narrative Christology* (Waco, TX: Baylor University Press, 2009). See Kelly R. Iverson, *The Gentiles in Mark: "Even the Dogs Under the Table Eat the Children's Crumbs,"* LNTS 339 (London: T&T Clark, 2007), 5-9. With special attention given to the discussion on page 9 as it relates to the revealing of character traits in J. F. Williams, *Other Followers of Jesus: Minor Characters as Major Figures in Mark's Gospel*, JSNTSup,102 (Sheffield: JSOT Press, 1994), 61–7.

[23] Brown, *The Gospels as Stories*, 70.

centurion but to assess his words and actions in the light of DPT and how that illuminates his characterization in Matthew.[24]

A. Characterizing the Centurion: Establishing Power Base(s)

One way that we might begin to understand the centurion as a character is by assessing the role of the Roman military presence in Palestine from roughly 37 BCE to 44 CE. This time frame covers the reigns of Herod the Great, Herod Antipas, and Agrippa I. It is interesting to note that there was not a significant Roman military presence (in terms of legions) in Galilee in this period, the period that covers the ministry of Jesus.[25] Zeichmann argues persuasively that the likely military role of the centurion in Mt. 8:5-13 would have been one of offering "protection to customs agents and toll collectors"[26] The location of Capernaum as a border town would have been an advantageous site for a "regional centurion" to oversee many of the issues that would be common to a town on international borders.[27] It is unlikely then that the centurion would have been attached to a specific legion (as there is little evidence to suggest one was stationed in Capernaum during the reign of Antipas); rather, he would have been one of a few centurions embedded in the royal army of Antipas and so his presence in Capernaum would have been somewhat distinct (if not unexpected) both due to his military role and his ethnicity (gentile).[28]

---

[24] I would also prefer to avoid static characterization and seek to view the centurion as somewhere on a spectrum of more or less complex. See Brown, *The Gospels as Stories*, 68–71. I am not arguing that DPT would necessarily have been recognized in the interactions of first-century Palestine nor that it would have been recognized by the actors (real or literary). However, DPT has the potential to draw out deeper meanings of the actions of the characters in this narrative.

[25] Christopher B. Zeichmann, *The Roman Army and the New Testament* (Lanham, MD: Lexington Books, 2018), 23–48; esp. the table on 32–3. Zeichman notes that there was no significant presence of Roman legions in Capernaum after the war (post-70 CE). He writes, "Given the tensions in Roman–Jewish relations after the war, it was deemed better to prepare for the worst than to attempt repair of the relationship. Legionaries were concentrated in massive garrisons with far fewer soldiers in minor sites; should another revolt break out, Rome would control access to financial resources, food stores, strategic sites, etc. These smaller detachments were placed to address concerns other than patrolling and policing. The Healing of the Centurion's Slave (Q/Luke 7:1-10, Matt. 8:5-13), for instance, is plausible in its depiction of an officer in Capernaum": Zeichmann, *The Roman Army and the New Testament*, 31. The pre-70 CE military presence in Capernaum (the time frame envisaged in the pericope) and the post-70 CE military presence in Capernaum (the likely time frame for the actual writing of Matthew) would be nearly identical. See Warren Carter, "Matthew 4:18-22 and Matthean Discipleship: An Audience-Oriented Perspective," *CBQ* 51, no.1 (1997): 58–75, for discussion of audience-oriented approaches to reading Matthew; and Charles L. Quarles, "The Oath Formulas of Matthew 23:16-22 as Evidence for a Pre-70 Date of Composition for Matthew's Gospel," *TynBul* 72 (2021): 1–24, for discussion of a pre-70 composition of the Gospel of Matthew.

[26] Zeichmann, *The Roman Army and the New Testament*, 67. Cf. figure 2.1 on page 30 for a map of pre- and post-70 CE Roman military sites in Palestine.

[27] Zeichmann, *The Roman Army and the New Testament*, 67–8.

[28] The ethnicity of the centurion is more specifically expressed in the parallel account in Lk. 7:1-10, where the centurion is contrasted with the Jewish elders he sends to Jesus on his behalf (Lk. 7:3-5). However, the ethnicity of the centurion may be established indirectly through Jesus' declaration concerning the faith of the centurion vis-à-vis Israel (Mt. 8:10-12). See Zeichmann, *The Roman Army and the New Testament*, 67.

The centurion as part of the narrative of the Gospel of Matthew would have an established base of power through "legitimate power, derived from holding a high-status position sanctioned by society" and likely some "referent power, held when others admire and emulate a person."[29] Given the role of the centurion as part of the royal army of Antipas as well as his duties of protection, it is not difficult to conceive of legitimate power as constituting his base of power. Referent power for the centurion might be more difficult to establish. However, if we entertain the reputational status of the centurion in the parallel account in Lk. 7:1-10, we could support the proposition that the centurion also derives power from his positive reputation in the community at Capernaum.[30] At the very least, his prominent role in the life of the local community (as a Roman centurion) could signal him as one worthy of emulation and that could establish a base of referent power. Thus, when the centurion approaches Jesus, he does so from an established base of power and is presented as one who speaks from within institutionalized power, albeit he is powerless to affect the healing he requires.

B. Characterizing the Centurion: Control Attempts and Counter-Control Attempts

As the narrative (8:5-13) opens, the centurion approaches Jesus as Jesus is entering the town (v. 5). Here, the centurion calls to Jesus and exhorts him to heal his servant (παῖς).[31] This exhortation to help is best understood as a control attempt and Dunbar has argued that, "when dyads are generally equal in power, the participants may be more likely to use control attempts."[32] The perceived power of the centurion leads him to initiate an exchange whereby he seeks a control outcome (compliance through healing) on the part of Jesus. It is interesting to note that the posturing of the centurion is not indicative of supplication, but rather that the use of the control attempt on his part appears to come from a powered position and not a disempowered position.[33] His reference to Jesus as "Lord" (Κύριε) indicates some deference to Jesus on the part of the centurion, but his interaction with Jesus does not model the deference of his address.[34] Glancy notes that in the Roman world, "the image of one person sunk on the ground

---

[29] Dunbar, "Dynamic Power Theory," 237. See Iverson, *The Gentiles in Mark*, 5-9, for a discussion of characters as both real and literary. See Seymour B. Chatman, *Story and Discourse: Narrative Structure in Fiction and Film* (Ithaca, NY: Cornell University Press, 1978), 96-145; esp. 119.

[30] It is widely accepted (even if the Q thesis is still under debate) that the narrative of the healing of the centurion's servant is derived from Q. See Steven R. Johnson (ed.), *Q 7:1-10: The Centurion's Faith in Jesus' Word*, Documenta Q (Leuven, Belgium: Peeters, 2002).

[31] The semantic range of παρακαλέω (translated in the NRSV as "appealing") is interesting here. It can carry the meaning of appeal but also the meaning of calling or summoning. It might be the case that as the narrative begins, the centurion summons Jesus to help, expressing his desire for healing from a position of power, utilizing that power to express a control attempt (according to DPT). Luz sees the centurion as "accosting" Jesus: Ulrich Luz, *Matthew 8-20: A Commentary on the Gospel of Matthew*, 3 vols., Hermeneia (Minneapolis: Fortress Press, 2001-7), 2:9.

[32] Dunbar, "Dynamic Power Theory," 241.

[33] See Jennifer A. Glancy, "Jesus, the Syrophoenician Woman, and Other First Century Bodies," *BibInt* 18 (2010): 342-63. According to DPT Proposition 4, "partners who perceive their relative power as equal or nearly equal will make more control attempts": Dunbar, "Dynamic Power Theory," 240.

[34] Davies and Allison, *Matthew*, 2:20.

in the presence of another person was the most common visual marker for submission to superior power and authority." Furthermore, "deference and authority are negotiated through posture and gesture as well as through words. Such negotiations of the hierarchies of power and social status would have been familiar to Mark's readers and indeed throughout the Roman Empire."[35] While Glancy is referencing the act of physical supplication in Mk 7:24-30, the implications would resonate in Matthew. For instance, In Mt. 15:25, after the Canaanite woman initiates a control attempt (shouting after Jesus; 15:22) and after Jesus initiates two counter-control attempts (silence—15:23; and rebuttal—15:24), the Canaanite woman kneels (προσεκύνει) before Jesus. The centurion in Matthew does not demonstrate such deference. Jesus' counter-control attempts reorients the woman who has "relative privilege."[36] Jesus' counter-control attempts will similarly reorient the centurion.

Jesus' response to the centurion in verse 7 may best be understood as a question ('Ἐγὼ ἐλθὼν θεραπεύσω αὐτόν—"Am I to come and heal him?").[37] Jesus would seem to be operating from a similarly powered position (referent power and expert power) and as such is more inclined to engage in counter-control attempts.[38] As Proposition 6 (DPT) suggests, those in relational exchanges will attempt more counter-control attempts as they see their relative power to be (more) equal to that of their relational exchange partner.[39] Two interesting observations follow from this:

> The logic of Proposition 6 and Proposition 7 rests on the assumption that the recipient of the control attempt chooses an appropriate response based on his or her perceptions of the power of the initiator of the original control attempt. If the initiator is perceived to be relatively powerful, then the control attempt is more likely to be met with compliance. If the initiator is perceived to be relatively powerless, then the recipient is more likely to make a counter-control attempt that reduces the effectiveness of the original control attempt ... Although, individuals extremely high in power do not necessarily need to make counter-control attempts to attain control, those same individuals will feel a need to respond to attempts to usurp their power by less powerful individuals.[40]

Jesus' responding question is appropriate given his relative power (an expert healer and one who manifests divine power; Mt. 3:13-17; 12:28) and the relative powerlessness of

---

[35] Glancy, "Jesus, the Syrophoenician Woman, and Other First Century Bodies," 354.
[36] Glancy, "Jesus, the Syrophoenician Woman, and Other First Century Bodies," 351–2.
[37] Davies and Allison, *Matthew*, 2:21-2; W. F. Albright and C. S. Mann, *Matthew: A New Translation with Introduction and Commentary*, 1st edn, AB 26 (Garden City, NY: Yale University Press, 1971), 93; Saldarini, *Matthew's Christian–Jewish Community*, 72, n. 16; Senior, "Between Two Worlds," 17 n. 36; and Jennings and Liew, "Mistaken Identities," 478–84.
[38] Jesus as an established healer (8:1-4, 5–13, 14–15, 16–17; 9:1-8, 20–2, 27–31, 32–4; 12:9-14, 22-3; 14:34-6; 15:21-8; and 17:14-20) would exhibit expert power; one caveat would be the establishment of that expertise by the time this narrative unfolds. See Matthew 4:23-5 and R. T. France, *The Gospel of Matthew*, NICNT (Grand Rapids, MI: Eerdmans, 2007), 299-300. Referent power could be established through Jesus' "ethical" teachings in Mt. 5:1–7:28.
[39] Dunbar, "Dynamic Power Theory," 242.
[40] Dunbar, "Dynamic Power Theory," 242.

the centurion in his current situation. Jesus' counter-control attempt is rather subtle in that he asks if he should come and heal the servant. This exposes both the cultural space Jesus is being asked to traverse (Jewish–gentile) and the power imbalance that the centurion has not yet fully acknowledged. Jesus reorients the interaction in such a way as to draw the centurion into a deeper understanding of his total powerlessness (an inability to heal) in this instance.

The centurion's counter-control attempt toward Jesus again stems from his understanding of his relative power being essentially equal to that of Jesus. In verses 8-9 the centurion again addresses Jesus as "Lord" (Κύριε), but this time the reference is contextualized within a greater understanding of the centurion's own powerlessness. Here he states that he is both disempowered ("under authority" —ὑπὸ ἐξουσίαν) and empowered as he has servants and soldiers under him. The centurion verbally acknowledges in this exchange that his relative power is diminished (vv. 8-9) and thus he is less likely to seek another control/counter-control attempt.[41] Combined with this is his recognition of both his own unworthiness (a voluntary verbal supplication) and that Jesus' relative power as it relates to healing far surpasses the centurion's own relative power in other matters. To draw this back to DPT, "a person's perception of relative power influences the number of control attempts he or she makes (and the type of strategies he or she uses) toward a partner, and those control attempts influence the amount of compliance obtained from the partner."[42] Jesus complies with the centurion, not because he is compelled by the centurion's use of power, but because of the centurion's demonstration of faith (vv. 10-13).[43]

The reading of the centurion as one who is faithful or demonstrative of faith is accurate. The move towards faith, however, may be a bit more complex than some of the flatter readings of this pericope have assumed. Certainly, the centurion is commended for his faith, and the connection between faith and powerful outcomes is a significant theme in Matthew's Gospel, one that is exhibited a number of times elsewhere (here in 8:10-13; 9:2—the healing of the paralytic; 9:22—the healing of the woman with irregular bleeding; 9:29—the healing of two blind men; 15:28—the healing of the Canaanite woman's daughter; 21:21-2—faith to "move mountains"). This connection between faith and dynamic power can also be seen in the examples of "little faith."[44] Perhaps there is a deeper connection between power and faith here, as these are not two mutually exclusive realms. For the centurion, the attempt to exert influence over Jesus from a position of power moves the centurion toward a more significant

---

[41] The centurion has the power to use his words to command soldiers and servants, but he does not have the power to use his words to command healing; only Jesus is able to do that.

[42] Dunbar, "Dynamic Power Theory," 242.

[43] Jennings and Liew, "Mistaken Identities," 484–92, see the faith of the centurion not as grounded in a correct understanding of who Jesus is as a divine representative of God. Rather, the centurion understands Jesus to have power over demonic forces in a way that is similar to the understanding of the Pharisees elsewhere in Matthew (12:22-32). Thus, according to Jennings and Liew, the centurion's faith is found in his actions (seeking healing for his beloved servant) over and against whatever his beliefs about Jesus and the source of Jesus' power might be.

[44] There is some chastisement to be found at 6:21 in reference to worry. But the more significant examples are at 8:26 (stilling of the storm); 14:31 (Peter walking on water); 16:8 (disciples worrying about having bread); and 23:23 (critique of the Pharisees for neglecting faith).

stance of faith. The centurion is more fully oriented toward his own powerlessness through the counter-control attempts of Jesus. His appeal moves from one based in power to one based in powerlessness. Jesus breaks the cycle of control attempts and counter-control attempts by acknowledging the faith of the centurion and shifting the interaction toward a positive outcome for both parties. Jesus demonstrates power, but in a way that is more equalizing than demoralizing, and the centurion's initial recognition of Jesus' capability to heal and his eventual verbalizing of his own powerlessness to heal (albeit through the language of power and authority) are indicative of his reorientation towards faith.

IV. Excursus on Power: The Centurion's Servant

It is difficult to conclude a discussion on power in interpersonal interactions in Mt. 8:5-13 without making some comments about the centurion's servant. Although there has been a fair amount written concerning the nature of the relationship between the centurion and the servant, the three most common suggestions are that the servant is a son, a servant, or a lover.[45] While it is difficult to know the exact nature of the relationship between the centurion and the παῖς, it should be remembered that there is broad evidence to suggest the use and abuse of servants for sexual ends by their owners in the ancient world.[46] And, while historically plausible, the idea that the centurion and his servant are in a pederastic relationship as suggested by Jennings and Liew has

---

[45] For "son," see Donald Hagner, *Matthew 1-13*, WBC 33A (Dallas: Word Books, 1991), 204; Luz, *Matthew 8-20*, 10; for "servant," see Albright and Mann, *Matthew*, 93; Davies and Allison, *Matthew*, 2:20-1; Craig Keener, *Matthew*, IVP New Testament Commentary Series (Downers Grove, IL: InterVarsity Press, 1997), 172. Keener also notes that centurions would not have been allowed families contra Hagner. See Zeichmann, *The Roman Army and the New Testament*, 10); Donald Senior, *Matthew*, ANTC (Nashville, TN: Abingdon Press, 1998), 98; France, *Matthew*, 310-31; and David L. Turner, *Matthew*, BECNT (Grand Rapids, MI: Baker Academic, 2008), 228; and for "lover," see Jennings and Liew, "Mistaken Identities," 468-78. See Christopher Zeichmann, "Rethinking the Gay Centurion—Sexual Exceptionalism, National Exceptionalism in Readings of Matt. 8:5-13//Luke 7:1-10," *Bible & Critical Theory* 11, no. 1 (2015): 35-54. Zeichmann notes, "Nevertheless, this reading is consistently overlooked in NT scholarship; no serialized commentaries even address the interpretation and Jennings and Liew's article (2004) in the Journal of Biblical Literature remains the only work in a major biblical studies journal to advocate the LGBT reading": Zeichmann, "Rethinking the Gay Centurion," 37. See Michael Gray-Fow, "Pederasty, the Scantian Law and the Roman Army," *Journal of Psychohistory* 13, no. 4 (1986): 449-60; Donald Mader, "The Entimos Pais of Matthew 8:5-13 and Luke 7:1-10," *Paidika: Journal of Paedophilia* 1 (1987): 27-39; "The Entimos Pais of Matthew 8:5-13 and Luke 7:1-10," in *Homosexuality and Religion and Philosophy*, ed. Wayne R. Dynes and Stephen Donaldson, Studies in Homosexuality 12 (New York: Garland, 1992), 223-35; J. Martignac, "Le centurion de Capernaüm," *Arcadie* 22 (1974): 117-28; Michel Mayer, "Le procurateur de Judée: Suite à la manière d'Anatole France," *Arcadie* 12 (1965): 63-71; Parker Rossman, *Sexual Experience Between Men and Boys: Exploring the Pederast Underground* (New York: Associations, 1965), 99; and Tom M. Horner, "Jesus" in *Encyclopedia of Homosexuality*, Vol. 2, ed. Wayne R. Dynes (New York: Garland, 1990), 635-9.

[46] Similar to Zeichmann, there is no indictment here nor is there an attempt to undermine Queer politics or interpretation: Zeichmann, *The Roman Army and the New Testament*, 68. There is significant evidence on the sexual abuse of slaves by their owners and that could also inform a reading of this narrative. Jennings and Liew assume that the sexual relationship is mutual and not coercive. The centurion may have had romantic feelings but did his servant? See Richard A. Horsley,

garnered little acceptance among New Testament scholars. For example, both Saddington and Zeichmann have offered rebuttals based primarily on Jennings and Liew's misapplication of primary Roman sources and military attitudes to the context of Mt. 8:5-13.[47] The crux of their arguments center on the fact that the centurion in this narrative would have been an auxiliary soldier and not a legionary and that the overall political and cultural contexts of the centurion would have differed significantly from the examples cited by Jennings and Liew.[48]

Regardless of the exact nature of the relationship between the centurion and his servant, this pericope is fundamentally one about power and its abuse. Here, Jesus and the centurion have engaged in an interpersonal encounter that is negotiated and mediated through control attempts and counter-control attempts, with the outcome being positive for both Jesus and the centurion. In the midst of this is an unnamed, silent, unempowered and immobilized παῖς. The servant is the one at the heart of the interaction but who has no agency in it. As our reading and characterization of the centurion has focused on the loci of power and faith, the disempowered and silent should be remembered, even if they cannot speak.

V. Conclusion

Recalling Brown, the assessment of any character can begin with the following concerns: 1) "what a character says"; 2) "what a character does"; 3) "what other characters say in relation to that character"; 4) "what other characters do in relations to that character"; 5) "the narrator's (implied author's) more direct characterization"; 6) "social realities outside the narrative relevant to the character, construed by readers"; and 7) "other potentially relevant points of comparison or illumination: settings, plot, themes."[49] Narrative approaches to characterization have yielded significant insights into the text by employing questions such as these. The reading of the centurion as one example of a faithful gentile in Matthew's Gospel is confirmed by the answers to these questions. The centurion speaks in such a way that exemplifies his faith (8:8-9); he acts

---

"The Slave Systems of Classical Antiquity and Their Reluctant Recognition by Modern Scholars," *Semeia* 83–84 (1998): 19–66; Margaret Y. Macdonald, "Slavery, Sexuality and House Churches: A Reassessment of Colossians 3.18–4.1 in Light of New Research on the Roman Family," *NTS* 53 (2007): 94–113; Joseph A. Marchal, "The Usefulness of an Onesimus: The Sexual Use of Slaves and Paul's Letter to Philemon," *JBL* 130, no.4 (2011): 749–70; Jennifer A. Glancy, "The Sexual Use of Slaves: A Response to Kyle Harper on Jewish and Christian *Porneia*," *JBL* 134, no.1 (2015): 215–29; and Matthew J. Perry, "Sexual Damage to Slaves in Roman Law," *Journal of Ancient History* 3, no.1 (2015): 55–75.

[47] D. B. Saddington, "The Centurion in Matthew 8:5-13: Consideration of the Proposal of Theodore W. Jennings, Jr., and Tat-Siong Benny Liew," *JBL* 125, no. 1 (2006): 140–2; and Zeichmann, *The Roman Army and the New Testament*, 67–70. See Holger Szesnat, "'Pretty Boys' in Philo's *De Vita Contemplativa*," *Studia Philonica Annual* 10 (1998): 87–107, for some discussion of Jewish attitudes toward Roman same-sex sexual practices.

[48] Saddington, "The Centurion in Matthew 8:5-13," 140–2; and Zeichmann, *The Roman Army and the New Testament*, 67–70.

[49] Brown, *The Gospels as Stories*, 72–3.

in such a way as to demonstrate his faith (not divorced from his speech) (8:5-6, 8-9); Jesus acknowledges the centurion's faith (8:10, 13); and Jesus heals the centurion's servant (8:13). In this way the centurion approaches with faith and his request is granted because of his faith. Yet, as has been suggested here, there is more to the narrative.

The interaction between the centurion and Jesus is a series of control attempts and counter-control attempts employed by two individuals who operate from similar but different bases of power. Historically, the centurion as representative of imperial power (legitimate and referent power) would have been understood as an empowered figure. Jesus as the one embodying the power to heal (referent power and expert power) would also have been read as an empowered figure. Yet, both figures would have experienced a certain disempowerment as well (Jesus as a member of an occupied people and minoritized ethnic group, and the centurion as powerless to heal). In their interaction, the centurion seeks to gain a positive outcome through power (compelling Jesus to heal) and Jesus resists the centurion's control attempt through his own counter-control attempt. The effect that his has on the centurion is to verbalize both Jesus' power to heal and the centurion's powerlessness. The result is the centurion's repositioning away from power and towards faith, with the desired outcome being achieved (healing for the servant). The centurion is a faithful gentile, but this faith is shaped by the entirety of the interaction with Jesus and not just the function of a foregone conclusion based on a flattened reading of his character traits.

If the present study has been successful, then it highlights the usefulness of careful interdisciplinary approaches to the interpretation of biblical texts. No single approach can hope to address the myriad questions presented in any single pericope. But more integrative approaches with integrative questions might get interpreters closer to addressing these questions. The current approach, and in particular the application of DPT to the interaction of Jesus and the centurion, could provide an interesting interpretative insight if applied to other narratives. The interaction between Jesus and the Canaanite/Syrophoenician woman in Mt. 15:21-8 and Mk 7:24-30 (as previously mentioned), Jesus' interactions with other empowered individuals (religious or political leaders), Jesus' interactions with disempowered individuals, and Jesus' interactions with his own disciples could all yield significant results if read through the lens of DPT. The prospect of new results and new insights should be appealing to interpreters of the gospels.

9

Peter: A Failed but Not False Disciple According to Saint Matthew

David Lertis Matson

Embarking upon a study of Peter in the Gospel of Matthew is like stepping into an exegetical minefield. Given the long legacy of Roman Catholic–Protestant polemics over Peter and the papacy, one would be well advised to walk gingerly lest he or she inadvertently detonate an ecclesiastical explosion.[1] Happily, more recent approaches to Peter tread on safer ground.[2] The picture that emerges, however, is largely the result of methodological procedure, privileging the historical and diachronic over the theological and ecclesiastical.[3]

---

[1] Jürgen Becker begins his study, "Wer sich urchristlichen Zeugnissen über Simon Petrus zuwendet, hat nicht nur die üblichen methodischen und historischen Probleme zu bedenken, sondern steht angesichts der römisch-katholischen Rezeptionsgeschichte der neutestamentlichen Aussagen zu Petrus, ob er will oder nicht, immer auch mitten in einer bis heute anhaltenden Debatte zwischen den christlichen Konfessionen"; *Simon Petrus im Urchristentum*, BTS 105 (Neukirchen-Vluyn: Neukirchener Verlag, 2009). Larry R. Helyer calls Jesus' words to Peter in Matthew 16:18-19 "some of the most bitterly disputed words in the New Testament": *The Life and Witness of Peter* (Downers Grove, IL: IVP Academic, 2012), 43.

[2] See the ecumenical study of Raymond E. Brown, Karl P. Donfried, and John Reumann (eds.), *Peter in the New Testament: A Collaborative Assessment by Protestant and Roman Catholic Scholars* (Augsburg, MN: Augsburg, 1973; repr., Eugene, OR: Wipf & Stock, 2002). Donald Senior, *What Are They Saying about Matthew?*, rev. and expand. edn (New York and Mahwah, NJ: Paulist, 1996), observes that "most exegetical studies of Matthew's gospel have moved beyond strident apologetics for later church positions, Catholic or Protestant" (95–6). Peter continues to fascinate on many levels as witnessed by two recently published colloquia: Helen K. Bond and Larry W. Hurtado (eds.), *Peter in Early Christianity* (Grand Rapids, MI: Eerdmans, 2015), and Judith Lieu (ed.), *Peter in the Early Church: Apostle—Missionary—Church Leader*, BETL 325 (Leuven, Belgium: Peeters, 2021). The latter volume appeared too late in my own editing process to be of use in this chapter.

[3] Rudolf Pesch compares the quest for the historical Peter to the quest for the historical Jesus, remarking, "Unleugbar ist die Petrusforschung durch die Wege der Jesusforschung mitbestimmt": *Simon-Petrus: Geschichte und Geschichtliche Bedeutung des Ersten Jüngers Jesu Christi* (Stuttgart: Anton Hiersemann, 1980). Jack Dean Kingsbury credits Oscar Cullmann's *Petrus: Jünger—Apostel*—Märtyrer*: Das historische und das theologische Petrusproblem* (Zürich: Zwingli, 1952) as establishing a "new trend" in Petrine scholarship centered on historical rather than dogmatic concerns; Jack Dean Kingsbury, "The Figure of Peter in Matthew's Gospel as a Theological Problem," *JBL* 98, no. 1 (1979): 67. More recent scholarship seeks a *via media* between Peter as a uniquely authoritative figure and Peter as spokesman and representative of the Twelve, both positively and negatively. Nevertheless, "old confessional divides remained firmly entrenched in Cullmann's day, as in some circles they continue into our own": Markus Bockmuehl, "Scripture's Pope Meets von Balthasar's Peter," in *Peter in Early Christianity*, ed. Helen K. Bond and Larry W. Hurtado (Grand Rapids, MI: Eerdmans, 2015), 331.

Just when all of Peter's interpretive children seemed to be playing nicely, Robert H. Gundry dropped a bombshell on the Matthean playground. In *Peter: False Disciple and Apostate according to Saint Matthew*, Gundry argued that Matthew presents Peter as failed and apostate on a par with Judas Iscariot.[4] As members of Matthew's visible church, Peter and Judas are false disciples, part of a *corpus mixtum* that awaits separation at the end of the age.[5] In Gundry's earth-shaking reading, Peter the Rock has fallen on rocky ground and can't get up. Peter is not only not the first Pope, he's not even a Christian. The book requires interaction with even the smallest of details, a tribute to a biblical scholar who reads Matthew's text closely and well: "Gundry's work on Peter is thoughtful and detailed yet concise and compelling."[6] Any work challenging his thesis will have to be at least equally compelling.[7]

That Peter is false and apostate would shock most readers. After all, the weight of the Christian tradition leans in the opposite direction: in Mark, the young man at the tomb marks Peter out for special mention (Mk 16:7); in Luke, Jesus tells Peter to strengthen his brothers after he has turned back again (Lk. 22:32); in John, Peter's post-resurrection threefold affirmation of his love for Jesus (Jn 21:15-17) counteracts his earlier threefold denial (Jn 18:17, 25, 27).[8] Readers influenced by this New Testament evidence tend to read that evidence into Matthew as well.

But a literary approach to the question will not allow for eating such a "gospel stew" diet of biblical interpretation.[9] Peter's repentance will have to be demonstrated on the

---

[4] Robert H. Gundry, *Peter: False Disciple and Apostate according to Saint Matthew* (Grand Rapids, MI: Eerdmans, 2015). Without defining the term more precisely, Gundry seems to equate "apostasy" with public defection in the face of persecution (vii, 97). Peter and Judas thus serve as pastoral warnings against apostasy in Matthew's church, particularly in Peter's case. If a disciple as estimable as Peter can apostatize, who is immune? In this chapter I am interacting with his second edition, *Peter: False Disciple and Apostate according to Saint Matthew. With Responses to Reviews* (Eugene, OR: Wipf & Stock, 2018), modeling my own title after his. The fuse was already lit in Gundry's first edition of *Matthew: A Commentary on His Literary and Theological Art* (Grand Rapids, MI: Eerdmans, 1982), e.g., 548-9.

[5] On the presence of false disciples in Matthew's church, see Mt. 7:15-20, 21-3; 13:24-30, 41-3, 47-50; 22:10-14; 25:1-2, 31-3, 41-6. See Robert H. Gundry, "In Defense of the Church in Matthew as a *Corpus Mixtum*," *ZNW* 91 (2000): 153-65.

[6] Sonya S. Cronin, review of *Peter: False Disciple and Apostate according to Saint Matthew*, by Robert H. Gundry, *RBL*, 03/2018.

[7] Disappointingly, a recent monograph by Gene L. Green fails to grapple with the implications of Gundry's proposal while contending that Peter is "the church's theologian, the Rock to whom we are all indebted for our understanding of the gospel of Christ": Gene L. Green, *Vox Petri: A Theology of Peter* (Eugene, OR: Cascade, 2019), 6. Likewise, a major recent commentary on Matthew proceeds unaware of Gundry's explosive thesis: R. Alan Culpepper, *Matthew: A Commentary*, NTL (Louisville, KY: Westminster John Knox, 2021).

[8] Peter's restoration figures more prominently in Luke and John than in Mark, but the singling out of Peter in Mk 16:7 makes such a possibility likely, particularly if καί is ascensive (*even* Peter). Gundry himself suggests as much (*Peter*, 4, 51, 63-7, 129). M. Eugene Boring sees a twofold restoration in Mk 16:7—the disciples and Peter—extending perhaps to Mark's own readers: M. Eugene Boring, *Mark: A Commentary*, NTL (Louisville, KY: Westminster John Knox, 2006), 446.

[9] I owe the metaphor to S. Scott Bartchy, who taught me years ago to respect the individual portraits of the New Testament gospels long before I encountered narrative criticism. More recently, Markus Bockmuehl argues for a synthetic approach, but he construes his project differently: Markus Bockmuehl, *Simon Peter in Scripture and Memory: The New Testament Apostle in the Early Church* (Grand Rapids, MI: Baker Academic, 2012), 20-1.

basis of the narrative itself, not on information extraneous to Matthew.[10] Even the discipline of sticking to one biblical text, however, is not likely to solve key interpretive differences arising from differences in methodology.[11] While both Gundry and I argue from a narrative-critical perspective, he assumes a first-time auditor; I assume a multiple implied reader.[12] What the reader knows or does not know at any given point is critical.[13] Redaction criticism also marks both of our approaches.[14] Any tradition that Matthew inherits from Mark, however, comprises Matthew's picture of Peter just as much as any material that Matthew might add.[15]

Which approach more clearly aligns with the goals of the implied author of Matthew?[16] The ending of Matthew, with its injunction to teach newly baptized disciples everything that Jesus has taught (Mt. 28:20), most naturally refers back to all the didactic material in the preceding narrative, which Matthew has punctuated with five skillfully placed discourses making up the structure of his gospel.[17] The closing scene thus invites the implied reader to go back and read the gospel again, this time as

---

[10] That more information exists about Peter than is necessary for the plot justifies a character analysis of Peter in Matthew: Fred W. Burnett, "Characterization and Reader Construction of Characters in the Gospels," *Semeia* 63 (1993): 20. Thus, my approach is closest to the "realistic" school of characterization. For a "defense" of classical narratology in light of more recent approaches, see Shlomith Rimmon-Kenan, *Narrative Fiction: Contemporary Poetics*, 2nd edn (London: Routledge, 2002), 138–49. My focus here is not so much on an accumulation of traits but on the question of a single trait: does Peter repent? Peter Dschulnigg counts some fourteen scenes involving Peter in Matthew: Peter Dschulnigg, *Petrus im Neuen Testament* (Stuttgart: Katholisches Bibelwerk, 1996), 32. I have selected those texts that sufficiently establish my thesis within the space limitations of this chapter.

[11] Warren Carter notes that the reading strategy or strategies one adopts largely determines what he or she sees in the text: Warren Carter, *Matthew: Storyteller, Interpreter, Evangelist*, rev. edn (Peabody. MA: Hendrickson, 2004), 1.

[12] Gundry confuses the issue somewhat when he says that Matthew wrote for first-time auditors but with the added expectation of repeated readings (*Peter*, 4). But a first-time reading can sometimes produce very different results and should be methodologically distinguished. For a first-time reading of Matthew, see Richard A. Edwards, *Matthew's Story of Jesus* (Philadelphia: Fortress, 1985); for multiple, see Jack Dean Kingsbury, *Matthew as Story*, 2nd edn (Philadelphia: Fortress, 1988).

[13] As Mark Allan Powell points out, "Many of the divergent perspectives in literary criticism today can be traced to different conceptions of the reader": Mark Allan Powell, *What is Narrative Criticism?* (Minneapolis: Fortress, 1990), 19.

[14] Assuming Markan priority. Narrative critics disagree on the combination of these two methodological approaches. For a critique, see Richard A. Edwards, *Matthew's Narrative Portrait of Disciples: How the Text-Connoted Reader Is Informed* (Harrisburg, PA: Trinity Press International, 1997), 4–7; see also Mark Allan Powell, "Toward a Narrative-Critical Understanding of Matthew," *Int* 46, no. 4 (1992): 341–6. If Matthew assumes that his readers know Mark, redactional analysis gains in importance.

[15] Gundry violates this principle when it suits his argument (*Peter*, 30, n. 47, 121–2, 127).

[16] As Powell observes, "The implied reader ... is not necessarily to be thought of as a first-time reader. In some instances, the narrative text apparently assumes the reader will come to an understanding only after multiple readings" (*What?* 20).

[17] Dale C. Allison, *Studies in Matthew: Interpretation Past and Present* (Grand Rapids, MI: Baker Academic, 2005), 218-19. Each of the five discourses (Mt. 5:1–7:29; 9:35–11:1; 13:1–53; 18:1–19:1; 23:1–26:1) is carefully demarcated. Matthew the scribe (Mt. 13:52) has carefully ordered his material: see Patrick Schreiner, *Matthew, Disciple and Scribe: The First Gospel and Its Portrait of Jesus* (Grand Rapids, MI: Baker Academic, 2019), 10, 16–17. This compositional structure, however, is not the same as Matthew's plot structure, which focuses on events (Powell, "Toward," 343–4).

a discipled scribe.[18] Matthew's readers are "pulled along to the end of the account, where they are commanded to hear it again."[19] The repetition demanded by the catechetical nature of Matthew's Gospel implies that "it might be reread and reviewed," particularly in a public setting.[20] This rereading moreover is no dull process: "the interpretation of a section of the Gospel is neither limited to nor permanently determined by a hearer's first reaction. A different reaction will occur and can be expected with every additional reading."[21] Even modern cinematic viewers know the difference between seeing a movie for the first time and seeing it for a second or even third time.

The above insights suggest then that we best interpret the Gospel of Matthew when we read it with a multiple implied reader clearly in mind.[22] Real readers read from the same location as the implied reader, that is, in the interval between the resurrection and Parousia, the period of Matthew's ecclesia (Mt. 16:18; 18:17; 28:19-20); privileged as such, the implied reader "oversees the story of the life and ministry of Jesus of Nazareth as Matthew conveys this through his voice as narrator, and he or she can comprehend the whole of this story."[23] The implied reader knows what happens in the past as well as in the future, including the fate of Jesus before it occurs.[24] This interpretive strategy reflects Matthew's own hermeneutical method of reading his sources backward and forward.[25] According to Patrick Schreiner, "The process of reading and interpretation is a complex interplay between a retrospective and prospective reading."[26] The reader knows and remembers everything of which he has been informed by the narrator and ably picks up on the subtleties of the text.[27]

---

[18] Schreiner, *Matthew, Disciple and Scribe*, 57. Ulrich Luz observes that "to go to 'school' with Jesus is the essence of discipleship": Ulrich Luz, *Matthew 8–20*, trans. James E. Crouch, Hermeneia (Minneapolis: Fortress, 2001), 366. Thus a "discipled scribe" (γραμματεὺς μαθητευθείς, Mt. 13:52) is every baptized and catechized disciple produced by the Great Commission (Mt. 28:19-20). The only other instance of μαθητεύω applies to Joseph of Arimathea, himself schooled to/by Jesus (Mt. 27:57).

[19] David P. Scaer, *Discourses in Matthew: Jesus Teaches the Church* (St. Louis: Concordia, 2004), 67.

[20] Scaer, *Discourses in Matthew*, claims that the five discourses provide a teaching outline to lead catechumens to baptism and the Eucharist (21).

[21] Scaer, *Discourses in Matthew*, 67–8. Wolfgang Iser observes that "a second reading ... often produces a different impression from the first": Wolfgang Iser, *The Implied Reader: Patterns of Communication in Prose Fiction from Bunyan to Beckett* (Baltimore, MD: Johns Hopkins University Press, 1974), 280. Allison contends that the implied hearers of Matthew can appreciate its intertextuality due to the recurrent hearing that the gospel invites (*Studies*, 218–19).

[22] Powell states that the aim of narrative criticism is "to read the text *as* the implied reader" (*What?*, 20, my italics).

[23] Kingsbury, *Matthew as Story*, 38. Kingsbury contends that the phrase "to this day" (Mt. 27:8; 28:15) and Matthew's explicit appeal to a post-Easter "reader" (Mt. 24:15) help to establish the reader's location.

[24] Matthew's description of Judas as ὁ παραδοὺς αὐτόν (aorist participle) in Mt. 10:4 assumes that the reader knows the end from the beginning: John Nolland, *The Gospel of Matthew: A Commentary on the Greek Text*, NIGTC (Grand Rapids, MI: Eerdmans, 2005), 413. Iser speaks of the implied reader receiving "a grandstand view of all the proceedings" (*Implied Reader*, 43).

[25] Schreiner, *Matthew, Disciple and Scribe*, 57. According to Schreiner, Matthew reads backward from Jesus' life to the Old Testament as well as forward from the Old Testament to Jesus' life.

[26] Schreiner, *Matthew, Disciple and Scribe*, 59.

[27] This *idealized* implied reader approximates the "paradigmatic reader" of Richard J. Cassidy, *Four Times Peter: Portrayals of Peter in the Four Gospels and at Philippi*, Interfaces (Collegeville, MN: Liturgical Press, 2007), 7, who borrows the terminology from Mark Stibbe.

I. Peter as Faithful Disciple

Peter figures prominently in the Gospel of Matthew as the first disciple called by Jesus (Mt. 4:18-20).[28] The call comes as Jesus is walking by the Sea of Galilee, allowing the narrator spatially to focalize the scene.[29] Peter's immediate and decisive response to Jesus' call shows the reader what an ideal disciple is like, "the kind of person Jesus is seeking."[30] The narrator underscores the totality of Peter's response when Peter later remarks to Jesus, "Look, we have left everything and followed you" (Mt. 19:27).[31] By understanding Jesus' cryptic summons to become a fisher of people, Peter, like his comrades, manifests such positive traits as "obedience, perceptivity, and quick reaction."[32] Moreover, the narrative placement of the disciples' calling, immediately following Jesus' summons to repentance (Mt. 4:17), demonstrates that positive trait as well.[33] But Peter's positive character is not the result of "showing" only. The narrator also "tells" the reader that Simon is called "Rock" (Πέτρος), a detail added to his Markan source (Mk 1:16).[34] The first-time auditor in Gundry's study may not know why Simon is called Peter, but a multiple implied reader of Matthew is aware of the meaning of Peter's name explained later in the narrative (Mt. 16:17-18).[35]

---

[28] Edwards notes that the call of the four fishermen is the first time that the disciples are "on scene" (*Matthew's Narrative Portrait*, 19). Their response qualifies as "character-shaping": Richard A. Edwards, "Characterization of the Disciples as a Feature of Matthew's Narrative," in *The Four Gospels*, Festschrift Frans Neirynck, ed. C. M. Tuckett et al., BETL 100 (Leuven, Belgium: Leuven University Press, 1992), 2:1313–14.

[29] Matthew's narrative "camera" moves from the Judean desert to "Galilee of the Gentiles" to the lakeside, homing in on a pair of brothers busy with the day's fishing. On the process of focalization, see Robert Funk, *The Poetics of Biblical Narrative*, Foundations and Facets (Sonoma, CA: Polebridge, 1988), 65–6, who helpfully employs the figure of a mobile camera. In today's cinematic world, a drone would do the trick.

[30] Edwards, *Matthew's Narrative Portrait*, 26.

[31] Peter's statement is not overly self-serving. Jesus recognizes the legitimacy of rewards, both in the immediate context (Mt. 19:28-9) and elsewhere (Mt. 5:12; 6:1; 10:41-2). Biblical citations are from the NRSV.

[32] Edwards, *Matthew's Narrative Portrait*, 22; also "Characterization," 2:1317.

[33] Edwards, *Matthew's Narrative Portrait*, 25-6, especially if ἀπὸ τότε temporally focalizes the scene. Kingsbury argues that the phrase is a structural marker (*Matthew as Story*, 40–2); if so, it goes with 4:18-22 rather than with 4:12-16 despite the paragraph headings in most major English translations (NCV excepted). Dschulnigg points out how Mt. 4:18-22 "ist die erste Erzählung nach der eröffnenden Zusammenfassung des öffentlichen Wirkens Jesu in Galaläa (4:17)" (*Petrus im Neuen Testament*, 33).

[34] In biblical thought a person's name fits his or her character. In literary theory, "character names often serve as 'labels' for a trait or cluster of traits characteristic of non-fictional human beings" (Rimmon-Kenan, *Narrative Fiction,* 33–4). On showing and telling as forms of characterization, see Powell, *What?*, 52–3.

[35] Gundry claims that Peter's name is not honorific in Matthew. Hence Jesus may be explaining for the first time the meaning of a surname that he has been using all along; see Carsten P. Thiede, *Simon Peter: From Galilee to Rome* (Exeter: Paternoster, 1986), 38. At this early juncture, "Peter" also serves to distinguish Simon from the other Simons that populate Matthew's story world, including Simon the Zealot, a fellow apostle (Mt. 10:4), Simon, a brother of Jesus (Mt. 13:55), Simon the leper (Mt. 26:6), and Simon of Cyrene (Mt. 27:32). Noted by R. T. France, *The Gospel of Matthew*, NICNT (Grand Rapids, MI: Eerdmans, 2007), 146. "Simon" was a popular Greek name among Jews in antiquity due to its correspondence to the Hebrew name Simeon (cf. Acts 15:14; 2 Pet. 1:1), but especially due to its political associations with Simon Maccabee. See Margaret H. Williams, "From Shimon to Petros—Petrine Nomenclature in the Light of Contemporary Onomastic Practices," in *Peter in Early Christianity*, ed. Helen K. Bond and Larry W. Hurtado (Grand Rapids, MI: Eerdmans, 2015), 32–3.

Thus the first image of Peter in Matthew is a positive image.[36] First impressions make lasting impressions.[37]

Gundry concedes Peter's prominence in this opening scene but minimizes its impact by pointing out the simultaneous calling of his brother Andrew, not to mention the brothers James and John who experience the same call.[38] Nevertheless, as Peter Dschulnigg observes, Simon's name still comes first, a sequence later reinforced by Matthew when he explicitly designates Peter the "first" (πρῶτος) of the apostles (Mt. 10:2).[39] The identical language and order between the two verses makes the connection explicit.[40] Certainly if Matthew wanted to mention Andrew ahead of Simon, nothing prevented him from doing so. John's Gospel does that very thing.[41]

The reader receives no prior knowledge to help explain the abrupt reaction of the disciples. The entire initiative rests with Jesus.[42] Richard A. Edwards notes how it is "puzzling to the reader to be told that these four men simply get up and leave their livelihood."[43] Unlike the disciples in John, for example, who have the prior benefit of the Baptist's testimony (Jn 1:35-42), the Matthean disciples have had no previous contact with Jesus. To what then does the reader attribute such efficacy? Edwards suggests that the reader "must supply a rationale and the only clue available is the assumption that they are aware of Jesus' message."[44] But nothing in the text hints at this prior knowledge and thus the reader has no framework for interpreting this "gap" in the text. Rather, the lack of a prior relationship is intentional since Matthew "wishes to emphasize Jesus' authoritative call and the disciples' immediate response."[45] Jesus' call

---

[36] Even Gundry admits that "Peter and Andrew's immediately leaving their nets and following Jesus in obedience to Jesus' command strikes a favorable note" (*Peter*, 7).

[37] Meir Sternberg calls this phenomenon the "primacy effect", in *Expositional Modes and Temporal Ordering in Fiction* (Indianapolis: Indiana University Press, 1978), 93–4, as opposed to the "recency effect." According to Edwards, "This first report about the followers is especially important for the reader. The initial appearance of a character has a lasting impact on the reader because it establishes a base or context of information … that can then be manipulated by the narrator as the story continues": Richard A. Edwards, "Uncertain Faith: Matthew's Portrait of the Disciples," in *Discipleship in the New Testament*, ed. Fernando F. Segovia (Philadelphia: Fortress, 1985), 53. This observation holds even for a multiple reader, formerly a first-time reader.

[38] Gundry, *Peter*, 7–9. Gundry claims that Peter's "firstness" comports with Jesus' later condemnation of the "first" who will be "last" (Mt. 19:30; 20:16). As one who has "left" everything, however, Peter is among the "last" who will be first, not vice-versa. A better connection is with Mt. 20:27, where Peter is reminded that his "firstness" (πρῶτος) is a call to sacrificial service (δοῦλος).

[39] Dschulnigg, *Petrus im Neuen Testament*, 33. Matthew's Markan source lacks the designation "first" (Mk 3:16). That the sequence of names in Mt. 10:2 corresponds exactly to Mt. 4:18-22 (contra Mk 3:16-18!) indicates that Matthew "attaches great importance to this order" (Kingsbury, "Figure of Peter," 70).

[40] Mt. 4:18: τὸν λεγόμενον Πέτρον; Mt. 10:2: ὁ λεγόμενος Πέτρος.

[41] In John, Simon is "first" only in that Andrew "first" (πρῶτον) found his brother Simon and brought him to Jesus (Jn 1:40-1).

[42] Grant R, Osborne, *Matthew*, ZECNT (Grand Rapids, MI: Zondervan, 2010), 148.

[43] Edwards, *Matthew's Story*, 18.

[44] Edwards, *Matthew's Story*, 18. Edwards appears to move away from this explanation in his later book, *Matthew's Narrative Portrait*, 20–2.

[45] Osborne, *Matthew*, 148. Kari Syreeni points out that with no prehistory in Matthew "Peter appears as a character only through Jesus' action": Kari Syreeni, "Peter as Character and Symbol in the Gospel of Matthew," in *Characterization on the Gospels: Reconceiving Narrative Criticism*, ed. David Rhoads and Kari Syreeni, JSNTSup 184 (Sheffield: Sheffield Academic, 2014), 121.

of the disciples is effectual, underscoring the compelling nature of Jesus' word.[46] The narrator heightens the efficacy of the call by having Peter and Andrew respond in the very act of casting their nets.[47] While one wonders what animates the two brothers, their motive remains inaccessible.[48] The text simply attributes their decisive reaction to divine initiative.[49]

The effectual nature of Jesus' word increases the reader's confidence that Peter and Andrew will in fact become "fishers of people." The prophecy first pronounced by Jesus finds fulfillment later in the narrative when Jesus sends them out to gather the lost sheep of the house of Israel (Mt. 9:37-10:6) and at story's end when they engage in discipling all the nations until the end of the age (Mt. 28:16-20).[50] Fishing for people, they will cast the gospel net far and wide, gathering fish of every kind (Mt. 24:14; 26:13), separated only at the last judgment (Mt. 13:47-50).[51] Since Matthew's reader is supremely confident in Jesus' ability to predict the future, as evidenced within the plotted narrative, internal predictive prolepses prepare the reader for Matthew's external predictive prolepses.[52] Jesus the "prophet" is a reliable narrator.[53]

---

[46] The calling of the disciples entails both conversion ("follow me") and commissioning ("I will make you fishers of people"). Both elements converge in a single call as in Paul's own calling on the Damascus Road (Gal. 1:15-16). The notion of "effectual calling" is particularly strong in Paul, where calling is tantamount to election (e.g., Rom. 8:28-30; 1 Cor. 1:9, 24, 26-8; 2 Thess. 2:13-14). D. A. Carson, *Matthew-Mark*, rev. edn, EBC (Grand Rapids, MI: Zondervan, 2010), 149, suggests that Matthew does not go as far as Paul, but the parable of the wedding feast (Mt. 22:1-14) distinguishes an effectual call from a more general call: "For many are called, but few are chosen" (22:14; cf. Mt. 9:13). This demarcation would certainly explain the presence of false disciples in Matthew's church. See R. T. France, *Matthew: Evangelist and Teacher*, New Testament Profiles (Downers Grove, IL: InterVarsity Press, 1989), 275; see also Gundry, *Peter*, 80, and Gundry, "In Defense," 154-6.

[47] Osborne notes the dynamic quality of the present participle βάλλοντας, "depicting the disciples in the act of fishing when the call came" (*Matthew*, 149).

[48] To try to determine otherwise is to psychologize the disciples. Even on a historical level, Peter's motivation remains elusive. See Sean Frye, "The Fisherman from Bethsaida," in *Peter in Early Christianity*, ed. Helen K. Bond and Larry W. Hurtado (Grand Rapids, MI: Eerdmans, 2015), 29. Robert E. Scholes and Robert Kellogg remind us that "we are not called upon to understand their [the disciples'] motivation as if they were whole human beings but to understand the principles they illustrate through their actions in a narrative framework"; Robert E. Scholes and Robert Kellogg, *The Nature of Narrative*, 1st edn (London: Oxford University Press, 1966), 83, cited in Mary Ann Tolbert, *Sowing the Gospel: Mark's World in Literary-Historical Perspective* (Minneapolis: Fortress, 1989), 199. The focus in this scene is on Jesus, the principal subject ("he saw," "he said," "he called"). Osborne notes that "Jesus is the creative force and the disciples passive participants" (*Matthew*, 149).

[49] Jesus is none other than "God with us" (Mt. 1:23), who comes powerfully proclaiming the gospel of the kingdom (4:17, 23a), effectively bracketing the call of the four fishermen and providing a key interpretive framework.

[50] So, correctly, France, *Gospel of Matthew*, 147. D. A. Carson speaks of a "straight line" here to the Great Commission (*Matthew-Mark*, 613).

[51] The fishing metaphor is therefore both positive and negative, resulting in both salvation and judgment (cf. Mt. 10:14-15). In using the predatory nature of fishing as a metaphor for judgment, particularly upon unbelieving Israel, Jesus is not alone (cf. Jer. 16:16; Amos 4:2).

[52] Internal predictive prolepses find fulfillment within the temporal frame of the narrative while external prolepses point beyond it. See Gerard Genette, *Narrative Discourse: An Essay in Method* (Ithaca, NY: Cornell University Press, 1990), 67-79; Funk, *Poetics*, 192-4; Cassidy, *Four Times Peter*, 3, 65-7. For Matthew's internal prolepses, see 4:19; 9:15; 16:21; 17:12, 22-3; 20:18-19; 21:2; 26:2, 12; 26:18, 21, 23-4, 31-2, 34; 28:10; for external, see 3:11; 5:4-9, 18; 7:11, 21-3; 10:19, 21-3, 25, 32-3; 11:22, 24; 12:31-2, 36-7, 41-2; 13:41-3, 49-50; 16:18-19, 27-8; 19:28-30; 20:23; 21:43; 23:34, 36, 39; 24:2, 9-11, 14; 25:31-46; 26:13, 29, 64; 28:20.

[53] Jesus has the status of prophet in Matthew (13:57; 21:11, 46).

II. Peter as Failed Disciple

The initial impression of the Matthean Peter is arguably positive. Peter is a faithful disciple, effectively called to follow Jesus and fish for people.[54] Peter also appears favorably, at least initially, in a further episode involving water: the story of Jesus walking on the sea (Mt. 14:22-33). Matthew has dramatically transformed the ending of his Markan source to make the scene an occasion for corporate worship (Mt. 14:33) rather than divine hardening (Mk. 6:52), signaling an overall positive intention. But Matthew also inserts a special incident involving Peter, who seeks Jesus' command to bid him to come to him on the water, a venture that will end in failure (14:28-31).[55]

A number of positive features characterizes Peter in the pericope, including the obvious but sometimes overlooked point that he actually walks on water.[56] Peter exercises at least a "little faith" (v. 31) as his address of Jesus in a first-class conditional sentence ("Lord, if it is you," Mt. 14:28) suggests.[57] Little faith does not mean lack of faith.[58] Peter's desire that Jesus command him (κέλευσόν με) to come to him on the water further recognizes the Lordship of Jesus, whom even the winds and sea obey (cf. Mt. 8:27).[59] Peter's coming to Jesus and subsequent crying out for salvation (σῶσόν με) become paradigmatic of all believers for, like the meaning of his name, Jesus "will save"

---

[54] As subsequent scenes in this section will show, Peter is a man of "little faith," but he exercises faith nonetheless. That Matthew deletes Mark's negative depiction of Peter subsequently hunting Jesus down (καταδιώκω, Mk 1:36) continues a favorable impression of Peter, at least for a first-time reader.

[55] This scene is one of three in Matthew that has no parallel in the other gospels (14:28-33; 16:16b-19; 17:24-7) and thus constitute Matthew's "principal contribution to the New Testament data on Peter": Brown et al., *Peter in the New Testament*, 78.

[56] While a baptismal wall fresco at a Dura-Europos (Syria) house church (c. 240 CE) depicts Peter walking on the water, later Christian artists were reluctant to do so, perhaps because "they felt the drama of the moment was his sinking or that the walking on the water should be reserved for Jesus": Heidi J. Hornik, "St. Peter's Crisis of Faith at Harvard: The Scarsellino Picture and Matthew 14," in *"A Temple Made with Hands": Essays in Honor of Naymond H. Keathley*, ed. Mikeal C. Parsons and Richard Walsh (Eugene, OR: Pickwick, 2018), 39.

[57] Contra Gundry, this condition is not a statement of doubt but of faith: "Since you are Lord over creation, tell me to participate in your miraculous power" (Osborne, *Matthew*, 575; so also Thiede, *Simon Peter*, 29-30). "Since" is an appropriate translation of the first-class condition *if* the context supports it—contra Daniel B. Wallace, *Greek Grammar Beyond the Basics: An Exegetical Syntax of the New Testament* (Grand Rapids, MI: Zondervan, 1996), 690-1, 711, who goes too far in ruling this translation out (cf. 708). Here the emphatic σὺ εἶ ("you are") corresponds to the emphatic ἐγώ εἰμι ("I am") in the previous verse (Nolland, *Gospel of Matthew*, 601). Contra Nolland, the christophanic context of the passage makes it likely that Jesus' utterance of ἐγώ εἰμι is a direct allusion to the divine name of Exod. 3:14: correctly, Donald A. Hagner, *Matthew 14-28*, WBC (Dallas: Word Books, 1995), 423. In that case, Peter's early recognition of Jesus' divine status sets the stage for the disciples' worship (προσκυνέω) at story's end (14:33).

[58] Surely Peter expresses some degree of trust in Jesus' ability to save and has already requested and acted upon Jesus' command. France argues that Matthew's ὀλιγόπιστος/ὀλιγοπιστία is tantamount to no faith (*Matthew: Evangelist and Teacher*, 273-5). I am not convinced of this reductionism either here or at Mt. 6:30 or 8:26. Why change Mark's "no faith" (4:40) to "little faith" (Mt. 8:26) if Mark's meaning was exactly what Matthew intended?

[59] Gundry questions whether Peter's address of Jesus as "Lord" is genuine (*Peter*, 10, 121), since the title appears on the lips of unbelievers and/or false disciples. Gundry is correct in some of his citations (Mt. 7:21-2; 8:2; 17:15; 25:11) but incorrect in others (Mt. 8:6, 8; 15:22, 25, 27; 20:30-1, 33). He further compares Peter's request to Satan's request for a stunt as in Mt. 4:3, 5-6 (*Peter*, 10-11), but Satan does not ask Jesus to command *him* (Satan) as Peter asks Jesus to command *him* (Peter). Peter is acting like a disciple.

(σώσει) his people from their sins (Mt. 1:21).⁶⁰ And Peter indeed demonstrates his sinfulness: when a strong wind arises he begins to sink. Anticipating Peter's later denial, the reader observes that "Peter's behavior can change radically due to fear."⁶¹ That Peter begins to doubt (διστάζω) suggests hesitancy or uncertainty.⁶² The choice of verb "indicates a divided mind brought about by a lack of an adequate measure of faith, not a lack of faith altogether."⁶³ Peter's faith is a saving faith as becomes clear when Peter lends his voice to the chorus of worshipping disciples in the boat: "Truly you are the Son of God" (Mt. 14:32).⁶⁴ This confession marks the first time human beings in Matthew recognize the divine sonship of Jesus, signaling a major Christological development.⁶⁵

The second occasion of Christological confession further demonstrates Peter as a failed disciple. Immediately after Peter confesses Jesus to be "the Christ, the Son of the living God" (Mt. 16:16), the fullest confession of Jesus in all of the gospels and directly attributable to the Father's revelation (Mt. 16:17; cf. 11:25-7), Peter takes Jesus aside to rebuke him for detailing the events of his Passion (Mt. 16:21-3). Jesus in turn addresses Peter as "Satan" and tells Peter to "get behind me" (ὕπαγε ὀπίσω μου), much like Jesus' earlier command to Satan at the temptation (Mt. 4:10).⁶⁶ In a case of narrative whiplash, Peter moves from being the mouthpiece of the heavenly Father to being the mouthpiece

---

⁶⁰ Culpepper notices how "Jesus acts to save his own," drawing attention to Mt. 1:21 (*Matthew*, 284). Moreover, Timothy Wiarda contends that Peter's directional focus "reinforces the Jesus-centered nature of his act": Timothy Wiarda, *Interpreting Gospel Narratives: Scenes, People, and Theology* (Nashville: B&H Academic, 2010), 181. See also Timothy Wiarda, *Peter in the Gospels: Pattern, Personality and Relationship*, WUNT 2nd Series 127 (Tübingen: Mohr Siebeck, 2000), 91–3.

⁶¹ Eric C. Stewart, *Peter: First Generation Member of the Jesus Movement*, Paul's Social Network: Brothers and Sisters in the Faith (Collegeville, MN: Liturgical Press, 2012), 46.

⁶² Gundry prematurely reads doubt into Peter's address of Jesus in Matthew 14:28 (*Peter*, 10); Peter's doubt arises only with the advent of the strong wind.

⁶³ Hagner, *Matthew 14-28*, 885. The only other appearance of this verb is at Mt. 28:17, where it retains this same essential meaning.

⁶⁴ Gundry, *Peter*, 12–13, 122, argues "those in the boat" (Mt. 14:33) excludes Peter, but the narrative sequencing indicates that both Jesus and Peter have climbed back into the boat (14:32; correctly, Cassidy, *Four Times Peter*, 64, 73). That 14:32 (εἰς τὸ πλοῖον) forms an *inclusio* with 14:22 (εἰς τὸ πλοῖον) means that Peter has rejoined the other disciples and thus is naturally part of the οἱ ἐν τῷ πλοίῳ in verse 33. Contra Gundry (*Peter*, 12), this phrase does not distinguish the other disciples from Jesus and Peter; the reader readily perceives that Jesus is the one worshiped, not one of the worshipers, as indicated by the subsequent αὐτῷ ("those in the boat worshiped *him*"). Peter's recognition of Jesus' divine status in 14:28 also argues for Peter's inclusion in the worshiping throng.

⁶⁵ Culpepper, *Matthew*, 285, points out the prior testimony of the voice from heaven (Mt. 3:17) and Satan's temptations (Mt. 4:3, 6; cf. 8:29), anticipating Mt. 16:16; 26:63; 27:40, 43, 54. According to Matthias Konradt, "Son of God" expresses a deeper knowledge of Jesus on the part of the disciples: Matthias Konradt, *The Gospel according to Matthew: A Commentary*, trans. M. Eugene Boring (Waco, TX: Baylor University Press, 2020), 251. Peter's later confession, however, will go even deeper, linking Jesus' divine status (ὁ υἱὸς τοῦ θεοῦ) to his human Messiahship (ὁ χριστός) in a way that the earlier confession does not (Mt. 16:16). By excluding Peter from the worshipers in the boat, Gundry privileges the other disciples who he asserts had no need of divine assistance (*Peter*, 16). But their confession is a response to Christophanic revelation, not human insight.

⁶⁶ Gundry, *Peter*, 28. Jesus says, "Away with you, Satan!" (ὕπαγε, σατανᾶ). By omitting Mark's "But turning and looking at the disciples" (Mk 8:33a), Matthew retains a singular focus on Peter.

of Satan in the span of a few verses.[67] Matthew intensifies Peter's failure by adding two key elements to his Markan source: Peter's direct address ("God forbid it, Lord! This must never happen to you"), with its emphatic οὐ μή negation (Mt. 16:22), and Jesus' calling Peter a σκάνδαλον (Mt. 16:23), a term in the emphatic first Greek position and reserved in Matthew for lawbreakers and apostates.[68] But the disciples as a whole will be scandalized (σκανδαλίζω) by Jesus' fate (Mt. 26:31, 33), as Gundry himself recognizes, so Peter's fate is not beyond repair.[69] Like the rest of the disciples, he can repent: "Peter had it in him to be a stone of stumbling or to be a foundation stone."[70]

Of course, the one disciple not relieved of his fate is Judas Iscariot, whom Gundry pairs with Peter as a false and apostate disciple. That Matthew intends some kind of relationship between them is clear from the juxtaposition of their respective failures— Peter's denial (Mt. 26:69-75) and Judas' suicide (Mt. 27:3-10), the latter unique to Matthew. Some debate exists whether Judas repents or whether he is lost forever, but the prior pronouncement of Jesus concerning Judas' fate (Mt. 26:24) strongly favors the latter.[71] Judas expresses regret for his actions, not repentance.[72]

Does Peter join Judas in his apostasy? Gundry affirms that he does. In Gundry's view, the denial scene in Matthew (26:69-75) "constitutes the heart of Matthew's portrayal of Peter as a false disciple who apostatized."[73] Like the seed sown on "rocky" ground (πετρώδης), Peter falls away in times of persecution and duress (Mt. 13:20-1),

---

[67] Sreeni quizzically asks, "How can Peter be the foundation of the church and Satan in one character?" ("Peter as Character," 130). Or, as Edwards puts it textually, "Peter, influenced by God in 16:17, is controlled by Satan in 16:22" (*Matthew's Story of Jesus*, 61). John R. Markley contends that Peter is functioning here not as a failed disciple but as an apocalyptic foil for divine revelation: John R. Markley, "Reassessing Peter's Imperception in Synoptic Tradition," in *Peter in Early Christianity*, ed. Helen K. Bond and Larry W. Hurtado (Grand Rapids, MI: Eerdmans, 2015), 106–8. There is something to be said for the role of human imperception in revelatory contexts, but Peter's alignment with Satan in this passage moves beyond mere human imperception to Satanic opposition. Markley objects to applying positive and negative categories to Peter, but a negative assessment here is inescapable, as it is in other contexts.

[68] The noun (σκάνδαλον) appears at Mt. 13:41; 16:23; 18:7 (3x), while the verb (σκανδαλίζω) occurs at 5:29, 30; 11:6; 13:21, 57; 15:12; 17:27; 18:6, 8, 9; 24:10; 26:31, 33 (2x). Cassidy notes the "conceptual affinity" between Peter the rock and Peter the stumbling stone (*Four Times Peter*, 77).

[69] Gundry seeks to minimize Mt. 26:31, 33 by pointing out their Markan origin (Mk 14:27, 29), but Matthew's *retention* of Mark's material is just as significant as any deletion of it (*Peter*, 30, n. 47). See n. 15.

[70] F. F. Bruce, *Peter, Stephen, James, and John: Studies in Non-Pauline Christianity* (Grand Rapids, MI: Eerdmans, 1979), 48.

[71] W. D. Davies and Dale C. Allison, *A Critical and Exegetical Commentary on the Gospel according to Saint Matthew*, ICC (Edinburgh: T&T Clark, 1997), consider Judas's apostasy "the interpretation of almost all commentators" (3:561). Nolland, however, argues that Judas repents and experiences only the loss of temporal life, but Nolland neglects the importance of the eschatological "woe" pronounced upon him by Jesus (*Gospel of Matthew*, 1153). Davies and Allison depart from the standard view themselves, though somewhat hesitatingly (3:562).

[72] Matthew uses the more ambiguous μεταμέλομαι (not μετανοέω) at 27:3, a term capable of expressing genuine repentance (Mt. 21:32), but also simply regret or a change of mind (Mt. 21:29; cf. 2 Cor. 7:8). France considers Judas an example of Paul's "worldly sorrow" rather than "godly sorrow" (*Gospel of Matthew*, 1039). Examples of regret but not repentance in Matthew include Herod (14:9) and the rich young man (19:22), albeit with different terminology.

[73] Gundry, *Peter*, 43. As Cassidy, *Four Times Peter*, 80-1, notes, Peter's threefold failure to "watch and pray" in Gethsemane (Mt. 26:36-46) anticipates Peter's threefold denial.

exemplified in his denial.⁷⁴ Matthew certainly intensifies Peter's rocky relationship with Jesus, as Gundry is wont to point out. For example, Peter's rejection is very public, denying Jesus "before all of them" (Mt. 26:70), a detail absent from Mark's account and reminiscent of Jesus' eschatological warning of people rejecting him "before others" (Mt. 10:33).⁷⁵ Matthew also adds a different servant girl before whom Peter denies Jesus a second time (Mt. 26:71), to which Matthew then attaches Peter's strong oath (Mt. 26:72), a move up from Mark, who reserves the oath for Peter's third denial (Mk 14:71).⁷⁶ That Matthew retains Mark's depiction of Peter's self-curse (Mt. 26:74; cf. Mk 14:71) means that Peter effectively swears an oath *twice* in violation of Jesus' prohibition on oaths (Mt. 5:33-7).⁷⁷

Despite these (and other) intensifications, Peter the Rock's future is not written in stone.⁷⁸ Peter may be temporarily sown on rocky ground, but he is not the only disciple withering in shallow soil.⁷⁹ That the dictum of Mt. 10:33 is not absolute becomes clear later when Jesus predicts Peter's denial in Mt. 26:34, a denial in which *all the disciples* participate by repeating Peter's very words (Mt. 26:35b).⁸⁰ In putting Peter's protest in the form of direct speech, Matthew once again presents Peter in his familiar role as spokesman and representative of the Twelve (Mt. 14:28; 15:15; 16:15-16; 17:4, 24-5a; 18:21; 19:27; 26:33). As examples of rocky ground, all the disciples, including Peter, will "fall away" (σκανδαλίζω), a term that Jesus closely associates with the denial (Mt. 13:21; 26:31) that transpires at Jesus' arrest in Gethsemane (Mt. 26:56b).⁸¹ Thus when Peter later denies his Lord, Peter acts on behalf of all the disciples and represents them.⁸²

---

⁷⁴ Gundry, *Peter*, 50.
⁷⁵ Gundry, *Peter*, 45-6. Gundry takes Mt. 10:33 in an absolute sense, with no possibility of repentance. But the verse functions as a generalized warning, not an individual promise.
⁷⁶ Gundry, *Peter*, 47.
⁷⁷ Yet Jesus himself appears to answer affirmatively under oath at his trial (Mt. 26:63-4; contra Gundry, *Peter*, 48), so the relevance of Mt. 5:33-7 is debatable.
⁷⁸ Frank Stagg helpfully distinguishes between willful denial and human weakness, in Craig L. Blomberg, *Matthew*, NAC (Nashville: Broadman Press, 1992), 179, n. 37.
⁷⁹ In a case of possible Matthean irony, the one sown on rocky soil is a temporary (πρόσκαιρος) disciple while Peter proves himself to be a temporary apostate. Gundry considers the parable of the soils (Mt. 13:3-9, 18-23) to represent hard and fast categories, but see Tolbert, *Sowing the Gospel*, 195-200, who argues that the disciples are much more fluid in their response to Jesus, at least in Mark (albeit in a more negative direction).
⁸⁰ In the form of indirect speech. Gundry ascribes similarity to Matthew's ὁμοίως rather than sameness, but it is doubtful that Matthew's redaction of Mark's ὡσαύτως (Mk 14:31) carries that sematic distinction. Both terms are capable of expressing both ideas (BDAG, 707, s.v. ὁμοίως; 1106, s.v. ὡσαύτως). Sameness is evident at Mt. 22:26 and possibly at Mt. 27:41, Matthew's only other usages of the term.
⁸¹ Jesus' prediction in Mt. 26:31 is emphatic: "*You all* [πάντες ὑμεῖς] will fall away." That the disciples' later fleeing the scene of Jesus' arrest (Mt. 26:56) is culpable rather than pragmatic (cf. Mt. 10:23; 24:16) is precisely the link to this verse. Notice that scandal (σκανδαλισθήσεσθε; 26:31) leads directly to denial (ἀπαρνήσῃ; 26:34) in Jesus' mind, the latter an example of the former. Certainly, Peter interprets their falling away as uniformly negative (v. 33).
⁸² A point missed by Gundry, *Peter*, 53. The bystanders accuse Peter of being "one of them" (σὺ ἐξ αὐτῶν εἶ) in Mt. 26:73, clearly associating Peter with the other disciples with the present tense indicating that Peter is still regarded as a disciple of Jesus, at least from an outsider's perspective (cf. Osborne, *Matthew*, 1001). Gundry says that the other disciples only *promise* denial. But was not their scandalous flight implicit denial, symbolized later in Peter's scandalous explicit denial? So Hagner: "Peter's guilt is not greater than that of the other disciples who abandoned Jesus and *who thus in effect also denied him*" (*Matthew 14-28*, 807, my emphasis). As Peter gives verbal expression to denial, so he gives physical expression to it as well.

Unless Gundry is prepared then to apply Mt. 10:33 to *all* the disciples and regard them *all* as hopelessly apostate, Peter's tomb is not sealed.[83] Peter may be walking on rocky ground, but he will regain his footing by narrative's end.[84] Moreover, Judas appears to have left the group before Jesus utters his prediction of eventual restoration (Mt. 26:32), so the betrayer is not included in Jesus' promise to regather his wavering and withering disciples in Galilee.[85]

The scene closes with Peter's third denial and bitter weeping (Mt. 26:74-5), the final image of the Matthean Peter. Matthew intensifies Peter's weeping with the addition of πικρῶς ("bitterly"), an addition he curiously shares with Luke (Lk. 22:62).[86] Gundry links this weeping not with repentance but with the "weeping and gnashing of teeth," used throughout Matthew for eschatological loss.[87] But "weeping and gnashing of teeth" is a syntagmatic expression; "weep bitterly" is the more relevant formula, connoting grief and lamentation (Isa. 22:4; 33:7 [LXX]; *Jos. Asen.* 10:14-15; *T. Abr.* 11:11; *Asc. Isa.* 1:10; *Gk. Apoc. Ezra* 5:8).[88] But is Peter repenting or mourning the loss of potential salvation?[89] Context must decide. Peter's weeping (no gnashing of teeth!) better comports with repentance at the remembrance of Jesus' word (Mt. 26:75), especially since that original word followed Jesus' promise to reconstitute his disciples in Galilee (Mt. 26:32; cf. 28:10).[90] The sheep may scatter, but they are still *his* sheep (Mt. 26:31).[91] The juxtaposition with Judas then is contrast, not comparison.[92] Fortunately

---

[83] One wonders if the plural πετρώδη ("rocky places") in Mt. 13:5 and 20 includes all the disciples.

[84] The dictum of Mt. 10:33 with Peter's threefold emphatic denial could imply a temporary loss of salvation. At the same time, indications exist that Peter has not forfeited his discipleship. Only Peter follows (ἀκολουθέω) Jesus to his trial, albeit at a distance (Mt. 26:58), and Peter is still convicted by the word of his Master (Mt. 26:75). See Dorothy Jean Weaver, *Matthew's Missionary Discourse: A Literary Critical Analysis*, JSNTSup 38 (Sheffield: Sheffield Academic, 1990), 149, cited in Carson, *Matthew–Mark*, 625. In Gundry's view, Peter's following "from a distance" (ἀπὸ μακρόθεν) negates his discipleship (*Peter*, 43), but in comparison with the geographical whereabouts of the other disciples (Mt. 26:73!), Peter is up close and personal.

[85] This important observation effectively strips Gundry of his consistent fallback position in dealing with promises of restoration. Matthew does not indicate exactly when Judas departed from the group as does John at the supper (Jn 13:30b), but Jesus and his disciples have reached the Mount of Olives in Mt. 26:30 and Gethsemane at 26:36, and Judas does not arrive at the latter until 26:47.

[86] Suggesting "a second source for the Petrine denials being available to both Matthew and Luke" (Nolland, *Gospel of Matthew*, 1143-4).

[87] Gundry, *Peter*, 51, citing Mt. 8:12; 13:41-2, 49-50; 22:13; 24:51; 25:30. In each instance, however, Matthew uses the adverb ἐκεῖ to denote the *place* of weeping and gashing of teeth: in the eschatological realm, not in the earthly where repentance is still possible—contra Gundry's emphasis on the location of Peter's weeping "outside" the courtyard of the high priest (51).

[88] Gundry's attempt to make Peter's weeping "bitterly" a stand-in for gnashing of teeth bears the marks of special pleading (*Peter*, 52, 125). Presumably all Matthew had to do to indicate Peter's damnation was to continue the use of a favorite stock phrase.

[89] Gundry argues the latter (*Peter*, 54).

[90] Gundry gives no attention to the promise of restoration in Mt. 26:32, a critical oversight (*Peter*, 39–41, 53).

[91] Not wolves in sheep's clothing (Mt. 7:15; 10:16)! Peter and the other disciples are sheep, albeit straying ones. Characteristic of Jesus the shepherd in Matthew, Jesus seeks to gather such straying sheep (18:12-13) so that they do not perish (18:14).

[92] If comparison, we have apparently two types of false disciples, one explicit and the other implicit, at least until Peter's public denial.

for Peter, denial of the Son of Man is not the unforgivable sin (cf. Mt. 12:31-2).[93] If Peter the effectually called fisherman repented once before, he will do so again.[94]

III. Peter as Future Disciple

Matthew's restoration of Peter is less than direct. When it comes time to narrate the empty tomb (Mt. 28:1-10), Matthew deletes Mark's explicit mention of Peter (Mk 16:7), preferring instead to lump Peter with the eleven disciples (Mt. 28:16).[95] For Matthew, Peter's calling as the first disciple is "much more important than is the first Easter appearance to him."[96] According to Gundry, Peter is a false disciple among true ones, a weed among wheat.[97] That Jesus calls the disciples "my brothers" (οἱ ἀδελφοί μου; Mt. 28:10), however, is strong evidence that Peter is in fact restored, since the phrase occurs elsewhere in Matthew for genuine believers in Jesus (12:49; 18:15[2x], 21, 35; 23:8; 25:40). The return to Galilee (Mt. 28:16; cf. 26:32; 28:7, 10), the scene of Peter's effectual calling and repentance (Mt. 4:18-20), and the future gentile mission (Mt. 4:12-17) also support this conclusion. Admittedly, Matthew muddies the waters when he says that some of the disciples in Galilee "doubted" (Mt. 28:17), recalling Peter's earlier hesitation on the sea (Mt. 14:31).[98]

But the reader does not approach the final chapter of Matthew unawares. The reader knows that Peter's future role as a fisher of people will result in the evangelization of the nations and the formation of the ἐκκλησία: "You are Peter [Πέτρος] and on this rock [πέτρᾳ] I will build my church" (Mt. 16:18). Whatever the meaning of this Greek word-

---

[93] Davies and Allison apply the logion of Mt. 12:32 to Peter so that "the judgment of 10:33 will not be spoken against him" (*Gospel according to Saint Matthew*, 3:55). So, too, Nolland asks, "Does 12:32 embed within Matthew's story the possibility of forgiveness for one who has behaved as Peter has here?" (*Gospel of Matthew*, 1144). See also France, *Gospel of Matthew*, 484; Osborne, *Matthew*, 477. But Gundry questions the relevance of Mt. 12:31-2 to Peter's situation (*Peter*, 45-6, 54-5).

[94] Hence the "recency effect" of Peter's weeping receives reinforcement from the "primacy effect" of Peter's initial calling (cf. Sternberg, *Expositional Modes*, 93). Given Peter's absence at the cross, the weeping here may mark the beginning of a process rather than its culmination.

[95] "Since Judas is dead by now, the reader will conclude that Peter is among the eleven" (Syreeni, 'Peter as Character', 147). Pheme Perkins attributes the lack of reference to Peter to Matthew's desire to show how Jesus "restores the whole group of disciples at the end of the Gospel": Pheme Perkins, *Peter: Apostle for the Whole Church* (Minneapolis: Fortress, 2000), 72 (orig. published by University of South Carolina Press, 1994). The reader knows that *all* the disciples had fled in fear (Mt. 26:31, 56b).

[96] Luz, *Matthew 8-20*, 368, referring to all the Synoptic Gospels. Bockmuehl comments that "it seems odd that Matthew's is the only one of the canonical gospels that fails to single out Peter as a resurrection witness" (*Simon Peter*, 83-4).

[97] Gundry, *Peter*, 55, 100. But since the weeds become apparent prior to harvest as evidenced in Peter's very public denial (*Peter*, 3, 25), one wonders how Peter can effectively exercise his ministry in a post-resurrection context if he has already been publicly exposed as false and apostate. I am anticipating my discussion below.

[98] "In light of all that the reader has learned about Peter, the question is inevitably raised whether Peter still has his doubts. No answer is given; but surely the reader is left with some doubts about Peter" (Syreeni, "Peter as Character," 147). On whether οἱ δὲ is partitive ("but some") or pronominal ("they"), see Hagner, *Matthew 14-28*, 884-5. He opts for the latter, contending that the tension of faith and doubt characterizes every believer.

play, the important point is the promised future role of Peter.[99] To this promise Jesus adds another: "I will give you the keys of the kingdom of heaven" (Mt. 16:19). Again, whatever the meaning of these words, and the binding and loosing they entail (v. 19b), Peter will play a future role as wielder of the keys.[100] The reiteration of this promise to the entire group of disciples (Mt. 18:18) does not cancel Peter's role, for "the keys belong to Peter alone."[101] Moreover, in response to Peter's question about eschatological reward, Jesus promises that Peter and his fellow disciples will participate in a new world order judging the twelve tribes of Israel (Mt. 19:27-8).

Are all these future predictions untrustworthy? Is Jesus an unreliable narrator? Characterization affects Christology.[102] Because Jesus has prophesied reliably within the story world of Matthew, the reader is confident in the future realization of these promises. None of the prophecies regarding Peter will materialize unless Peter repents.[103] Peter may be an "open-ended" character, but the reader can fill in the gap.[104] Gundry seeks to mitigate these and similar passages by appealing to Judas's presence among the disciples who collectively receive the promises.[105] But the narrator has sufficiently prepared the reader for Judas's treachery and false discipleship, consistently telling the reader that Judas is "the betrayer" and marking him out as "that man" with a

---

[99] Becker, *Simon Petrus*, 83. The literature on Mt. 16:17-19 is vast (for a history of interpretation, see Luz, *Matthew 8–20*, 370–5). Gundry equates the foundation of the church not with Peter but with Jesus' words, linking ἐπὶ ταύτῃ τῇ πέτρᾳ in Mt. 16:18 to ἐπὶ τὴν πέτραν in Mt. 7:24 (*Peter*, 20-4). Gundry justifies this interpretive maneuver partly by appealing to the switch in pronouns (from σὺ to ταύτῃ), but the immediate context is Peter's Christological revelation, not Jesus' teachings. His view also seemingly requires an adversative force to καί, which is unlikely. More likely, ταύτῃ is pointing back to Peter's confession. As spokesman for this confession, "Peter becomes the foundation stone for the church" (Nolland, *Gospel of Matthew*, 669). Chrys C. Caragounis considers Peter's confession as the church's foundation "the only real option": Chrys C. Caragounis, *Peter and the Rock* (Berlin: de Gruyter, 1990), 106.

[100] Gundry identifies the "keys" of binding and loosing with conveying the words of Jesus without the aid of interpretation (*Peter*, 25). In Matthean terms, however, "A teacher who does not understand what he himself teaches is a blind man leading the blind": Ulrich Luz, "The Disciples in the Gospel according to Matthew," in *The Interpretation of Matthew*, 2nd edn, ed. Graham Stanton (Edinburgh: T&T Clark, 1995), 120; cf. Mt. 15:14. If the keys involve Peter in determining matters of halakha (Mt. 15:15; 17:24-7; 18:21), interpretation would be essential (see Perkins, *Peter*, 66–67). Nowhere in Matthew is κλείς or its verbal cognate κλείω associated with the teachings of Jesus.

[101] Stewart, *Peter*, 44. Peter is also the only disciple singularly called "blessed" in Matthew (16:17). Note also the emphatic σοι and σὺ at Mt. 16:18. Brown et al.'s question is pertinent here: "If all the authority is meant for the body of disciples, why is Peter so often the one singled out by Matthew?" (*Peter in the New Testament*, 105).

[102] Gundry admits that Jesus as an "unreliable character" is "not at all the image of Jesus that Matthew wants to project" and goes on to affirm Jesus as in fact reliable (*Peter*, 59).

[103] Gundry's view that Peter continues in the post-Easter period as a false disciple strains credulity in light of Peter's public exposure at his denial and the stupendous nature of these promises. Moreover, the promise of a throne in Mt. 19:28 occurs *after* the eschatological harvest when the weeds have already been separated (Mt. 13:30). Jesus will therefore have to reconstitute Peter to prepare him for his future role (Brown et al., *Peter in the New Testament*, 94). As with his earlier experience on the sea, the sinful Peter "kehrt auch in Reue um, und der Kleingläubige ruft zum Hern, und wird gerettet" (Dschulnigg, *Petrus im Neuen Tetsament*, 55).

[104] Seymour Chatman, *Story and Discourse: Narrative Structure in Fiction and Film* (Ithaca, NY: Cornell University Press, 1978), 131-2.

[105] Particularly at Mt. 18:18 (Gundry, *Peter*, 24), but also see his wider application (88-9). As previously noted, Judas was likely not present to hear Jesus' promise of restoration in Mt. 26:32.

scripturally assigned fate (Mt. 26:24).[106] This explicit identification of Judas restricts his polemical value.[107] Nor is Judas ever singled out by name by Jesus for a post-Easter role. This narrative competence enables the reader to discriminate the generalizing plurals accordingly.[108] Of course, if the Betrayer genuinely repents, the image of "Judas the apostate" must fall away.

IV. Conclusion

A character analysis of Peter in the Gospel of Matthew offers another way around the polemical treatments that have dominated discussions in the past. But ecclesiology is not the only framework that has shut Peter's character up in prison; some literary approaches, as Seymour Chatman observes, would hold Peter hostage as well, viewing characterization only as a function of plot.[109] In contrast to Judas, without whose treachery the passion of Jesus does not come to pass, Peter's denial does not seem to advance the storyline at all.[110] So what is the point of the denial? A lapsed but not ultimately failed disciple, Peter is symbolic of the kind of discipleship "that is never completed, is likely to be in constant flux, and cannot be idealized."[111] If Judas, "the quintessential false disciple and apostate" (to use Gundry's words), represents false disciples in Matthew's church, the hesitant and even failed Peter represents those of "little faith." Apostasy is not the only possible response in times of persecution. It is the repentant and confessing Peter upon whom Jesus builds his church.

Gundry helpfully points out the many negative features of Matthew's characterization of Peter otherwise neglected or ignored. In doing so, however, Gundry runs the risk of

---

[106] Judas is known as "the betrayer" in every mention of his name (Mt. 10:4; 26:25, 47-8; 27:3) with the exception of Mt. 26:14, which depicts Judas in the very act of betrayal. By contrast, Peter is never labeled "the denier" as if denial were a permanent trait. Gundry's claim that Matthew is bound by common tradition in not labeling Peter a denier (121) is methodologically flawed from both a redactional and narrative-critical point of view. See n. 15.

[107] As a "marked man," Judas cannot function as a warning to the possibility of closet false disciples in the church in the way that Peter's implicit falsity can. But even Peter's falsity is eventually exposed, so his polemical value is limited as well. Judas's being marked out opens up the possibility that since Peter is not so marked he is capable of repentance.

[108] The disciples often function simply as a group character in Matthew (Powell, *What?*, 51). While the number twelve at Mt. 19:28 is clearly conventional (Luz, "Disciples," 116), does the reader anticipate a replacement for Judas beyond Matthew's narrative? Since Matthew is not writing a second volume, a replacement for Judas is not part of his story as it is for Luke (Acts 1:15-26). On narrative competence, see Genette, *Narrative Discourse*, 77.

[109] Chatman, *Story and Discourse*, 111: "They wish to analyze only what characters do in a story, not what they are."

[110] Burnett, "Characterization," 21; Kingsbury, *Matthew as Story*, 13. Peter's failure may bear important implications for Matthew's church, but that is different from saying that Peter's denial is essential to Matthew's plot. In contrast, without Judas's betrayal, there is no arrest, and without an arrest, there is no crucifixion and subsequent resurrection. Judas's "repentance" (Mt. 27:3-10), on the other hand, is extraneous to the plot and functions as a foil for Peter's restoration.

[111] Edwards, "Uncertain Faith," 59. On Peter's potential as a symbolic character, see Syreeni, "Peter as Character," 106-52.

reducing Peter to a decidedly "flat" character, at least soteriologically.[112] Though Peter can exemplify both positive and negative aspects of discipleship, he was never truly a disciple in the first place.[113] By contrast, Peter is a sufficiently "round" character that functions as an example *par excellence* of a disciple both lapsed and repentant.[114] Peter "is confessor *and* tempter, denier *and* penitent, courageous *and* weak."[115] In this way Peter represents the Matthean disciples as a whole, who manifest the same conflicting traits.[116] Like them, Peter is unpredictable.[117] Thus the ever-vacillating Peter in Matthew is a failed but not a false disciple.

---

[112] Gundry's Peter is "round" in so far as he appears (to a first-time reader) as a false disciple in disguise, exposed over time. But from the perspective of a multiple implied reader who already knows Peter's falsity going in, Peter is soteriologically flat, incapable of salvation.

[113] Gundry speaks of Peter's "loss of salvation" as having to do with "the loss of a salvation that might have been had in the end, not with the loss of salvation that was *truly had in the first place*" (*Peter*, vii, my emphasis). But then one wonders in what sense Peter is an apostate. Even if the distinction between flat and round characters is relative at times (Rimmon-Kenan, *Narrative Fiction*, 40-1), Peter's ultimate fate is never left open by Gundry. Of course, one could object that my reading of Peter as an effectually called disciple makes him soteriologically flat as well, *unless* Peter experiences a temporary loss of salvation (see n. 84). Whether Matthew thinks of the elect as potentially susceptible to a temporary loss of salvation is not entirely clear (see εἰ δυνατόν at Mt. 24:24). As Osborne points out, it is not possible to deceive the elect in any *final* sense (*Matthew*, 887, my emphasis). In Peter's case, his repentance confirms his election.

[114] "Jede Jüngerin und jeder Jünger Jesu kann sich im je eigenen Versagen als Glaubende(r) im ersten Jünger wiedererkennen" (Dschulnigg, *Petrus im Neuen Testament*, 54).

[115] Luz, *Matthew 8-20*, 366 (italics in original). Wiarda observes how the sequence of faith and failure characterizes many of Matthew's Petrine stories (*Interpreting*, 180).

[116] Luz, *Matthew 8-20*, 366. On the disciples as a group character in Matthew, see Jeannine K. Brown, *The Disciples in Narrative Perspective: The Portrayal and Function of the Matthean Disciples*, SBL Academia Biblica 9 (Leiden and Boston: Brill, 2002), who notes widespread agreement on the "mixed" traits of the disciples in Matthew (18).

[117] As Chatman observes, round characters "possess a variety of traits, some of them conflicting or even contradictory; their behavior is not predictable—they are capable of changing, of surprising us" (*Story and Discourse*, 132).

10

The Corporate Portrayal of Women in the Gospel of Matthew as Narrative Disciples

Jeffrey W. Aernie

I. Introduction

The portrayal of women in Matthew's Gospel represents a unique contribution to the narrative of Jesus. Although no individual woman has a sustained presence in the gospel, women feature throughout Matthew's narrative. Women appear prominently in the extended introduction to the life and ministry of Jesus (Mt. 1–2). Women benefit from the restorative power of Jesus' ministry (Mt. 8:14-15; 9:18-26). Women engage with Jesus concerning the inclusive and sacrificial nature of God's kingdom (Mt. 15:21-8; 20:20-8). And women are central participants in the narration of Jesus' crucifixion and resurrection (Mt. 26:6-13; 27:55-6, 61; 28:1-11). The narrative presence of these women provides Matthew's audience—both ancient and contemporary—with a distinct set of characters with whom they can interact and from whom they can learn. The intent in this chapter is to examine the narrative significance of these women as a corporate character who contribute to Matthew's narrative portrayal of the messianic king Jesus.

II. The Women as a Corporate Character

One of the primary ways in which Matthew's Gospel develops its theological narrative of Jesus' inauguration of God's kingdom is through its portrayal of Jesus' engagement with other characters. For this reason, the study of characters is a crucial component in the analysis of the meaning and impact of the gospel.[1] The women in Matthew's Gospel function primarily as minor characters.[2] For example, they feature as imagined

---

[1] See Cornelis Bennema, *A Theory of Character in New Testament Narrative* (Minneapolis: Fortress, 2014).

[2] Within studies of character and characterization, there is a general distinction between "major" and "minor" characters. Major characters are those who have a sustained or recurring presence in the narrative, while minor characters are those who lack a sustained or recurring presence in the narrative. See Elizabeth Struthers Malbon, "The Major Importance of the Minor Characters in Mark," in *The New Literary Criticism and the New Testament*, ed. Elizabeth Struthers Malbon and Edgar V. McKnight, JSNTSup 109 (Sheffield: Sheffield Academic, 1994), 58–86 (60).

actors within Jesus' parables (e.g., Mt. 25:1-13), as distinct participants in single scenes (e.g., Mt. 8:14-15), or as late additions to the narrative (e.g., Mt. 27:55-6). An essential contribution to the understanding of minor characters is the analysis of character and characterization by Joel Williams.[3] Of particular importance is Williams's application of the concept of narrative analogy to the study of characters in the gospels.[4] Narrative analogy describes the way in which an author invests individual scenes with similar story components so that the audience identifies connections between them and evaluates the impact of their similarities and differences. With respect to characters, narrative analogy allows us to consider both how characters function within their individual scenes and how they may relate to other characters at other points of the narrative. While discussions of characterization normally focus on the portrayal of a single individual such as Mary or a single group such as the disciples, the concept of narrative analogy suggests that it is fruitful to consider the connection between distinct individuals who appear at different stages in the narrative. This is especially important for minor characters, such as the women in Matthew's Gospel, who lack a sustained or recurring presence in the narrative. Narrative analogy suggests that even though these minor characters have limited narrative presence, their connection with one another extends their narrative impact.

Building on the concept of narrative analogy with respect to characters in Matthew's Gospel, I argue in this chapter that the inclusion and portrayal of women in Matthew's narrative creates a corporate connection between them as women.[5] The women are essential both to the development of the narrative at the point at which each appears and in coordination with one another. As the narratives of women in the gospel are read in concert with one another, their narrative impact is extended.[6] In other words, the narratives of women in Matthew's Gospel function in analogous concert—as narratives of women—to create a corporate character which contributes to the development and portrayal of several of the gospel's central themes. Matthew's portrayal of women illuminates the identity of Jesus (Mt. 1), demonstrates the restorative impact of Jesus' ministry (Mt. 8–9), accentuates the paradoxical and sacrificial inversion of Jesus' ministry (Mt. 15 and 20), and illustrates faithful

---

[3] Joel F. Williams, *Other Followers of Jesus: Minor Characters as Major Figures in Mark's Gospel*, JSNTSup 102 (Sheffield: JSOT Press, 1994).

[4] Williams, *Other Followers*, 36–54.

[5] For studies of the women in Matthew's Gospel, see especially Janice Capel Anderson, "Matthew: Gender and Reading," *Semeia* 28 (1983): 3–27; E. Anne Clements, *Mothers on the Margin? The Significance of the Women in Matthew's Genealogy* (Eugene, OR: Pickwick, 2014); Jane Kopas, "Jesus and Women in Matthew," *TTod* 47 (1990): 13–21; Stuart L. Love, *Jesus and Marginal Women: The Gospel of Matthew in Social-Scientific Perspective* (Eugene, OR: Cascade, 2009); Baby Parambi, *The Discipleship of Women in the Gospel according to Matthew: An Exegetical Theological Study of Matt 27:51b–56, 57–61 and 28:1–10* (Rome: Editrice Pontificia Università Gregoriana, 2003); and Elaine M. Wainwright, *Towards a Feminist Critical Reading of the Gospel according to Matthew*, BZNW 60 (Berlin: de Gruyter, 1991).

[6] This chapter will not explore the narratives of every woman that appears in Matthew's Gospel. My aim is not to suggest that women are portrayed uniformly or simplistically in Matthew's Gospel, but rather to show that Matthew's portrayal of certain women in the narrative extends his portrait of Jesus' inauguration of God's kingdom.

commitment to the crucified and resurrected Jesus (Mt. 26–8). The following sections survey the individual portraits of these women to highlight their collective contribution to Matthew's narrative portrayal of Jesus.

III. Women in Jesus' Genealogy (Matthew 1)

Matthew's genealogy is an intentionally crafted theological statement that establishes the messianic framework for the gospel's narrative portrayal of Jesus. A unique aspect of Matthew's genealogy is its inclusion of women.[7] In the first section of the genealogy, Matthew explicitly names three women—Tamar (Mt. 1:3), Rahab (Mt. 1:5), and Ruth (Mt. 1:5)—and in the second section implicitly refers to another—"she of Uriah" (Mt. 1:6), that is, Bathsheba. In the conclusion of the genealogy, Matthew then names Mary (Mt. 1:16) and stresses her essential role in Jesus' birth. The presence of these women demonstrates the inclusive nature of Jesus' messianic ministry and provides an introductory lens through which to understand the wider portrayal of women in Matthew's narrative. The unique, and perhaps unexpected, inclusion of women in Matthew's genealogy is regularly seen as evidence that there is a specific thread uniting them.[8] For example, Peter-Ben Smit suggests that the annotated references to Tamar, Rahab, Ruth, and Bathsheba are an integrated feature of the genealogy that provides insight into Jesus' messianic identity and foreshadows Mary's distinct role in the narrative.[9] This interpretative framework is constructive in so far as it demonstrates that Matthew's portrayal of women in the narrative is intentional. The unique introduction of these women at the beginning of the gospel indicates their foundational importance for understanding how women throughout the rest of the narrative relate to Jesus and represent characteristics of his messianic ministry.[10]

However, the interpretative framework which emphasizes the connection between Tamar, Rahab, Ruth, Bathsheba, and Mary requires at least three qualifications. First, the inclusion of these women is not an isolated revision to the genealogy, but rather a further instance of Matthew's intentional shaping of the material (cf. Mt. 1:1-2, 6, 11, 16-17). The annotations involving women are essential, but they function only within the wider narrative and theological formation of the genealogy.[11] Second, it is important to avoid oversimplifying the purpose for which Matthew refers to the four Old Testament women. The diversity of both their scriptural portrayals and their historical

---

[7] See especially Clements, *Mothers*; and Jason B. Hood, *The Messiah, His Brothers, and the Nations: Matthew 1.1-17*, LNTS 441 (London: T&T Clark, 2011), 88–138.
[8] For example, Ulrich Luz, *Matthew 1-7*, trans. James E. Crouch, Hermeneia (Minneapolis: Fortress, 2007), 82.
[9] Peter-Ben Smit, "Something about Mary? Remarks about the Five Women in the Matthean Genealogy," *NTS* 56 (2010): 191–207.
[10] Cf. Clements, *Mothers*, 268: "Read as intertexts to the Gospel the five women establish the narrative tone concerning women as a gender group, setting the terms of reference that guide the implied reader's response towards women in the ensuing gospel narrative."
[11] John Nolland, "The Four (Five) Women and Other Annotations in Matthew's Genealogy," *NTS* 43 (1997): 527–39 (533).

reception suggest that it is unlikely that Matthew includes the women for a uniform reason. The common interpretative traditions which portray the women as sinners, as "irregular" in some way, or as non-Israelites all fail to account for the diversity of the women as individuals and the unique contributions they make to Matthew's genealogy.[12] Third, it is important to avoid oversimplifying Matthew's unique reference to Bathsheba as "she of Uriah" (Mt. 1:6). Several of the challenges inherent in the common interpretative traditions concerning the women stem precisely from their inability to account for Bathsheba. The narrative portrayal of her abuse by David highlights his moral failure, not hers. Her later conception of Solomon is never characterized as "irregular" in any way. And she is likely the daughter of an Israelite (Eliam in 2 Sam. 11:3; Ammiel in 1 Chron. 3:5).[13] As Jason Hood argues, it seems more plausible that Matthew specifically names Uriah, along with Tamar, Rahab, and Ruth, to develop the positive position of those outside of Israel within Jesus' genealogy.[14]

These qualifications all suggest the need for a nuanced discussion of Matthew's inclusion of named women in the genealogy. Anne Clements demonstrates how the individual narratives of Tamar, Rahab, and Ruth provide positive examples of women who embody traits that evoke Yahweh's own character—righteousness, mercy, and fidelity.[15] In their representation of these characteristics, the named women coordinate with the subsequent narratives of women in Matthew's Gospel, especially as they embody representations of Jesus' mercy (e.g., Mt. 8:14-15; 9:18-26) and demonstrate the persistent allegiance demanded of Jesus' disciples (e.g., Mt. 9:22; 15:28; 27:55-6).[16] The collective identity of Tamar, Rahab, and Ruth (along with Uriah) evokes the inclusive reality of Jesus' messianic identity and ministry.[17] In this way the named women prepare us not only for portrayals of presumably Israelite women in the narrative, such as Peter's mother-in-law (Mt. 8:14-15), but also those outside of Israel who demonstrate remarkable awareness of the in-breaking of God's kingdom. Here Matthew's identification of the woman in Mt. 15:22 as a Canaanite is significant. The thematic emphasis in Mt. 15:21-8 on the direction and boundaries of Jesus' mission highlights the same focus on Israel and the nations present in Matthew's genealogy. Jesus' messianic identity impacts both "the brothers" (Mt. 1:2, 11)—a wide reference to Israel—and the nations. The presence of the named women in Mt. 1:3-5 helps to introduce this important dimension of Jesus' ministry.

Matthew's reference to Mary at the conclusion of the genealogy emphasizes her unique role as the bearer of the messiah (Μαρίας, ἐξ ἧς ἐγεννήθη Ἰησοῦς ὁ λεγόμενος Χριστός; Mt. 1:16). Although Mary's introduction into the genealogy is distinct from that of the women in Mt. 1:3-6, who are all introduced with the same grammatical

---

[12] For an overview of these interpretative traditions and their weaknesses, see Hood, *Messiah*, 88–118.
[13] The frequent assertion that Mt. 1:6 refers to Bathsheba as "she of Uriah" (ἐκ τῆς τοῦ Οὐρίου) specifically to highlight her connection with a non-Jewish tradition seems to stem from the desire to link the women with the theme of inclusion, not from an examination of Bathsheba herself.
[14] Hood, *Messiah* 119–38.
[15] Clements, *Mothers*, 179–93.
[16] Cf. Clements, *Mothers*, 179–93.
[17] On the complexity of Tamar's ancestry, see Richard Bauckham, "Tamar's Ancestry and Rahab's Marriage: Two Problems in the Matthean Genealogy," *NovT* 37 (1995): 313–29.

formula (ἐκ τῆς plus name), Smit argues that the resonance between the forms outweighs their differences.[18] The distinct reference to these women coordinates their presence in the genealogy. Although Matthew's subsequent characterization of Mary does not emphasize the same dimensions of Jesus' ministry foreshadowed by Tamar, Rahab, Ruth, and Bathsheba (cf. Mt. 1:18–2:21; 12:46-50; 13:55-6), her unique naming in the genealogy connects the women's narratives together as women.

Furthermore, the dramatic events of the birth narrative—both Mary's conception of Jesus and the immediate political danger of Jesus' birth—connect Mary with the tumultuous experiences portrayed in the narratives of Tamar, Rahab, Ruth, and Bathsheba. Together these women demonstrate that Jesus' messianic ministry impacts people across ethnic, social, political, relational, and biological divides. Importantly, Mary also bridges the divide between the genealogy and the narrative material in Matthew's Gospel. Her narrative portrayal represents an essential component of Matthew's characterization of women. With Tamar, Rahab, Ruth, and Bathsheba, Mary forms the basis of a corporate character that extends throughout Matthew's wider narrative. These women provide the genealogical foundation for Matthew's characterization of women.

IV. Healed Women (Matthew 8–9)

Matthew twice describes Jesus' ministry with a threefold structure: teaching in the synagogues, proclaiming the gospel of the kingdom, and healing every sickness and disease (Mt. 4:23-5; 9:35-8). In broad terms, Matthew 8–9 provides an extended portrait of the restorative impact of Jesus' proclamation of the kingdom. An element of Matthew's structured portrayal of this dimension of Jesus' ministry is the healing narratives of three women: Peter's mother-in-law (Mt. 8:14-15), a woman enduring chronic bleeding (Mt. 9:20-2), and the daughter of a local leader (Mt. 9:18-19, 23-6). The healing narratives of these three women are closely associated with the ministry of Jesus, not merely in the portrayal of the direct interaction between the women and Jesus, but in the way that each narrative emphasizes characteristics of discipleship. The language that Matthew uses to describe each of these women creates key linguistic connections to the in-breaking of God's kingdom.[19]

A. Peter's Mother-in-law (Matthew 8:14-15)

Within Mt. 8:1-17 Jesus heals three individuals: an individual with a skin disease (Mt. 8:2-4), a slave (Mt. 8:5-13), and a woman (Mt. 8:14-15). Each of the healings resonates with the inclusive portrait of the kingdom developed in Jesus' genealogy (Mt. 1:1-17). Matthew's structural foreshadowing in the genealogy that Jesus' messianic ministry would impact people across social, ethnic, and relational boundaries is here brought to

---

[18] Smit, "Mary," 198.
[19] See especially Elaine M. Wainwright, *Women Healing/Healing Women: The Genderization of Healing in Early Christianity* (London: Equinox, 2006), 139–59.

fruition in the healing of three individuals who, for different reasons, could be conceived of as outsiders.[20] The relationship of these healings to Jesus' messianic ministry is further established in Mt. 8:16-17, where Matthew positions them within an Isaianic framework that expresses the expansive reality of Jesus' inauguration of the kingdom as being for both Israel and the nations.[21]

Within this context, Matthew's concise description of Jesus' interaction with Peter's mother-in-law accentuates both Jesus' restorative authority over sickness and the importance of her response to him. When Jesus enters Peter's house and sees the suffering of Peter's mother-in-law, he acts decisively with immediate effect—"he touched her hand and the fever left her" (Mt. 8:14). Peter's mother-in-law responds in an equally decisive manner—"she got up and served [διηκόνει] him" (Mt. 8:15). The narration of Jesus' action reiterates the restorative reality of the kingdom exhibited in the healings of the individual with a skin disease and the centurion's slave. And the narration of the woman's action emphasizes her embodiment of kingdom service. Within Matthew's Gospel the language of service is especially connected with Jesus' ministry in his dramatic declaration that "the son of Man did not come to be served [διακονηθῆναι], but to serve [διακονῆσαι], and to give his life as a ransom for many" (Mt. 20:28). Apart from Jesus, the only human agents to whom the language of service is attributed in Matthew's Gospel are women—Peter's mother-in-law (Mt. 8:15) and the women who follow Jesus to the cross (Mt. 27:55). Although the specific location of Jesus' act of restoration in Matthew 8 suggests that the service that Peter's mother-in-law offers is primarily domestic, this does not diminish its significance. That Jesus' ministry is defined using language regularly associated with the domestic responsibilities of women and slaves inverts its value, with the service that Peter's mother-in-law offers functioning in the narrative as a representative act of discipleship.[22]

B. The Bleeding Woman and the Leader's Daughter (Matthew 9:18-26)

The final section of Matthew 8–9 includes three further healing miracles: the restoration of two women (Mt. 9:18-26), two blind men (Mt. 9:27-31), and a single mute man (Mt. 9:32-4). The first of these narratives, the combined restoration of a bleeding woman and the daughter of a local leader (Mt. 9:18-26), appears as an intercalated narrative throughout the Synoptic tradition (cf. Mk 5:21-43; Lk. 8:40-56). Within the narrative context of Matthew's Gospel, the healing of these two women initiates a series of scenes which illustrate Jesus' preceding comments to the Pharisees about the merciful shape of his ministry and those to the disciples of John the Baptist about its newness (Mt. 9:9-17). Jesus' interaction with each of these women provides a key example of the restorative newness of his ministry.

---

[20] R.T. France, *The Gospel of Matthew*, NICNT (Grand Rapids, MI: Eerdmans, 2007), 305.
[21] On the Isaianic framework in this section, see especially Jeannine K. Brown and Kyle Roberts, *Matthew*, THNTC (Grand Rapids, MI: Eerdmans, 2018), 86–7.
[22] Brown and Roberts, *Matthew*, 86; Donald A. Hagner, *Matthew*, 2 vols., WBC 33 (Nashville, TN: Thomas Nelson, 1995–2000), 1:209; cf. Jeffrey W. Aernie, *Narrative Discipleship: Portraits of Women in the Gospel of Mark* (Eugene, OR: Pickwick, 2018), 52–5.

Matthew's succinct narration of Jesus' revivification of the leader's daughter (Mt. 9:25) echoes his earlier interaction with Peter's mother-in-law (Mt. 8:14-15). In each scene, Jesus enters the room, grasps the woman by the hand, and restores her to life (ἠγέρθη). Although Matthew does not narrate the young woman's subsequent response, the linguistic parallels between her narrative and that of Peter's mother-in-law may suggest that the young woman's experience also evokes the way in which she embodies aspects of Jesus' ministry.[23] More cautiously, the portrayal of this young woman's restoration confirms that the restorative impact of Jesus' ministry will not be bound by gender, age, or circumstance.

Matthew's equally concise narration of Jesus' restoration of the woman with chronic bleeding (Mt. 9:20-2) also evokes Jesus' interaction with Peter's mother-in-law (Mt. 8:14-15). In a reversal of that earlier narrative where Jesus enters a private dwelling and touches the woman, the action of the bleeding woman is here placed in the narrative foreground, as she goes out to a public space and touches Jesus in the hope that it will bring relief from her extensive ailment. There are also narrative connections between the portrayal of the bleeding woman and the young woman's father. Matthew introduces each with the same language (ἰδοὺ ἄρχων in Mt. 9:18; ἰδοὺ γυνή in Mt. 9:20), but the way in which they approach Jesus is manifestly different. The father approaches Jesus and makes a direct request for his daughter, while the woman approaches from behind and seeks restoration indirectly. Despite these distinctions, each initiates their engagement with Jesus and embodies certainty in their belief in his restorative ability. The woman's internal certainty that if she merely touches Jesus' garment she will be restored is confirmed in Jesus' declaration that her "faith" (πίστις) has saved her. That it is the woman's πίστις which brings about her restoration and positions her narrative within the wider context of Matthew's portrayal of discipleship. The language of πίστις is used throughout Matthew's Gospel to highlight the importance of allegiance to Jesus (Mt. 8:10; 9:2, 29; 15:28). The centrality of allegiance is reinforced in Matthew's repeated references to the disciples' "little faith" (ὀλιγόπιστος), which provide negative examples meant to encourage Matthew's audience to embody consistent trust in Jesus (Mt. 6:30; 8:26; 14:31; 16:8; cf. ὀλιγοπιστία in Mt. 17:20). In contrast to the disciples, the bleeding woman embodies the requisite allegiance that defines kingdom participants.

The woman's narrative also highlights an important transition with respect to her identity. In her introduction into the narrative, she is defined only by the reality of her chronic ailment (καὶ ἰδοὺ γυνὴ αἱμορροοῦσα δώδεκα ἔτη; Mt. 9:20), but when Jesus turns and sees her, he identifies her immediately as daughter (θύγατερ; Mt. 9:22). This familial description places her alongside the disciples whom Jesus defines as brother, sister, and mother in Mt. 12:50. This woman's initiative in approaching Jesus positions her not as someone excluded from the community but as its representative.[24] That Jesus describes the

---

[23] See, for example, Wainwright, *Women Healing*, 148. The young woman's father also provides an important narrative portrait of discipleship. His concern for his daughter embodies the compassion that defines Jesus' ministry (Mt. 9:36; 14:14; 15:32; 20:34) and his certainty concerning Jesus' restorative authority embodies the faith demonstrated by other kingdom participants (e.g., Mt. 9:10; 15:28).

[24] On the cultic implications of the woman's narrative, see Matthew Thiessen, *Jesus and the Forces of Death: The Gospels' Portrayal of Ritual Impurity within First-Century Judaism* (Grand Rapids, MI: Baker Academic, 2020), 69–96.

woman's restoration with the holistic language of "salvation" (σέσωκέν σε; Mt. 9:22) may also suggest this emphasis on her inclusion in the community. She is restored physically, socially, and spiritually.[25] In this way she joins Peter's mother-in-law and the daughter of the leader as narrative representatives of restoration and those called to embody that restoration.

V. Unexpected Women (Matthew 15 and 20)

Women feature in several ways in the extended material between Jesus' mission discourse (Mt. 9:35–11:1) and his triumphal entry into Jerusalem (Mt. 21:1-11). There are broad references to women in Jesus' description of the significance of John the Baptist (Mt. 11:11), in his teaching on the purity regulations and divorce (Mt. 15:6; 19:1-11), and in relation to the extensive crowds for which he provides (Mt. 14:21; 15:38). Jesus' mother and sisters are mentioned briefly (Mt. 12:46-50; 13:55-6), and Mt. 14:1-12 refers to the infamous role of Herodias and her daughter in the murder of John the Baptist.[26] Beyond these references, the narratives of two women in this section of the gospel extend Matthew's portrait of the way in which women relate to Jesus: those of the Canaanite woman (Mt. 15:21-8) and the mother of Zebedee's sons (Mt. 20:20-8). Each of these women engages with Jesus in unexpected ways and with unexpected results. Both the Canaanite woman and the mother of Zebedee's sons participate in stark verbal engagements with Jesus which elucidate the nature of both God's kingdom and discipleship. Jesus' initial rebuke of each woman highlights the unexpected nature of their response. The Canaanite woman persists in her dialogue and demonstrates her great faith (Mt. 15:28) and the mother of Zebedee's sons persists in following Jesus and demonstrates her service to him (Mt. 27:55-6).

A. The Canaanite Woman (Matthew 15:21-8)

After the extended parables discourse in Matthew 13 there is a series of narratives that center on an evaluation of Jesus' Christological identity, framed by both negative (Mt. 13:53-8) and positive (Mt. 16:13-20) valuations. In this context, Matthew narrates a dramatic encounter between a Canaanite woman and Jesus in the regions of Tyre and Sidon (Mt. 15:21-8). Their interaction ultimately highlights the inclusive nature of Jesus' messianic kingship and the necessity of allegiance to him.[27] However, there are

---

[25] Cf. David L. Turner, *Matthew*, BECNT (Grand Rapids, MI: Baker Academic, 2008), 259–60; Gerhard Maier, *Das Evangelium des Matthäus: Kapitel 1-14*, HTA (Wuppertal: Brockhaus, 2015), 525.

[26] On the characterization of Herodias and her daughter in Mk 6:14-29, where Herodias is more prominent in the narrative, see Susan Miller, "Women Characters in Mark's Gospel," in *Character Studies and the Gospel of Mark*, ed. Christopher W. Skinner and Matthew Ryan Hauge, LNTS 483 (London: T&T Clark, 2014), 182–4.

[27] On Matthew's unique portrayal of the Canaanite woman, see, for example, Glenna Jackson, *Have Mercy on Me: The Story of the Canaanite Woman in Matthew 15:21–28*, JSNTSup 228 (Sheffield: Sheffield Academic Press, 2002), and Nancy Klancher, *The Taming of the Canaanite Woman: Constructions of Christian Identity in the Afterlife of Matthew 15:21–28*, Studies in the Bible and Its Reception 1 (Berlin: de Gruyter, 2013). On the relationship between Mt. 15:21-8 and Mk 7:24-30, see Kara Lyons-Pardue, "A Syrophoenician Becomes a Canaanite: Jesus Exegetes the Canaanite Woman in Matthew," *JTI* 13, no. 2 (2019): 235–50.

several unexpected elements of this encounter which speak to its importance both for Matthew's narrative portrayal of women and his wider conception of discipleship: (1) the woman's identification as a Canaanite, (2) Jesus' harsh rejection of her request, and (3) Jesus' acknowledgement of her faith.

Jesus' entry into the regions of Tyre and Sidon (Mt. 15:21) evokes both his earlier exhortation that the disciples should not engage with those outside Israel (Mt. 10:5) and his use of Tyre and Sidon as paradigmatically negative cities (Mt. 11:21-2). In this context, Matthew's unique description of the woman as a Canaanite from those regions (Χαναναία ἀπὸ τῶν ὁρίων; Mt. 15:22) seems to function pejoratively.[28] Kara Lyons-Pardue, however, argues insightfully that Matthew's unique terminology creates ambiguity, forcing Jesus to interpret the woman through the lens of Israel's scriptures. Lyons-Pardue suggests that given the (geographical and narrative) context, Jesus may reasonably interpret the woman negatively, in connection with Jezebel; or positively, in connection with Rahab or the widow of Zarephath. The narrated complexity of their encounter portrays Jesus engaging in an act of contextual exegesis as he seeks to understand the identity of the woman and the purpose of her approach.[29] As with those evaluating Jesus in Mt. 13:53-16:20, Jesus here evaluates the Canaanite woman. The conclusion of their interaction demonstrates that Jesus ultimately interprets her positively. The woman and her daughter are drawn into the inclusive messianic kingdom foreshadowed in Matthew's genealogy.

The positive conclusion of the narrative, however, should not immediately overshadow the harsh treatment of the woman in Mt. 15:23-6. Her introduction (ἰδοὺ γυνή) in Mt. 15:22 parallels that of both the young woman's father (ἰδοὺ ἄρχων) and the bleeding woman (ἰδοὺ γυνή) in Mt. 9:18-26. Although Matthew regularly uses ἰδού, the linguistic parallel here emphasizes the unexpected nature of what follows. Jesus has already provided restoration to a woman who approaches him and to a parent seeking the restoration of a daughter in dire circumstances. Surprisingly, Jesus here responds to the woman's sustained pleas first with silence (Mt. 15:23) and then with stark statements of cultural exclusion (Mt. 15:24, 26). The contextual dissonance is heightened by the woman's own language. She repeatedly identifies Jesus as "Lord" (Mt. 15:22, 25, 27) and refers to him as the "son of David" (Mt. 15:22). Her persistent awareness of Jesus' identity functions as a catalyst for Jesus' progressive re-evaluation of the situation, from silence to rejection to acceptance. It is within the complexity of their encounter that an appropriate evaluation of Jesus' ministry and of the woman's identity emerge. Jesus' ministry extends beyond the boundaries of Israel and the woman embodies allegiance to Jesus.

Jesus' final speech-act in Mt. 15:28 again demonstrates the restorative impact of the kingdom. Jesus heals the woman's daughter with immediate effect (ἀπὸ τῆς ὥρας ἐκείνης; cf. Mt. 9:22). In the light of their strained dialogue, however, Jesus' declaration concerning the woman herself provides a dramatic conclusion to her narrative portrayal. Jesus' unique identification of the woman's "great faith" (μεγάλη σου ἡ πίστις)

---

[28] W. D. Davies and Dale C. Allison, *A Critical and Exegetical Commentary on the Gospel according to Saint Matthew*, 3 vols., ICC (Edinburgh: T&T Clark, 1988–97), 2:547.

[29] Lyons-Pardue, "A Syrophoenician Becomes a Canaanite," 247–9.

positions her in direct contrast with the general characterization of the disciples.[30] Although the disciples' earlier request that Jesus send the woman away (Mt. 15:23) may be interpreted positively,[31] this final declaration of her faith seemingly increases the divide between their respective portrayals. As noted in the discussion of the bleeding woman, Matthew regularly narrates the disciples' "little faith" (ὀλιγόπιστος) to provide a negative portrait of the requirements of discipleship (Mt. 6:30; 8:26; 14:31; 16:8; cf. ὀλιγοπιστία in Mt. 17:20). Along with the bleeding woman, the Canaanite woman is an extraordinary exemplar of the requisite allegiance that defines kingdom participants.

B. The Mother of Zebedee's Sons (Matthew 20:20-8; 27:56)

Jesus' arrival in Jerusalem in Matthew 21 leads to a series of provocative encounters between Jesus and the religious and political leaders that function as a catalyst for the events of the passion narrative in Matthew 26–7. Immediately prior to Jesus' entry into Jerusalem, however, Matthew narrates two scenes which provide insight into the nature of discipleship. On his way from Jericho to Jerusalem, Jesus heals two blind men who, upon the immediate restoration of their sight, follow Jesus (ἠκολούθησαν αὐτῷ; Mt. 20:34), becoming positive narrative exemplars of discipleship (cf. Mt. 9:27-31). The two blind men function as narrative foils for Zebedee's sons who, in the preceding scene (Mt. 20:20-8), seek positions of leadership in the kingdom only to be rebuked for their ignorance of the extensive sacrifice required of kingdom participants. Importantly, Jesus' engagement with Zebedee's sons is framed by two statements about the identity and mission of the "son of man" (ὁ υἱὸς τοῦ ἀνθρώπου) which emphasize the sacrificial reality of Jesus' ministry (Mt. 20:18-19, 28). In responding to the controversy that results from his engagement with Zebedee's sons, Jesus applies this dimension of his ministry directly to his followers, calling them to embody the sacrificial service that characterizes his ministry (Mt. 20:26-7).

Matthew's portrayal of the engagement between Jesus and Zebedee's sons is unique within the Synoptic tradition for its inclusion of their mother in the narrative. In distinction from Mk 10:35-45, it is the mother of Zebedee's sons who approaches Jesus, kneels before him in the same manner as the Canaanite woman (προσκυνοῦσα; cf. Mt. 15:25), and requests that her sons take up positions of authority in Jesus' kingdom (Mt. 20:20-1). Interpreters often see the stark conversation that follows her request to pertain only to the portrayal of her sons.[32] However, some interpreters transpose the lack of understanding implicit in the behavior of Zebedee's sons implied by Jesus' response—"you do not know what you are asking" (οὐκ οἴδατε τί αἰτεῖσθε; Mt. 20:22)— and the controversy it creates among the rest of the disciples (Mt. 20:24) onto the

---

[30] The woman's faith is also parallel to that of the centurion (Mt. 8:5-13), whom Jesus describes as having "such faith" (τοσαύτην πίστιν) that he has not found elsewhere in Israel (Mt. 8:10).
[31] See France, *Matthew*, 593.
[32] For example, Hagner, *Matthew*, 2:581; John Nolland, *The Gospel of Matthew*, NIGTC (Grand Rapids, MI: Eerdmans, 2005), 820–1; Turner, *Matthew*, 486.

portrait of their mother.³³ That is, she is seen to embody her sons' ignorance concerning the inverted nature of the kingdom and the significance of Jesus' impending crucifixion. The limitation of this reading is that it does not account for Matthew's subsequent portrayal of these characters. Whereas Zebedee's sons join the rest of the disciples in abandoning Jesus after his arrest in Gethsemane (Mt. 26:56), their mother follows Jesus to the cross (Mt. 27:56). Matthew's unique inclusion of the mother of Zebedee's sons in the passion narrative, where she joins a large group of women as vital witnesses to the gospel's climactic events, suggests that she responds to her engagement with Jesus in Matthew 20 in a way that aligns more closely with the narrative portrayal of the two blind men. Her request—on behalf of her sons—demonstrates a lack of understanding about the nature of the kingdom, but her response—in contrast to her sons—develops a positive narrative portrait of discipleship.³⁴

VI. Faithful Women (Matthew 26-8)

Matthew 26-8 is intricately structured to signify the importance of the climactic events of the gospel—Jesus' death and resurrection—for understanding the wider impact of Jesus' ministry.³⁵ The gospel's concluding commission emphasizes the theological direction of these chapters, with the crucified and resurrected Jesus exhorting his followers to extend the mission of the kingdom to all nations (Mt. 28:18-20). Women are essential characters in these climactic events.³⁶ The central scene in the first section of the passion narrative (Mt. 26:1-19) focuses on the dramatic action of an anonymous woman who anoints Jesus to prepare him for his burial (Mt. 26:6-13). Another group of women then feature prominently in the specific events of the passion. A large group of women, including Mary Magdalene, Mary the mother of James and Joseph, and the mother of Zebedee's sons, witness the events of the crucifixion (Mt. 27:55-6) and Mary Magdalene and "the other Mary" (ἡ ἄλλη Μαρία) observe Jesus' burial in the tomb of Joseph of Arimathea (Mt. 27:61). The presence and importance of these women continues in the narrative of Jesus' resurrection. As Mary Magdalene and "the other Mary" return to the tomb, they learn of Jesus' resurrection through their encounter with an angel (Mt. 28:1-7) and with the risen Jesus himself (Mt. 28:8-10). In each encounter the women are commissioned to proclaim the resurrection to the disciples in Galilee, becoming the first narrative participants in the commission to proclaim the gospel. These women are key narrative voices who proclaim the essential reality of Jesus' death (Mt. 26:6-13; 27:55-6, 61) and resurrection (Mt. 28:1-10).

---

[33] For example, Grant R. Osborne, *Matthew*, ZECNT 1 (Grand Rapids, MI: Zondervan, 2010), 739; Turner, *Matthew*, 486.
[34] On this reading, see especially Wainwright, *Towards a Feminist Critical Reading*, 118-21, 252-7; cf. Clements, *Mothers*, 251-4.
[35] For an overview of the structure of Matthew's passion and resurrection narrative, see Nolland, *Matthew*, 60-2.
[36] In addition to the women discussed here, Matthew's passion narrative also uniquely includes two female servants interacting with Peter in the temple courtyard (Mt. 26:69-71) and the wife of Pilate recounting her dream to her husband (Mt. 27:19).

A. The Woman who Anoints Jesus (Matthew 26:6-13)

Matthew's passion narrative begins with a final prediction of Jesus' death and a concise statement of the plot to kill him (Mt. 26:1-5). As the narrative portrays others scheming to bring about Jesus' death, a woman approaches Jesus at the home of Simon the leper and anoints his head with a jar of expensive ointment (Mt. 26:6-7). Jesus' disciples respond to the woman's action indignantly (cf. Mt. 15:23), perceiving it as the destruction of a valuable economic resource that could have been used to support the poor (Mt. 26:8-9). But Jesus rebukes the disciples and positions the woman's action within the narrative of his imminent death and as a remembered element of the ongoing proclamation of the gospel of the kingdom (Mt. 26:10-13).

The unique importance of the woman's action is established by both the structural development of her narrative and Jesus' interpretation of its significance. The woman functions as a key foil for other characters in Matthew 26. For example, while it may be possible to affirm the economic rationale of the disciples' indignant response to the woman's action, Jesus' description of it as a "good work" (ἔργον ... καλόν; Mt. 26:10; cf. Mt. 5:16) demands its positive evaluation. Despite their consistent engagement with Jesus and their awareness of his repeated predictions of his death (Mt. 16:21; 17:22-3; 20:17-19; 26:2), Jesus' framing of her action as preparation for his burial highlights the limitation of the disciples' awareness of their proximity to the crucifixion.[37] In contrast, the totality of the woman's action highlights her exclusive focus on Jesus and his death. The woman's dramatic action is also framed by the scheme of Judas and the religious leaders in Jerusalem to arrest and kill Jesus (Mt. 26:3-5, 14-15). While this unnamed woman enters Simon's house to pour expensive ointment over Jesus for his burial, one of Jesus' named followers leaves the house to deliver Jesus over to the religious leaders for money. This direct contrast between the woman and Judas positions her action as a positive narrative model for Jesus' followers.

Jesus' decisive interpretation of the woman's action in Mt. 26:10-13 further clarifies its importance. Jesus' declaration that the anointing was preparation for his burial (πρὸς τὸ ἐνταφιάσαι με ἐποίησεν; Mt. 26:12) emphasizes the central place of his death in defining the shape of the kingdom. That the woman's action will be remembered throughout the world in connection with the proclamation of the gospel positions Jesus' death as an inescapable component of the ministry of the kingdom. Furthermore, Jesus' interpretation of the woman's act of devotion positions his death as a key component of the identity of his followers. Jesus asserts that the woman's action will be remembered as her own funerary inscription (εἰς μνημόσυνον αὐτῆς; Mt. 26:13), establishing her act of anointing not only as a narrative precursor to Jesus' death but also as a narrative portrayal of her own embodiment of the sacrifice that Jesus will endure on the cross.[38] Her act of anointing is a narrative portrayal of discipleship.

---

[37] Cf. Turner, *Matthew*, 618.
[38] See Aernie, *Narrative Discipleship*, 99–100.

B. The Women who Remain with Jesus (Matthew 27:55-6, 61; 28:1-10)

Women are the only characters in the narrative who serve as consistent witnesses of the climactic events of Matthew's Gospel—Jesus' death, burial, and resurrection. Although Jesus is deserted by his male disciples (Mt. 26:56), a large group of women who followed Jesus from Galilee to serve him remain with him (Mt. 27:55-6). The introduction of these women into the narrative draws together a consistent thread of characters throughout the gospel. As with the preceding narratives of women that emphasized key aspects of Jesus' identity and mission, the actions and testimony of these women coordinate with central elements of Matthew's narrative—the crucifixion of Jesus and the vindication of the crucified Jesus in the resurrection. Further, Matthew's identification of three specific women from within the larger group present at the crucifixion—Mary Magdalene, Mary the mother of James and Joseph, and the mother of Zebedee's sons—creates an extended narrative bracket with the women in Matthew 1. The news of the authority of the resurrected Jesus of which these women bear initial witness is the culmination of the inclusive messianic kingship emphasized by the presence of Tamar, Rahab, Ruth, Bathsheba, and Mary in Matthew's genealogy.

The specific narrative function of the women in Matthew 27–8 is to serve as faithful witnesses of the gospel's climactic events.[39] In each of the scenes in which Matthew explicitly identifies the women, there is an emphasis on their visual proximity to the narrated events. The women watch the crucifixion from a distance (ἀπὸ μακρόθεν θεωροῦσαι; Mt. 27:55), they sit directly opposite the tomb (καθήμεναι ἀπέναντι τοῦ τάφου; Mt. 27:61), they return to look at the tomb (θεωρῆσαι τὸν τάφον; Mt. 28:1), and they are invited to see the place (ἴδετε τὸν τόπον; Mt. 28:6) where Jesus was laid but no longer remains. This emphasis suggests a focus in the narrative on the validity of the women's identity as witnesses.[40] This validation is further established in the women's experience both at the tomb and immediately after they depart from it. Their double commission from the angel and the resurrected Jesus (Mt. 28:7, 10) accentuates the certainty of the message they are called to deliver to the disciples. Although Matthew's Gospel does not narrate the subsequent interaction between the women and the disciples, the disciples' return to Galilee confirms that the women faithfully fulfilled their commission (Mt. 28:16). In contrast to the guards stationed at the tomb who, in their fear, become marked by metaphorical death (ἐγενήθησαν ὡς νεκροί; Mt. 28:4), the women, in both fear and joy, become the first human agents to proclaim the news of Jesus' resurrected life (Mt. 28:5-10).

The women's faithful outworking of their commission positions them as crucial characters within the narrative progression of the gospel. Matthew's introduction of the women into the narrative to serve as witnesses to Jesus' crucifixion and burial and as recipients of the news of his resurrection allows them to function as narrative representations of those who are faithful to the crucified and resurrected Jesus. The emphasis in Mt. 27:55 on the women's identification as disciples—those who "followed

---

[39] France, *Matthew*, 1085.
[40] See Richard Bauckham, *Gospel Women: Studies of the Named Women in the Gospels* (Grand Rapids, MI: Eerdmans, 2002), 277–9.

to serve" (ἠκολούθησαν ... διακονοῦσαι)—is enhanced as the narrative progresses and the women become not only narrative witnesses but also faithful preachers.[41] Their testimony to the disciples—rooted in their visual and spatial proximity to Jesus' death, burial, and resurrection—provides the necessary foundation both for Matthew's rendition of the final commission to the eleven and for the whole of the narrative. Without the witness and proclamation of these women, the gospel of the kingdom does not progress to all nations.

VII. Conclusion

Matthew's portrayal of women contributes to the narrative progression of the gospel. Individual scenes which feature women throughout the narrative sections of the gospel emphasize key dimensions of Jesus' identity and mission. Women illuminate Jesus' identity (Mt. 1), demonstrate his restorative authority (Mt. 8–9), illustrate the nature of his kingdom (Mt. 15 and 20), and embody faithful allegiance to him (Mt. 26-8). Matthew's unique inclusion of women in his genealogy and his portrayal of the sustained presence of women in the climactic events of Jesus' passion and resurrection provide a frame in which to evaluate the characterization of women throughout the gospel. This frame suggests that the scenes which feature women can be read together, forming a corporate character through their analogous portrayal of women. Although limited in terms of narrative space, the narratives of women in Matthew's Gospel create an integrated portrait of faithful engagement with Jesus. The women in the genealogy provide a foundation for the inclusive nature of Jesus' ministry. The women restored by Jesus portray and embody the impact of Jesus' ministry. The women who converse with Jesus help to define the shape of Jesus' ministry. And the women in the passion and resurrection narratives proclaim the cruciform and resurrected reality of Jesus' ministry. The combined narrative portrait of these women extends their significance in the gospel and unites them as narrative representations of discipleship.

---

[41] Cf. Love, *Marginal Women*, 213.

11

The Characterization of the Crowds in the Gospel of Matthew

J. R. C. Cousland

James L. Resseguie writes that, "The crowds in the Gospels are ... undifferentiated characters that may be considered part of the setting rather than characters in their own right." He adds that the "crowd also act like an ancient Greek chorus, voicing complaints about Jesus' association with sinners (Luke 19:7)."[1] Here Resseguie raises a vital question: are the gospel crowds characters in their own right or merely literary "extras" who impart verisimilitude to the story of Jesus? Careful consideration of the issue suggests that Resseguie is mistaken about all the gospel crowds, and that this assessment is especially applicable to the Gospel of Matthew for a variety of reasons.

First of all, Resseguie undercuts his own argument by comparing the crowds to the chorus of Greek tragedies. He appears unaware that Greek choruses are construed as characters with a distinct corporate persona that actively engage with the figures onstage.[2] Second, he does not seem to take account of the various qualities that distinguish characters in narratives. While there is considerable variation and limited agreement as to the precise nature of these distinguishing features, the Matthean crowds possess a substantial number of them.[3] These typically include consistency in identification, the prominence accorded to the figure(s), distinctive actions and reactions attributed to them, repeated sayings or thoughts imputed to them, and development or change on their part over the course of the work. As will become

---

[1] James L. Resseguie, *Narrative Criticism of the New Testament* (Grand Rapids, MI.: Baker Academic, 2005), 125.
[2] See J. R. C. Cousland, "The Choral Crowds in the Tragedy according to St. Matthew," in *Ancient Fiction: The Matrix of Early Christian and Jewish Narrative*, ed. Jo-Ann Brant, Charles W. Hedrick, and Chris Shea, SBL Symposium Series 32 (Atlanta: Society of Biblical Literature, 2005), 255–73.
[3] For a very useful survey of various ways of construing characterization and how this has been done with particular reference to the gospels, see S. A. Hunt, D. F. Tolmie and R. Zimmermann, "An Introduction to Character and Characterization in John and Related New Testament Literature," in *Character Studies in the Fourth Gospel: Narrative Approaches to Seventy Figures in John*, ed. S. A. Hunt, D. F. Tolmie and R. Zimmermann, WUNT 314 (Tübingen: Mohr Siebeck, 2013), 1-33. Cf., as well, Uta Poplutz, *Erzählte Welt. Narratologische Studien zum Matthäusevangelium*, BTS 100 (Neukirchen-Vluyn: Neukirchener, 2008), 57–75.

apparent from the following discussion, many—if not all—of these features definitely apply to the crowds in Matthew's Gospel.[4]

Matthew Hauge raises the vital question of how character traits would have been construed by ancient authors. He lists how various ancient authors such as Theon of Alexandria and Cicero would have conceptualized the characteristics of a person. While the crowds as a corporate entity do not embody all of these characteristics (such as "death" and "what followed death"), they nevertheless display more than half of the eleven traits that Hauge outlines.[5]

A final indication that the crowds are a distinct character—as will become evident below—is that they are consistently distinguished and contrasted with the other two major groups who figure as characters in the gospel, namely the disciples and the Jewish leaders.[6] Denying the status of a character to the crowds, while attributing it to the other two groups seems methodologically problematic.[7] Even though the precise constitution of the Jewish leadership changes—as for instance in the Pharisees' absence in the passion narrative—there is still a definite persona that characterizes all the Jewish leaders in Matthew. The same can be said for the disciples, who are mentioned as a corporate group even before they are formally identified (5:1 with 10:2-4). Nor is it clear that the disciples are always the same as the "twelve disciples," but regardless they are usually treated as a distinct persona.

Hence, by identifying Matthew's crowds as a "character," I am necessarily implying that Matthew has shaped the "historical crowds" according to his own predilections.[8] This is not to deny that his presentation is ultimately indebted to historical traditions, but Matthew is arguably at several removes from these traditions and this chapter, therefore, assumes that his (re-)construction of the character of the crowds is chiefly dominated by his theological concerns.[9]

---

[4] Matthew Ryan Hauge, "The Creation of Person in Ancient Narrative and the Gospel of Mark," in *Character Studies and the Gospel of Mark*, ed. Christopher W. Skinner and Matthew Ryan Hauge, LNTS 483 (London: Bloomsbury/T&T Clark, 2014), 57–77 (61–3).

[5] Hauge, "Creation of Person," 62. These traits include: origin/race, nature, disposition, morality, action, and speech. The oft-repeated cliché that ancient characters are "flat" (not "round") because they do not develop deserves to be shelved, and is refuted as early as Homer in the portrayals of the characters of Achilles and Odysseus.

[6] Poplutz, *Erzählte Welt*, 101–39. For a detailed pericope-by-pericope overview of the three groups in the gospel, cf. Detlev Dormeyer, "Die Rollen von Volk, Jüngern und Gegnern im Matthäusevangelium," in *"Dies ist das Buch ..." Das Matthäusevangelium: Interpretationem—Rezeption—Rezeptionsgeschichte; FS H. Frankemölle*, ed. R. Kampling (Paderborn and Zurich: Ferdinand Schöningh, 2004) 105–28 (110–13).

[7] Poplutz, *Erzählte Welt*, 101–39.

[8] It needs to be acknowledged that the arguments advanced here about the Matthean crowds and their characterization are still contested by scholars. Robert J. Myles, *The Homeless Jesus in the Gospel of Matthew* (Sheffield: Phoenix Press, 2014), 169, for instance, remarks that "the identification of the crowds in Matthew's Gospel, including their characterization and function, has gained little consensus in recent scholarly opinion." For discussion of some these scholarly opinions, see J. R. C. Cousland, *The Crowds in the Gospel of Matthew*, NovTSup 102 (Leiden: Brill, 2002), 9–19.

[9] Robert J. Myles has recently sought to isolate the "historical crowds" in "Crowds and Power in the Early Palestinian Tradition," *Journal for the Study of the Historical Jesus* 18 (2020): 124–40. His attempt is laudable, but his exclusive focus on social-scientific realia omits the most essential feature of Matthew's crowds—namely their characterization. As I have argued before, "the most distinctive feature of the crowds is how unlike crowds they actually are." Cf. Cousland, *Crowds*, 43.

I. Matthew's Crowds

Among the four canonical gospels, Matthew's crowds are most pronounced, both in terms of the frequency in which they are mentioned—some fifty times—but also terminologically. Where the crowds are given other designations by the other evangelists, Matthew confines himself almost exclusively to the term ὄχλος (though see 12:15 πολλοί v.l).[10] His ascription of a definite designation to the crowds suggests that he has also ascribed a more definite character to them, as opposed to the more amorphous and variegated representations that can be seen in the other gospels.

That being said, the precise constitution of the crowds continues to engender discussion. Beate Kowalski, for instance, speaks of a *corpus permixtum* of Jews and gentiles, whereas Joel Willetts would identify them as the remnant of the former Northern Kingdom of Israel.[11] For his part, Herman Waetjen makes the interesting suggestion that the crowds may be transparent for "the general Jewish community of Antioch."[12] All of these proposals provide valuable insights into the nature of the crowds, but need qualification. Gentiles certainly figure in Matthew's crowds, but the evangelist deliberately has Jesus focus on the crowds' identity as the "lost sheep of the house of Israel" (9:36 with 10:5; 15:24). Likewise, it is the house of Israel conceived as a whole—remnant terminology is not a distinctive feature of the gospel.[13] As for the crowds serving as a cipher for the "general Jewish community of Antioch" of Matthew's day, it is certainly a possibility, but apart from 4:24, the gospel itself furnishes little warrant for the supposition.

Most satisfactory is Alan Culpepper's recent assertion that the crowds are the "surrogate for 'the people,' who follow Jesus from 'Galilee, the Decapolis, Jerusalem, Judea, and across the Jordan': all the areas inhabited by the twelve tribes of Israel."[14] They, along with their leaders, constitute the people of Israel—the λαός. Culpepper

---

[10] On "crowd" terminology in the gospels, see Christiane Zimmermann, "Jesus und das Volk," in *Jesus Handbuch*, ed. Jens Schröter and Christine Jacobi (Tübingen: Siebeck Mohr, 2017), 333–8; John P. Meier, *A Marginal Jew: Rethinking the Historical Jesus*, Vol. 3 (New York: Doubleday, 2001), 19–39. On Matthew's use of ὄχλος, cf. Cousland, *Crowds*, 31-43. According to Martin Meiser, *Die Reaktion des Volkes auf Jesus*, BZNW 96 (Berlin and New York: de Gruyter, 1998), 258, Matthew's vacillation between the singular and plural forms of ὄχλος corresponds to Rabbinic usage.

[11] B. Kowalski, "Wunder bei den Heiden. Der heidnische Hauptmann (MT 8,5-13) und der Kanaanäische Frau (MT 15:21-28)," in *The Gospel of Matthew at the Crossroads of Early Christianity*, ed. Donald Senior, BETL 243 (Leuven: Leuven University Press, 2011), 537–59 (547). Rebekah Eklund, "From 'Hosanna!' to 'Crucify!' The Fickle Crowds in the Four Gospels," *BBR* 26, no.1 (2016): 21–41 (21), makes a similar suggestion.

[12] Herman C. Waetjen, *Matthew's Theology of Fulfillment, its Universality and its Ethnicity. God's New Israel as the Pioneer of God's New Humanity* (London: Bloomsbury, 2017), 59, 125.

[13] Joel Willitts, *Matthew's Messianic Shepherd-King. In Search of 'The Lost Sheep of the House of Israel,'* BZNW 147 (Berlin and New York: de Gruyter, 2007), 184, 200, would contend that the crowds are "the oppressed and marginalized remnant of the former Northern Kingdom of Israel." His supposition that Matthew's term addresses this group tends to overlook the fact that Matthew's Galilean focus is largely beholden to Mark for this emphasis on "the northern regions of the land" (218).

[14] R. Alan Culpepper, *Matthew*, NTL 1 (Louisville, KY: Westminster John Knox, 2021), 79; cf. Carolin Ziethe, *Auf seinem Namen werden die Völker Hoffen. Die Matthäische Rezeption der Schriften Israels zur Begründung des universalen Heils*, BZNW 233 (Berlin: de Gruyter, 2018), 137, n. 174.

further observes that over the course of Jesus' ministry the two groups of the λαός are diffracted, and that after 4:23 "'the people' do not reappear until the passion narrative (26:3,5,47; 27:1,25,64; 21:43) except in biblical quotations (Isa 6:10 // Matt 13:15; Isa 29:13 // Matt 15:8)."[15] On this reading, the crowds may certainly be construed, as Anders Runesson suggests, as the "majority of Jews in any given place," but they also embody a corporate ethnic status. They are "people," but also "the people."[16]

It is in their relation with their leaders, with the disciples, and with Jesus himself that the crowds' character comes to its fullest expression, so the discussion that follows will base its findings on the interactions of the crowds with the other main characters in the gospel. The most fundamental of these interactions is Jesus' involvement with the crowds and their responses to him.

II. Jesus and the Crowds

The crowds constitute a central focus of Jesus' ministry in the Gospel of Matthew. Apart from teaching the disciples, and contending with the Jewish leaders, a great portion of Jesus' ministry is directed at remedying the needs of the crowds: "Then Jesus went about all the cities and villages, teaching in their synagogues, and proclaiming the good news of the kingdom, and curing every disease and every sickness. When he saw the crowds, he had compassion for them, because they were harassed and helpless, like sheep without a shepherd" (9:35-6; on Jesus' compassion, cf. 14:14; 15:32; cf. 20:34). He feeds them (14:13-21; 15:29-39). He proclaims parables to them (13:3, 10, 34), and furnishes them with guidance (15:10-14).[17] Most characteristically, perhaps, he heals them (cf. 15:30-1), as well as offering them forgiveness (9:6). From a global perspective, Jesus assumes the role of the Davidic Shepherd who shepherds the "lost sheep of the House of Israel" (9:36).[18] With the failure of the Jewish leaders to live up to their responsibilities to the people, Jesus intervenes to compensate for the leaders' deficiencies. In this capacity, therefore, the crowds function as one of the primary objects of Jesus' earthly ministry. Their need is strongly highlighted so that Jesus can be portrayed as requiting that need. As with the historical Jesus, Jesus' reputation for performing miracles and exorcisms would have attracted needy crowds.[19]

The crowds respond to Jesus in characteristic fashion. The evangelist describes the reactions of the crowds, using a variety of terms that signal the crowds' amazement, astonishment, and marveling at what Jesus says and does, namely θαυμάζω,

---

[15] Culpepper, *Matthew*, 78.
[16] Anders Runesson, *Divine Wrath and Salvation in Matthew* (Minneapolis: Fortress, 2016), 215.
[17] Waetjen, *Matthew's Theology of Fulfillment*, 178–80, has sought to revive the notion of a gentile crowd at Mt. 15:29-39. For a critique of this view, see J. R. C. Cousland, "The Feeding of the Four Thousand *Gentiles* in Matthew? Matthew 15:29-39 as a Test Case," *NovT* 41 (1999): 1–23.
[18] Most recently, Carolin Ziethe, "Notwendige Davidsohnschaft für das Heil des Volkers?" in *The Composition, Theology, and Early Reception of Matthew's Gospel*, ed. J. Verheyden, J. Schröter, and D. C. Sim, WUNT 477 (Tubingen: Mohr Siebeck, 2022), 195–222 (196).
[19] For more on Jesus' ministry to the crowds, cf. Cousland, *Crowds*, 101–23.

ἐκπλήσσομαι, ἐξίστημι, and φοβέομαι. All of these terms denote a similar sort of reaction—a fundamental shock and awe at the unprecedented character of the sayings and actions performed by Jesus. The crowds aver that they have never experienced anything comparable before (9:33) and are, accordingly, dazzled at the extraordinary implications of these events. That being said, these reactions are precisely that—reactions—which represent a spontaneous and preliminary response to an epiphany without constituting a considered or faith-based response to Jesus' actions.[20]

Exceptions to this set of circumstances occur when the astonished reaction of the crowds extends to a glorification of (δοξάζω) God. So, for instance, when Jesus heals a paralyzed man, the crowds "were filled with awe, and they glorified God, who had given such authority to human beings" (9:8). Likewise, when Jesus heals a multitude of illnesses, "the crowd was amazed when they saw the mute speaking, the maimed whole, the lame walking, and the blind seeing. And they praised the God of Israel" (15:31). In both instances, their ecstatic reaction culminates in the glorification of God. So, even though their reactions make no explicit evaluation of Jesus, they nevertheless make the fundamental recognition that Jesus' authority and deeds are God-given—in contrast, say, to the Pharisees, who impute Jesus' marvels to Beelzebul (12:12, 24, cf. 9:34).[21]

It is also noteworthy that the disciples do not usually react to Jesus' words and deeds as the crowds do, with a few exceptions. They are overcome by amazement (ἐθαύμασαν) at the withering of the fig tree (21:20), and struck (ἐξεπλήσσοντο) by Jesus' teaching at 19:25. Most notably, after the wind and the sea had threatened to swamp their boat, they marvel (ἐθαύμασαν) and ask, 'What sort of man is this, that even the winds and the sea obey him?' (8:27). Even though this episode causes the disciples to question Jesus' identity, the general tenor of the gospel indicates that they do not need to anxiously question who Jesus is (unlike the disciples in Mark, for instance)—they have already largely come to understand who he is. A case in point is when Jesus walks on the water. At the end of the episode, "the disciples in the boat worshipped him, saying, 'Truly you are the Son of God'" (14:33).[22] So, while the crowds come to an awareness that Jesus is an emissary of God, the disciples recognize Jesus as "the Messiah,—the Son of the living God" (16:16), a confession that "marks a major christological development" in Matthew.[23]

The remarks that are presented in direct speech by the crowds also speak to the limited but growing awareness of the crowds: when Jesus heals a mute demoniac, they exclaim, "'Never has anything like this been seen in Israel'" (9:33). A further healing of a blind and mute demoniac again prompts amazement, stirring them to ask, "'Can this be the Son of David?'" (12:23). Here, it is generally recognized that their phrasing of the question—beginning with μήτι—expresses some doubt about the answer, "This can't be

---

[20] Michael Theophilos, *Jesus as the New Moses in Matthew 8–9: Jewish Typology in First Century Greek Literature*, GSPT 4 (Piscataway, NJ: Gorgias, 2011), 164, aptly refers to the crowds' "superficial wonder." Cf. Meiser, *Die Reaktion des Volkes*, 247.

[21] For more detailed assessments of the crowds' reactions, see Meiser, *Die Reaktion des Volkes*; Cousland, *Crowds*, 125–44; Matthias Konradt, *Israel, Church, and the Gentiles in the Gospel of Matthew* (Waco, TX: Baylor University Press, 2014), 89–101.

[22] Konradt, *Israel*, 292–3.

[23] Culpepper, *Matthew*, 284.

the Son of David, can it?"²⁴ Nevertheless, their query demonstrates the direction that the crowd is moving in—a direction that is deliberately negated by the Pharisees in their counterclaim that Jesus is associated with Beelzebul. The crowds' surmise about Jesus is a significant one. Not only does their suggestion correspond to authorial assertions about Jesus' identity (1:1), but it also corresponds to the particular relationship they have with the Son of David. As Ezekiel 34 makes especially clear, the Son of David is the Davidic shepherd whose primary function is to tend the abused flocks of Israel.²⁵ The crowds in their guise as the lost sheep of the house of Israel instinctively come to recognize their Davidic ruler. In this way, Matthew points to an idyll that should have ensued, an idyll, however, that—apart from the two feeding narratives—never happens.²⁶

The crowds' surmises about Jesus begin to coalesce at the Triumphal Entry, when Jesus enters Jerusalem: "The crowds that went ahead of him and that followed were shouting, 'Hosanna to the Son of David! Blessed is the one who comes in the name of the Lord! Hosanna in the highest heaven!'" (21:9). Here the crowds have moved from their earlier surmise about Jesus to the concrete recognition that he is, in fact, the God-sent Son of David. They have seemingly built on their earlier recognition that Jesus is a divine emissary and further recognized that his advent was an occasion for rejoicing. What is somewhat less clear is their understanding of the term. Is it merely a spontaneous outburst of popular enthusiasm without express theological significance or does it have more explicit messianic connotations, reflecting the popular expectation of an anointed and kingly ruler?²⁷ It is noteworthy that when the refrain of Hosanna is repeated by children, Jesus accepts it as appropriate praise (21:16).

The crowds' subsequent identification of Jesus as "the prophet Jesus from Nazareth in Galilee" (21:11) is more definite than their surmise about the Son of David, but still lacking in clarity. Jesus is a prophet, but they say the same of John the Baptist fifteen verses later (21:26). Given the proximity of the two passages, this parallel terminology can be regarded as part of Matthew's larger parallelism between the Baptist and Jesus.²⁸ This parallelism seems to imply that the crowds consider Jesus to be *a* prophet rather than *the* prophet. For this reason, scholars tend to regard the designation "prophet" as a title that is correct, but inadequate.²⁹

This raises the question of "Jerusalem crowds." Drawing on the opposition that Matthew makes between Galilee and Jerusalem, a number of scholars have posited a

---

²⁴ BDAG s.v. μήτι.
²⁵ Cf. Cousland, *Crowds*, 184–91; H. Daniel Zacharias, *Matthew's Presentation of the Son of David: Davidic Tradition and Typology in the Gospel of Matthew* (London: T&T Clark, 2017), 129–32; Willitts, *Matthew's Messianic Shepherd-King*.
²⁶ On the strong associations of the feeding of the four thousand with the fulfilment of Isaianic motifs, see Culpepper, *Matthew*, 299-301; Craig A. Evans, *Matthew*, NCBC (New York: Cambridge University Press, 2012), 305–6.
²⁷ Zacharias, *Matthew's Presentation of the Son of David*, 132. On the role of the Son of David in Matthew, see Cousland, *Crowds*, 175–99.
²⁸ Dale C. Allison, *Studies in Matthew: Interpretation Past and Present* (Grand Rapids, MI: Baker, 2005), 225–6.
²⁹ David L. Turner, *Israel's Last Prophet: Jesus and the Jewish Leaders in Matthew 23* (Minneapolis: Fortress, 2015), 154–6; Meiser, *Die Reaktion des Volkes*, 251. Cf., more broadly, Cousland, *Crowds*, 208–25.

further opposition between the "Galilean crowds" who accompany Jesus and figure in the triumphal procession and the alleged "Jerusalem crowds" who query them about Jesus' identity (21:10).[30] The latter tend to be hostile, and it is they who ultimately persecute Jesus, as Jesus acknowledges in his apostrophe against Jerusalem at 23:37-9. An armed crowd from the chief priests and elders come to Gethsemane to arrest him (26:47, 55), and it is these "Jerusalem" crowds that appear before Pilate at Jesus' trial and ultimately cry out for Jesus' crucifixion at 27:25 and assume responsibility for his death. The "Jerusalem" crowds end up coalescing with their leaders, a factor that may explain why the risen Jesus appears to his disciples in Galilee rather than in Jerusalem (as happens in Luke–Acts).

As intriguing as this reading is, it is not without difficulties. The biggest problem is that Matthew makes no mention of the "Jerusalem crowds." This viewpoint assumes that the reference to "the entire city" at 21:10 must be a reference to the "Jerusalem" crowds, even though Matthew makes no such identification. Moreover, it presupposes that all the references to crowds up to the time of Jesus' passion must be to "Galilean" crowds, because they regularly make up Jesus' audience—even in the temple. The only indication of a malign crowd is the description of the armed crowd sent "from the chief priests and elders of the people" (26:47). Yet this is Matthew's only portrayal of a hostile crowd prior to the trial scene, and the fact that he includes a qualification that expressly identifies the origin and provenance of this particular crowd implies that the "arresting" crowd is meant to be distinguished from the crowds in general.

Strikingly, however, there is no indication that this "arresting" crowd is the same crowd as the one in the passion narrative before Pilate. Matthew explicitly relates that these crowds are not the same as the arresting crowds. The crowds of the passion narrative come together or assemble (συνηγμένων οὖν αὐτῶν; 27:17) before Pilate to secure the release of a prisoner. It is only at this point that the "chief priests and the elders *persuaded* [ἔπεισαν] the people to ask for Barabbas and destroy Jesus" (27:20). Yet, if this crowd was basically the same as the "arresting" crowd, why would they need to be persuaded? All of which leads one to ask, where are the hostile "Jerusalem" crowds? The more one searches for them, the more chimerical they become.

These two representations of the crowds, therefore, result in potentially different characterizations of them. If it be supposed that there are two sets of crowds—a favorable "Galilean" crowd versus a negative, "Jerusalem crowd," then it is not possible to impute a unified single character to Matthew's crowds. The crowds would have at least two distinct personae. The characters of both would be static, and their central dispositions—positive and negative—would remain unchanged. If, on the other hand, one understands Matthew to be describing a major transformation on the part of a single group, then this portrayal is certainly significant, and would mean that of the three corporate characters within the gospel, the disposition of only one of them changes. Although the disciples and the Jewish leaders do not essentially change in character, the crowds alone of these three groups do. I regard this understanding of the crowds as the likelier of the two possible representations and will provide my rationale below.

---

[30] Poplutz, *Erzählte Welt*, 119–20; Konradt, *Israel*, 159–66; Runesson, *Divine Wrath*, 293–307.

III. The Crowds and the Disciples

First, however, it is necessary to confirm that Matthew regards the crowds and the disciples as distinct entities.[31] Recently, there has been a trend to downplay the differences between the two. For instance, Anders Runesson in his 2016 book, *Divine Wrath and Salvation in Matthew*, seeks to argue that the crowds' understanding of Jesus and the kingdom is on a par with that of the disciples.[32]

To substantiate his notion of the crowds' understanding, Runesson appeals to Matthew Chapter 13. Here Runesson assumes that the crowds understand all the parables they are told, and places special emphasis on Matthew 13:34: "Jesus told the crowds 'all these things' [ταῦτα πάντα] in parables; without a parable he told them nothing." Runesson claims that this citation displays the "revelatory" character of the parables spoken to the crowds.[33] But this assumption misconstrues the chapter fundamentally.[34] Matthew's summation, drawing on Psalm 78:2, is intended as a negative counterpart to the conclusion of the chapter, where the disciples affirm that they understand "all these things" (ταῦτα πάντα). The repetition of the key phrase ταῦτα πάντα indicates that the two summaries are designed to be read in relation to each other—one negatively and one positively.

For the crowds, Jesus' teaching remains "in parables" because they remain without understanding.[35] In contrast to the disciples (13:10, 36, 49; cf. 15:15), Jesus does not ever provide the crowds with *any* interpretations and, as a consequence, they remain devoid of understanding. Rather, Jesus stresses again and again that the crowds do *not* understand (13:12-14). Jesus speaks to them in parables *because* (ὅτι 13:16) they do not understand. He gives private interpretations to the disciples with the result that they do understand the parables (13:52). And while Jesus once elsewhere adjures the crowds to understand (15:10), the gospel never asserts that the crowds understand Jesus. Only the disciples understand him (notwithstanding 21:45).

But if the crowds don't understand Jesus as the disciples do, is it not the case that they follow Jesus just as the disciples do? Charles H. Talbert, for one, argues "that the crowd that follows Jesus is best understood as part of [a] wider circle of disciples," and contends that the crowds are attracted to and favorably disposed toward Jesus, and that they follow (ἀκολουθέω) Jesus just as his disciples do.[36] This argument, however, is

---

[31] See, also, Meiser, *Die Reaktion des Volkes*, 232-42.
[32] Runesson, *Divine Wrath*, 270–308.
[33] Runesson, *Divine Wrath*, 278. It is no wonder that he discerns a "patent contradiction" between 13:13-15 and 13:34-5.
[34] Céline Rohmer, *Valeurs et Paraboles. Une lecture du discourse en Matthieu 13, 1-53*, Études Bibliques 66 (Pendé: Gabalda, 2014), 107–8; Jürgen Roloff, *Jesu Gleichnisse im Matthäusevangelium. Ein Kommentar zu Mt 13, 1–52*, BTS 73 (Neukirchen-Vluyn: Neukirchener, 2005), 66-9; Ulrich Luz, *Matthew 8–20*, Hermeneia (Minneapolis: Fortress, 2001), 265; cf. Peter Yaw Oppong-Kumi, *Matthean Sets of Parables*, WUNT 340 (Tübingen: Mohr Siebeck, 2013), 368.
[35] See the excellent analysis in Konradt, *Israel*, 244–63.
[36] Charles H. Talbert, *Matthew*, Paideia 1 (Grand Rapids, MI: Baker Academic, 2010), 74. See also Charles H. Talbert, *Reading the Sermon on the Mount* (Grand Rapids, MI: Baker Academic, 2006), 12–13.

based on a faulty analogy. The following of the crowds is literal, while that of the disciples is chiefly metaphorical. Upon closer inspection, the apparent similarity between them emerges as profoundly different. In the Gospel of Mark, anyone can become a follower of Jesus and, within that gospel, the literal and metaphorical dimensions are distinctly blurred. But such is emphatically not the case in Matthew. In Matthew, Jesus never enjoins the crowds to follow him—this invitation is only ever extended to the disciples, who are expressly called upon to take up their cross and follow him. The demands and rigors of being Jesus' disciples are uniquely theirs, as Jesus' chosen followers.[37]

The crowds, by contrast, are invited *to come to* Jesus (11:28), so that he can assuage their needs as the "lost sheep of the house of Israel" (9:36). When the crowds do follow Jesus, as in the feeding narratives, it is precisely so that Jesus might feed them, heal them, preach the news of the kingdom to them. They follow Jesus, just as sheep follow their shepherd, in order to be cared for. Matthew 9:27-31 makes this distinction especially clear. Two blind men follow Jesus, entreating him to heal them. Once he has done so, they do not continue to follow him, but go away and, what is more, explicitly disobey Jesus' adjuration not to tell anyone of the healing. Their behavior is hardly a paradigm of discipleship.[38]

The distinction between the crowds and disciples becomes particularly vivid in the context of the feedings, because here the disciples join Jesus in tending the crowds. They follow Jesus' instructions implicitly, arranging for the crowds to break into small groups upon the grass, and then distributing the loaves and fishes to the hungry multitudes. The disciples function as co-workers of Jesus by joining him in his pastoral ministry. For them, as for Jesus, the crowds are the needy object of their ministry.

The same can be said for the disciples' attempts to heal the epileptic boy while Jesus is away on the mountain of transfiguration (17:14-21). Although the disciples prove themselves unequal to the task on this occasion, the fact that they sought to help needy members of the crowds again points to their status as the co-workers of Jesus who have been empowered by him to engage in public ministry (10:6-8).

Finally, it is certainly evocative that the crowds and the disciples do not use the same Christological titles to refer to Jesus.[39] The disciples refer to Jesus as the Messiah and Son of God (16:16), whereas the crowds identify Jesus as the Son of David and a prophet (12:23; 21:9-11).

All of these features make it evident that Matthew draws very clear distinctions between the crowds and the disciples. The latter receive a special call to follow him, and are granted special authority to engage in their mission, as well as special insights into the Kingdom of Heaven. The crowds, by contrast, lack this special gift of understanding, and remain profoundly and perennially needy. Their sheer need highlights how effectively Jesus and his disciples are able to remedy it. In sum, therefore, the crowds resemble the disciples in displaying a positive predisposition toward Jesus, but they share none of the disciples' radical commitment.

---

[37] Cousland, *Crowds*, 145–73.
[38] This is especially noteworthy since Matthew's source, Mark 10:46-52, explicitly indicates that Bartimaeus does follow Jesus once he is cured (v. 52; cf. Mt. 20:34).
[39] Meiser, *Die Reaktion des Volkes*, 235.

IV. The Crowds and the Jewish Leaders

The crowds' engagement with the Jewish leaders is expressed in two ways in the gospel: first, in the warning that Jesus gives the crowds about their leaders; and second, in the actual attempts made by the leaders to subvert the crowds. With regard to the former, it is notable that the crowds figure along with the disciples as the audience for Jesus' anti-Pharisaic discourse. Although Matthew's Jesus begins by urging the crowds and disciples to "do whatever they teach you and follow it" (23:3), it soon emerges that he regards the scribes and Pharisees as supremely flawed exponents of God's teaching. The leaders are "blind guides" who will lead their charges into a pit, "hypocrites" who teach their followers to misinterpret God's demands, ultimately turning them into sons of hell, religious guides who exhaust their adherents with unnecessary religious burdens (cf. 11:30) and consistently abuse their own authority (21:13, 45; 23:4-5, 13, 34, 37). In short, Matthew's Jesus is adamant that the words and deeds of the scribes and Pharisees embody the very antithesis of what the crowds and disciples ought to be doing (5:20; 15:13-14). Their teaching and examples are destructive, and they will lead the crowds to destruction.

As examples of this destructive behavior, the Jewish leaders are portrayed as systematically subverting the crowds' enthusiasm for Jesus. It is no coincidence that most of the favorable utterances and positive reactions made by the crowds in response to Jesus are directly countermanded and denigrated by the Jewish leadership. Matthew has constructed his gospel in such a way that the toxicity of the leaders is made palpable.

This toxicity culminates in the manipulation of the crowds by the Jewish high priests and elders to accomplish their bidding during the arrest and trial of Jesus. The arresting crowd that seizes Jesus in the Garden of Gethsemane has been sent by them. More seriously, it is they who "persuade the crowds" (ἔπεισαν τοὺς ὄχλους) before Pilate to condemn Jesus to death and to liberate Barabbas. This is not a "stirring up" of the crowd, as happens in Mark,[40] but a deliberate misguiding of them, culminating, famously, in the crowds' proclamation, where "the people as a whole [πᾶς ὁ λαὸς] answered, 'His blood be on us and on our children!'"[41] The passage's representation of the crowds intensifies the crowds' involvement, and it is at this juncture that Matthew drops his use of the word ὄχλος and reverts once more to the word λαός.[42] As Culpepper astutely notes, the only time that "the people" (ὁ λαός) actually act in Matthew is in their rejection of Jesus.[43]

---

[40] As in Mark 15:11: οἱ δὲ ἀρχιερεῖς ἀνέσεισαν τὸν ὄχλον ἵνα μᾶλλον τὸν Βαραββᾶν ἀπολύσῃ αὐτοῖς.
[41] The bibliography on this verse is extensive. For recent discussion, see Walter T. Wilson, *The Gospel of Matthew*, Eerdmans Critical Commentary (Grand Rapids, MI: Eerdmans, 2022), 2.397; Hans M. Moscicke, "Jesus, Barabbas, and the Crowd as Figures in Matthew's Day of Atonement Typology (Matthew 27:15-26)," *JBL* 139, no. 1 (2020): 125–53; Turner, *Israel's Last Prophet* 257–65; and cf. Ulrich Luz, *Studies in Matthew* (Grand Rapids, MI, and Cambridge: Eerdmans, 2005), 29–30.
[42] Meiser, *Die Reaktion des Volkes*, 260.
[43] Culpepper, *Matthew*, 78. On the crowds' role in the Passion narrative, cf. Cousland, *Crowds*, 227–39.

But even though the crowds cease to be mentioned after this point in the gospel, this same misdirection, uniquely among the gospels, recurs when the chief priests and elders invent the story of the theft of Jesus' body from the tomb by the disciples. Matthew relates that this fraud had attained such currency that "this story is still told among the Jews to this day" (28:15).

So even though the evangelist's focus moves between the scribes and Pharisees and the chief priests and elders, their impact on the crowds is consistently toxic. Whether it resides in the misguided teaching and example of their leaders, or in the express manipulation of the crowds to perform evil, Matthew indicates that their influence is malign.

It goes without saying that the Jewish leadership is presented in such an unrelentingly negative light to serve as a foil to Jesus (and, as most scholars agree, the later Christians associated with the gospel). In almost every respect, the conduct of the Jewish leadership towards the crowds is portrayed as the antithesis of that of responsible leaders. And it is important to recognize that Matthew's characterization is not primarily historical but theological: his design is to construct a polarity between Jesus and the Jewish leadership—one that situates the crowds clearly in the middle.[44] Meiser rightly discerns an apologetic dimension in the contrast between the crowds and their leaders. If the crowds were on the brink of discerning Jesus' messianic identity, how much more should this discernment have been expected from their leaders, who were steeped in the prophets and fixated on Torah.[45]

V. Conclusions

This chapter has focused on the character(s) of the crowds in relation to Jesus, and the characters of the disciples and Jewish leaders. The crowds have interactions with all of these figures, and the juxtaposition of the crowds with the other main characters of the gospel helps to establish their own character. What emerges particularly from these juxtapositions is the extent to which Matthew has laid down clear distinctions between the groups: the parameters are clearly demarcated, as are the groups' attributes and defining characteristics. This process is especially highlighted in the crowds' engagement with Jesus.

What is particularly vivid in many of the interactions among the gospel's characters is that the crowds are often the object and focus of the others, and thereby contribute a dynamic element to the plot. Jesus and the disciples seek to help and benefit the crowds, whereas the Jewish leaders seek to control them and negate Jesus' influence over them. The crowds, for their own part, seek to penetrate Jesus' identity even as they gravitate towards him and the disciples for aid. The picture that emerges of the crowds over the course of the gospel is of a group that is poised uneasily between opposing forces

---

[44] Poplutz, *Erzählte Welt*, 48-51. It cannot be stressed sufficiently strongly that Matthew's characterization of the Jewish leaders and the Jewish people is extraordinarily partisan. Polemic has replaced historicity, and with this caveat in mind, the gospel must be read with corrective lenses.

[45] Meiser, *Die Reaktion des Volkes*, 256.

before they finally succumb to their leaders, with a resultant change in their allegiance and the abrupt disappearance of them as a distinct character.[46]

The chief reason that Matthew portrays this change is theological. He wants to demonstrate that the crowds' volte-face is momentous and has profound repercussions for all the characters associated with the crowds. While he likely regards this change as historical, he may also have apologetic reasons for attributing the crowds' downfall to the Jewish leaders. Matthew repeatedly has Jesus accuse the Pharisees of being blind guides and warns that "if one blind person guides another, both will fall into a pit" (15:14). Jesus' apophthegm serves as a profound encapsulation of the fate of the crowds, and a harsh condemnation of the hubris and ignorance of the Jewish leaders.

Earlier, of course, there is also a change in the character of the crowds as they become increasingly aware of Jesus as the messianic shepherd and Son of David. This transformation functions as a foil to Matthew's Christology and also promotes an increased awareness of Jesus' identity on the part of the hearer or reader of the gospel. The above points can be summarized as follows:

1. The crowds in Matthew's Gospel are a distinct character. It is possible that they actually comprise two groups—a "Galilean" and a "Jerusalem" crowd, but this reading is less likely.
2. The crowds are essentially Jewish and, together with their leaders, corporately represent the λαός of Israel.
3. The crowds and the other characters—Jesus, the disciples, and the Jewish leaders—act as foils to each other, although the crowds' chief role is to serve as a foil to Jesus.
4. In contrast to the more static representations of the other two groups in the gospel, the crowds' character is dynamic insofar as it likely undergoes a change. This change reflects an agonistic dimension to the gospel, where Jesus and his disciples are ranged against the Jewish leadership. Here, the gospel's characterization is closely bound up with its plot.
5. The characterization of the crowds, which depicts them as being fascinated by Jesus, yet ultimately beguiled by their leadership, allows Matthew to develop an apology that condemns the Jewish leaders categorically.

---

[46] If one presupposes two sets of crowds, the "Jerusalem" crowds would also be arrayed against the "Galilee" crowds together with the Jewish leaders.

12

The Gentile Other in Matthew: A Theo-Ethnic Teaching Tool for Israel about to be Transformed

Anders Runesson

I. Introduction

Gentiles, or "the nations" (τὰ ἔθνη), or simply non-Jewish characters, occupy a somewhat odd and seemingly contradictory narrative position in Matthew's Gospel. This has led to diverse reception in both ancient and modern scholarship. On the one hand, they seem to be models of πίστις ("faithfulness," "loyalty"), drawing near to Jesus in obeisance (2:1-12) and asking for assistance, convinced that he has the power to help them (the centurion, 8:5-13; the Canaanite woman, 15:21-8). In addition, when compared explicitly with certain Jewish towns in Galilee, a selection of gentile cities is brought forth as producing superior would-be reactions to Jesus' message (11:21-4). On the other hand, when addressed in more general terms, everything gentiles do and say is seen as examples of what Jews must *not* do or say (e.g., 5:47; 6:7, 32; 18:17). Indeed, Jesus' disciples, all of whom are Jews (cf. 10:5-6), are warned that they will be hated by all the nations (πάντα τὰ ἔθνη; 24:9).

In this chapter, my aim is to explain how these distinct traits in fact make sense and present us with a strategically coherent narrative. Named gentile individuals and collectivities highlight what needs to be done in *Israēl*, but they are (surprising) exceptions to a negative rule. It is precisely the fact that their words and actions are unanticipated that constitute the core of the message communicated through these characters. In addition, the apparent contradiction between the two mission commands in terms of their gentile component (10:5-6; 28:18-20) will be addressed through an analysis of how the plot develops, such that certain actions or happenings change fundamental cosmic and therefore also earthly realities and preconditions for human life.

We shall proceed in three steps. After a brief discussion of the nature of Matthew's text, we shall look at how the author(s) deploy non-Jewish individuals as the story is told. Then, we shall proceed to see what, if anything, changes and why when non-Jewish collectivities—cities and general universalizing statements, respectively—are called upon to perform certain functions in the text. We shall structure the discussion by taking into account the narrative past, present, and future, since this will assist us in uncovering certain patterns of use with regard to these characters and what they may tell us about the nature of the ultimate concern of the story: the Kingdom of Heaven.

II. The Gentile in Matthew's Story

The first and perhaps the most important observation to be made as we approach Matthew is that it is a unified narrative telling a story.[1] As with most narratives, the text describes a beginning, a middle, and an end,[2] moving characters (which in my view are often neither "flat" nor "round")[3] through its landscapes and applying various techniques in order to effectively communicate the overall message of the story. The message is this: the Kingdom of Heaven has been initiated in *Israēl* through a series of battles between the Messiah, the agent of the God of *Israēl*, and evil cosmic forces affecting the human condition, and will now be globally implemented based on the unlimited divine powers given to Jesus after his resurrection. Along the way, as this message is carefully construed employing Jewish ancestral traditions,[4] the rhetorical force of which is taken for granted, the audience becomes privy to specific information which is communicated through the narrator's voice, the characters, and events ("plot"),[5] all of which make (positive and negative) sense within the world conjured up by the author. While there are certain pieces of information describing the conditions within which the (human and non-human) characters go about their business that remain constant throughout the story, the narrative also describes a development in which the basic preconditions for life change.

In the story Matthew is telling, there are two such radical transformations of (cosmic) realities towards which characters are inescapably moved, and in relation to which everything in the story (events, existents) builds. The first is the sacrificial death of the Messiah, which saves the Jewish people from destruction in the wake of the pollution (and predicted ruin) of the Jerusalem temple that, in turn, initiates the

---

[1] See the important but now slightly dated study by J. D. Kingsbury, *Matthew as Story*, 2nd edn (Minneapolis: Fortress, 1988), which traces the storyline of Jesus, the "religious leaders," and the disciples. On Matthew as a unified narrative and on how its story (what it is about) relates to its discourse (how the story is told), cf. W. D. Davies and D. C. Allison, *Matthew: A Critical and Exegetical Commentary on the Gospel according to Saint Matthew*, 3 vols. (London: T&T Clark, 1991–8), 96: "devises such as foreshadowing, repetition, and *inclusio* show up the impressive unity of the gospel." For S. Chatman, *Story and Discourse: Narrative Structure in Fiction and Film* (Ithaca, NY: Cornell University Press, 1978), 19 (cf. 26), "story" divides further into "events" and "existents," where the former refers to actions and happenings, and the latter to characters and settings.

[2] I would identify these, structurally/thematically, as a) the birth of the Messiah within the context of the history of *Israēl* divided into four epochs (the Messiah initiates the fourth and final/the present [cf. *m. 'Abot* 5:2 on generations from Adam to Noah to Abraham; Mt. 1:1-25), b) the Messiah's march on Jerusalem after successfully gathering large crowds (ὄχλοι πολλοί) in Galilee prepared to follow him to the "city of the great king" (5:35; cf. Ps. 48:3, LXX 47:3), as Matthew identifies this city (19:1-2; cf. 20:17-19), and c) the transformation of the Messiah into a cosmic ruler with universal powers (28:1-20).

[3] See discussion in C. Bennema, *A Theory of Character in New Testament Narrative* (Minneapolis: Fortress, 2014).

[4] See J. Nolland, *The Gospel of Matthew: A Commentary on the Greek Text* (Grand Rapids, MI: Eerdmans, 2005), 29–38, for a brief overview of Matthew's use of Jewish tradition, including but not limited to the Hebrew Bible.

[5] Defined as happenings or actions that are arranged in specific temporal and causal ways and extend throughout the story; cf. Chatman, *Story and Discourse*, 19–27 (diagrams on 19, 26); Kingsbury, *Matthew as Story*, 3.

apocalyptic end-time and the suffering associated with it.[6] The second transformation, which follows from the first, is the resurrection of the Messiah, which reinvents him from being an embodied agent of God's Spirit[7] to becoming a cosmic (co-)ruler of the universe and extends his previously limited powers accordingly.[8] What interests us here is that the second transformation of celestial realities, the enthronement of Jesus as a cosmic Messiah, also changes the reality on the ground for non-Jews, from having been excluded from direct messianic interest (10:5-6; 15:24) to becoming the center of attention (28:19-20). This interweaving of the non-Jewish world into one of the two key transformational sequences of the story suggests that the gentiles have been part of the ultimate aim of the narrative from the very beginning; the end point explains the construction of the narrative as such, even as the story's focus has been almost exclusively on the Jewish people and their redemption until these last two verses.

In which way has this been achieved? Following the gentile characters in Matthew from individual to collective portrayals and noting their words, actions, motifs, and relationships to other characters in the story will reveal the complexity of the issue, but still signal a consistent approach to them as they assist the protagonist and narrator in making theo-ethnic points and moving the plot forward to its—in hindsight—inescapable conclusion.

III. Non-Jewish Individuals and Groups in (Narrative) History, Present, and Future

In order to lead the audience toward the principal message of the story—that the basic conditions for human life have changed and Ἰσραήλ ("Israel") and τὰ ἔθνη ("the nations") need to be aware of that to survive the divine judgment soon to come—Matthew works with a layered use of gentile characters. There are two basic axes on this "narrative grid," at the intersection of which the author(s) give expression to their theo-ethnic convictions: time (past/present/future) and dimension (individuals/collectivities). If we isolate the relevant passages, the following image presents itself (p. 178).

This "map" does not, however, exhaust Matthew's use of the non-Jewish. In addition to the features of time and dimension that are listed in Figure 1, we also find general and generalizing statements in the First Gospel, which reveal how the protagonist portray and approach the non-Jewish world, and how people move about in that world. Figure 2 below outlines these basic characteristics (p. 179).

---

[6] The pollution/destruction of the temple (23:35-24:2) is thus the reason why Jesus has to die to save his people (1:21). For discussion of this central aspect of Matthew, which in my view explains the story as such, see A. Runesson, *Divine Wrath and Salvation in Matthew: The Narrative World of the First Gospel* (Minneapolis: Fortress, 2016), 233-56, where the narrative role of "the Pharisees" in this regard is highlighted.

[7] Cf. Mt. 12:28, 32.

[8] Compare Mt. 4:8, implying that the devil controls the world (see W. Carter, *Matthew and the Margins: A Socio-Political and Religious Reading* [Sheffield: Sheffield Academic Press, 2000], 110-11), with the transformational resurrection-effects extending far beyond the powers of the devil in Mt. 28:18, the latter now finally about to lose influence.

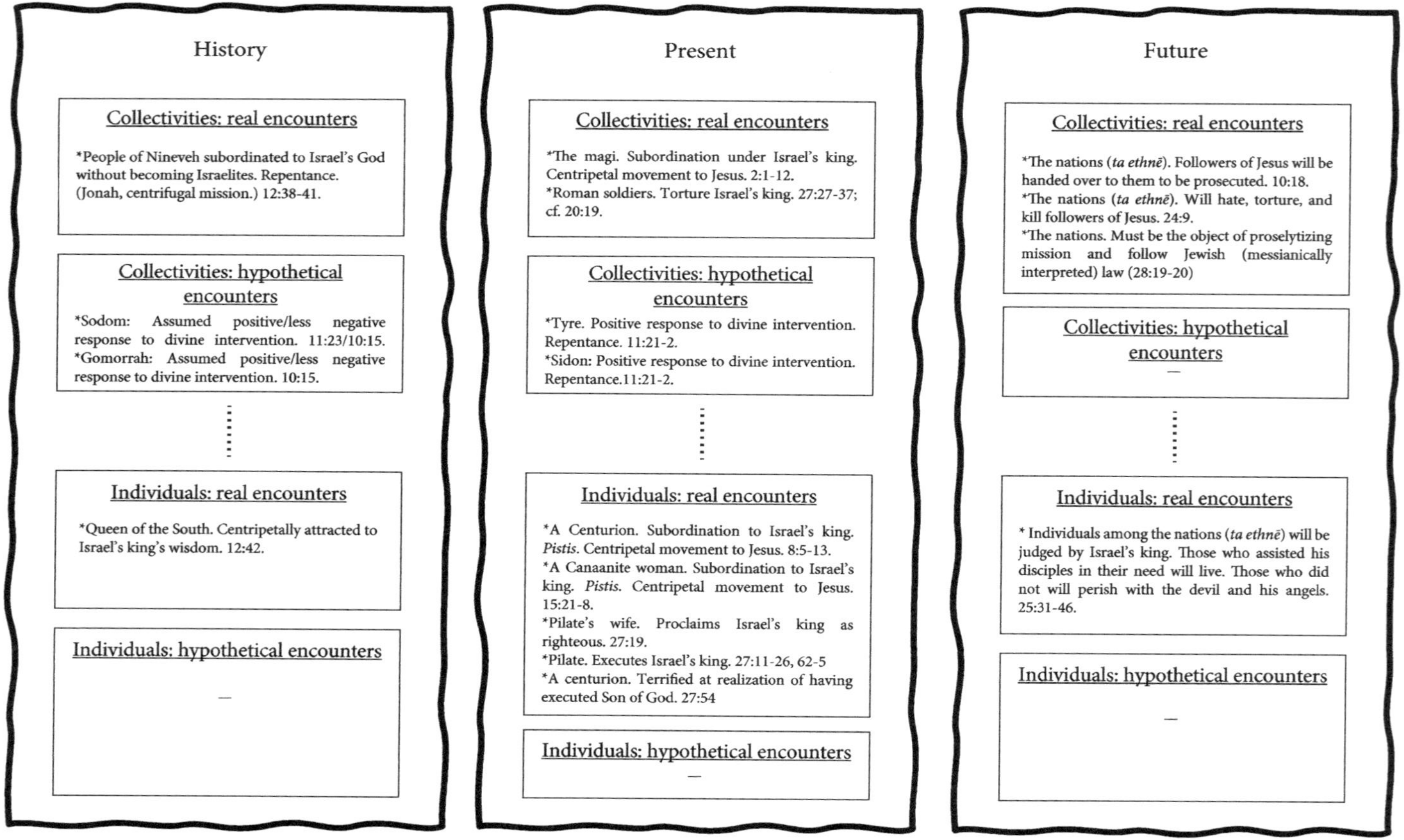

History

Collectivities: real encounters

*People of Nineveh subordinated to Israel's God without becoming Israelites. Repentance. (Jonah, centrifugal mission.) 12.38-41.

Collectivities: hypothetical encounters

*Sodom: Assumed positive/less negative response to divine intervention. 11:23/10:15.
*Gomorrah: Assumed positive/less negative response to divine intervention. 10:15.

Individuals: real encounters

*Queen of the South. Centripetally attracted to Israel's king's wisdom. 12.42.

Individuals: hypothetical encounters

—

Present

Collectivities: real encounters

*The magi. Subordination under Israel's king. Centripetal movement to Jesus. 2.1-12.
*Roman soldiers. Torture Israel's king. 27:27-37; cf. 20:19.

Collectivities: hypothetical encounters

*Tyre. Positive response to divine intervention. Repentance. 11:21-2.
*Sidon: Positive response to divine intervention. Repentance.11:21-2.

Individuals: real encounters

*A Centurion. Subordination to Israel's king. *Pistis*. Centripetal movement to Jesus. 8.5-13.
*A Canaanite woman. Subordination to Israel's king. *Pistis*. Centripetal movement to Jesus. 15:21-8.
*Pilate's wife. Proclaims Israel's king as righteous. 27:19.
*Pilate. Executes Israel's king. 27:11-26, 62-5
*A centurion. Terrified at realization of having executed Son of God. 27:54

Individuals: hypothetical encounters

—

Future

Collectivities: real encounters

*The nations (*ta ethnē*). Followers of Jesus will be handed over to them to be prosecuted. 10:18.
*The nations (*ta ethnē*). Will hate, torture, and kill followers of Jesus. 24:9.
*The nations. Must be the object of proselytizing mission and follow Jewish (messianically interpreted) law (28:19-20)

Collectivities: hypothetical encounters

—

Individuals: real encounters

* Individuals among the nations (*ta ethnē*) will be judged by Israel's king. Those who assisted his disciples in their need will live. Those who did not will perish with the devil and his angels. 25:31-46.

Individuals: hypothetical encounters

—

Figure 1. Gentiles in Matthew; aspects of time and dimension within the narrative world.

The general character of gentile behavior	Ideal approaches to gentiles A. Before Jesus's death and resurrection	Ideal approaches to gentiles B. After Jesus's death and resurrection

They:
 	
* Engage in unremarkable inter-human interaction based on the principle of love of friends, not of enemies, which is insufficient for the (Jewish) *ekklēsia* (5:45).
 	
* Pray to their deities with a multitude of empty words of no consequence (6:7).
 	
* Worry and strive to attain worldly possessions and sustenance, ignorant of the coming kingdom of the God of Israel within which divine care will see to all these things (6:32).
 	
* Function as representatives for people who are outsiders to the (Jewish) *ekklēsia*, and from whom one cannot expect divinely ordained behavior, such as asking for and extending forgiveness (18:17).
 	
* Organize their societies in hierarchical ways contrary to the egalitarianism and ideal of assisting others that must characterize the (Jewish) *ekklēsia* (20:25).
 	
* Represent the Other, to whom the Jerusalemite leaders will hand over Jesus for execution (20:19; 26:2, 45).
	* Non-Jews must not be actively missionized (10:5-6). This decision withholds from gentiles:
	   – awareness that the kingdom of the God of Israel is coming (v.7);
	   – healing,
	   – resuscitation of their dead,
	   – purification of those with *lepra*,
	   – and exorcism of those who are demon possessed (v.8).
	
	* Non-Jews who are centripetally drawn to Jesus asking for help must not be rejected (8:5-13; 15:21-28). This decision makes available to such gentiles:
	   – healing from paralysis and pain (8:6, 13),
	   – and liberation from demon possession (15:22, 28; cf. 8:28).
		* The nations (*ta ethnē*) need to be actively missionized and in that process go through water immersion to become disciples (28:19). This decision is based on the need for non-Jews to learn and keep Jewish law (*nomos*), which is what Jesus has been teaching his own (Jewish) disciples throughout the narrative to open the way for them to the kingdom (28:20; cf. 5:17-20; 19:16-17).
		
		   – This teaching of Jewish law is what the gentiles have been in need of since the time of the prophets; it is their only hope (12:18-21).
		   – It will be implemented not by Jesus but by his followers (24:14; 26:13; 28:19-20). This mission is made possible through a) Jesus's post-resurrection unlimited cosmic powers (28:18) and b) his presence among the members of the *ekklēsia* as they perform these tasks (28:20; cf. 18:20; 1:23). By implication, without the resurrection there would be no gentile mission (10:5-6; cf. 1 Cor 15:13-14, 17-18).

Figure 2. The general character of gentile behavior beyond named individuals or groups, and how to approach them.

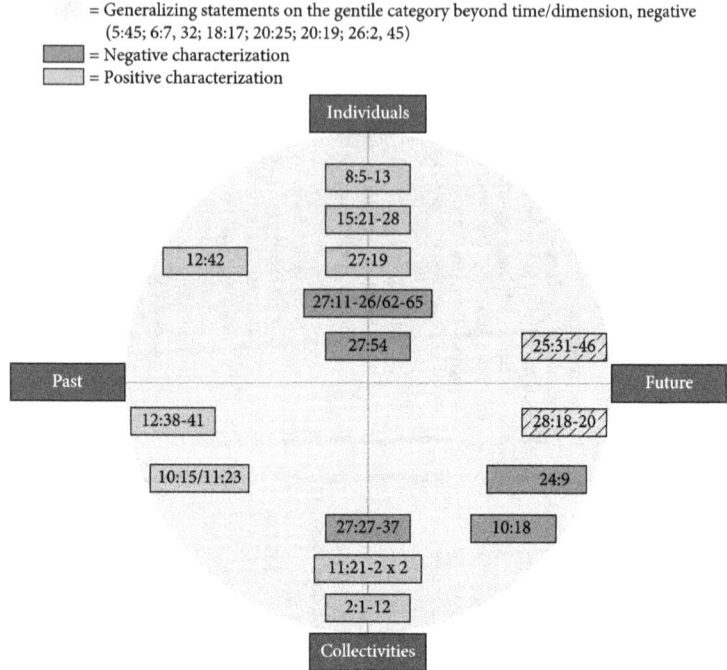

Figure 3. Time and dimension in relation to generalization and characterization.

With these "maps," what emerges is a rather complex picture. If we combine the information of Figs. 1 and 2, the above chart (Fig. 3) details what the Matthean world looks like in relation to all things gentile.

The first thing to note on a most basic level is that the nations (τὰ ἔθνη) and the individuals that belong among them (the gentiles) are construed as the outsider, the Other. "They" are people who in various ways compare with *Israēl* (i.e., *Israēl* and the nations are two distinct entities between which comparisons can be made); "they" are the ones to whom the Jerusalemite leadership (the chief priest, elders, and scribes)[9] will hand over Jesus; and "they" are dependent on *Israēl* for understanding justice and sustaining hope (12:18-21). This basic ethno-religiously oriented dividing line between insiders and outsiders does *not*, then, distinguish between approved and disapproved characters. There is evil in Matthew's world among the insiders (those who do not properly observe Jewish law/ancestral customs [νόμος] [e.g., 5:20; 13:41-2; 23:29-34]), as well as good (e.g., 7:28-9; 10:40-2; 15:31; 21:8-11), and the same applies to outsiders (disapproved: e.g., 18:17; 20:25; 27:27-37; approved: e.g., 2:1-12; 8:5-13; 15:21-8).

Looking at how the gentile character is constructed, we need, therefore, to approach the question beyond the more simplistic, or "flat," and look at this narrative "edifice" from different angles, including how the plot affects characterization. In which way do actions, words, deeds, and motives in the narrative past, present, and future contribute to bringing

---

[9] All of these characters are thus presented as insiders; cf. Mt. 16:21; cf. 20:18.

these characters to life, and in which way do the gentiles reflect the values and vision of the ultimate message of this Gospel, the Kingdom of Heaven? In order to answer such questions, we shall search for patterns based on a) time/dimension, and b) generalizing characterizations, using time as the primary sorting instrument.

A. Historical Gentiles

Historical actors are brought forth only rarely, and in a rather limited part of the text (chapters 10–12). Looking first at what is described as real historical events, with references to scriptures considered authoritative by all parties concerned (characters, narrator, author, intended audience; Jon. 3:5; 1 Kgs 10:1-10), we have two examples: one involving a collectivity (the people of Nineveh; 12:38-40) and one focusing on the actions of an individual (the Queen of the South; 12:42).

The two passages, one following on the other, have some things in common but describe different movements altogether. The action defining the people of Nineveh as righteous is their repentance, but this repentance is entirely dependent on an Israelite, Jonah, warning them of coming doom. For the Queen of the South, the movement is centripetal; based on rumors about the king of *Israēl*, she takes the initiative to seek out his wisdom. This initiative defines her as righteous and allows her a place in the coming kingdom.[10] What unites the people of Nineveh and this Queen is their Otherness in relation to the people of *Israēl*, and their positive response to, a) divine intervention, preventing their own doom, and b) rumors about the greatness of the king of *Israēl*, respectively. It is precisely this Otherness that constitutes the key to unfold Matthew's narrative technique here and at other places in the gospel. For, while at first glance the Other is held forth as an example for the insiders, the Jewish people, to follow, the rhetorical impact lies in a shared understanding between the protagonist and his audience of the ethno-religiously Other as, on a fundamental level, poorly equipped to understand right from wrong; to understand when the God of *Israēl* intervenes in history. It is a *qal-vaḥomer* argument of sorts that is being made.[11] If even these people, from whom we cannot expect much, could see and understand and act upon information received from, or rumors about, an Israelite agent of the God of *Israēl*, how much more should not the learned among God's people itself—the Pharisees and the scribes associated with them who are his interlocutors in this setting (12:38)[12]—have been able to see and understand when this god intervenes in history through this Messiah, who signifies something far more important, namely the arrival of the

---

[10] In the Hebrew source text, and the LXX, referred to by the protagonist, the Queen of Sheba in fact travels to Solomon in order to test him, as she doubts what she has heard. Once there, she becomes convinced and praises the God of *Israēl* for bestowing such gifts on this king. Thus, if we assume that this story was known by the author(s)' audience, the aspect of repentance is indeed echoed also in this story, even if her initiative remains the key to the argument made.

[11] A type of argument, common also in rabbinic literature, *a minore ad maius*, from the minor to the major. As M. J. Bernstein and S. A. Koyfman, "The Interpretation of Biblical Law in the Dead Sea Scrolls," in *Biblical Interpretation at Qumran*, ed. M. Henze (Grand Rapids, MI: Eerdmans, 2005), 61–87 (79), describe it, "[f]undamentally, it is an argument from analogy supported by logic."

[12] On the meaning of "this generation" in this passage and in Matthew more generally, see Runesson, *Divine Wrath*, 271–307.

Kingdom of Heaven? In the Matthean world, the generalized ethnic Other is, thus, a negatively evaluated group, but from this group individual heroic exceptions may still be brought forth and thus shame those within God's people, who have access to genuine and approved ancestral traditions but do not understand what is happening around this Messiah.

This negative evaluation of gentile culture and ancestral customs comes through in several other passages,[13] and presents the protagonist's (Jewish) audience in the narrative with a basic point of departure for assessing the shame attributed to those within the people, the in-group, who do not pay attention to, or reject, the work of God's spirit through the Messiah. They are also, through these gentile examples, given a tool for measuring the ultimate danger they are in as the kingdom is approaching around Jesus. The rhetorical technique applied in these cases to gentile characters thus indicates that the gentiles are not in and of themselves of interest here; their function is to put the spotlight on *Israēl*, which is also the purpose of the narrative as a whole.[14]

If we stay within the (narrative) historical, two more cases, both of them referring to collectivities, further this same point, based on the same logic: Sodom and Gomorrah (11:23; 10:15). These passages suggest that both of these proverbially evil cities, which were destroyed by the wrath of the God of *Israēl*, *would*, hypothetically, have reacted more positively than the protagonist understands Capernaum, his home base, to do in the present, *if* they had been privileged to witness the deeds of power through him that Capernaum has (11:23-4). The same logic underlies the position taken in 10:15, where the target is those who would reject the disciples when they visit; if they do, they will fare worse than the people of the land of Sodom and Gomorrah (γῇ Σοδόμων καὶ Γομόρρων).

B. Gentiles in the Present

As we enter the story world's present (and future), we see that the same general understanding of the gentile as Other applies, as we have noted in Figure 2, leaflet 1 (5:45; 6:7, 32; 18:17; 20:25; 20:19; 26:2, 45). That is, the general statements about gentile culture, politics, and ancestral customs are consistent and negative, constituting a rhetorically important part of the story as the plot develops. The generalized gentile character is part of the negative background against which *Israēl* is measured; when its few specific collective and individual exceptions perforate the backdrop and enter the scene, they highlight what should—indeed must—happen in *Israēl*. The focus is on repentance as well as on recognition of and/or subordination to the lawful king of *Israēl*, who rules at the center of the world.[15] In the narrative present, this takes different forms, but the message is essentially the same: if even gentiles can approach and submit

---

[13] See leaflet one in Figure 2 above (Mt. 5:45; 6:7, 32; 18:17; 20:25), and further discussion below.

[14] The focus is, throughout, on the Jewish people—the Matthean Jesus' own people—and their salvation, from 1:21 onwards, as also emphasized explicitly in Mt. 10:5-6. We shall return to discuss Mt. 28:18-20 below.

[15] Like Rome, from a Roman perspective, was the center of the inhabited world. On empire, see further below.

themselves to the authority of the Messiah, how much more should not *Israēl*'s own be able to understand and do the same?

The first example is the story of the magi (μάγοι) from the East (2:1-12). These gentiles, representative of the "provinces" of the East, have been able to interpret the celestial signs that a new king has been born, who, quite obviously, is being perceived as having authority far beyond his own territory (Ἰσραήλ), and thus understood to be an emperor.[16] The movement is centripetal: from the margins to the center. But the magi have no knowledge of the ancestral traditions of *Israēl*. Consequently, they ask the current king in Jerusalem, Herod, who, ignorant of both the celestial signs and his own holy scriptures, in turn asks his chief priests and scribes. The latter, ignorant of the celestial signs but knowledgeable of their scriptures, point to Bethlehem. Adding revelatory insight from the scriptures of *Israēl* to the universally available (celestial) knowledge allows these magi to find the young child and, when they do, prostrate (προσκυνέω) themselves before him as representatives of an empire's provinces would before their emperor (2:11).

These gentile characters' actions signal, from the very beginning of the story, that this Messiah will have universal authority, and that the appropriate posture of the non-Jewish world is recognition of and subordination to this Jewish ruler. Again, however, the gentiles highlight how miserable the state of things are in the political world of the land; they are used to highlight the state of things in the land of *Israēl*.[17] The current king is not only more ignorant than gentiles, he is illegitimate, and murders innumerable children of Abraham[18] in order to find and kill the lawful king that would replace him on the throne.

Something similar happens when a centurion, a representative of the Roman Empire, and thus Rome in the West,[19] approaches Jesus (8:5-13). The movement is again centripetal, from the margins to the center, and recognition of the superior powers of,[20] and the appropriate subordination to, this Messiah are thematized. And again, this recognition and trust (πίστις; 8:10) is contrasted with the lack of such strong trust in *Israēl*, including, by necessary implication, among his own disciples.[21] The rhetorical point of the passage, which supports the overall case here that the protagonist operates with *qal-vaḥomer* arguments when calling upon gentile characters to exercise influence

---

[16] For more discussion of the magi and Herod in this regard, see Runesson, *Divine Wrath*, 356-61.
[17] A designation employed by Matthew for Judaea and Galilee (γῆ Ἰσραήλ), but possibly not Samaria, since Jesus orders his disciples to avoid Samaritan cities specifically and still talks about the entire area that they will travel as the cities of *Israēl* (10:5, 23). Cf. R. T. France, *The Gospel according to Matthew: An Introduction and Commentary* (Leicester: Inter-Varsity Press, 1985), 90. In any case, as Davies and Allison, *Matthew*, 272, point out, γῆ Ἰσραήλ is a "biblical" designation.
[18] Cf. Mt. 3:9, which likely signals what the Messiah, in contrast, will accomplish, i.e., more children of Abraham brought in from the non-Jewish world. For discussion, see Runesson, *Divine Wrath*, 361.
[19] Note the mention of East and West in Mt. 8:11, as if summing up the combined effect of the Eastern magi and the centurion.
[20] The power the centurion is convinced Jesus has access to is clarified through an analogy with human powers (his own, 8:9). In Jesus' case it is, however, a matter of exorcizing an illness from a person, i.e., in the worldview of this narrative, a cosmic power, or demon, which is less powerful than this agent of the God of *Israēl* (*theou Israēl*; cf. 15:31) and, consequently, must obey.
[21] On Jesus' critique of his own disciples' lack of πίστις, cf. Mt. 17:16-17, 20. For the disciples as part of—and future rulers of—*Israēl*, see Mt. 19:28.

on the story, is further emphasized by Jesus' expression of surprise and astonishment at the centurion's words (θαυμάζω); these are words that, it is implied, would be easier to understand had they been spoken by someone within his own people.

A third case of a centripetal movement from the gentile margins to the Jewish Messiah is found in 15:21-8, where a Canaanite woman begs Jesus to heal her daughter by exorcizing the demon that torments her. Here, as in other passages where non-Jews are introduced to Jesus, *Israēl* is brought up as a comparative entity, indicating, as we have argued, that the basic dividing line between in-group and out-group is ethnic in character. In this case, Jesus reiterates what the narrator told the audience in 1:21, namely that Jesus' program is focused on the salvation of his own people, the people of *Israēl* (*laou Israēl*), and more specifically, those within the people who are described as "lost" (τὰ πρόβατα τὰ ἀπολωλότα οἴκου Ἰσραήλ; 15:24).[22] The pattern we saw with the magi and the centurion is repeated: the woman prostrates (προσκυνέω) herself before the Jewish Messiah, calling him lord (κύριε; 15:25), very explicitly confirming to him that she understands her position as subordinated to him and his people (15:27). The exchange of words between Jesus and the woman is repugnant and offensive to most modern, and probably some ancient, readers,[23] but the point is clear: the gentile is *and remains* the Other, but πίστις—of which subordination to the Jewish Messiah is an integral part—perforates the ethnic boundary and allows—even forces—Jesus to expel her daughter's demon. The difference in this episode compared to the centurion-passage is that the Canaanite's πίστις is not compared to the lack of such trust in *Israēl*; the lost among the Jewish people, in this incidence, is a positive entity which deserves the full attention of their soon-to-be-enthroned king.[24]

These non-Jews, the magi, the centurion, and the Canaanite woman, all understand what is happening in *Israēl* and act accordingly (πίστις/subordination). None of them, though, join the movement and they all remain outsiders; they are *not* among Jesus' followers in this story.[25] The point in this case is precisely that *even outsiders* will have a share of the blessings of the kingdom when the Messiah is present in their midst, *if* they approach him with the right attitude and resolve.

---

[22] Mt. 2:6. The issue is one of lack of leadership, leaving the people (οἱ ὄχλοι; the crowds) vulnerable and lost: Mt. 9:36.

[23] Indeed, one wonders how late-first-century non-Jews interested in Jesus but not joining the Jewish people as (messianic) proselytes would have understood these verses, especially in settings like the Matthean where Christ-oriented Jews constituted the core of the movement, and, conversely, how the latter would have understood the former in light of the same passage. We know from Romans 11 and Acts 15 that the interrelationship between such members of Christ-groups was controversial and debated. This is not the place to further discuss the socio-religious setting of our narrative, but see A. J. Saldarini, *Matthew's Christian-Jewish Community*, CSHJ (Chicago: University of Chicago Press, 1994), and D. C. Sim, *The Gospel of Matthew and Christian Judaism: The History and Social Setting of the Matthean Community*, Studies of the New Testament and Its World (Edinburgh: T&T Clark, 1998). On the importance of historical context for the understanding of literary characters, cf. discussion in J. Rüggemeier and E. E. Shively, "Introduction: Towards a Cognitive Theory of New Testament Characters: Methodology, Problems, and Desiderata," *BibInt* 29 (2021): 403–29.

[24] Although his enthronement will take place in an unexpected way, post resurrection.

[25] This, of course, corresponds logically with the messianic program and orientation of Mt. 10:5-6, indicating narrative consistency. (There are, in fact, no non-Jewish followers of Jesus in any of the gospels. As with the hint in Jn 12:20-3, non-Jews as members of the movement belongs to another, post-resurrection phase of the story, which Matthew is also very clear about in 28:18-20.)

This message is, implicitly, also communicated through the brief mention of Pilate's wife (27:19). While she does not ask the Messiah for help as the other gentile individuals do, she recognizes that he is righteous and fears the consequences for her and her husband should Jesus be punished or executed. This fear is the reverse side of what surfaces as πίστις in the other passages discussed above. Lack of respect and subordination will result in a nightmare; πίστις, on the other hand, is a prerequisite for the good life, that is, the kingdom. Pilate himself is, far from common Christian interpretation, described as a weak leader, who is ultimately a tool in the hands of the God of *Israël*. As the story carefully reasons, a non-Jew could never offer the sacrifice needed after the pollution and (future) destruction of the Jerusalem temple (23:35–24:2)—a sacrifice (which is Jesus, 1:21; 20:28; 26:28) for the forgiveness of sins. This is the role of the chief priests in the temple, whose duty is precisely to bring atonement for their people.[26]

So far, we have looked at gentiles in the narrative past and present, but what happens as we turn the spotlight to the future? Is this character developed in new directions as the story moves towards its post-resurrection climax? I would have liked to respond "yes," or "yes and no," but, ultimately, I must land on "not really." There is change there, but transformation happens in the world around the gentiles, and to this new reality they must adapt.

C. Future Gentiles

First, a comment on the aspect of continuity between present and future. Gentiles in the future post-resurrection world of the narrative, the world the story points towards but which is not developed in the text itself, primarily represent danger to the (Jewish) followers of Jesus. This is a logical development based on the general statements on the unprincipled culture, politics, and worship of the gentile world that we discussed above (5:45; 6:7, 32; 18:17; 20:25; 20:19; 26:2, 45). Not surprisingly, then, in the time ahead, followers of Jesus will be handed over to the gentiles to be prosecuted (10:18) and the nations (τὰ ἔθνη) will hate, torture, and kill them (24:9). But here, precisely, lies the crux of the matter. It is the general corrupt nature of the gentile world that necessitates their reform in light of the messianic era and, more specifically, the coming judgment. In Matthew, such reform of the nations is both possible and desirable, and in fact, it is their only hope; they need to be taught what justice[27] is (12:18-20), and if they are, and if they reform, the kingdom will be opened for them too.

---

[26] While the Pharisees and the scribes associated with them are accused of causing the pollution and destruction of the temple (23:1–24:2), a catastrophe which only the Messiah can solve through his self-sacrifice, restoring the Mosaic covenant (1:21; 26:28), the Pharisees disappear from the story when they have filled this narrative function. Enter instead the chief priests, who, unknowingly, bring forth the necessary sacrifice. Gentiles cannot have a theo-ritual role in this atonement drama— they are simply the executioners—and, consequently, must be presented as without guilt (27:24). See further, A. Runesson, "Who Killed Jesus and Why? The Jewish Nature of Matthew's Anti-Imperial Polemics," in *The Gospel of Matthew: Its Composition, Theology, and Early Reception*, ed. J. Verheyden, J. Schröter, and David C. Sim, WUNT 477 (Tübingen: Mohr Siebeck, 2022); cf. Catherine Sider Hamilton, *The Death of Jesus in Matthew: Innocent Blood and the End of Exile*, SNTSMS 167 (Cambridge: Cambridge University Press, 2017).

[27] That is, torah, upon which judgment (κρίσις) is based (Mt. 12:18).

This is what the so-called Great Commission is all about (28:19–20). But as the God of *Israēl* enthrones Jesus as a cosmic Messiah with unlimited and unprecedented powers on earth and in heaven, and thus changes the entire cosmic order in favor of those who thirst for justice (5:6; 12:18), long for comfort (5:4), embody mercy (5:7) and pureness of heart (5:8), and work for peace (5:9), non-Jews have to change their nature too in order to share in this new world order. It is not enough to teach them; they need to go through change ritually, through baptism.[28] This ritual implies, by necessity, that what they then become is something they were not before; they change their ritual status and will, as a consequence, be in a position to follow Jewish ancestral customs, the Jewish νόμος as taught by Jesus (5:17; 28:20).[29] In brief, regardless of whether one understands 28:20 as implying circumcision for male converts[30] or not, this water ritual indicates in and of itself the same change of status as circumcision would have done; that is, it communicates that the salvation of gentiles depends on them becoming Jews and following Jewish ancestral customs.[31] The outsider, indeed the enemy (24:9), is thus conquered through offering them—through incorporation—an escape from certain destruction in the coming divine judgment, a solution consistent with what is taught elsewhere on loving the enemy (5:43-8; cf. 24:12-13).

Looking at past, present, and future aspects of Matthew's narrative world thus reveals some consistency with regard to the gentile character, even as the story develops and changes the preconditions for life both within and beyond the Jewish people. The most significant change is what happens after the resurrection. Prior to Jesus' enthronement as cosmic ruler (28:18), the blessings of the kingdom leaked through ethno-religious boundaries and improved the lives of those individual gentiles who actively approached Jesus and asked for supra-human assistance. After the resurrection, the nations are called upon to ritually transform their nature and join the Jewish people in the ways of justice that lead to and constitute the Kingdom of Heaven.

There is, however, one aspect of gentile ways of being that seems consistent and decides the issue of salvation for certain individuals: their willingness to help followers of Jesus when they suffer (25:31-46). In ways similar to later rabbinic theologies of the Other, Matthew's Jesus keeps open the possibility of the non-Jewish Other entering into the kingdom based on their showing mercy and compassion towards Jesus' disciples; salvation by association, as it were.[32] This option does not, however, cancel

---

[28] No Jews are baptized by Jesus or his disciples in Matthew's Gospel. The πάντα τὰ ἔθνη of 28:19 have been the object of scholarly debate, but it seems clear to me that this expression refers to non-Jews, not the Jewish people, as T. L. Donaldson, "'Nations,' 'Non-Jewish Nations,' or 'Non-Jewish Individuals,'? Matthew 28:19 Revisited," in *Matthew Within Judaism: Israel and the Nations in the First Gospel*, ed. Anders Runesson and Daniel M. Gurtner, ECL 27 (Atlanta: Society of Biblical Literature, 2020), 169–94, has recently argued; cf. J. Kampen, *Matthew Within Sectarian Judaism* (New Haven, CT: Yale University Press, 2019), 184–202.

[29] 28:20. On this interpretation, see Sim, *The Gospel of Matthew*, 250–5; Runesson, *Divine Wrath*, 350, n. 16, 364–88.

[30] Referring, e.g., to general statements on the enduring validity of the Jewish νόμος in all its parts; 5:17-20; 23:23.

[31] A position taken also by others in the early Jesus movement, as Acts 15:1, 5, and Paul's opponents in Galatia show.

[32] See discussion in Runesson, *Divine Wrath*, 414–28. Cf. the theology expressed in Gen. 12:3; *2 Bar.* 72.4.

out the call to proselytize the nations, as this missionizing takes place, narratively, before the final judgment described in 25:31-46.

IV. Named and Unnamed Individuals and Collectivities: Different but Complementary Functions

What comes through most clearly, perhaps, in the above discussion is that the gentile in Matthew is used in different ways narratively depending on what point the author(s) want to make. When spoken of in non-specific and generalizing ways, their ways of life are in deep need of being reformed (5:45; 6:7, 32; 18:17, 20:25; 24:9); the Jewish Messiah is their only hope (12:18; 28:19-20). These passages indicate the protagonist's understanding of the non-Jewish world.

When spoken of in specific terms, both individual characters and named collectivities (towns and cities), their function is to show how strange it is that Jesus' own compatriots do not seem to understand what is happening around and through him (e.g., 2:1-12; 8:5-13; 15:21-8; 11:21-2). The narrator's and the protagonist's interest is not here in the gentile himself or herself, but they are used as a tool to address those in *Israēl* who do not heed the call to repentance; to highlight perceived deficiencies in levels of πίστις within Jesus' own people as they encounter him in different settings. The gentile-specific is, thus, the exception to the general rule, and the rhetorical force of the arguments made lies precisely in the Otherness of these individuals and towns.

Except for the theology of the gentile Other expressed in 25:31-46, it is not really until the last three verses of the gospel that the nations, as a general category, come into view in their own right, and when they do the message is that they need to change their nature through a water ritual in order to be taken up among those destined for the kingdom (28:18-20). After the resurrection, and contrary to Paul and Acts, then, Matthew's Gospel tears down all ethno-religious barriers within the Jesus movement through messianically opening the Sinaitic covenant between God and *Israēl* for proselytes—that is, for those who were not born Jews but who wished, in light of the coming divine judgment, to choose life.[33] In other words, the basic *understanding* of the gentile and "their" culture is consistent throughout the Matthean narrative—generally negative, with exceptions brought forth only to shame those of limited πίστις in *Israēl*— but the *approach* to the gentile Other changes as the story reaches its climax, from a closed ethnic position to an open ethnic and actively missionizing stance.[34]

---

[33] On Matthew's difference compared to Paul, see A. Runesson, "Beyond Universalism and Particularism: Rethinking Paul and Matthew on Gentile Inclusion," in *Paul and Matthew among Jews and Gentiles: Essays in Honour of Terence L. Donaldson*, ed. R. Charles, LNTS 628 (London: T&T Clark, 2021), 99–111. Of course, opening the covenant for proselytes also became the majority position within rabbinic Judaism, and has remained so until the present day. The path chosen by Paul and Acts maintains difference within the Christ-groups, a path that was abandoned, as was Matthew's approach, by the emerging mainstream non-Jewish churches.

[34] On this terminology, see A. Runesson, *Judaism for Gentiles: Reading Paul Beyond the Parting of the Ways Paradigm*, In collaboration with Rebecca Runesson, WUNT 494 (Tübingen: Mohr Siebeck, 2022), Ch. 2. A closed-ethnic approach rejects inclusion of proselytes in an ethno-religious group; an open-ethnic stance maintains the socio-religious validity of ethnicity, but is open to proselyte converts.

V. Conclusion

So, which vision of the Kingdom of Heaven, the ultimate concern of the narrative towards which everything—story (events, existents) and discourse (structure and manifestation)—gravitates, is communicated through gentile characters in Matthew? In order to answer this question, first-century ethnic reasoning related to peoples and gods need to be taken into account, as this was the context within which the text was written and first understood.[35] As Paula Fredriksen has shown,

> [e]thnicity, like divinity, was a category that spanned heaven and earth: gods and their humans formed family groups, and gods often shared in the ethnicity of the people who worshipped them. In this regard, the Jewish god was no exception. What was exceptional was the Jewish god's claims to cross-ethnic supremacy: at the end of days, the gods of the other nations as well as their peoples would acknowledge Israel's god alone.[36]

The author(s) of the Matthean narrative operate with precisely these two parameters: a god interwoven with an ethnos, on the one hand, and, on the other, what happens as this god initiates an apocalyptic-eschatological process in which his cross-ethnic supremacy, long acknowledged especially in the poetic and prophetic scriptures of *Israēl*, is about to materialize on a global scale as heaven merges with earth. These two components, indeed, form the backbone of the story; they are the reason the story was written and why it was written the way it was.

The Kingdom of Heaven, seen through named gentile characters' or cities' perspective, represents, as the previous discussion has shown, the good life; a time/place where bodies heal (8:13), where wisdom rules (12:42), where their hopes for justice are realized (12:18-21), and where the devil and his demons are restrained and kept in check before they are finally destroyed (15:28; 25:41). It is a world where Jewish ancestral customs have come to full fruition and in all aspects, big and small, express the core value of loving God and neighbor (7:12; 22:34-40; cf. 23:23). It is into this world, this time/place, the gentiles have been invited, transformed through baptism and, perhaps implied, circumcision (for men), to share it with the Jewish people (28:18-20). Notably, as the good life is proclaimed to the nations, an unnamed Jewish woman is to be held forth as a model disciple, possessing an understanding of Jesus and what he is about to go through that goes beyond what his own (male) disciples can fathom (26:13). She acts on her insight with compassion and generosity, and for this she will always be remembered wherever the good news of the kingdom is proclaimed throughout the world.[37] Not all

---

[35] Cf. Rüggemeier and Shively, "Introduction," 403–29, here 416: "meaning-making is a complex process of production, reception, and interpretation involving text-internal and text-external phenomena. As a result, a cognitive approach, not only enables but also requires a historical-culturally oriented literary study of NT narratives."

[36] P. Fredriksen, "How Jewish is God? Divine Ethnicity in Paul's Theology," *JBL* 137, no. 1 (2018): 193–212 (193).

[37] Here, thus, a Jewish woman is held forth as an example for the gentiles to follow, in contrast to the gentile men and women to whom the protagonist referred as exemplary, as we discussed above,

gentiles, however, will find delight in the message about such global transformation, and those who have the power to do it will persecute, inflict suffering on, and kill Jesus' followers (10:18; 24:19).

While the invitation to share the good life comes only at the very end of the narrative, in hindsight the audience of this gospel realizes that it has been signaled from early on, not only through the words and actions of gentile characters who are centripetally drawn to the Messiah, but also in the way the narrator and the protagonist comment on or respond to their behavior. The time/place in which the characters live is the fourth of the historical epochs of the Jewish people listed in the genealogy (1:17).[38] Commentators commonly discuss only the number fourteen, the number of generations that make up each epoch according to our text, and how it (uneasily) structures the first three epochs; that is, the focus is on (narrative) history.[39] The awkwardness of the theological mathematics that categorizes the epochs strongly suggests that the author(s) aimed to convey a deeper meaning than statistics. R. T. France rightly suggests that the focus lies beyond the number fourteen and points to the royal dimension of the genealogy; it is a dynastic document, aiming to signal the restoration of the monarchy.[40] In other words, while the historical is certainly about the past, it is much more about the future, and this suggests that we redirect out attention from the first three epochs to the fact that the current (narrative) epoch is the fourth and final one that completes (Jewish) history. This completion is, as Warren Carter notes, the beginning of a new creation (cf. παλιγγενεσίᾳ in 19:28).[41] In light of the focus on new creation elsewhere in Matthew, the significance of the number four in the genealogy is, in my view, best understood as related to the four cardinal directions.[42]

---

when previously engaging his own people in his Galilean campaign. On this passage, see E. Schüssler Fiorenza, *"In memory of her": A Feminist Reconstruction of Christian Origins* (New York: Crossroad, 1983).

[38] The structuring of history in generations, or using other parameters, forming epochs is common in ancient Jewish texts, apocalyptic or otherwise; see, e.g., 1 Chron. 1-2; Dan. 9:24-7; *1 En.* 91:12-17; 93:1-10; *2 Bar.* 53-74; 4 Ezra 14:11; *m. 'Abot* 1:1-12.

[39] See, e.g., Davies and Allison, *Matthew*, 163–5; Nolland, *The Gospel of Matthew*, 86–7.

[40] R. T. France, *The Gospel according to Matthew: An Introduction and Commentary* (Leicester: Inter-Varsity Press, 1985), 32. To be sure, this interpretation can be merged with Davies and Allison, *Matthew*, ad loc., who point to the numerical value of the Hebrew name David (*dwd*), the ideal king, which is 4+6+4, i.e., fourteen; cf. M. Konradt, *Das Evangelium nach Matthäus* (Göttingen: Vandenhoeck & Ruprecht, 2015), 30, who notes the dynastic element, but suggests that we can only assume, not ultimately know, if the name *dwd* is intended by these numbers (28).

[41] W. Carter, *Matthew and the Margins: A Socio-Political and Religious Reading* (London: T&T Clark, 2000), 65.

[42] Cf. the four rivers of Gen. 2:10-14. As already G. von Rad, *Genesis: A Commentary*, 2nd rev. edn (London: SCM Press, 1972), 79, noted regarding Genesis, "The author projects a picture of the great river system that surrounded the world he knew, for the number 'four' circumscribes the entire world." See also J. C. Gertz, *Das Erste Buch Mose: Genesis. Die Urgeschichte, Gen 1-11*, ATD 1 (Göttingen: Vandenhoeck & Ruprecht, 2018), 113, who adds Isa. 11:12 ("the four corners of the earth"); Jer. 49:36 ("the four winds from the four quarters of heaven"); Ezek. 37:9 ("the four winds," which will resurrect the dead"); Zech. 6:5 ("the four winds/spirits of heaven"), noting that, in the Bible, the number four signifies completeness ("Vollständigkeit"). Matthew's proven preference for Genesis when discussing interpretation and application of Torah (*nomos*) more generally indicates further both a global perspective and the theme of re-creation (cf. Mt. 19:4, 8, 28). The river motif from Genesis is also elaborated on, in different ways, in, e.g., Ezek. 47:1-12; cf. Rev. 22:1-3, where the nations (*ta ethnē*) are said to benefit from the transformation about to happen to Jerusalem.

The global perspective that comes with the re-creation of the world, and which finds its *inclusio* in the very last verses of the gospel where all nations are drawn into this rebirth of social and political life, is thus dependent on the universal cosmic powers given to the Messiah at this point (28:18-19).[43] In other words, the narrative goal of global inclusion was there from the beginning of the story, and controls the movements of characters and developments of events.

This does not mean, however, that gentiles are the main characters of the story.[44] The goal is universal, but the core, the hub around which the past, present, and future world turns, is the Jewish people and their ancestral traditions in the service of the God of *Israel*. What is to be proclaimed to the nations is Jewish justice, Jewish compassion for fellow human beings, a Jewish longing for peace and righteousness (cf. 5:3-9). It is this narrative focus and frame that ultimately explains the role of gentile characters in this story, as it moves history toward its consummation.

I dedicate this study to the memory of my friend and fellow Matthean, David C. Sim (1957–2023). Fearless in interpretation, David played a major role in changing the way we read Matthew's Gospel, pointing to the Jewish character of the text. He will be missed by many.

---

[43] The theological logic of Matthew's story thus describes a movement from cosmic transformation of power relations to change on earth, in that order; nothing can change in the world until the cosmic battle is won and the Messiah is enthroned.

[44] *Pace* much previous scholarship on Matthew, which describe a transfer of divine election from the Jewish people to a "new people of God"; cf. A. Y. Collins, "Polemics Against the Pharisees in Matthew 23," in *The Pharisees*, ed. J. Sievers and A.-J. Levine (Grand Rapids, MI: Eerdmans, 2021), 148–69. There is narrative progression in Matthew, but it is not based on replacement (of the Jewish people) but of inclusion (of the gentiles).

13

Between Straw Man and Punching Bag: "Pharisees" as a Character in the Gospel of Matthew

Eric Ottenheijm

I. On Studying Character and Genre

Fiction has a strange way of dealing with reality. As it purports to tell a story without claiming historical truth, in drawing elements from reality, it at times shapes our perception of this reality as well. Canonical stories such as those contained in the gospels add to this effect, as they convey religious truth claims and their characters are considered by readers to be "truer than truth."[1] Moreover, aspects of what modern readers would label as literature were employed by authors of late antiquity as well: predictability, repetition, and coherence of a character.[2] Indeed, as Mieke Bal notes, readers' inclination to see stories as complete and reliable also tends to view characters as such.[3] The implied reader of Matthew is expected as well to comprehend details and fill out the gaps, and in doing so construe a fitting picture.[4] And even when the modern discernment of "flat characters" versus "round characters" may falter in the face of ancient modes of storytelling, the Pharisees certainly belong to the "type," being a highly recognizable figure, often in comic or absurd situations.[5] However, there is

---

[1] Uri Margolin, "Character," in *The Cambridge Companion to Narrative. Cambridge Companions to Literature*, ed. David Herman (Cambridge: Cambridge University Press, 2007), 119: "[T]he character is an effect that makes us believe in the human nature of a creature that is constantly resisting that humanity, in favour of other important insights it has to offer. This is the game of make-believe in fiction—a game that is, according to the specific insights it produces, truer than truth."

[2] Predictability is also repetition of content: Mieke Bal and Christine van Boheemen, *Narratology: Introduction to the Theory of Narrative*, 3rd edn (Toronto: University of Toronto Press, 2009), 126. Indeed, Janice Capel Anderson, *Matthew's Narrative Web: Over, and Over, and Over Again* (Sheffield: JSOT Press, 1994), emphasizes Matthew's verbal repetitions.

[3] Bal and van Boheemen, *Narratology*, 114: "But relying on the analogy between character and human being, readers tend to attach so much importance to coherence that this material is easily reduced to a psychological 'portrait' that has more bearing on the reader's own desire to 'recognize' the character than on the interchange between story and fabula."

[4] Margolin, "Character," 67, 76. Cf. Bal and van Boheemen, *Narratology*, 125: "A character's predictability is closely related to the reader's frame of reference in which it seems to 'fit.'"

[5] The notion of "flat character" was applied to Pharisees, as "antagonists," in Jack Dean Kingsbury, *Matthew as Story*, 2nd edn, rev. and enlarged (Minneapolis: Fortress Press, 1988), 115ff., and,

nothing comic here: the impact of blurring narrative and reality was paramount in Matthew's biographical story about the life and teachings of Jesus embedded in a sacred history of biblical Israel, as such close to a *Roman a thèse*, and if Pharisees entered dictionaries as the prototype of hypocritical, treacherous or inhuman persons, Matthew to a large extent contributed to this effect.[6] Of course, not all of this is the fault of Matthew, but scholarly mimicking of the characterizing of Pharisees by Matthew would amount to falling into a trap. This is all the more so since the Pharisees, in due course, became synonymous with Jews and Judaism in the eyes of Christian commentators on Matthew, and any current reader should be warned against reading the stories about them in the gospel as reliable.[7]

In Matthew, the word Pharisees occurs twenty-nine times, mostly in relation to a group (plural "Pharisees"), or in combination with "Scribes" (ten times),[8] Sadducees (five times)[9] or Chief Priests (twice).[10] They represent one faction of what scholars have labeled "Jewish Leaders," but in this chapter I refrain from lumping them together with Sadducees, scribes, or priests, for reasons that will gradually become clear.[11] The evangelist neither names nor emotionally profiles any individual Pharisee in the Gospel of Matthew. Matthew departs from the relatively neutral renderings in Mark and skips their ambiguous role in Luke.[12] The task of the critical commentator sensitive to text and *Wirkungsgeschichte* is to ask how and why the Pharisees are depicted as they are, and to look for contextual knowledge that helps this character to "resist" (Bal) their presence as caricature in the text. This involves asking historical questions. If reading Matthew is a matter of literary aesthetics, which I think to a certain extent it is, critical commentary should supply counter-readings that help us understand not only how, but why the Pharisees are portrayed as such.[13] This also fits the communicative setting of Matthew, since polemics, irony, and conflict were regular writing techniques in (late) antique biography. Synoptic criticism, as well as reading Matthew in its Jewish, Greco-

---

nuanced, Anderson, *Narrative Web*, 81. The notion of "types" signifies "limited, fixed sets of co-occurring properties, which can be exemplified with additions and variations by numerous individual figures" (Margolin, "Character," 70). Pharisees indeed function as a "type" and are subject to "a degree of flattening." Unlike Peter, for example, Pharisees lack "individuation" (Margolin, "Character," 72), and therewith, emotional depth and recognizability. However, as we will see, neither "flatness" nor "type" preclude rhetorical necessity and ideological proximity.

[6] Ulrich Luz, *Matthäus (18–25)*, Evangelisch-Katholischer Kommentar zum Neuen Testament I/3 (Neukirchen-Vluyn: Vandenhoeck & Ruprecht, 1997), 293, n. 13. Compare the gloomy picture of these evil "antagonists" in Kingsbury, *Story*, 115-27; Anderson, *Narrative Web*, 97–109.

[7] Luz, *Matthäus*, 311–14, 345–51, offers examples from the history of interpretation. Roland Deines, *Die Pharisäer: ihr Verständnis im Spiegel der christlichen und jüdischen Forschung seit Wellhausen und Graetz*, WUNT 101 (Tübingen: Mohr Siebeck, 1997), traces engrained anti-Judaism in nineteenth- and twentieth-century scholarly studies of Pharisees.

[8] Mt. 5:20; 12:38; 15:1; 23:2, 13, 15, 23, 25, 27, 29 (the "woe sayings").

[9] Mt. 3:7; 16:1, 6, 11, 12 (three of which relate to the "yeast of the Sadducees and the Pharisees").

[10] Mt. 21:45; 27:61.

[11] The notion of "Jewish Leaders," introduced by Sjef van Tilborg's redaction critical study in 1972, dominates subsequent scholarly treatments of the Pharisees, e.g., Anderson, *Narrative Web*.

[12] Cf. Lk. 13:31, where Pharisees warn Jesus to escape Herod. In Acts 5:34-40 it is "a Pharisee in the council called Gamaliel [τις ἐν τῷ συνεδρίῳ Φαρισαῖος ὀνόματι Γαμαλιήλ]" who comes to the rescue of the community.

[13] Cf. Bal and van Boheemen, *Narratology*, 114.

Roman and material culture contexts, is of the utmost importance in filling narrative gaps. These tools will accompany us in the following sections.

II. Matthew and the "Historical" Pharisees

Matthew is not the only source where we find critical appraisals of "Pharisees." Stereotyping "Pharisees" as untrustworthy teachers and expounders of the Law or as religious extremists appears, to a certain extent, as a *topos*. But are all of these texts talking about the same social reality?[14] Our main source for the Pharisees as a historical group or movement is Josephus. Josephus describes them in his well-known School passages (*War* 2:119-66; *Ant.* 13:173; 13:297ff.; 18:15) as the most popular of the three "schools of philosophy" (φιλοσοφεῖται καὶ τοῦ μὲν αἱρετισται; *War* 2:119) in the Second Temple era, next to the introverted and ascetic Essenes, and the temple elite, the Sadducees. His depictions of the Pharisees yield a picture of a pre-70 CE "school" of mostly non-priestly Torah teachers who uphold purity laws as much as possible in daily life and believe in angels and in bodily resurrection. They take a middle road between Sadducees and Essenes in the debate on fate and free will. Josephus' schematized picture follows the frame of the three main philosophical schools in the Graeco-Roman world, with the Pythagoreans as the Essenes, Stoics as Pharisees, and Epicureans as Sadducees. It surely does not cover all existing groups or networks.[15] Josephus also mentions a "fourth philosophy" as a faction closely related to the Pharisees, distinct only in their uncompromising yearning for political freedom. Pharisees are praised as most highly accurate interpreters of the Law (οἱ μετὰ ἀκριβείας δοκοῦντες ἐξηγεῖσθαι τὰ νόμιμα; *War* 2:162), who "teach to the people laws of the tradition of the fathers that are not written in the Laws of Moses."[16] Some of these elements recur in the New Testament.[17] Their scribal versatility and reliance on traditions is similar to the view espoused in Mk 7 *et par* and by Paul in Acts 22:3.[18] We should, however, be cautious not to take any occurrence of the term as signifying the same, delineated, group. The name both means "separatists" and "interpreters," in the sense of "specifiers."[19] The term "seekers of smooth things" (דורשי חלקות) in Qumran (4QpNah 3:1-5; 1QH 2:15, 32), according to some scholars, may be a word pun on "teachers of laws" (דורשי ההלכות) and refer to "Pharisees" in a negative sense.[20] The term

---

[14] Cf. Craig S. Keener, *A Commentary on the Gospel of Matthew* (Grand Rapids, MI: Eerdmans, 1999), 538–40.
[15] Steve Mason, *Josephus and the New Testament* (Peabody, MA: Hendrickson, 2003), 68.
[16] νόμιμά τινα παρέδοσαν τῷ δήμῳ οἱ Φαρισαῖοι ἐκ πατέρων διαδοχῆς ἅπερ οὐκ ἀναγέγραπται ἐν τοῖς Μωυσέως νόμοις (*Ant.* 13:297).
[17] Mason, *Josephus*, 145. The Pharisee Gamaliel in Acts 5:34-40 is a "a teacher of the law [νομοδιδάσκαλος] held in honor by all the people."
[18] Cf. Phil. 3:5. Josephus' sympathy for the Essenes may underlie his defense of a pragmatic, if not opportunistic, choice for the Pharisaic ways in his own life (*Life* 10–11); Mason, *Josephus*, 143.
[19] Albert I. Baumgarten, "The Name of the Pharisees," *JBL* 102, no. 3 (1983): 420, 423. Compare Keener, *Matthew*, 538ff.
[20] Baumgarten, "Name of the Pharisees," 421. The pun as referencing Pharisaic halakha is, however, contested among scholars; compare Anthony J. Saldarini, *Pharisees, Scribes, and Sadducees: A Sociological Approach* (Edinburgh: T&T Clark, 1989), 278–80.

"separatists" could also be used as criticism of the Pharisees for not taking their own policies serious enough, while the expression "You know that we have separated [שפרשנו] ourselves from the many" in the halakhic "letter" (4QMMT, C 7-8) has been read as a response to Pharisaic policies.[21]

A similar ambiguity occurs in Rabbinic traditions that mention Pharisees with a topical form of vitriolic criticism: "A foolish man of piety, and a conniving wicked person, and an abstinent woman; the blow of the Pharisees [מכת פרושים], these wear out the world" (m. *Soṭah* 3:4, ms. Kaufmann).[22] The attribution of this tradition to the first-century CE Rabbi Yoshua makes sense, but the issue remains whether Joshua referred to actual "Pharisees" or to religious extremists. In a *baraita*, he issues a measure against extreme abstinence from wine, sex, and food among those refraining themselves from these commodities after the fall of the temple, when "*pherushin* multiplied in Israel" (t. *Soṭah* 15:11: רבו פרושין בישראל). The word used here refers to ascetics refraining from procreative activities and thus, according to R. Joshua, endangering the fate of the Jewish community.[23] Clearly, this is not the social group known for their expertise in scriptural interpretation.[24] The word itself became ambivalent and Rabbis initially avoided any association with "separatists" to identify themselves.[25] Nonetheless, "Pharisees" existed and some of them connect with the emerging Rabbis after 70 CE. The Rabbinic movement reaches back to some teachers, not all, who were labeled as Pharisees in non-Rabbinic sources (m. *Avot* 1:4-14, m. *Hagiga* 2:2).[26] Josephus mentions Shimon ben Gamliel (*Life* 191) and Acts 5:34 features the Pharisee Gamaliel, both known from Rabbinic sources.[27] Moreover, in terms of geography, these sages are located in Jerusalem and in a position of power. In Galilee, the region of the narrated conflicts between Jesus and the Pharisees in Matthew's Gospel, only after the fall of the temple do sages appear, such as Rabban Yohanan ben Zakkai, that were associated with

---

[21] Compare the comments in Elisha Qimron and John Strugnell, *Qumran Cave 4*. DJD 10 (Oxford: Oxford University Press, 1994), 99, 111, 114–15, and Roland Deines, "The Pharisees between 'Judaisms' and 'Common Judaism,'" in *Justification and Variegated Nomism*, Vol. 1: *The Complexities of Second Temple Judaism*, ed. D. A. Carson, P. T. O'Brien, and M. A. Seifrid (Tübingen: Mohr Siebeck, 2001), 494.

[22] So also Ms Parma; Ms Cambridge and b. *Soṭah* 22 read plural "blows," referring to overly pious behavior.

[23] t. *Soṭah* 15:10, ms. Vienna presents these same practices as a rule discussed by R. Ishmael, ms. Erfurt to Rabban Shimon ben Gamliel; see for the better reading "Shimon ben Gamliel": Saul Lieberman, *Tosephta Ki-Pheshuta* 8 (New York: JTS, 1995), 771. Lieberman, *Tosephta*, 772, discusses the motifs not to procreate as connected with religious oppression. Baumgarten, "Name of the Pharisees," 412, 417.

[24] Baumgarten, "Name of the Pharisees," 424–6, 427–8.

[25] Cf. Baumgarten, "Name of the Pharisees," 425. The seven types of "Pharisees" in Avot of Rabbi Nathan a, 37/b, 45; p. *Berakhot* 9:7 (14b) and p. *Soṭah* 5:7 (20a), only two of which are positive, reflect this ambiguity as well.

[26] Hayim Lapin, "The Rabbinic Movement," in *The Cambridge Guide to Jewish History, Religion, and Culture*, ed. Judith R. Baskin and Kenneth Seeskin (Cambridge: Cambridge University Press, 2010), 76. A topical hint criticizing a "pharisaic" separation may be present in a famous saying of Hillel: "Do not separate [אל תיפרוש] yourself from the community" (m. *'Abot* 2:5 following ms. Cambridge and codex Munich).

[27] It is possible that he names Hillel's teacher Avtalyon (*Pollio*) and Shammai's teacher Shemaya (*Sameas*) as Pharisees as well (*Ant.* 14:9; 15:3-4). Sameas is, however, the only Pharisee worthy of praise: Mason, *Josephus*, 141.

Pharisees.²⁸ In summary, the maximalist picture that conflates Rabbinic Judaism and Pharisaic Judaism as reflective of practices and views of "common Judaism" has become untenable.²⁹ The minimalist approach, however, which denies any connection between Pharisees and the later Rabbis, negates the influence of the Pharisees as attested by Josephus and limits any knowledge of them due to Josephus' political rhetoric or the late editing of Rabbinic texts, may not be convincing either.³⁰

Matthew, edited in the last decades of the first century CE, mentions both "Pharisees" and the title "Rabbi" (Mt. 23:8) and reflects a transition period of reigning religious authorities. Matthew's depictions of these "Pharisees" reflect a deep conflict and one that still affects the context of his (implied) audience. "Pharisees" appear to be the natural opponents for this community, and in particular regarding scriptural interpretation or legal tradition. In this respect, the approximately 219 disputes attributed to the Houses of Hillel and Shammai form an impressive corpus that is highly relevant for Matthean studies as well.³¹ These disputes have undergone Rabbinic editing in the generation of Rabbi Akiva and his disciples, but they draw on traditions that show striking convergences with unique Matthean terms and legal phraseology.³² The Houses operated in the decades between 40 and 70, and their debates show a highly divided movement which in the last years before the Jewish war was at loggerheads.³³ Comparative study of their legal teachings on the Sabbath, divorce, and purity, as well as theological tenets, shows ideational alignments with Matthean views espoused in the teachings of Jesus, or with halakhic positions lurking behind his debates with Pharisees. If we identify the Houses of Hillel and Shammai as Pharisaic factions, which I think we have good reason to do, a movement emerges that consisted of two branches, as suggested by Josephus.³⁴ These findings contradict the cohesive image we might gain from Matthew, since Pharisaic

---

²⁸ Roland Deines, "Religious Practices and Religious Movements in Galilee: 100 BCE–200 CE," in *Galilee in the Late Second Temple and Mishnaic Periods*, Vol. 1: *Life, Culture, and Society*, ed. David A. Fiensy and James Riley Strange (Minneapolis: Fortress Press, 2014), 93: Yohanan migrated to Arav in Galilee (p. *Shabbat* 16:8, 15d).

²⁹ This issue is connected with Rabbinic authority. The Rabbinic movement as a dominating force from the late first century onwards has yielded to viewing Rabbis as local networks of teachers and disciples only gaining authority after the fourth century CE, during the Christianization of the Roman Empire: Lapin, "Rabbinic Movement," 82. Stuart S. Miller, *Sages and Commoners in Late Antique 'Erez Israel: A Philological Inquiry Into Local Traditions in Talmud Yerushalmi* (Tübingen: Mohr Siebeck, 2006), argues, however, that by the fourth century CE, Rabbis and their disciples constituted local networks effectively reaching out to non-Rabbinic Jews as well.

³⁰ The notion of "revealing hidden things" (Deut. 29:28) in Qumran and Rabbinic sources strengthens connections: Aharon Shemesh and Cana Werman, "Hidden things and their revelation," *Revue de Qumran* (1998): 409–27.

³¹ Jacob Neusner, *The Rabbinic Traditions about the Pharisees before 70*, Part III: *The Houses* (Leiden: Brill, 1973), 303. However, Shmuel Safrai, "Beith Hillel and Beith Shammai," *Encyclopedia Judaica* 4 (1973): 737, mentions a number of more than 350, including parallel versions. Compare my discussion of some relevant House traditions in Eric Ottenheijm, "Matthew and Yavne: Religious Authority in the Making?" in *Jews and Christians in the First and Second Centuries: The Interbellum 70–132 CE*, ed. Joshua J. Schwartz and Peter J. Tomson (Leiden: Brill, 2017).

³² Compare Saldarini, *Pharisees*, 201–3.

³³ m. *Shabbat* 1:4 (ms. Kaufmann 1:7); t. *Shabbat* 1:16; p. *Shabbat* 1:4 (3c); b. *Shabbat* 17a/153b.

³⁴ Joseph. *Ant.* 18:23. Compare the reflection of this diversity in the House debate on a "Pharisee who suffers a flux [venereal disease, auth.]" (זב פרוש); t. *Shabbat* 1:15; p. *Shabbat* 1:5 (3c).

Law was not only flexible, as Josephus suggests, but also pluralistic both in its outlooks and practices.[35] Nonetheless, given the little knowledge we may have of "real" Pharisees, the leading question in reviewing Matthew's storyline will be what role did these "specialists" play in the gospel, and what rhetorical function did they perform? We will now review these issues in topically arranged sections.

III. Pharisees in the Opening of the Gospel (Mt. 2–3)

Herod's policies to crush any possible rivalry of a newborn child as "king of the Jews" involves the "Chief priests and the Scribes" (Mt. 2:4), but no Pharisees. This simple observation is useful, as Matthew also refrains from associating them with the political powers ultimately responsible for the trial of Jesus (high priests, Romans), and this absence resists a reading of the Pharisees as *the* archenemies of Jesus from the outset. That conflict lies elsewhere, and Matthew, who hints at their enmity towards Jesus at several places (Mt. 12:14; 21:45-6; 22:15), does not associate Pharisees with the arrest and trial of Jesus. Matthew reveals his religio-political agenda in his editorial chiseling of Q 3:7-8, the first time that Pharisees appear, together with the Sadducees, as attending the preaching of John the Baptist. In Luke, John aims his call for repentance at the "outgoing masses" (τοις ἐκπορευομένοις ὄχλοις,; Lk. 3:7—compare v. 10) who flock to see him.[36] Matthew, however, lumps "Pharisees and Sadducees" together as the object of the upcoming divine verdict:

But when he saw many Pharisees and Sadducees coming for baptism, he said to them, You brood of vipers! Who warned you to flee from the wrath to come? Bear fruit worthy of repentance. (Mt. 3:7-8).	Ἰδὼν δὲ πολλοὺς τῶν Φαρισαίων καὶ Σαδδουκαίων ἐρχομένους ἐπὶ τὸ βάπτισμα αὐτοῦ εἶπεν αὐτοῖς· γεννήματα ἐχιδνῶν, τίς ὑπέδειξεν ὑμῖν φυγεῖν ἀπὸ τῆς μελλούσης ὀργῆς; ποιήσατε οὖν καρπὸν ἄξιον τῆς μετανοίας.

In Matthew the "Pharisees and Sadducees" will not be able to escape the upcoming verdict. This is a telling move. Obviously, the rhetorical function is to carry the basic value that is unique in Matthew's rendering of John's preaching: repentance. However, they do so in a purely negative way, as representing those groups apparently not bringing forth, in Matthew's parabolic saying, "fruits worthy of repentance" (Mt. 3:8).[37] It simultaneously opposes the masses (ὄχλοι), Matthew's prime audience of Jesus' teaching and a character pending in its attitude towards Jesus until the Passion

---

[35] The theorem of "Yavne" as a consolidation of Rabbinic hegemony after 70 CE—known in Matthean studies through William D. Davies, *The Setting of the Sermon on the Mount* (Cambridge: Cambridge University Press, 1966)—has yielded to a layered and chronologically protracted view of Rabbinic authority: see essays in Joshua J. Schwartz and Peter J. Tomson (eds.), *Jews and Christians in the First and Second Centuries: The Interbellum 70-132 CE* (Leiden: Brill, 2017).

[36] Q 3:7a follows Lk. 3:7: James M. Robinson, Paul Hoffmann, and John S. Kloppenborg, *The Critical Edition of Q* (Minneapolis: Augsburg Fortress Publishers, 2000), 8.

[37] Anderson, *Narrative Web*, 107.

narrative.[38] The narrative, however, has not informed the reader as to why these "Pharisees and Sadducees" do not yet show repentance, and here we encounter one of Matthew's narrative gaps which offers a glimpse into the social setting of this gospel. There may be a rhetorical anti-establishment ring to Matthew: John, the synoptic precursor of Jesus, engages with the Jerusalem elite (represented here as "Pharisees and Sadducees") in similar terms to those of Jesus later.[39] According to Josephus, John enjoyed a reputation as a "good man," and the Jews denounced his execution by Herod. John preached "justice [δικαιοσύνη] towards their fellows and piety [εὐσέβειᾰ] towards God."[40] He criticized the Pharisees' (and Sadducees') misguided trust in their Abrahamic lineage: "Do not presume to say to yourselves, We have Abraham as our ancestor; for I tell you, God is able from these stones to raise up children to Abraham" (Mt. 3:9). In the oral stage of the Q tradition, this saying may have contained a Hebrew word pun on אבן ("stone") and בן ("son").[41] The rhetoric of "sons" in Matthew denotes a binary worldview in which disciples of Jesus are opposed to the disciples of the Pharisees, as Greek "sons" will recur in "sons of the Kingdom" (υἱοὶ τῆς βασιλείας; Mt. 13:38) as opposed to the "son(s) of hell" produced by the Pharisees (υἱὸν γεέννης; Mt. 23:15).[42] Opposing John's preaching of the Kingdom with Pharisees (and Sadducees) is, in terms of narrative, an effective way of presenting the Pharisees as compromised from the start. Here, concomitantly, the grounds are prepared for a clash between Jesus and these religious authorities in Galilee and later in Jerusalem.

Again, however, the Passion narrative shows a fissure: Matthew suggests Pharisaic enmity in his staging of the final conflict with the temple authorities (Mt. 21:34), but, and this is remarkable, the "bad Pharisees" leave the stage when Matthew narrates the arrest and execution of Jesus. Now it is the "Scribes and high priests," representing the temple elite, who act. Pharisees enter again only after Jesus' execution (Mt. 27:62), but they are omitted again in Mt. 28:11.[43] It is in the use of the word "Impostor" (πλάνος; Mt. 27:63), where Matthew's Pharisees reference the resurrection as an act of treachery, that the implicit author reveals himself again in addressing a lingering rumor in the environment of his readers.[44] In sum, the author denounces Pharisees in the

---

[38] Robert. C. J. Cousland, *The Crowds in the Gospel of Matthew* (Leiden: Brill, 2002). The notion of bringing forth fruits as a defining social quality will recur in Matthew's addition to the parable of the bad tenants in Mt. 21:34: "Therefore I tell you, the kingdom of God will be taken away from you and given to a people producing its fruits" (ἔθνει ποιοῦντι τοὺς καρποὺς αὐτῆς).

[39] Mason, *Josephus*, 155.

[40] Joseph. *Ant.* 18.116-19; Mason, *Josephus*, 152–3. "Righteousness" (δικαιοσύνη) is a key word in Matthew.

[41] Keener, *Matthew*, 125. Azan Yadin-Israel, "Late Ancient Jewish Languages," in *A Companion to Late Ancient Jews and Judaism: 3rd Century BCE-7th Century CE*, ed. Gwynn Kessler and Naomi Koltun-Fromm (Hoboken NJ: Wiley Blackwell, 2020), 63–6, points to the "language ideology" behind the multilinguistic practices and the—limited—use of Hebrew.

[42] Craig A. Evans, *Matthew*, NCBC (New York: Cambridge University Press, 2012), 72, mentions, e.g., Josephus, *War* 5:272; Targum Onqelos Gen. 49:24 and Targum Onqelos Ps. 118:22 (!). A related wordplay ("sons"/ "builders," בונים\\בנים) occurs in Rabbinic midrash (b. *Ber.* 64a, on Isa. 54:13) to address the disciples of the Rabbis as (re)builders of Jerusalem.

[43] The combination of Pharisees with the Chief Priests is clumsy and, tellingly, the Pharisees are absent when the "chief priests and elders" devise a plan to spread false rumors: Mt. 28:11-15.

[44] Anderson, *Narrative Web*, 119. For Matthew's community located in Galilee or Syria, see discussion in David C. Sim, "Reconstructing the social and religious milieu of Matthew: methods, sources, and possible results," in *Matthew, James, and Didache: Three Related Documents in their Jewish and Christian Settings*, ed. Huub Van de Sandt (Atlanta: Society of Biblical Literature, 2008), 19–25.

environment of his readership' community by featuring them in clashes between John and Jesus with a Jerusalem-based religious elite, even if Pharisees, ultimately, have little to do with the arrest and execution of Jesus. Their appearance in these clashes reflects the contemporary situation of the author.

IV. Debating the Law (Mt. 5-7; 12:1-12;15:1-14; 22:34-46)

The role of Pharisees in Matthew's interpretation of Mosaic Law is ambiguous, as they share basic values, such as the love commandment (Mt. 22:34-40), but also function as legal antagonists. The Sermon of the Mount, where Jesus teaches his interpretation of Moses, mentions Pharisees only in Mt. 5:20: "For I tell you, unless your righteousness exceeds that of the Scribes and Pharisees, you will never enter the Kingdom of Heaven."[45] This saying is remarkable as it requires the disciples and readers not to oppose or to dismiss their teachings, but rather to exceed their levels of conduct. The stress on righteous behavior as being more important than obedience to teachings recurs in the imagery of "fruit," especially "good fruit" (καρπὸν καλὸν; Mt. 3:10; 7:15-20, esp. 16; and the "fruits of the Kingdom"; τοὺς καρποὺς αὐτῆ; Mt. 21:43). The parable of the building of the house stresses performing above acclaiming authority (Mt. 7:21-7).[46] Their teachings are attractive, nonetheless, and Jesus warns against the teachings of the Pharisees: "Watch out, and beware of the yeast of the Pharisees and Sadducees" (Mt. 16:6).[47]

The Pharisees clearly represent a power, either real or imagined, of religious knowledge and social ethos. This is notable in Matthew's editorial interventions in scenes where Pharisees approach the disciples or Jesus to question a mode of behavior or ask about a detail of the law. Matthew emphasizes the Pharisees as "looking" at actions or "hearing" a teaching, which suggests spatial nearness and watchfulness: "When the Pharisees *saw* this, they said to his disciples, Why is your master dining with sinners and tax collectors" (Mt. 9:11); "When the Pharisees *saw* it, they said to him, Look, your disciples are doing what is not lawful to do on the sabbath" (Mt. 12:2); "Then Pharisees and scribes came to Jesus from Jerusalem and said, Why do your disciples break the tradition of the elders? For they do not wash their hands before they eat" (Mt. 15:1-2). Moreover, and in a typically Matthean doubling of interlocution, the disciples approach Jesus to explain to them what he meant to say, motivated by their awe of the Pharisees: "Then the disciples approached and said to him, Do you know that the

---

[45] Mt. 6:5 mentions "hypocrites" and Mt. 7:29 refers to "their scribes," but it is unclear to whom this refers.

[46] Eric Ottenheijm, "Learning and Practising: Uses of an Early Jewish Discourse in Matthew (7:24-27) and Rabbinic Literature," in *Interaction between Judaism and Christianity in History, Religion, Art and Literature*, Jewish Christian Perspectives 17, ed. Marcel Poorthuis, Alberdina Houtman, Yossi Gal, and Joshua Schwartz (Leiden: Brill, 2009), 45–64.

[47] The editor makes a great effort to explain what is meant by this metaphor: "Then they understood that he had not told them to beware of the yeast of bread, but of the teaching of the Pharisees and Sadducees" (Mt. 16:12).

Pharisees took offense when they *heard* what you said?" (Mt. 15:12).[48] The atmosphere is tense, and one of social and spatial nearness and watchfulness. Matthew's editing of the legal debates between Jesus and Pharisees (and their scribes) continues in this atmosphere of hostility, and has led early scholars on Matthew's narratology to interpet these disputes as a religious rift.[49] In the debate on rinsing hands, Jesus indeed rejects the Pharisees' position and reproaches them that they, "for the sake of your tradition" (διὰ τὴν παράδοσιν ὑμῶν; Mt. 15:3, 6—compare Mk 7:13) "make void the Word of God" (Mt. 15:6), However, despite this reproach, Mt. 23:2-3 emphasizes Pharisaic authority and gives the impression that Matthew is primarily waging a war against an all too close, religiously competing foe.[50] Indeed, Matthew's legal terminology and concepts reflect awareness of proto-Rabbinic halakha that may be close to the Pharisaic stance.[51] Moreover, these disputes reflect the urgency of these matters for the Matthean community. This is manifest in biblical quotes and in legal principles or legal logic which, as scholars assume, suggest a scribal elite at work in the community of Matthew.[52] Jesus' sole authority in interpreting Moses (Mt. 12:8) does not negate the need of biblical legitimation, as in Matthew's quote of Hos. 6:6, added to the saying "those who are well have no need of a physician, but those who are sick" (Mt. 9:12), concluding the debate on dining with "tax collectors and sinners" (Mt. 9:9-13).[53] Hosea 6:6 is quoted again in the midst of two Sabbath disputes (Mt. 12:7).[54] Furthermore, Matthew shows legal versatility in his use of the legal comparison in raising a sheep fallen into the pit (Mt. 12:11-12) as well as in his legitimation of healing as an example of "doing good" (Mt. 12:13). In the purity debate, the question of Peter and the subsequent explanation (Mt. 15:15-20) of Jesus' "saying" (παραβολὴν; Mt. 15:15) reflect communal interests. Moreover, tackling issues in the form of controversy is, in itself, a genre and not by definition conflict-ridden. This rhetoric may even inform our reading of the repeatedly used πειράζω ("tempting" or "testing"—compare Mt. 22:35), commonly understood as expressing a hostile bias.[55] It also denotes probing another teacher's knowledge and

---

[48] The doubling of a dialogue, where a teacher adds explanation in the private company of his disciples recurs in Matthew (e.g. Mt. 13:10-15; 19:1-12), and is a mode of teaching in Rabbinic sources as well: David Daube, "Public Pronouncement and Private Explanation in the Gospels," *ExpTim* 57, no. 7 (1946): 175–7.

[49] Kingsbury, *Story*, 62–8; Anderson, *Narrative Web*; 123–6.

[50] Compare the implicit acceptance of Pharisaic regulations on tithing mint, dill, and cumin in Mt. 23:23b, where the polemic aims at Pharisees neglecting the "weighty things." As already noted in Kingsbury, *Story*, 67.

[51] This was aptly noted by Davies, *Setting*, 93–108; cf. John Kampen, *Matthew within Sectarian Judaism* (New Haven: Yale University Press, 2019), 92–111.

[52] Luz, *Matthäus (1–7)*, 60–1.

[53] Mark mentions "Scribes of the Pharisees," while Luke refers to "Pharisees and Scribes." Eric Ottenheijm, "The Shared Meal—a Therapeutical Device: The Function and Meaning of Hos. 6:6 in Matt 9:10-13," *NovT* 53, no. 1 (2011): 16, argues that "within the threefold structure of the answer which Jesus provides, Hos. 6:6 offers scriptural legitimation for his behaviour and indicates a legally scholastic discourse." Jesus embodies the principle to be emulated by his disciples in eating together with "publicans and sinners." These findings refute the observation of Anderson, *Narrative Web*, 109, that the repetition points to the Pharisees not having learnt its proper meaning.

[54] Lutz Doering, "Sabbath Laws in the New Testament Gospels," in *The New Testament and Rabbinic Literature*, ed. Reimund Bieringer, Florentino García Martínez, Didier Pollefeyt, and Peter. J. Tomson (Leiden: Brill, 2009), 223, argues that Hos. 6:6 not only points at Christological fulfilment but also at the principle of mercy.

ideological stance in scholarly exchanges. In Matthew, "testing" always implies assessing a deep knowledge of biblical interpretation and legal logic, and even if it bears a negative connotation, it retains this rhetoric of scriptural knowledge.[56]

V. Matthean Disputes on Law and Ethics

It is not only a matter of form. Legal proximity to Pharisaic Law is apparent in the debate on divorce: "Some Pharisees came to him, and to test him they asked, 'Is it lawful for a man to divorce his wife *for any cause?*'" (Mt. 19:3). The clause "for any cause" (κατὰ πᾶσαν αἰτίαν) reiterates the Hillelite position on divorce (m. *Gittin* 9:10), and Matthew's unique allowance for divorce in the case of adultery (Mt. 19:9) may even reflect or resemble the Shammaite stance.[57] As to the Sabbath, Matthew defends plucking ears of grain or healing on the Sabbath as authorized by the Messianic presence of Jesus (Mt. 12:8). However, given the fact that Matthew's audience kept the Sabbath (Mt. 24:20) nonetheless, the legal logic that "it is allowed to do good on the Sabbath" (ἔξεστιν τοῖς σάββασιν καλῶς ποιεῖν; Mt. 12:12) deviates from this Christological presence. Matthew prioritizes "doing good," a category of ethical and pious acts in early Jewish halakha, and a regulatory principle of the Hillelites in Sabbath debates. Matthew sees this principle as embodied in the acts of Jesus, but teaches it as a general principle nevertheless.[58] Finally, when Jesus emphasizes the moral dimensions of purity and objects to the Pharisaic practice of rinsing hands, Matthew is positively interested in purity, especially where he criticizes the Pharisaic innovation of washing the hands before dinner.[59]

Tannaitic Rabbinic traditions shed light on elliptic teachings of Jesus in the Sermon on the Mount, suggesting a proto-Rabbinic discourse partly echoed in Matthew. Quoting the biblical prohibition of murder (Exod. 21:12—compare Gen. 9:6), Jesus teaches that it includes verbal insults as well (Mt. 5:21-2). The morality of ire or verbal insults as equal to manslaughter is a *topos* in late antiquity that recurs in Christian sources (1 Jn 3:15). However, its exegetical underpinnings and therewith its relation to

---

[55] Anderson, *Narrative Web*, 116–18.
[56] The verb is used for the devil "tempting" Jesus (Mt. 4:3), but here Jesus quotes scripture to neutralize the attempts! Compare also the explicitly negative term for "testing" (παγιδεύσωσιν) in Mt. 22:15.
[57] Peter J. Tomson, "Divorce Halakhah in Paul and the Jesus Tradition," in *The New Testament and Rabbinic Literature*, ed. Reimund Bieringer, Florentino García Martínez, Didier Pollefeyt, and Peter. J. Tomson (Leiden: Brill, 2009), 324. It should be noted, moreover, that this issue troubles the disciples of Jesus (Mt. 19:10-12).
[58] Such is the case in the house dispute on performing certain acts on the Sabbath: t. *Shabbat* 16 (17):22 (ed. Lieberman, 79-80); b. *Shabbat* 12a. These "acts of charity" (גמילות חסדים), on the border of legally structured Mosaic commandments and social ethics, are associated with Hos. 6:6: Davies, *Setting*, 307. On this ethical-legal concept and its rhetoric in Mt. 12:12, as proposed in Eric Ottenheijm, "Genezen als goed doen. Halachische logica in Matt 12, 9-14," *Bijdragen* 63, no. 3 (2002): 356ff., see the debate in Doering, "Sabbath Laws," 222-3, 235-6.
[59] Cf. Friedrich Avemarie, "Jesus and Purity," in *The New Testament and Rabbinic Literature*, ed. Reimund Bieringer, Florentino García Martínez, Didier Pollefeyt, and Peter. J. Tomson (Leiden: Brill, 2009), 272, n. 77.

Exod. 21:12, quoted in Matthew, remain elusive.[60] A Rabbinic midrash on a related verse (Deut. 19:11) shows a chain of emotions leading up to murder and reveals a manner of reading close to the one in Matthew. The midrash comments on the biblical cities of refuge, addressing a verse that exempts someone who intentionally killed his fellow man from the right of refuge:

> "And if a man hates his neighbour, and lies in wait for him, and rises up against him (and strikes him a fatal blow)" (Deut. 19:11). From here they taught: If a man transgressed a light commandment, in the end he will transgress a grave one. If he transgressed "You shall love your neighbor as yourself" (Lev. 19:18) he is poised to transgress "You shall not hate" (Lev. 19:17). "You shall not take revenge" (Lev. 19:18), "You shall not bear a grudge" (Lev. 19:18) and, in the end, "and your brother shall live with you" (Lev. 25:36); until he arrives at bloodshed.[61]

Whereas Jesus simply equates slander, a verbal expression of anger or jealousy or dismay, with murder (compare also *Did.* 3:2), the midrash explicates how murder is the end result of transgressing the love commandment.[62] Moreover, a shared legal logic recurs here as well, in a distinction of "light and heavy" commandments, echoing the "great" and "least" commandments in Mt. 5:19 and Mt. 22:36.38, pointing to a legal logic that extends the law beyond its literal meaning to include additional dimensions of human agency, such as thought or modesty.[63] Both traditions assess biblical law as not limited to juridical dimensions but including human emotions and intentions.

VI. Authority and Accusations

Such proximities notwithstanding, Matthew's debates are never accompanied by any appraisal of the Pharisees' views. On the contrary, Matthew' editorial interventions create an atmosphere of growing conflict. Matthew exacerbates legal exchanges in his editing of the Sabbath debate and the purity debate, where he adds enmity towards Jesus on the part of the Pharisees: "But the Pharisees went out and conspired against him, how to destroy him" (Mt. 12:14).[64] Debates and teachings are tools to establish law,

---

[60] For Graeco-Roman and Jewish sources on anger, see Keener, *Matthew*, 183, n. 69.

[61] Sifre Deut. 176–7 on Deut. 19:11 (ed. Finkelstein, 226) Parr. in Avot of Rabbi Natan a, 26; t. *Soṭah* 5:11 (ed. Lieberman, 302); m. *Makkot* 2:6; b. *Makkot* 10b; Sifre Numbers 160 (ed. Horowitz, 220; and shorter version in Derekh Eretz Rabbah XI:15 (ed. Higger, 312/3).

[62] Note the proximity of the love commandment and "evading hatred" in Mt. 5:44 and *Did.* 2:7-3:1-2; Huub Van de Sandt and David Flusser, *The Didache: Its Jewish Sources and Its Place in Early Judaism and Christianity* (Minneapolis: Fortress Press, 2002), 227.

[63] Van de Sandt and Flusser, *Didache*, 231. Christine Hayes, "Were the Noachide Commandments Formulated at Yavne? Tosefta Avoda Zara 8:4-9 in Cultural and Historical Context," in *Jews and Christians in the First and Second Centuries: The Interbellum 70–132 CE*, ed. Joshua J. Schwartz and Peter J. Tomson (Leiden: Brill, 2017), 243–56, points, however, to a different rhetorical use. "Christian" sources distinguish between ethical and cultic; tannaitic sources distinguish quantitatively within one class of commandments. Exceptions occur (253–5), however, and, as I would argue, Mt. 23 does not negate the cultic practices criticized here, but is expressive of Pharisaic public visibility.

[64] Anderson, *Narrative Web*, 114, notices that this plotting is commented upon in a lengthy condemnation by Jesus (Mt. 12:25-37).

but here they are also establishing communal borders by delegitimizing other authorities. In this sense, Matthew's rhetoric of the unique authority of Jesus reflects or extends "sectarian" politics of the Second Temple Period.[65] Jesus as the Messianic Teacher of the Law requires others to either join ranks or remain relegated to the outside. Matthew's version of the love commandment is another instance where he finds ground to strengthen the sole authority of Jesus. The debate starts after the Sadducees have been rebuked for their refusal to believe in the resurrection of the dead. Now the Pharisees huddle together (Mt. 22:34) and "one of them, a lawyer, asked him a question to test him" (Mt. 22:35).[66] In the end, both parties agree in principle, but whereas Mark's scribe is assured to be close to the Kingdom of Heaven (Mk 12:34), Matthew describes (Mt. 22:40) "all the Law and the prophets" as "hanging" (κρέμαται) on these two commandments, and omits the positive reply of Jesus.[67] There is no mention of rapprochement, merely another instance of Jesus' scriptural versatility.[68]

This uniqueness also appears in Matthew's editing of the debate on David and the Messiah, right after the great love commandment. Jesus questions the Pharisees about what they think of the Messiah, "whose son is he?" (Mt. 22:42). As a reply to their answer, "David's son," Jesus asks them what they think of Ps. 110:1: "The Lord said to my Lord: sit at my right hand, until I put your enemies under my feet." The Psalm as quoted here suggests a person next to but also superseding David. This divine Messiah-king is, according to early Christian tradition, represented in Jesus, and the Psalm is a *topos* in early Christian sources (e.g., 1 Cor. 15:25; Heb. 1:13; 10:12-13; Acts 2:34-5).[69] However, none of these sources, neither Mark nor Luke, present it as a matter of dispute with the Pharisees. Matthew, deviating from Mark and Luke, emphasizes Pharisaic presence here to articulate their non-acceptance of Jesus' Messianic authority while being so close on the issue of the great commandment. He even adds their inability to raise objections: "no one was able to give him an answer, nor from that day did anyone dare to ask him any more questions" (Mt. 22:46). Messianic anxieties surrounded Ps. 110 in Qumran, and Matthew may have addressed these as well, but he evokes a clear answer from the implied reader that contrasts with the Pharisees' silence.[70] The reader has to choose a side.

---

[65] Cf. Kampen, *Matthew*, 47-59. Anders Runesson, "Rethinking Early Jewish–Christian Relations: Matthean Community History as Pharisaic Intragroup Conflict," *JBL* 127, no. 1 (2008): 95–132, argues for protracted sectarian policies after 70 CE, in which Matthew took part.

[66] Lk. 15:25 uses the same verb in the scribe's question about the meaning of "Love your neighbor" in Lev. 19:18, as prelude to the parable of the Good Samaritan.

[67] The rhetorical function of and proximity of κρέμαται in Mt. 22:40 to Rabbinic תלוי is argued in Terence L. Donaldson, "The law that hangs (Matthew 22:40): rabbinic formulation and Matthean social world," *CBQ* 57, no. 4 (1995): 689–709.

[68] On the "basic hermeneutical pattern" of the double love commandment in Mt. 22:34-40, see Serge Ruzer, *Mapping the New Testament: Early Christian Writings as a Witness for Jewish Biblical Exegesis* (Leiden: Brill, 2007), 71–99.

[69] Martin Hengel, "'Setze dich zu meiner Rechten!' Die Inthronisation Christi zur Rechten Gottes uns Psalm 110,1," in *Studien zur Christologie* (Tübingen: Mohr Siebeck, 2006), 281–367.

[70] Keener, *Matthew*, 532-4, points to Rabbinic tradition, but Messianic motifs occur as well in Qumranic readings of Ps. 110:4 (Q246 and 11Q *Melchizedek*). Anderson, *Narrative Web*, 64, points to Matthew's use of the historical present alternating with the past tense to make the dispute an appeal to the implied reader.

The Pharisees' inability or unwillingness to assess the proper identity of Jesus is also present in their request for signs: "The Pharisees and Sadducees came, and to test Jesus, they asked him to show them a sign from heaven" (Mt. 16:1). This is one of the many instances where Pharisees and Jesus clash over authority, an issue which must have bothered the readers as well: who was this teacher? Clearly, the rebuttal of this request is also an implicit teaching for the community itself (Mt. 24:5, 23-4!, 29-30), and the Pharisees act as a punching bag in this respect.[71]

VII. Parables about the Pharisees

As Anderson aptly notes, "If the Jewish Leaders told as many powerful parables as Jesus does in Matthew, the (Implied) Reader would view them differently. Indeed, the reader would be reading a different text."[72] The fact is that in all Synoptic Gospels, it is only Jesus who tells parables.[73] We assume, nonetheless, that the genre must have existed and that some teachers within the Pharisaic movement made use of these tales as well. Indeed, no one is surprised to hear parables, and disciples question details of their application or why Jesus teaches parables to the general public (Mt. 13:10). They appear by the hundreds in Rabbinic sources and may have been used by Jewish teachers as well, as a regional genre and especially in Galilee.[74] The standardized form of the Matthean parables, such as openings (ὡμοιώθη; ὁμοία, ὅμοιός, e.g. Mt. 13:24, 31, 52), "transfer signals" of application (οὕτως, e.g. Mt. 13:40, 49; γάρ, connecting a parable to a saying, e.g. Mt. 22:14), as well as scriptural embeddedness reflect proximity to the Rabbinic *mashal*.[75] The social rhetoric is not so dissimilar as well, even if the applications differ: the Jesus parables address the Kingdom of Heaven, authority, or pending crisis.[76] Remarkably, Pharisees are also among the addressees. The failing authority of the

---

[71] This rhetoric may likewise apply to the Pharisees explaining exorcisms performed by Jesus as expressive of his demonic power, a polemic to deride any competitive teacher: "But the Pharisees said, 'By the ruler of the demons he casts out the demons'" (Mt. 9:34; cf. Mt. 12:14).

[72] Anderson, *Narrative Web*, 62.

[73] One exception might be the legal analogy offered by the Sadducees in Mt. 22:24-8. Note that the genre term παραβολή can also denote a "saying."

[74] Eric Ottenheijm and Marcel Poorthuis (eds.), *Parables in Changing Contexts: Essays on the Study of Parables in Christianity, Judaism, Islam, and Buddhism*, JCP 35 (Leiden: Brill, 2020), 4. The transitional figure Rabban Yohanan ben Zakkai, who witnessed the Jewish War (66-70 CE) and whose disciples are the first carrying the title "Rabbi," is known to have taught parables: Jacob Neusner, *A Life of Rabban Yohanan Ben Zakkai: Ca. 1-80 CE* (Leiden: Brill, 1970), 122-3.

[75] Proximity in form of Jesus' parables to Rabbinic parables was noted first by Paul Fiebig, *Altjüdische gleichnisse und die Gleichnisse Jesu* (Tübingen: JCB Mohr/Paul Siebeck, 1904), 13. Compare Rudolph Bultmann, *Die Geschichte der synoptischen tradition. Mit einem Nachwort von Gert Theissen*. 10e Auflage (Göttingen: Vandenhoeck & Ruprecht, 1995), 194-5. As Peter Tomson says of the synoptics, "Matthew shows most of a stereotyped formulary similar to the rabbinic one": Peter J. Tomson, "Fables, Proverbs, Parables, Allegories: Ancient Border-Crossing Lore," in *Overcoming Dichotomies: Parables, Fables, and Similes in the Graeco-Roman World*, WUNT 483, ed. Albertina Oegema, Jonathan Pater, and Martijn Stoutjesdijk (Tübingen: Mohr Siebeck, 2022), 154, n. 111.

[76] On social location, see Christian Münch, "Parabeln im Matthäusevangelium. Einleitung," in *Kompendium der Gleichnisse Jesu*, ed. Ruben Zimmermann and Detlev Dormeyer (Gütersloh: Gütersloher Verlagshaus, 2007), 385-9; Ottenheijm and Poorthuis, *Parables*, 21-2.

Pharisees in legal matters is addressed in a double parable: "Every plant that my heavenly Father has not planted will be uprooted. Let them alone, they are blind guides of the blind. And if one blind person guides another, both will fall into a pit" (Mt. 15:13-14). The irony of this addition in a legal context is clear, as falling into a pit was a legal rhetorical motif in the Sabbath controversy (Mt. 12:11).[77] The ability of Jesus, over against that of his Pharisaic opponents, to explain the Law is at stake in these editorial additions, reducing the prospects of agreement or harmonization. The issue here is—again —less a historical conflict but rather a clash of communal authorities, as some scholars have noted by the repeated Matthean expression "their synagogues."[78]

This clash aims at winning the hearts of the masses. At the end of the Sermon on the Mount, following the parable of the house built on the rock, the narrator adds a summative response of the masses: "the crowds [οἱ ὄχλοι] were astounded at his teaching, for he taught them as one having authority, not as their scribes" (Mt. 7:28-9). This positive response, however, will not tilt the fate of the masses to acclaim Jesus as the Messiah in the very end, and this failure has to be accounted for as well. Pharisees come into view again in this respect in Matthew's editing of the parable of the bad tenants (Mt. 21:33-46). In Matthew, it is the third and final one discussing Jesus' authority as a response to the "chief priests and elders" questioning "by what authority are you doing these things, and who gave you this authority" (Mt. 21:23). The section concludes somewhat astonishingly, "When the chief priests and the Pharisees heard his parables, they realized that he was speaking about them" (Mt. 21:45). Matthew's editorial hand is visible in changing the parties here, but especially in the added saying that "Therefore I tell you, the Kingdom of Heaven will be taken from you and given to a people that produces its fruits" (Mt. 21:34). The key issue is not so much Matthew's alleged substitution theology but rather the fate of the temple and its leading authorities ("chief priests and elders").[79] Grouping the Pharisees with these "chief priests" (v. 45) is also surprising from a historical perspective, as Pharisees had no political alliance with the chief priests in the decades before the Jewish War. Their juxtaposition with chief priests should rather be understood as a comment on the two crises Matthew's community has to face: Jesus being rejected by the "the people as a whole" (πᾶς ὁ λαὸς;

---

[77] Peter asks Jesus to "explain the parable to us" (φράσον ἡμῖν τὴν παραβολὴν); Mt 15:15. Notably, Lk. 6:39 offers only the latter saying, to illustrate that "a disciple is not above the teacher" (Luke 6:40)!

[78] Mt. 4:23; 9:35; 10:17; 12:9; 13:54; and 23:34. Anderson, *Narrative Web*, 57-9, marks it as inscribing an us-versus-them mentality. Graham Stanton, *A Gospel for a New People: Studies in Matthew* (Louisville, KY: Westminster John Knox Press, 1993), 97, 124, points to the opposition of synagogue to *ekklesia* (Mt. 17:18; 18:16). The suggestion of Deines, "Movements," 89, that "their" may refer to any synagogue presupposes a rift in the community ("extra muros") from its Jewish context and reiterates the old scholarly opinion. However, David C. Sim, *The Gospel of Matthew and Christian Judaism: The History and Social Setting of the Matthean Community* (Edinburgh: T&T, 1998), following the lead of Saldarini, *Pharisees*, 157-73, and John Andrew Overman, *Matthew's Gospel and formative Judaism: The Social World of the Matthean Community* (Minneapolis: Fortress Press, 1990), assesses it as social competition *within* a religious field. Moreover, ἐκκλησία is a rendering of the Hebrew קהל and used for local Jewish assemblies, but could, as such, denote synagogues as well: Anders Runesson, Donald Binder, and Birger Olsson, *The Ancient Synagogue from its Origins to 200 CE: A Source Book* (Leiden: Brill, 2007), 10, n. 21 and 252-3 (Jas 2:2-4), 260.

[79] Anderson, *Narrative Web*, 108. Note that the response of the people differs from that of the "chief priests and Pharisees": they "regarded him as a prophet" (Mt. 21:46).

Mt. 27:25) and the fall of the temple.[80] Combining these events is the role the Pharisees or their Rabbinic successors seek in Galilee, before and after 70 CE.[81] Their position and Matthew's response to it come to the fore, veiled in polemics, in Matthew's "woe sayings."

VIII. Polemic against "Scribes and Pharisees" in Mt. 23

Jesus' speech in Mt. 23 offers Matthew's most vitriolic response to the "Scribes and Pharisees." It is based on Mk 12:37-40 and sparse material derived from Q, with some unique Matthean additions that call for our attention here.[82] The speech is structured in three parts.[83] Verses 1-12 address the members of the Matthean community as the intended audience and describe practices of the "Scribes and Pharisees" (where Mark only addresses the scribes) as a proof of the initial reproach that they do not practice what they teach. The second part, verses 13-36, addresses the same "Scribes and Pharisees," but now in a second-person singular speech: "Woe to you"! Traditions deriving from Mark and Q and aimed at the "Scribes and Pharisees" are reconfigured in a speech setting, bridging the Jerusalem-based discourses against "chief priests and Pharisees" with the "Olivet" speech (Mt. 24-5).[84] Finally, verses 37-9 depict the fate of Jerusalem and the disastrous consequences of its misbehavior. However, even though Jesus teaches on the Temple Mount (Mt. 21:23), and the polemic of Chapter 23 addresses the Jerusalem elite, it does not only feature a Jerusalem context. Its rhetoric is also aimed at a rival elite operative in synagogues (Mt. 23:6, 34), and while issues related to the temple are invoked (Mt. 23:16-22, 35) or Jerusalem is lamented (Mt. 23:29, 37), the elite discredited here is Galilean.[85] Matthew polemicizes on two levels and the discourse addresses a pre- and post-70 CE environment.[86] This double agenda becomes visible in additions to Mark and Q that mirror the social reality of his community.[87] The relevant passage runs as follows:

---

[80] On the intertextuality with Isa. 5 and readings that refer to the temple, see Wim J. C. Weren, "The Use of Isaiah 5, 1-7 in the parable of the tenants (Mark 12, 1-12; Matthew 21, 33-46)," *Biblica* (1998): 1–26. Matthew ends with a prophecy about the "desolate house" of Jerusalem (Mt. 23:37-9), and note how in Mt. 24:1-2 the prophecy on the fate of the temple and its buildings is followed by prophecies about the fate of the disciples in Judea and Galilee.

[81] Deines, "Movements," 85–93.

[82] Luz, *Matthäus*, 292–3.

[83] William D. Davies and Dale C. Allison, *Matthew, 19–28*, Vol. 3 (London: T&T Clark, 1988), 264, argue for two parts; verses 37–9 on Jerusalem, however, clearly show a thematic break with the foregoing "woes" against the Pharisees.

[84] On the literary unity of this speech with Mt. 24–5, see Luz, *Matthäus*, 25–6. Despite the distinct narrative opening of Mt. 24:1, Keener, *Matthew*, 535, stresses the topic of judgment as a *topos* linking Mt. 23 to the Olivet speech (Mt. 24–5) and sees Mt. 23–5 as constituting a speech roughly similar in size to the Sermon on the Mount, ending with the summary statement in Mt. 26:1.

[85] Likewise Keener, *Matthew*, 536: "The harshness of Matthew's language does not imply his alienation from his Jewish heritage—only from rivals for religious power within Syro-Palestinian Judaism."

[86] Yair Furstenberg, "Jesus against the Laws of the Pharisees: The Legal Woe Sayings and Second Temple Intersectarian Discourse," *JBL* 139, no. 4 (2020): 769–88, discusses the reproaches on vows, tithes, and purity as reflective of a Second Temple sectarian discourse.

[87] Verses 11 and 12 are proverbial and unrelated to the polemic. On sources and additions, see Davies and Allison, *Matthew*, 265.

> The scribes and the Pharisees sit on Moses' seat; therefore, do whatever they teach you and follow it; but do not do as they do, for they do not practice what they teach. They tie up heavy burdens, hard to bear, and lay them on the shoulders of others; but they themselves are unwilling to lift a finger to move them. They do all their deeds to be seen by others; for they make their phylacteries broad and their fringes long. They love to have the place of honor at banquets and the best seats in the synagogues, and to be greeted with respect in the marketplaces, and to have people call them rabbi. But you are not to be called rabbi, for you have one teacher, and you are all students. And call no one your father on earth, for you have one Father—the one in heaven. Nor are you to be called instructors, for you have one instructor, the Messiah.
>
> Mt. 23:1-10

The reproach regarding hypocrisy—not practicing what you preach—is well known in Qumranic and Rabbinic sources.[88] Matthew's examples feature body practices—donning specific shapes of phylacteries (τὰ φυλακτήρια) and wearing long fringes (according to most translations), addressing the size of the tassels attached to the robes (τὰ κράσπεδα)—which are additions to the Markan reproach for wearing long robes (Mk 12:38-9; compare Lk. 11:43; 20:46). Secondly, the "seat of Moses" (Mt. 23:1) is added to the reproach to those seeking the best places in synagogues and banquets (Mk 12:39; Lk. 20:46). Finally, the social address *rabbi* (Mt. 23:7-8) is added to the reproach to those seeking public salutations (Mk 12:38; Lk. 20:46). The expression "sitting on the seat of Moses" has been argued as indicating Pharisaic authority in first-century CE synagogues, but as Lee Levine has succinctly put it, "there is no shred of evidence" for this.[89] However, Pharisees are attributed an authority that has to be discredited by pointing to their alleged ostentatiousness. Matthew's implied audience does, nonetheless, share the very same criticized cultic practices: they don garments with tassels (ציצית) and wear phylacteries (תפילין) while praying, albeit of a different size. Public salutation of a teacher is a highly sensitive issue for Matthew: Jesus is called a "teacher" (διδάσκαλος) only by Pharisees and other leaders, or by Judas.[90] This being the case, the scribes (οἱ γραμματεῖς, often mentioned together with Pharisees, as noted) represent a function of the Matthean community as well: he is only not to be called a "rabbi" (ῥαββί; Mt. 23:8).[91] Indeed, the phrase "Scribes and Pharisees" occurs seven

---

[88] For example, t. *Yebamot* 8:7; p. *Shabbat* 1:5 (3b). Cf. Moshe Weinfeld, "The Charge of Hypocrisy in Matthew 23 and in Jewish Sources," in *Normative and Sectarian Judaism in the Second Temple Period* (London: T&T Clark, 2005), 279–85; Kampen, *Matthew*, 162–3.

[89] Lee I. Levine, *The Ancient Synagogue: The First Thousand Years* (New Haven, CT: Yale University Press, 2008), 41. Compare the assessments in *The Synagogue in Ancient Palestine: Current Issues and Emerging Trends*, ed. Rick Bonnie, Raimo Hakola, and Ulla Tervahauta (Göttingen: Vandenhoeck & Ruprecht, 2021), 50, 100. "Sitting on the seat of Moses" most probably is a saying associated with the honor attributed to Torah Scrolls by teachers. See the discussion in Ottenheijm, "Matthew and Yavne," 388–94.

[90] Kingsbury, *Story*, 63, n. 6.

[91] On social and religious backgrounds, see Ottenheijm, "Matthew and Yavne," 394–7.

times in Chapter 23, in verses where Mark and Luke mention only scribes.[92] The Matthean community had their own scribes, nonetheless, as is apparent from the Matthean parable of the "Scribe who has become a Disciple of the Kingdom" (πᾶς γραμματεὺς μαθητευθεὶς τῇ βασιλείᾳ τῶν οὐρανῶν; Mt. 13:52).[93] In short, Mt. 23 represents the necessity to distance a community that is quite close to Pharisaic-Rabbinic practices yet is engaged in struggles against Pharisaic or early Rabbinic elites. Proximity requires fierce polemic to sustain this community's claim to solely embody the biblical Covenant.[94] The fierceness with which Matthew delegitimizes religious opponents reveals a deeply felt threat: these "enemies" are close, socially and, to a certain extent, even religiously.

IX. Discussion and Conclusions

Scholarly readings of Matthew emphasize Matthew's depiction of Pharisees as "Jewish Leaders" who are the prime antagonists of Jesus, inherently "evil," constantly planning to obstruct Jesus, plan his downfall, and refusing to acknowledge this Messiah. Pharisees by their actions and by their sheer presence operate as a negative type in the story. Their depiction follows the principle that "Repetition, accumulation, relations to other characters, and transformations are four different principles which work together to construct the image of a character."[95] Matthew seems to deny the possibility of the Pharisees' transformation. Even the Gospel of John, with its infamous anti-Jewish passages (e.g., Jn 8) presents us with the highly sympathetic Pharisee Joseph of Arimathea (Jn 19:38) as a "Disciple of Jesus," or the empathic Pharisaic teacher Nicodemus (Jn 3). Moreover, lumping them together as "chief priests and Pharisees," or "Pharisees and Sadducees" appears to be a necessary corollary to Matthew's rhetoric, connecting Jerusalem-based authorities rejecting Jesus as Messiah with the elites surrounding Matthew's communities. Matthew's apocalyptical-ethical and social dualism, however, does not explain sufficiently why the narrative focuses on Pharisees in specific contexts, or why their opinions resonate in disputes where they are not mentioned explicitly. In explaining the Law of Moses (e.g., divorce, Sabbath, murder), Matthew's disputes and teachings attest to proto-Rabbinic legal logic and concepts, even if he anchors the law and ethics or teaching in parables on the Messianic and final

---

[92] Davies and Allison, *Matthew*, 267, assume a lack of knowledge on the part of the (last) editor. Cousland, *Crowds*, 268–9, argues that the lumping together with "Scribes" is reflective of acute tensions with the (emerging) Jewish leadership of his day. "Scribes" is a designation for literate professionals active in villages or cities, denoting teachers, priests, or Pharisees: see Daniel R. Schwartz, "'Scribes and Pharisees, Hypocrites.' Who were the Scribes?" in *Studies in the Jewish Background of Christianity* (Tübingen: Mohr Siebeck, 1992), 89–101; Keener, *Matthew*, 537–8; Deines, "Movements," 89. In Mt. 23 it operates as a *hendyadis*.

[93] Patrick Schreiner, *Matthew, Disciple and Scribe: The First Gospel and Its Portrait of Jesus* (Grand Rapids, MI: Baker Academic, 2019), 9–33, argues, mainly over the ground of sapiential traditions, that Matthew reveals himself as a "discipled scribe" in this parable. I am less convinced, however, by the identification of the implicit author with a historical "Matthew."

[94] Stanton, *Gospel*, 103ff., 113–14. Compare his compelling comparison of Mt. 18 with the sectarian *Damascus Covenant*, 85–107.

[95] Bal and van Boheemen, *Narratology*, 127.

presence of Jesus. In his polemic against "Scribes and Pharisees," Matthew surprisingly acknowledges their authority (Mt. 23:1) but undercuts their standing by pointing to their hypocrisy. Furthermore, this chapter shows some practices that are rather close to Pharisaic ones, and here, the necessity to distance the community from these proximities becomes most clear. Competitiveness may explain this ambiguity: both Matthew and the Pharisees operate in a similar social field. This cannot be explained by pointing to Matthew being *extra muros*. Matthew's proximity to Pharisees in terms of legal logic and religious culture necessitates a vigorous policy creating a "space of attention," a niche filled in by the community.[96] Pharisees also deflect questions, anxieties, or tensions among the implied Matthean readership such as concerning the identity of Jesus. Pharisees are the rhetorical intimate Other in articulating Jesus' Messianic identity. They represent a deviant scriptural and legal authority, yet are close to Matthew's own positions. As such, Matthew's Pharisees serve the author addressing the implied reader. In this respect, his story hinges on the Pharisees as punching bags or strawmen. In exacerbating "historical" debates between Jesus and his disciples and the Pharisees, Matthew continued sectarian struggles typical of the Second Temple Period, now as one of the factions contesting Jewish leadership after 70 CE.[97] Claiming to be the righteous heir of biblical Israel (Mt. 1:1-17), and with a new scribal elite, Matthew delegitimizes Pharisaic competitors and their early Rabbinic successors. For Matthew's story, Pharisees remain indispensable.

---

[96] Randal Collins, "On the Acrimoniousness of Intellectual Disputes," *Common Knowledge* 8 (2002): 51.
[97] Runesson, "Rethinking Early Jewish–Christian Relations," argues, starting from Mt. 12:9, that Matthew parted from the Pharisees; Ottenheijm, "Matthew and Yavne," stresses Matthew's leadership as competing with rising Rabbinic elites. Lapin, "Rabbinic Movement," 76, following Martin Goodman, *Judaism in the Roman World: Collected Essays* (Leiden: Brill, 2007), 153–62, argues that even the Rabbis continued sectarian policies.

14

Roman Rulers as Characters in Matthew's Gospel: Characterization, the Tyrant Trope, and Political Critique

Adam Winn

I. Introduction

The last several decades have produced a significant number of narrative critical assessments of Matthew's Gospel, most of which give ample consideration to the gospel's construction of characters.[1] Yet, few studies give significant attention to the gospel's characterization of Roman rulers.[2] The relative absence of such studies is surprising, as Roman rulers are granted more space in Matthew than any of the other canonical gospels. In fact, Roman rulers feature prominently at the beginning (Herod the Great and Archelaus), middle (Herod Antipas), and end (Pontius Pilate) of the gospel. While they are no doubt best understood as "minor characters," such characters can indeed play an important role in advancing narrative aims.[3] The present chapter seeks to fill this void in Matthean scholarship by offering a character analysis of these

---

[1] See, for example, J. D. Kingsbury, *Matthew as Story* (Philadelphia: Fortress, 1986); J. C. Anderson, *Matthew's Narrative Web: Over, and Over, and Over Again* (Sheffield: JSOT, 1994); Mark A. Powell, "Toward a Narrative-Critical Understanding of Matthew," *Int* 46, no. 4 (1992): 341–6; R. A. Edwards, "Reading Matthew: The Gospel as Narrative," *List* 24, no. 3 (1989): 251–61; D. Cortés-Fuentes, "Not Like the Gentiles: The Characterization of Gentiles in the Gospel according to St. Matthew," *JHLT* 9, no. 1 (2001): 6–26; Masashi Sawamura, "The Gentiles in Matthew," *AJBI* 41 (2015): 107–18; Jeannine K. Brown, *The Gospels as Story: A Narrative Approach to Matthew, Mark, Luke, and John* (Grand Rapids, MI: Baker, 2020); David Rhoads and K. Syreeni (eds.), *Characterization in the Gospels: Reconceiving Narrative Criticism* (Sheffield: Sheffield Academic, 1999).

[2] See L. J. Lawrence, "'Fearing Within.' 'The Herods' of Matthew's Gospel," *Theology in Scotland* 8 (2001): 39–52; F. P. Vijoen, "Power and Authority in Matthew's Gospel," *AcT* 31, no. 2 (2011): 329–45; Warren Carter, *Pontius Pilate: Portraits of a Roman Governor* (Collegeville, MN: Liturgical Press, 2003); Helen K. Bond, *Pontius Pilate in History and Interpretation* (New York: Cambridge University Press, 1998), 120–37.

[3] On the significance of minor characters in gospel narratives, see Elizabeth Struthers Malbon, "The Major Importance of Minor Characters in Mark," in *The New Literary Criticism and the New Testament*, ed. E. S. Malbon and Edgar V. McKnight, JSNTSup 109 (Sheffield: Sheffield Academic and Valley Forge, PA.: Trinity, 1994), 58–86.

Roman rulers, paying particular attention to what they say, what they do, and, where relevant, what other characters (including the narrator) says about them. This analysis should yield fruitful results as to how these characters function in Matthew's narrative.

Yet, this chapter will also push beyond the strictures of Matthew's narrative and consider how these characters might function to communicate meaning to a first-century Jewish-Christian audience living in a Greco-Roman world.[4] In the Greco-Roman world, character creation and depiction not only functioned to depict that which had happened in the real and/or narrative world but also functioned heuristically to speak to the situation of the audience. To this end, the chapter will consider the common trope of the tyrant and the ways in which Matthew's Gospel draws on this trope in its creation of characters. It will also consider the strategies used in the Greco-Roman world for critiquing tyrants as well as the possibility that Matthew's depiction of Roman rulers might be employing one such strategy.

II. Matthew's Characterization of Herod the Great

The first Roman ruler one encounters in Matthew's Gospel is Herod the Great, whom the evangelist simply calls "King Herod." The first reference to "King Herod" comes in the first verse of Chapter 2, with no additional information provided to the reader. Such an introduction suggests that the author presumes the audience's basic familiarity with this figure, including the general time frame of his reign, his basic reputation, and the nature of his kingship. Thus, though Matthew does not identify Herod as a distinctly Roman ruler or even mention any Roman association, it seems safe to assume that the first-century audience knows that this Herod was in fact a client king who represented Roman authority.

Much of the scholarship on the Matthean Herod focuses primarily on the historical veracity of his depiction by the evangelist, in particular his order to execute all male children in Bethlehem who were under the age of two.[5] Such historical concerns are not within the purview of this chapter. However, knowledge of the historical Herod, that which would likely be possessed by Matthew's readers, may at times be drawn upon in consideration of Matthew's characterization.

After Jesus' birth, Matthew reports that astrologers traveling from the East arrive in Jerusalem asking where they might find the child that has been born "king of the Jews," with their ultimate purpose being to give him reverence or perhaps even worship.[6] It is unclear whether these men come to Herod directly asking for the location of the child king or whether the text describes a general arrival in Jerusalem accompanied by

---

[4] That the Gospel of Matthew is written for a Jewish-Christian audience is a widely held position among Matthean interpreters and commentators and is presumed here.

[5] See, for example, Barry J. Beitzel, "Herod the Great: Another Snapshot of His Treachery," *JETS* 57, no. 2 (2014): 309–22; M. Vogel, "Herodes: Kindermörder: Hintergründe einer Rollenbesetzung," *ZNT* 8, no.16 (2005): 42–7; R. T. France, "Herod and the Children of Bethlehem," *NovT* 21 (1979): 98–120.

[6] For discussion and debate, see R. T. France, *The Gospel of Matthew*, NICNT (Grand Rapids, MI: Eerdmans, 2007), 69; Donald Hagner, *Matthew 1-13*, WBC 33a (Nashville, TN: Thomas Nelson, 1993), 28; John Nolland, *The Gospel of Matthew*, NIGTC (Grand Rapids, MI: Eerdmans, 2005), 111.

widespread questioning of those in the city. Regardless, hearing of their questioning troubles (ἐταράχθη) both Herod and the entire city of Jerusalem. Whether the reader is to understand that both Herod and the entire city are troubled in the same way or for the same reason is unclear. Yet, what becomes clear as the story progresses is that Herod is troubled by the threat of a possible challenger to his position and authority (see Mt. 1:16). For readers familiar with Herod's reputation for extreme paranoia, particularly paranoia over plots to usurp him, such a response is not at all surprising. In fact, such familiarity would likely shape the readers' understanding of Herod's reaction to the endeavors of the astrologers. This potential challenge to Herod's position is presumably the catalyst for a series of machinations intended to eliminate the threat. Herod begins by calling together the Chief Priests and scribes to question them as to where the "Messiah" was to be born. Interestingly, Matthew depicts a Herod who both trusts the Jewish sacred texts as reliable guides to the future, and yet, at the same time, attempts to thwart the plans of the God who communicates through them. In this way, Matthew depicts Herod as an intentional enemy of Israel's God, one who is willing to stand against that God for his own gain.

After Herod discovers that the Messiah is to be born in Bethlehem, he moves his plan forward through a covert meeting with the astrologers. The secret nature of this meeting seems to draw further on the historical Herod's reputation for paranoia, as the Matthean Herod presumably desires to keep his plan to remove the infant king from any who might thwart it. In this secret meeting, Herod ascertains when the star first appeared, knowledge that the reader will soon realize gives Herod information regarding the possible age of his infant challenger. The meeting concludes with Herod instructing the visiting astrologers to search for the child and when them have found him, to report back to Herod so that he too can pay homage to the new king. The cunning of these instructions is not immediately obvious, but becomes so soon enough.

After finding the child, the astrologers are warned in a dream not to return to Herod, and thus they depart for home without alerting him to the child's location. Similarly, Joseph himself through a dream receives a warning from an angel. It is in this warning where it first becomes clear to the reader that Herod's actions are sinister in nature, as the angel tells Joseph that Herod is about to search for the infant Jesus in order to destroy him. Joseph heeds this warning and flees to Egypt per the angel's instructions.

After the narration of the departure to Egypt, the narrative describes Herod's realization that, ironically, he has been tricked by the astrologers that he himself had tried to deceive, a realization that produces what might be best described as an intense rage (ἐθυμώθη λίαν). This emotional response manifests itself in an extreme act of violence, as Herod, drawing on the information he has gleaned regarding the birthplace of the Messiah and the appearance of the star, orders that all children in Bethlehem under the age of two be killed. Here the nature of Herod's fear at hearing of the astrologers and their mission as well as the purpose of all his subsequent actions become crystal clear: the protection of his own power. The paranoid Herod of history, who killed one of his wives and three of his sons to protect his position and authority, becomes the paranoid Matthean Herod, who kills innocent children for the same reason (see Joseph. *Ant.* 15.231; 16.392-4; 17.187).

Regardless of what one concludes about the actual historicity of this Matthean episode, Matthew's Herod is one that bears historical verisimilitude. Such verisimilitude enables the evangelist to believably construct Herod as a paranoid despot who takes extreme and unjust measures to maintain his power and authority. By means of such actions, Matthew's Herod is depicted as both an enemy and pawn of the God of Israel. Herod schemes to kill God's Messiah but in doing so he is actually advancing God's purposes and bringing about the fulfillment of Israel's scriptures. Through Herod's actions the story of God's Messiah recapitulates the story of Israel herself, as the Messiah goes into and returns from Egypt (see Mt. 2:15), an exile that like Joseph's exile to Egypt and Israel's exile to Babylon is accompanied by mourning (see Mt. 2:18). Additionally, Herod's actions (and those of his son Archelaus) are the catalyst to move the locus of the narrative from Bethlehem of Judea to Nazareth of Galilee, yet another event that Matthew identifies with the fulfillment of Israel's scriptures (see Mt. 2:23).

III. Matthew's Characterization of Herod Antipas

The next Rome ruler one encounters in Matthew's Gospel is Herod Antipas (from here on Antipas, to avoid confusion with his father), who, contra the Gospel of Mark, is rightly identified in Matthew as "the tetrarch" (compare Mt. 14:1 and Mk 6:14). Again, as with Herod the Great, Matthew does not note any connection between Antipas and Rome. Yet, it again seems safe to assume that Matthew's readers are familiar with Antipas: that he was the son of Herod the Great and that he was the representative of Roman authority in both Galilee and Perea for over four decades (4 BCE–39 CE). Matthew's use of the title "tetrarch" ("ruler over one fourth"), without any explanation, supports such a conclusion.

The Matthean Antipas is first introduced in the context of his hearing a report about Jesus and his miraculous deeds (Mt. 14:1-2). In response to the report, Antipas errantly identifies Jesus as John the Baptist who has risen from the dead, an identity to which he attributes Jesus' miracles (Mt. 14:2).[7] This lack of understanding of Jesus' identity establishes Antipas as an outsider previously described by Matthew; he is one who hears but fails to understand (Mt. 13:13). Yet, it quickly becomes clear that Antipas is not only an outsider who fails to rightly recognize Jesus, but he is also a direct enemy of God, his kingdom, and those associated with its coming.

After relaying Antipas' reaction to Jesus, the gospel offers a flashback to Antipas' arrest, imprisonment, and execution of John the Baptist. The catalyst for the events described in the flashback is Antipas taking his brother Philip's wife Herodias as his

---

[7] What is meant by Antipas' belief that Jesus had risen from the dead is unclear. In her discussion of the Markan parallel, Adela Yarbro Collins contends that the text reflects the popular belief that either a very good or evil person could return from the dead through a mysterious process, offering Nero *redivivus* as a close analogy: Adela Yarbro Collins, *Mark*, Hermeneia (Minneapolis: Fortress, 2007), 304. Bruce Longenecker suggests that rather than reflecting the belief in the actual physical return of a dead person, Antipas' fear reflects the belief that the *genius* of John had now come upon Jesus: Bruce Longenecker, *In Stone and Story: Early Christianity in the Roman World* (Grand Rapids, MI: Baker, 2020), 86.

own, an act with which Matthew's readers would likely already be familiar. John the Baptist responds to Antipas' action by condemning it as "unlawful," a claim likely based on Leviticus 18:16: "Do not uncover the nakedness of your brother's wife; it is your brother's nakedness." Thus, from a Jewish perspective, Antipas has engaged in a direct violation of the Torah. Though not technically illegal in the Greco-Roman world, the act of taking the wife of a living brother would have violated deeply ingrained notions of piety. Greco-Roman piety required one to maintain their obligations not only to gods and country, but also to their family. Romans in particular saw such piety as the ultimate basis for their imperium over the world.[8] Within familial relationships, none was seen as being stronger than the fraternal bond.[9] Cynthia Bannon argues that one could not separate the treatment of one's brother from his political reputation.[10] Thus, not only do Antipas' actions violate the sacred Law of the Jews, they also abandon a fundamental aspect of Greco-Roman piety, one that would raise significant questions about Antipas' ability as a ruler.

In response to John's condemnation of Antipas' unlawful marriage, Antipas has John arrested and imprisoned. According to Matthew, Antipas wanted to execute John, but he feared the people's response for killing one they esteemed as a prophet (Mt. 14:5). Here Matthew's redaction of Mark is noteworthy. In the Markan parallel, it is Antipas' wife, Herodias, that desires John's death, while Antipas himself is described as knowing that John was a "righteous and holy man" (Mk 6:20). Mark even describes Antipas meeting with John in prison and being both glad to hear him as well as being perplexed. Matthew omits Herodias' desire for John's execution and places that desire on Antipas himself. The detail of Antipas fearing to kill John because he was a "righteous and holy man" is transformed into his fear of the response of his subjects, while the detail of Antipas meeting with John in prison is completely omitted. Thus, Matthew's redaction produces a more negative view of Antipas, removing elements in Mark's account that might be regarded as sympathetic. According to Matthew, Antipas himself opposes God's messenger from the beginning and wishes to eliminate him, with the fear of the people being his only restraint. Ultimately, Antipas' arrest of John is an act of injustice, as John had violated no law in condemning Antipas for violating God's laws.

But Antipas' restraint is both undermined and overcome by a confluence of events that take place at his birthday celebration. It is noteworthy that Second Temple Jews did not celebrate birthdays and that the practice was condemned by Jewish rabbis and early Christian voices.[11] Thus, the mere mention of a celebrated birthday would likely

---

[8] See L. R. Lind, "Concept, Actions, and Character: The Reasons for Rome's Greatness," *Transactions and Proceedings of the American Philological Association* 103 (1972): 235–83; R. M. Henry, "'*Pietas*' and '*Fides*' in Catullus," *Hermathena* 75 (1950): 63–8; Martin Percival Charlesworth, "*Pietas and Victoria*: The Emperor and the Roman Citizen," *JRS* 33 (1943): 1–10.

[9] On the fraternal bond in Roman thought, see Cynthia J. Bannon, *The Brothers of Romulus: Fraternal Pietas in Roman Law, Literature and Society* (Princeton, NJ: Princeton University Press, 1997), 3–11.

[10] Bannon, *The Brothers of Romulus*, 3–11, 189–93.

[11] For discussion and primary sources, see Joel Marcus, *Mark 1-8: A New Translation with Introduction and Commentary*, AB 27 (New York: Doubleday, 2000), 21.

be perceived negatively by Jewish-Christian readers. If the birthday itself was not perceived negatively, the events that unfold during the celebration most certainly would be.

At the birthday, Antipas's stepdaughter dances for him and his guests. The nature of this dance has been the subject of debate. In verse 11, the stepdaughter is identified as a κοράσιον, which usually refers to a young girl, likely between the ages of six and fifteen. Such an identification has led some to conclude that the dance was not of a sexual or provocative nature, with the contention being that a young girl would not be placed in such a situation.[12] Yet, others have argued that Matthew offers a restrained depiction of a depraved Herodian party, one in which Antipas takes offensive sexual pleasure in the dancing of his stepdaughter.[13] Κοράσιον is a flexible term that can refer to a prepubescent girl but can also refer to an unmarried girl that is of a marriable age, between twelve and fifteen—such an identification would make the notion of an erotic dance more plausible. Additionally, Matthew follows Mark in using the verb ἀρέσκω to describe Antipas's reaction to the dance, a word that in the LXX frequently connotes sexual arousal or gratification (see Gen. 19:8; Judg. 14:1, 2; Est. 2:4; Job 31:10).[14] That Greco-Roman parties, including birthday celebrations, were frequently associated with drunkenness and erotic behavior might further shape the way Matthew's readers would perceive the nature of this dance.[15] Thus, while not certain, there are strong reasons to conclude that Matthew's description of this dance and Herod's response to it would be understood as sexual in nature. Because the object of Herod's sexual desire is the daughter of his wife, Jewish readers would equate it with a desire for incest and thus an extreme abrogation of Torah (see Lev. 18:17), one akin to his illegal marriage to Herodias.

What is likely Antipas' incestuous response to an erotic dance is followed by a foolish oath in which he promises his stepdaughter anything she desires. In both Greco-Roman and Jewish literature, oaths of this nature are a common trope, often illustrating the foolish character of the oath-maker.[16] The degree to which Antipas' power would be limited as a client of Rome might serve to enhance the foolishness of his oath, as he would not be in a position to truly grant anything his stepdaughter requested.[17] As is often the case in this common trope, the oath forces Antipas into an undesirable position. His stepdaughter, at the urging of her mother, makes the macabre

---

[12] See Nolland, *Matthew*, 583–4; France, *Matthew*, 556; Harold W. Hoehner, *Herod Antipas*, SNTSM 17 (Cambridge: Cambridge University Press, 1972), 151–7; David L. Turner, *Matthew*, BECNT (Grand Rapids, MI: Baker, 2008), 364.

[13] See A. Schlatter, *Der Evangelist Matthäus: Sein Sprache, sein Ziel, seine Selbständigkeit*, 6th edn (Stuttgart: Calwer, 1963), 460; Craig Keener, *A Commentary on the Gospel of Matthew* (Grand Rapids, MI: Eerdmans, 1999), 399–401; Ulrich Luz is somewhat noncommittal on this issue, but in a footnote comments that Greeks would perceive the scene as "totally unseemly": Ulrich Luz, *Matthew*, Hermeneia (Minneapolis: Fortress, 2001), 307, n. 16.

[14] See Gerd Theissen, *The Gospels in Context: Social and Political History in the Synoptic Tradition* (Edinburgh: T&T Clark; 1992), 91–7; Collins, *Mark*, 309.

[15] See Keener, *Matthew*, 401; Joseph. *Apion* 2.204.

[16] See Keener, *Matthew*, 401; Nolland, *Matthew*, 584.

[17] Here Matthew redacts Mark, removing the stipulation of up to half of the kingdom in Antipas' promise to grant his stepdaughter whatever she wishes. This redaction increases the scope of Antipas' promise, making it even more foolish.

request for the head of John the Baptist on a platter. Matthew describes Antipas' reaction to the request as one of grief, though given the previous statement that he wanted to kill John, the grief cannot be understood in terms of concern for the prophet himself. Rather, the reaction is best understood in terms of grief over his foolishness and the political fallout it might incur, related to his fear of the masses (see Mt.14:5). This grief, however, does not prevent Antipas from granting the request, as the greater force is the desire to maintain his honor in front of his dinner guests. Thus, trapped by his foolish oath, Antipas orders the gruesome beheading of John and that the head be presented to his stepdaughter.

In light of this analysis, Matthew's Gospel clearly characterizes Herod Antipas as an opponent of God and his messengers. His unjust arrest of John is the first link in a chain of both foolish and immoral actions that culminates in his execution of God's penultimate prophet (Mt. 11:11). Narratively, Antipas' execution of John follows rejection of Jesus in his hometown of Nazareth and foreshadows Jesus' own execution.

IV. Matthew's Characterization of Pontius Pilate[18]

Pilate is first introduced in Matthew's narrative when, after trying Jesus themselves, the Chief Priests and elders of the people bring him before Pilate. Pilate, who is identified as a governor (Mt. 27:1), appears rather abruptly in the narrative, with no information provided to the reader regarding his history or reputation. The lack of such information indicates that the author presupposes some knowledge on the part of the reader regarding Pilate's identity. While Pilate is first named at the outset of Chapter 27, the narrative cuts away from him to briefly recount the repentance of Judas. After this brief divergence, Pilate appears again, with Jesus standing before him (Mt. 27:11). Their interaction begins with Pilate asking Jesus "Are you the king of the Jews?" (Mt. 27:11). Though not explicitly stated, this question is best understood to stem from the charges brought to Pilate by the Chief Priests and elders, namely that Jesus is one who identifies himself as a messianic figure (see Mt. 26:63-8). Such a charge would no doubt be taken seriously by a Roman governor, as it would carry implications for one's loyalty to Rome as well as for the stability of the region. Pilate's question is thus natural and expected, as interrogating the accused and hearing their testimony would have been a necessary component of a Roman trial. The question is best understood as neutral in nature, as there is no indication in the narrative that Pilate assumes a particular answer or has a

---

[18] Because of the sensitive nature of the gospel passion narratives, it is important to note that the following assessment is particularly focused on the Matthean narrative and its characterization of Pilate. It is decidedly not an historical assessment of the death of Jesus and Pilate's role therein. There are significant reasons to conclude that Matthew's depiction of the passion narrative is at best an incomplete historical picture of the realities surrounding the crucifixion of Jesus, one that in my estimation is likely influenced by intra-Jewish conflict between Matthew's Jewish community and the larger Jewish community in which it found itself. For a narrative treatment of the complex historical realities surrounding the arrest, trial, and crucifixion of Jesus, see Adam Winn, *Killing a Messiah: A Novel* (Downers Grove, IL: IVP, 2020).

particular agenda. Jesus' response to the question is similar to his response to the Jewish council, though instead of using the aorist tense ("You have said so") it is now in the present tense ("You say so"). The nature of this response is debated. It is widely understood in terms of equivocation, with some understanding it as an equivocation that leans toward an affirmation, others that it leans toward negation (or at least an implied correction to a faulty messianic understanding), and still others who understand it in terms of intentional ambiguity.[19] Jesus' similar response to Judas in Matthew 26:25 and to the high priest in Matthew 26:64 are often drawn upon to support various conclusions. Yet, what seems most telling for understanding this particular iteration of the answer is the response of Pilate. In verses 13-14, Pilate asks Jesus about the many accusations being brought against him and is amazed at his refusal to respond. Such an interaction strongly suggests that Pilate does not draw from Jesus' response in verse 11 either an affirmation or a negation. Pilate's question of "what evil has he done" in verse 23 seems at the very least to suggest that in the narrative Pilate does not understand Jesus' initial response (Mt. 27:11) as an affirmation. Thus, Pilate's initial interaction with Jesus seems to be neutral in nature, with Pilate questioning the accused Jesus and giving him an opportunity to respond to the charges against him. In this respect, Matthew seems to be presenting Pilate as a dutiful governor.

After this initial interaction, the narrative introduces Pilate's custom of releasing to the people any prisoner they desired at the Passover festival. Regardless of the historical veracity of this narrative detail, its narrative function seems to be that of attributing to Pilate an act of generosity to the people or perhaps an opportunity to correct a perceived injustice. This custom of Pilate could, on its own, contribute positively to Matthew's characterization of Pilate. Yet, Pilate's use of this custom in regard to Jesus, namely giving the people a choice between Jesus Barabbas and Jesus, will ultimately prove foolish, as by offering this choice Pilate places himself in difficult position. Before exploring this position further, we must first consider Pilate's assessment of the charges against Jesus.

It seems clear in the narrative that Pilate finds Jesus to be innocent of the charges brought against him and would like to set him free. Many details in the story point to this conclusion. First, in verse 18, the reader is told explicitly that Pilate knew that the motivation of the Chief Priest and elders was envy, a narrative claim that implies that Pilate perceives a lack of veracity in the charges they have brought. Second, as noted above, in verse 23, Pilate asks the crowd what evil Jesus has done, a question that is not answered and which strongly implies Jesus' innocence. Third, the detail of Pilate's wife urging him not have anything to do with Jesus, who she describes as a "righteous man," is likely provided to suggest something about Pilate's own attitude toward Jesus' innocence. Fourth, Pilate's act of washing his hands and claiming his own innocence

---

[19] For those who see equivocation with a positive leaning, see Nolland, *Matthew*, 1162; Daniel J. Harrington, *The Gospel of Matthew*, SP 1 (Collegeville, MN: Liturgical, 1991), 388; Donald Senior, *The Passion Narrative according to St. Matthew*, BETL 39 (Louvain: Louvain University Press, 1975), 228; Hagner, *Matthew*, 818; France, *Matthew*, 1051–2. For an example of equivocation with a negative leaning, see Bond, *Pointius Pilate*, 129–30; for an example of one who sees ambiguity, see Turner, *Matthew*, 653.

regarding Jesus' blood clearly implies his perception of Jesus' innocence. Finally, though perhaps less telling, is that on two occasions, Pilate refers to Jesus as "the one who is called Christ" (27:17, 22). Here it seems that "Christ" has replaced Pilate's earlier use of "King of the Jews." Who Pilate understands as calling Jesus the Christ is unclear, whether the people of the city or simply Jesus' accusers, but it seems significant that Pilate does not say that Jesus is the Christ or claims to be the Christ. The wording suggests that Pilate understands the charge against Jesus of claiming to be "the King of the Jews" or "the Christ" to be unsubstantiated.[20]

After determining that the Matthean Pilate finds Jesus to be innocent, Pilate's use of the custom to release a prisoner can be explored further. By giving the gathered crowd a choice between Jesus and the notorious prisoner Jesus Barabbas, Pilate appears to be trying to find a way to free the innocent Jesus. Yet, what Pilate seemingly fails to account for is what unfolds in the narrative, namely the Chief Priests and the elders persuading the crowd to choose Jesus Barabbas for release instead of Jesus. This failure in foresight places Pilate in the difficult position of choosing justice or pleasing the crowd. As Antipas could not retract his promise without losing honor in front of his guests, so too Pilate cannot retract the choice he has offered without angering the crowd.

Pilate must now deal with the repercussions of his misguided decision to offer the crowd a choice between Jesus Barabbas and Jesus. When he asks what he should do with Jesus, the crowd tells Pilate that he should be crucified., Pilate appears reluctant to grant this demand, since he asks the crowd for a justification: "Why? What evil has he done?" (Mt. 27:23). The crowd does not reply with an answer but is depicted as increasingly shouting that Jesus be crucified (Mt. 27:24). The text then describes Pilate as accepting that he could do nothing, a statement explained in terms of Pilate perceiving the beginning of a riot within the crowd. Pilate is depicted as trapped between a decision for justice for Jesus or facing a riot by the crowd. Pilate's approach to the dilemma is to abdicate his authority in this situation. Instead of fighting for Jesus' innocence, Pilate declares his own innocence with regards to Jesus' blood, a declaration that is also manifest in the symbolic washing of his hands. He then grants the crowd permission to crucify Jesus. Thus, Pilate fails in what could arguably be considered his most important role as a Roman governor, namely the enactment of justice. Rome prided itself on the virtue of justice and promised such justice to the provinces. In condemning an innocent man out of a fear of mob violence, Pilate is grossly failing in his role as governor.[21] Thus, Matthew characterizes Pilate as a governor who not only foolishly offers the crowd before him a choice in which injustice is an option, but also, when the crowd chooses injustice, lacks the moral courage to resist the pressure of the mob.[22]

---

[20] For a similar conclusion, see France, *Matthew*, 1053. Contra Gundry who argues that Matthew has Christianized Pilate and that Pilate is making a Christian confession: R. H. Gundry, *Matthew: A Commentary on His Literary and Theological Art* (Grand Rapids, MI: Eerdmans, 1982), 561–2.

[21] Justice was considered a foundational virtue among Romans, and one on which they based their divine right to rule. For discussion, see Lind, "Concept, Action, Character," 236–4. Cicero claims that the provinces were the theatre in which Roman rulers demonstrated virtue, with justice being a central virtue (Cic. QFr. 1.1.42). The Matthean Pilate clearly fails in his theatrical performance.

[22] It should be noted that Warren Carter has argued that Matthew's Pilate is not weak, but rather strong and that he manipulates the audience: Warren Carter, *Pontius Pilate: Portraits of a Roman Governor* (Collegeville, MN: Liturgical, 2003), 75–99.

Pilate's handwashing is worthy of discussion, as it may contribute to a negative characterization. Many interpreters have noted that washing one's hands as an act of declaring the innocence of another's blood finds a strong parallel in Deuteronomy 21:1-9. Here, when the community cannot find the culprit who committed a murder, the elders of the community wash their hands over a heifer whose neck has been broken as a means of removing the guilt from the shedding of innocent blood. While many see this Jewish legal custom as a background to Pilate's handwashing, some contend that Matthew employs a satirical parody of the custom, a parody in which Pilate misunderstands and misuses it.[23] Callie Callon rightly notes that the custom is one by which people demonstrate they are innocent of a murder that has already taken place.[24] Yet, in Matthew, Jesus is still alive, and though Pilate washes his hands of Jesus' blood, he ultimately hands Jesus over to be executed. On this basis, Callon claims that Pilate, who has legal authority over Jesus' life, washes his hands of shed blood of which he is not innocent and, in this way, violates and disrespects the custom.[25] Therefore, not only does Pilate fail to enforce justice by preserving Jesus' life, but he also breaks and makes a mockery of the Torah in his efforts to declare his innocence in Jesus' death.

Matthew's characterization of Pilate is more complicated than that of King Herod and Antipas. It seems the Matthean Pilate does indeed perceive Jesus to be innocent of the charges brought against him by the Jewish authorities, with Pilate even trying to free Jesus. But like Antipas, he makes a foolish offer that places him in a difficult position and instead of enforcing justice, Pilate allows the will of the mob to override it. Finally, in an attempt to absolve himself of his complicity in Jesus' death, he violates and mocks God's law. Thus, Matthew's Pilate is characterized negatively, as a foolish and weak ruler who is manipulated by the Jewish Chief Priests and elders into permitting the execution of God's Messiah and who in so doing contravenes the Torah. Narratively, Pilate's perception of Jesus' innocence is widely recognized as a foil used by the evangelist to magnify Jewish guilt. Yet, Pilate himself is also complicit and thus is also used to move the gospel to its climax, the death of Jesus.

V. Matthew's Roman Rulers and the Tyrant Trope

The concept of the tyrant was well established in the ancient Mediterranean world, with a substantial history among both Greeks and Romans. The Greek concept of the tyrant likely finds its origins in the archaic period (seventh to sixth century BCE), while the Roman variant finds its origins in the history of Tarquinius Superbus (sixth century BCE).[26] The Greek distinction between the "good philosopher" king and the bad tyrant

---

[23] For those who see a parody, see Nolland, *Matthew*, 1177; Callie Callon, "Pilate the Villain: An Alternative Reading of Matthew's Portrayal of Pilate," *BTB* 36 (2006): 62–71; Andrew Simmonds, "Mark's and Matthew's *Sub Rosa* Message in the Scene of Pilate and the Crowd," *JBL* 131 (2012): 748–53.

[24] Callon, 'Pilate the Villain', 68–70.

[25] Callon, 'Pilate the Villain', 68–70.

[26] For discussion of the tyrant trope in the Greek world, see Helmut Berve, *Die Tyrannis bei den Griechen*, 2 vols. (Muenchen: C. H. Beck'sche Verlagsbuchhandlung, 1967), esp. 1:476-509 and 2:737-

was a common motif in both ancient philosophy and history.[27] For Romans, the hatred of the tyrant, often inseparable from the concept of a king, resulted in the formation of a republican form of government that lasted over five centuries and greatly shaped the nature of the early principate.[28] Such histories of tyrants produced common tropes in both Greco-Roman and Jewish literature. The tyrant was a common figure in plays, novels, political invective/philosophies, and histories.[29] In his analysis of the Markan Herod, Abraham Smith notes four common features of the tyrant trope: 1) paranoia; 2) possession of a bodyguard; 3) displays of excess; and 4) interaction with a philosopher.[30] Yet to these features others could also be added, including the abrogation of law/justice, association with vices, and immoral behavior such as murder, rape, or incest.[31]

Here I bring this trope to bear on Matthew's characterization of Roman rulers. A number of the above noted features can be seen in Matthew's depiction of Herod the Great: 1) his actions seem driven by paranoia related to the birth of a child that might threaten his own reign; 2) he seems to engage philosophers (the magi) who are actually seeking to honor a true king; 3) he seeks to deceive these philosophers and make them unwitting accomplices in his efforts to eliminate a perceived political challenger; and 4) his efforts to secure his own power culminates in the execution of all the infants in the town of Bethlehem. The presence of such features makes a strong case that Matthew's Gospel has intentionally sought to depict Herod the Great as a tyrant.

A similar case can be made for the characterization of Herod Antipas, as a number of features of the tyrant trope litter Matthew's depiction of the tetrarch: 1) paranoia that one he has executed—John—has returned to oppose him in Jesus; 2) the stealing of his brother's wife; 3) engagement with a philosopher figure in John the Baptist; 4) the unjust arrest and imprisonment of a righteous man who speaks out against his actions toward his brother's wife; 5) possible displays of excess in a birthday celebration; 6) sanctioning an erotic dance from his stepdaughter, one which elicits sexual arousal;

53; Abraham Smith, "Tyranny Exposed: Mark's Typological Characterization of Herod Antipas (Mark 6:14-29)," *BibInt* 14, no. 3 (2006): 269-71. For a thorough discussion and bibliography of the tyrant trope in the Roman world, see Mark Lamas, "Did Mark's Jesus 'Live Like a King?': Roman Rex and Imperial Ideology in Mark's Gospel" (PhD diss., University of Edinburgh, 2020), 82-162; and Adam Winn, "Tyrant or Servant? Roman Political Ideology and Mark 10.42-45," *JSNT* 36, no. 4 (2014): 330-9.

[27] See, for example, Dio Chrysostom's *Discourses on Kingship* 1-4; Plut. *C. Gracch.* 19. For discussion and further primary references, see E. R. Goodenough, *The Political Philosophy of Hellenistic Kingship*, Yale Classical Studies (New Haven, CT: Yale University Press, 1928), 55-102; Oswyn Murray, "Philodemus on the Good King according to Homer," *JRS* 55 (1965): 161-82; Elizabeth Rawson, "Hellenistic Heritage: Hellenistic Kings and Their Roman Equals," *JRS* 65 (1975): 148-59; J. R. Dunkle, "The Greek Tyrant and Roman Political Invective of the Late Republic," *TAPA* 98 (1967): 151-71; J. M. C. Toynbee, "Dictators and Philosophers in the First Century," *Greece and Rome* 13 (1944): 43-58.

[28] Again, see Lamas, "Roman Rex," 82-162; Dunkle, "Roman Political Invective"; A. Wallace-Hadrill, "Civilis Princeps: Between Citizen and King," *JRS* 72 (1982): 32-48.

[29] See discussion and examples in Smith, "Tyranny Exposed," 269-71.

[30] Smith, "Tyranny Exposed," 271-7.

[31] Wallace-Hadrill lays out the features that would distinguish an emperor from a tyrant or make him one ("Civilis Princeps," 32-48). Note that Nero's tyranny is associated with the abrogation of laws and the murder of those perceived to be political threats, including both his mother and Seneca. Caligula's tyrannical behavior included, among other abhorrent behaviors, incestuous relations with his sisters.

and 7) the unjust and grotesque execution of an innocent and righteous figure. Thus, in Matthew's Gospel, the Herodian apple does not fall far from the tree, as Herod the Great's son Antipas also bears a great many of the traits of a tyrant.

Unlike the Matthean Herodians, Matthew's characterization of Pilate lacks most of the significant traits often found in the tyrant trope. Matthew's Pilate is ultimately a weak ruler who abandon's justice by giving into the desires of a mob, but such behavior alone does not merit the label "tyrant." Thus, in Matthew's portrayal of Roman rulers, all are characterized negatively, while two out of three are depicted as tyrants.

VI. The Tyrant Trope and Political Critique

Among postcolonial theorists and New Testament scholars engaged in empire criticism, it is widely recognized that resistance from the powerless colonized against the powerful colonizer is rarely open and direct.[32] Because resistance would generally incur a negative response from the colonizer (often a violent one), resistance must regularly be covert, veiled, and indirect.[33] Evidence of such a hidden or veiled critique of the powerful is widespread in both the Hellenistic and Roman political worlds. Perhaps the best example is the political critique of a reigning monarch or emperor. To critique such figures openly and directly could bring about harsh retribution. During the Roman Principate, laws were instituted by various emperors to criminalize defamation of the imperial family (*crimen maiestatis*), and such defamation was frequently prosecuted and punished.[34] Punishments were severe, including *damnatio memoriae*, exile, forced suicide, and execution.[35] Imperial informants were perceived to be rampant throughout the empire, leading to people taking great care in what they said or wrote, not only publicly but privately.[36] The fear of informants and imperial reprisal led the employment of the art of figured speech as a means of critiquing the powerful. The art of figured speech was a common component of ancient education in rhetoric (see Quint. *Inst.* 9.2; Demetr. *Eloc.* 287–95; Hermog. *Inv.* 4.13; and Dion. *Rhet.* 8–11). Figured speech involved arguing for the opposite of what one actually intended to say or implying something that was not actually spoken through the way in which a

---

[32] For example, see Richard Horsley (ed.), *Hidden Transcript and the Arts of Resistance: Applying the Work of James C. Scott to Jesus and Paul*, SemeiaSt 48 (Atlanta: SBL, 2004); Adam Winn, "Striking Back at the Empire: Empire Theory and Responses to Empire in the New Testament," in *An Introduction to Empire in the New Testament*, ed. Adam Winn, RBS 84 (Atlanta: SBL, 2016), 1–14; Brigitte Kahl, "Acts of the Apostles: Pro(to)-Imperial Script and Hidden Transcript," in *In the Shadow of Empire*, ed. R. Horsley (Louisville, KY: WJK, 2008), 137–57.

[33] Such claims are prominent in the works of postcolonial theorist James C. Scott. See Scott, *Domination and the Arts of Resistance* (New Haven, CT: Yale University Press, 1990), 2–8.

[34] For discussion, see Drew Strait, *Hidden Criticism of the Angry Tyrant in Early Judaism and the Acts of the Apostles* (New York: Lexington/Fortress, 2019), 141–3. Strait notes the work of Jane McCarthy, who records thirty-nine defamation cases between the early first century BCE and early second century CE: Jane McCarthy, "Speech and Silence: Freedom of Speech and Processes of Censorship in Early Imperial Rome" (PhD diss., King's College London, 2013), 285–97.

[35] Again, see McCarthy, "Speech and Silence," 285–97.

[36] See Strait, *Angry Tyrant*, 139–41.

speech was composed.[37] Such a rhetorical device was widely recognized as the ideal way to critique the powerful, particularly a reigning monarch or emperor. See, for example, the following words from Ps-Demetrius:

> Often when what we say is directed toward a tyrant or someone who is violent in some other way, and when we want to censure him, we are compelled to use figured speech ... Flattery is shameful. Direct criticism is risky. The best course is the middle course: figured speech.
>
> Demetr. *Eloc.* 289, 294[38]

Quintillian further evinces such a strategy for critiquing the tyrant:

> You can speak well and make open statement against the tyrants we were discussing, provided the statement can be understood in another way. It is only danger you are trying to avoid, not giving offense. If you can slip by through ambiguity of expression, there's no one who won't enjoy your verbal burglary.
>
> Quint. *Inst.* 9.2.66-7[39]

One particular means of critiquing a ruling figure through figured speech was referencing other figures of the past who had acted in similar way as the current tyrant.[40] Such a strategy is outlined clearly in Ps-Demetrius:

> Since powerful men and women dislike hearing their own faults mentioned, we will not speak openly, if we are advising them against a fault, but we will either blame others who have acted in similar way, for example, in addressing the tyrant Dionysius, we will attack the tyrant Phalaris and the cruelty of Phalaris...
>
> Demetr. *Eloc.* 292 [Innes, LCL]

Similarly, deceased rulers who were widely esteemed as good could be used as examples to highlight the failings of a tyrant or to motivate them to change their course of action. For example, Philo praises the actions of the ideal Augustus in his attempt to dissuade Gaius Caligula from erecting a statue in the Jerusalem temple (Philo, *Leg.* 153–8).[41] By using deceased rulers of the past (good or bad), one could engage in figured political invective without the appearing to do so.

---

[37] For discussion of figured speech, see Jason Whitlark, *Resisting Empire: Rethinking the Purpose of the Letter to "the Hebrews"*, LNTS 484 (London: Bloomsbury/T&T Clark, 2014), 21–48; Strait, *Angry Tyrant*, 143–50.
[38] Translation from Frederick Ahl, "The Art of Safe Criticism in Greece and Rome," *AJP* 105 (1984): 186–7.
[39] Translation from Ahl, "Art of Safe Criticism," 193.
[40] See discussion of this strategy in Strait, *Angry Tyrant*, 144–5, who draws heavily on Ps-Demetrius, particularly Demetr. *Eloc.* 291–5.
[41] For other examples, see Strait, *Angry Tyrant*, 51–2.

VII. Matthew's Tyrants, Figured Speech, and Political Critique

The practice of figured speech for the purpose of political critique, particularly the strategy of using deceased rulers as a means of critiquing present rulers, opens interesting interpretive possibilities for assessing Matthew's characterization of both King Herod and Herod Antipas. Beyond the possibilities of Matthew engaging in historical remembrance or character creation to serve literary or theological functions, we must consider the strong possibility that Matthew's depiction of Herodian tyrants is an example of figured speech and a means of critiquing current Roman rulers. The Greco-Roman literati, of which the Matthean evangelist was most certainly a part, were trained in the art of figured speech. Thus, Matthew's depiction of two deceased Roman clients as tyrants who opposed God and his agents may very well function as a narrative form of figured speech, one that intends to critique living Roman rulers. That audiences were trained to look out for such forms of critique means that whether intended by the evangelist or not, many readers/hearers of Matthew's Gospel could perceive a creative political invective.

Given the uncertainty regarding the date and provenance of Matthew's Gospel, the target of such a political critique remains equally uncertain. Yet, it is not difficult to imagine likely possibilities. If the gospel was written in the mid-80s as many suggest, a figure like Domitian, one widely regarded as a tyrant both during and after his reign, would be an obvious choice. In depicting both King Herod and Antipas as tyrants who oppose God and his agents, Matthew would be able to indirectly critique the current tyrant Domitian for doing the same. Though the reign of Nero seems far too early for most Matthean interpreters, for those that favor such an early date, Nero would be a perfect target for such a figured critique. And while Vespasian and Titus were not remembered as tyrants by Roman or Christian historians, it is indeed possible that the Matthean evangelist could perceive them in this way, particularly given their role in destroying Jerusalem and its temple. Regardless of the specific target, that Matthew's characterization of Herodians functioned as a figured critique of a reigning figure is a strong interpretive possibility and one that should be considered in assessing not only Matthew's response to the Roman imperial order but also the response of early Christianity as a whole.

Index of References

HEBREW BIBLE/OLD TESTAMENT

Genesis
9:6	200
12	56
12:3	17
17:19	17
19:8	214
38	90
49:9	90
49:9-10	90, 97
49:10	97

Exodus
2:2	91
4:19	18
13:21-22	38
14:19, 24	38
15:15-16	91
16:10	38
19:16-18	38
20:12	104
21:12	200–1
21:17	104
23:20	57–8, 65
23:23	64
33:9-10	38
34:29 LXX	78

Leviticus
16:1-4	37
18:16	213
18:17	214
19:17	201
19:18	201
25:36	201

Numbers
6:1-21	37
17:7	38
17:16-26	38
22–24	43
24	49

24:8	97
24:17	97

Deuteronomy
8:3 LXX	101
9:9	78
19:11	201
21:1-9	218
22:13-22	19
22:23-9	19
26:5	105
28:15	56
28:63-8	56
30:15-20	59

Joshua
2	91
2:3-4	91
2:4	91
2:9	91
2:10	91
2:11	91

Judges
11:29-40	46
14:1	214
14:2	214

Ruth
1:16	91
3:9-10	91
4:11	92
4:11-12	92
4:17	92

1 Samuel
1–2	36
1:28	37
2:11	37
2:18	37
3:1	37

16:1-13	16	*Ezekiel*	
17:12, 15	16	34	168
		36:16-21	56
2 Samuel			
7	56	*Hosea*	
11–12	93	6:6	199
11:3	152	11:1	105, 116
12:9-10	93		
		Jonah	
1 Kings		3:5	181
10:1-10	181		
11:1-8	42	*Micah*	
11:14-22	42	3:1	57
17–21	46	5:2	16
1 Chronicles		*Malachi*	
3:5	152	3:1	58, 64–5
		3:22 LXX	65

APOCRYPHA/ DEUTERO-CANONICAL BOOKS

2 Chronicles			
36:14-21	56		
Esther		*Judith*	
2:4	214	12:10–13:16	46
7	46		
		Baruch	
Job		1:15–3:8	56
31:10	214		

DEAD SEA SCROLLS

Psalms		*1QH*	
78:2	170	2.15	193
110:1	202	2.32	193
Isaiah			
6:10	166	*4QMMT*	
7:13-16	95	C 7–8	194
7:14	20, 26, 32, 102		
7:16	95	*4QpNah*	
7:17	95	3.1-5	193
8:23–9:1 LXX	59		

PSEUDEPIGRAPHA

9:1-2	59	*Ascension of Isaiah*	
11	57	1:10	144
22:4	144		
29:13	166	*1 Enoch*	
33:7 LXX	144	89:73-5	56
40	58, 62		
40:3	57	*Greek Apocalypse of Ezra*	
		5:8	144
Jeremiah			
31:15	96	*Joseph and Aseneth*	
32:23-35	56	10:14-15	144

Index of References

Testament of Abraham
11:11   144

Testament of Joseph
17.1-2   18

Testament of Simeon
5.1   18

NEW TESTAMENT
Matthew
1   25, 150, 162
1–2   16, 24, 29–31, 39, 49, 149
1:1   16, 23, 56, 85, 89, 94, 96, 168
1:1-2   151
1:1-17   15, 153, 207
1:1-18   12
1:1–4:16   7
1:2   93, 96, 152
1:2-4   57
1:2-11   93
1:3   151
1:3-5   152
1:3-6   152
1:4   58
1:5   151
1:6   97, 151–2
1:11   93, 151–2
1:11-12   57, 94
1:16   10, 16–18, 33, 94–5, 151–2, 211
1:16-17   151
1:17   10, 23, 32, 56–7, 94, 189
1:18   17–18, 20, 22, 25, 85, 95
1:18-19   21
1:18-25   10, 15
1:18–2:21   153
1:19   17–19, 25
1:20   16, 20–1, 29, 33
1:20-1   29
1:20-5   21
1:21   17, 33, 56, 58, 62, 94, 102, 141, 184–5
1:22   31–2, 95, 101
1:23   22, 31, 35, 58, 81, 95, 96, 102, 179
1:24   20
1:24-5   21
1:25   21, 26, 33
2   26–7, 42, 47, 49, 83, 91, 210
2:1   10, 11, 16, 85
2:1-6   41
2:1-12   23, 175, 178, 180, 183, 187
2:1-14   57
2:1-15   96
2:1-18   45–7
2:2   85, 91, 96–7, 99–100
2:3   97
2:4   196
2:6   16, 92
2:11   15, 33–4, 183
2:12   21
2:13   21–23, 34
2:13-15   21
2:13-23   10, 15
2:14   34
2:14-15   21–2, 57
2:15   22, 31, 57, 101, 105, 116, 212
2:16   53, 97
2:16-18   23
2:17   31
2:17-18   23, 53, 98
2:18   96, 212
2:19   10, 21
2:19-21   21–2
2:19-23   23
2:20   21–2, 34
2:21   21–2
2:22   21
2:23   22–3, 31, 57–8, 212
3   57–8, 65
3:1   11, 57–9
3:1-3   57
3:2   66, 68, 102
3:4   65
3:3   59
3:7   58, 60, 65, 67, 192
3:7-8   196
3:7-10   58

3:8	196	5:20	24, 57, 172, 180, 192, 198
3:8-10	57		
3:9	101, 197	5:21-2	200
3:10	66, 198	5:21-48	78
3:11	61	5:31-2	25
3:11-12	59	5:32	25
3:13-17	57, 127	5:33-7	143
3:14	62, 87	5:43-8	186
3:15	11, 57	5:44-5	107
3:16	102	5:45	24, 103, 112, 179–80, 182, 185, 187
3:17	110, 116		
4–10	63		
4:1-11	57	5:47	175
4:4	101	5:48	57, 102–3, 107, 112–13
4:7	101		
4:10	101, 141	6:1	24, 65, 103, 107, 112–13
4:12	60, 65		
4:12-17	145	6:4	103, 107, 112–14
4:13	15, 59	6:6	103, 107, 112–14
4:15-16	59	6:7	175, 179, 180, 182, 185, 187
4:17	59, 102, 137		
4:17–16:20	7	6:8	103, 106, 112, 114
4:18	138		
4:18-20	137, 145	6:9	103, 112, 114-16
4:21-2	102	6:9-13	115
4:23	166, 204	6:14	103, 112, 114
4:23-5	153	6:14-15	107
4:24	165	6:14–7:21	115
5	25	6:15	103, 112, 114
5–6	16, 24	6:18	103, 107, 112–14
5–7	63, 75, 78, 82	6:19-21	65, 82
5:1	57, 78, 164	6:24	102
5:1-12	65	6:25-33	65
5:3-9	190	6:26	103, 106, 112–13
5:4	186	6:26-30	101
5:6	24–5, 186	6:30	155, 158
5:7	25, 186	6:32	103, 107, 112–13, 175, 179–80, 182, 185, 187
5:8	186		
5:9	186		
5:10	24–5	6:33	24
5:11-12	66	7:6	77
5:14	107	7:9-11	107
5:16	103, 106, 107, 112, 160	7:11	103, 112
		7:12	188
5:16–6:8	115	7:15-20	198
5:17	186	7:21	103, 107, 109, 112, 115
5:17-18	43		
5:17-20	75, 78, 179	7:21-7	198
5:19	75–6, 81, 201	7:24	75

7:24-7	64, 75	9:27-8	63
7:26	75, 77	9:27-31	154, 158, 171
7:28-9	79, 180, 204	9:29	128, 155
8	154	9:32-4	154
8–9	12, 63, 150, 153–4, 162	9:33	167
		9:34	167
8:1	78	9:35	204
8:1-4	78	9:35-6	166
8:1-17	153	9:35-8	153
8:2	63, 78	9:35–11:1	156
8:2-4	153	9:36	165–6, 171
8:3	78	9:37–10:6	139
8:4	78	10–12	181
8:5-6	131	10:2	138
8:5-13	119, 123–6, 129–30, 153, 175, 178–80, 183, 187	10:2-4	164
		10:5	157, 165
		10:5-6	175, 177, 179
8:6	179	10:6-8	171
8:8	63	10:7	60, 179
8:8-9	128, 130–1	10:8	179
8:10	131, 155, 183	10:15	178, 180, 182
8:10-13	128	10:16-23	68
8:13	131, 179, 188	10:17	204
8:14	154	10:17-20	107
8:14-15	149–50, 152–5	10:18	178, 180, 185, 189
8:15	154	10:20	103
8:16-17	154	10:20-33	115
8:21	102	10:21	104
8:22	104	10:24	80
8:26	155, 158	10:24-5	80
8:27	140, 167	10:28	107
8:28	179	10:29	103, 106
9:2	128, 155	10:30	107
9:6	166	10:31	107
9:8	167	10:32	103, 106
9:9-13	199	10:32-3	108–9
9:9-17	154	10:33	103, 143–4
9:11	198	10:35-7	104
9:12	199	10:35-45	158
9:14-15	64	10:36	104
9:18	63, 155	10:40-2	180
19:18-19	153	11:1-6	66
9:18-26	149, 152, 154, 157	11:2	60
9:20	155	11:2-30	60
9:20-2	153, 155	11:2	63
9:22	128, 152, 155–7	11:2-6	64
9:23-6	153	11:3	63, 66
9:25	155	11:4	66
9:27	98	11:7	65–6

11:7-15	66	12:50	103, 109, 155
11:8	60	13	170
11:9	66, 68	13:3	166
11:9-11	64	13:10	166, 170, 203
11:10	64	13:12-14	170
11:11	65, 156, 215	13:13	212
11:12	60, 68	13:15	166
11:13	66	13:16	170
11:14	64–5, 68	13:20-1	142
11:18	60	13:21	143
11:18-9	64	13:23	76
11:19	66	13:24	203
11:21-2	157, 178, 180, 187	13:31	203
11:21-4	175	13:34	166, 170
11:23	178, 180, 182	13:36	170
11:23-4	182	13:38	197
11:25	66, 101, 103, 115	13:40	203
11:25-6	115	13:41-2	180
11:25-7	141	13:43	103, 108
11:26	103	13:47-50	139
11:26–26:29	115	13:49	170, 203
11:27	103, 106, 109, 116	13:52	170, 203, 207
11:28	171	13:53–16:20	157
12:1–13:58	60	13:54	204
12:2	198	13:54-7	105
12:7	199	13:54-8	61
12:8	199–200	13:55	15, 17, 24
12:9	204	13:55-6	153, 156
12:11	204	13:57	66
12:11-12	199	14	48
12:12	167, 200	14:1	212
12:13	199	14:1-2	212
12:14	196, 201	14:1-12	45–7, 51–3, 61, 65, 156
12:15	165		
12:18	186–7	14:2	212
12:18-20	185	14:3-4	51
12:18-21	179–80, 188	14:5	51, 213, 215
12:23	167, 171	14:9	53
12:24	167	14:13-21	166
12:28	101–2, 127	14:14	166
12.31-2	145	14:21	156
12:33	76	14:22-33	140
12:38	181, 192	14:28	140, 143
12:38-40	181	14:28-31	140
12:38-41	178, 180	14:31	140, 145, 155, 158
12:42	178, 180–1, 188	14:32	141
12:46-50	15–16, 26, 104, 153, 156	14:33	117, 140, 167
		15	12, 150, 162
12:49	145	15:1	192

15:1-2	198	16:21	160
15:3	102, 199	16:21-3	141
15:4	104	16:21–28:20	8
15:6	156, 199	16:22	142
15:8	166	16:23	142
15:10	170	16:27	103, 108
15:10-14	166	17:4	143
15:12	199	17:5	110, 116
15:13	103, 109	17:11-12	68
15:13-14	172, 204	17:14-21	171
15:14	108, 174	17:20	155, 158
15:15	143, 170, 199	17:22-3	160
15:15-20	199	17:24-5	143
15:21	157	18:10	103, 108, 110
15:21-8	131, 149, 152, 156–8, 175, 178–80, 184, 187	18:14	103, 106
		18:15	145
		18:15-20	77
15:22	98, 127, 152, 157, 179	18:17	136, 175, 179–80, 182, 185, 187
15:23	127, 157, 158, 160	18:18	146
15:23-6	157	18:19	103, 108, 110
15:24	127, 157, 165, 177, 184	18:20	81, 102, 179
		18:21	143, 145
15:25	63, 99, 127, 157–8, 184	18:35	103, 108, 110, 145
		19	21, 26
15:26	157	19:1-10	24
15:27	157, 184	19:1-11	156
15:28	99, 128, 152, 155–7, 179, 188	19:1-12	16, 25, 78
		19:3	26, 78, 200
15:29-39	166	19:3-12	78
15:30-1	166	19:4-6	78
15:31	167, 180	19:7	78
15:32	166	19:8	78
15:38	156	19:9	25, 200
16:1	192, 203	19:10	26
16:3	66	19:12	26
16:6	192, 198	19:16	76
16:8	155, 158	19:16-22	104
16:11	192	19:16-26	76
16:12	192	19:16-17	179
16:15-16	143	19:17	101
16:16	101, 117, 141, 167, 171	19:17-19	76
		19:21	76, 82
16:17	103, 108–9, 141	19:25	167
16:17-18	137	19:26	101
16:17-19	8	19:27	137, 143
16:18	136, 145	19:27-8	146
16:18-19	12	19:28	189
16:19	146	19:29	104

20	12, 150, 159, 162	22:36-8	201
20:17-19	160	22:37	102
20:18-19	158	22:40	202
20:19	178, 180, 182, 185	22:42	202
20:20-1	158	22:46	202
20:20-8	149, 156, 158	23	68, 79–80, 205, 207
20:22	158	23:1	77, 80, 206, 208
20:23	103, 108, 110	23:1-3	43
20:24	158	23:1-10	206
20:25	179–80, 182, 185, 187	23:1-12	205
		23:2	79, 192
20:26-7	158	23:2-3	78, 199
20:28	154, 158, 185	23:3	76, 79, 172
20:30	98	23:4-5	172
20:34	158, 166	23:6	205
21	158	23:7	80
21:1-11	156	23:7-8	206
21:8-11	180	23:8	80–1, 145, 195, 206
21:9	99, 168	23:9	103, 108–9
21:9-11	171	23:10	77, 80–2
21:10	169	23:13	79, 172, 192
21:11	168	23:13-36	205
21:13	172	23:15	79, 192, 197
21:15	99	23:16-22	79, 205
21:16	168	23:23	188, 192
21:20	167	23:23-4	79
21:21-2	128	23:24	80
21:23	204–5	23:25	192
21:23-7	61	23:25-8	79
21:26	168	23:27	192
21:28-32	61	23:28	25
21:32	64	23:29	192, 205
21:33-44	61	23:29-33	67
21:33-46	67, 204	23:29-34	180
21:34	197, 204	23:30-3	105
21:40-3	61	23:31-2	80
21:43	166, 198	23:33	67
21:45	170, 172, 192, 204	23:34	172, 204–5
21:45-6	196	23:34-5	68
22:1-14	67	23:35	205
22:6	67	23:35–24:2	185
22:14	203	23:37	172, 205
22:15	196	23:37-9	169
22:21	102	24-5	205
22:29	101	24:5	203
22:32	101	24:9	175, 178, 180, 185, 187
22:34	202		
22:34-40	188, 198	24:12-13	186
22:35	199, 202	24:14	139, 179

24:19	189	26:47	166, 169
24:20	200	26:53	103, 108
24:23-4	203	26:53–28:19	115
24:29-30	203	26:55	169
24:36	103, 108–9	26:56	143, 159, 161
24:43-4	76	26:63	101
25	75	26:63-8	215
25:1-13	150	26:64	216
25:13	76	26:69-75	142
25:31-46	74–5, 82, 102, 178, 180, 186–7	26:70	143
		26:71	143
25:34	103, 108, 110	26:72	143
25:40	75, 145	26:74	143
25:41	188	26:74-5	144
25:45	75	26:75	144
25:46	75	27	215
26	160	27-8	161
26–7	158	27:1	166, 215
26–8	12, 151, 159, 162	27:3-10	142
26:1-5	160	27:11	215–16
26:1-19	159	27:11-26	178, 180
26:2	160, 179–80, 182, 185	27:13-14	216
		27:17	169, 217
26:3	166	27:18	216
26:3-5	160	27:19	45, 87, 178, 180, 185
26:3-6	99		
26:5	166	27:20	45, 169
26:6-7	160	27:22	217
26:6-13	149, 159–60	27:23	45, 216–17
26:7	99	27:24	217
26:8-9	160	27:24-5	45
26:10	160	27:25	166, 169, 205
26:10-13	160	27:27-37	178, 180
26:12	160	27:37	11, 100
26:13	139, 160, 179, 188	27:46	110
26:14-15	160	27:51-2	45
26:18	80	27:54	11, 117, 178, 180
26:24	142, 147	27:55	154, 161
26:25	216	27:55-6	149–50, 152, 156, 159, 161
26:28	62, 185		
26:29	103	27:56	159
26:31	142–4	27:61	149, 159, 161, 192
26:32	144–5	27:62	197
26:33	142–3	27:62-5	178, 180
26:34	143	27:63	197
26:35	143	27:64	166
26:39	103, 110, 115	28:1	161
26:42	103, 110, 115	28:1-7	159
26:45	179, 180, 182, 185	28:1-10	145, 159

28:1-11	149	1:28	29
28:4	161	1:31	29
28:5-10	161	1:42	29
28:6	161	2:30	30
28:7	145, 161	2:32	30
28:8-10	159	3:7	196
28:10	144–5, 161	6:35	112
28:11	197	6:36	113
28:15	173	6:46	112
28:16	145, 161	7:1-10	126
28:16-20	81, 139	8:40-56	154
28:17	145	11:2	114
28:18	81, 179, 186	11:13	112
28:18-19	190	11:43	206
28:18-20	159, 175, 180, 187–8	12:24	113
		12:30	113
28:19	81, 103, 106, 116, 179	19:7	163
		20:46	206
28:19-20	136, 177–8, 186–7	22:32	134
28:20	32, 81, 102, 135, 179, 186	22:62	144

John

Mark		1:135-42	138
1:4	56, 62	3	207
1:7	62	3:30	62
1:7-8	58–9	8	207
1:16	137	18:17	134
5:21-43	154	18:25	134
6:14	53, 212	18:27	134
6:16	52	19:38	207
6:17-29	51–3	21:15-17	134
6:20	213		
6:25	53	*Acts*	
6:27	53	2:34-5	202
6:52	140	5:34	194
7	193	22:3	193
7:13	199		
7:24-30	127, 131	*Romans*	
11:25	114	10:9	109
12:34	202		
12:37-40	205	*1 Corinthians*	
12:38	206	12:3	109
12:38-9	206	15:13-14	179
12:39	206	15:17-18	179
14:71	143	15:25	202
16:7	134, 145		
		2 Corinthians	
Luke		4:5	109
1:26-38	29		

Hebrews
1:13	202
10:12-13	202

1 John
3:15	200

EARLY CHRISTIAN LITERATURE
Didache
3.2	201

Protevangelium of James
1:1–7:10	29
2:2-4	34
2:5	34
2:6	34
2:9	34
3:1-8	34
4:2	36
5:5–6:5	35
5:9	37
6:1-5	37
6:2-7	34
6:4	35
6:4-5	37
6:8	34
6:9	34
7:1-3	35
7:2	37
7:7	34
8:1-2	37
8:7-9	38
9:1	35
9:1-7	29
9:5-6	38
10:1	35
11:1-8	29
11:2	34
11:6	30
11:9	30
12:5	34
12:6	30
12:15	34
13:1	35
13:8	30
15:2	35
15:13	30
16:1	35
17:9	30
17:10	30
19	35
19-20	34
19:3	35
19:13-16	29
20:13-18	38
22:5-7	34

PHILO
Legatio ad Gaium
153–8	221

BABYLONIAN TALMUD
Sanhedrin
100	80

MISHNAH
Avot
1.4-14	194
1.15	74
4.5	74

Hagigah
2.2	194

Gittin
9.10	200

Sotah
3.4	194

TOSEFTA
Sotah
15.10-11	194

GREEK/ROMAN/CLASSICAL WORKS
Aristotle
Poetics
1–4	4
15	4

Politics
8	73

Cassius Dio
Roman History
60.31.8	51
60.32.4	51

60.35.1	49
60.33.6	50
61.2.1	50
62.14.1	51
66.9.2	50
66.17.2	50
67.3.2	51
67.12.2	50
67.14.4	50
67.15.6	50

Cicero
De invention rhetorica

1.25.36	86

Demetrius
De Elocutione

287–95	220
289	221
292	221
294	221

Dionysius Halicarnassensis
Ars rhetorica

8–11	220

Hermogenes
Περὶ εὑρέσεως

4.13	220

Josephus
Antiquities

1.154	84
13.173	193
13:297	193
14.403	42
15.231	211
16.392-4	211
17.187	211
18.15	193
18.118-19	48

Jewish War

1.181	42
1.429	84
2.119-66	193

Life of Josephus

191	194

Philo
De vita Mosis

1.6.25	86
1.6.28-9	86

Plutarch
Alcibiades

1.1	85, 88

Alexander

39.1	86

Pericles

3.2	85

Tiberius Gracchus

1.2	84

Quintilian
Institutio oratoria

9.2	220–1

Suetonius
Augustus

79.1	84

Domitian

10.4	51
14.1	50
16–17	50
16.1	50

Tacitus
Agricola

1.1	86
4	85
4.2-3	85
44-6	85

Annals

13.45	86

History

3.49	85

Index of Subjects

Abraham 10, 16–18, 27, 32, 56, 64, 83–85, 87–92, 94, 98, 101, 116, 197
Abrahamic 57, 197
abrogation 214, 219
accusation 45, 201, 216
adultery 19, 24–5, 51, 93, 200
Agricola 85, 88
Agrippina 50–1
Ahab 46, 68
Ahasuerus 46
Ahaz 95–6
Alcibiades 85, 88
Alexander and Aristobulus 47
Alexander the Great 86–7
ambiguity 23, 157, 194, 208, 216, 221
Ammiel 152
ancestral 176, 180, 182–3, 186, 188, 190
ancestry 57, 85, 88, 116
Andrew (Jesus' disciple) 138–9
angel 16–17, 20–1, 23, 29, 34, 37, 49, 102, 159, 161, 211
anoint 11, 16, 83, 93–4, 98–100, 102, 159–60, 168
antagonist 198, 207
Antioch 43, 165
Antipater I 42, 49
Antipater II 47
antithesis 25, 60, 78, 172–3
Antonius Primus 85
Antony 100
apostate 134, 142, 144, 147
Archelaus 22, 209, 212
arrest 51, 143, 159–60, 169, 172, 196–8, 212–13, 215, 219
Assyria 95
astrologer 47, 49–50, 52, 210–11
audience 4, 6, 19, 41, 46–9, 65, 72, 75, 77, 81–2, 149–50, 155, 169, 172, 176–7, 181–2, 184, 189, 196, 200, 210
    implied audience 77, 81–2, 195, 206
    intended audience 101, 181, 205

auditor 135, 137
author 1, 3–4, 21, 32, 34, 49, 74, 82, 101, 106, 116–17, 124, 150, 164, 175–7, 181, 187–9, 191, 197–8, 208, 210, 215
    implied author 2–3, 9, 100, 124, 130, 135
authority 11, 31, 43–5, 52–3, 55, 61, 67, 77, 79–82, 87, 107, 110, 119, 122–3, 127–9, 154, 158, 161–2, 167, 171–2, 183, 198–9, 202–4, 206, 208, 210–12, 217–18

Babylonian deportation 32, 93–4, 98
Babylonian exile 56, 93
Babylonian Talmud 80
Balaam 43, 65, 97
Balak of Moab 43, 46
banquet 46, 206
    (see also "feast")
baptism 55, 57–9, 61–3, 67, 109, 186, 188, 196
baptize 11, 55, 57–9, 62, 81, 86–7, 135
Barabbas 169, 172, 216–17
Bathsheba 32, 92–3, 151–3, 161
Beelzebul 167–8
behavior 26, 77, 121–2, 141, 158, 171–2, 179, 189, 198, 205, 214, 219–20
behead 46, 48, 52, 215
    (see also "decapitate")
beloved (see "love")
Berenice 48–9
Bethlehem 10, 16, 23, 53, 85, 92, 97–9, 183, 210–12, 219
birthday 51, 65, 213–14, 219
blessing 37, 56–7, 92, 184, 186
blind 98–9, 128, 154, 158–9, 167, 171–2, 174, 204
blood 33, 45, 47, 62, 67–8, 92–4, 97–100, 105, 109, 172, 201, 217–18
boat 141, 167

Boaz 91
brood of vipers 58, 65, 67, 105, 196
brother 15, 26, 47–9, 51, 93–4, 104–5, 109–10, 134, 138–9, 145, 152, 155, 201, 212–13, 219
burial 99, 159–62

Caesarea Philippi 109
Caligula 48, 221
Canaanite woman 11, 98–100, 127–8, 131, 152, 156–8, 175, 184
Capernaum 59, 125–6, 182
cardinal directions 189
Cato 86
celestial 177, 183
centurion 11, 119–21, 123–31, 154, 175, 183–4
character 1, 3–13, 15–16, 18, 20–3
    flat character 5, 9–11, 22, 120–21, 131, 148, 176, 180, 191
    minor character 11, 13, 22, 149–50, 209
    round character 5, 9, 148, 176, 191
character analysis 4, 6–7, 9–10, 86, 147, 209
characterization 5, 9–10, 15–19, 21–5, 30, 34, 39, 45, 47, 55, 57, 59, 61–3, 65–8, 71–2, 74, 79, 81, 83–4, 87–8, 100–1, 106, 108, 111, 115–17, 120–1, 124–5, 130, 146–7, 150, 153, 158, 162–3, 169, 173–4, 180–1, 209–10, 212, 215–16, 218–20, 222
    direct characterization 18, 21, 88, 124, 130
    indirect characterization 21, 111
characterize 18, 24, 60–1, 66, 68, 81–2, 88, 96, 101, 106, 108, 110, 140, 152, 158, 164, 215, 217–18, 220
chiasm 111, 113–14, 116
chief priest (see "priest")
chorus 64, 141, 163
Christ 42, 57, 63, 83, 85, 88, 91, 93–8, 100, 141, 217
Christian 10, 44–5, 48, 68–9, 102, 134, 173, 185, 192, 200, 202, 210, 213–14, 222
Christology 55–6, 59, 62, 64, 66, 69, 87, 108, 117, 141, 146, 156, 167, 171, 174, 200
church 8, 12, 59, 77, 81, 134, 145, 147
Cicero 86, 164
circumcision 186, 188

city 11, 16, 157, 166, 169, 175, 182, 187–8, 201, 211, 217
Claudius 49–51
Cleopatra VII 49
client 72, 210, 214, 222
cloud 38–9, 61
cognitive understanding 71–2, 74–7, 82
command 21–2, 41, 78, 81, 136, 140–1, 175
command-execution (see "execution")
commandment 75–6, 81, 104, 198, 201–2
commission 17, 81, 116, 159, 161–2, 186
compassion 166, 186, 188, 190
compliance 122, 126–8
confess 82, 141, 147–8
confession 107–9, 141, 167
conflict 1, 91, 98, 100, 122–3, 148, 192, 194–7, 199, 201, 204
control 2, 11, 30, 34, 36–7, 39, 44, 51, 72, 80, 86, 89, 102, 121–3, 126, 127, 131, 173, 190
    control attempt 122–4, 126–31
    counter-control attempt 122–4, 127–31
controversy 60, 78, 158, 199, 204
corporate 12, 140, 149–50, 153, 162–4, 166, 169, 174
cosmic 44, 175–7, 186, 190
covenant 26, 57, 62, 64–5, 87, 187
cross 11, 69, 100, 154, 159–60, 171
crowd 6, 8, 12, 26, 45, 51, 66–7, 77, 80, 99, 104, 119, 156, 163–74, 204, 216–17
crucifixion 12, 45, 65, 69, 149, 159–61, 169
Cyrus 46

dance 37, 51, 53, 214, 219
daughter 33, 36–7, 46, 51, 99, 104, 128, 152–7, 184, 214
    stepdaughter 214–15, 219
David 10, 16–17, 26–7, 32, 42–3, 53, 56, 64, 85, 88, 90–5, 98–100, 152, 166, 168, 202
decapitate 47, 51
    (see also "behead")
Decapolis 165
decision 9, 35, 58, 72, 77, 122, 217
deed 11, 17, 63, 69, 76–7, 79, 81–2, 86–7, 94, 102, 105, 167, 172, 180, 182, 206, 212
demon 184, 188
demoniac 167
denial 109, 134, 141–5, 147

Index of Subjects

depravity 88, 100
devil 5, 188
didactic 79, 80, 82, 135
disciple 1, 7–8, 11–12, 24, 26, 41, 63, 66, 77,
    81, 99, 102, 104, 106–9, 115–16, 119,
    131, 134–48, 150, 152, 154–5,
    157–62, 164, 166–7, 169–75, 182–3,
    186, 188, 195, 197–8, 203, 207–8
discipleship 8, 12, 62–4, 68–9, 77, 80–1,
    102, 117, 146–8, 153–60, 162, 171
discourse 2, 7, 76, 79, 135, 156, 172, 188,
    200, 205
disease 153–4, 166
disempower 126, 128, 130–1
disobedience (see "obedience")
dispute 195, 199–200, 202, 207
divine 10, 23–4, 26, 30–1, 33–6, 38–9, 61,
    64, 87, 101–2, 106–11, 115–17, 127,
    139–41, 168, 176, 181, 196, 202
    divine judgment 109, 177, 186–7
    divine will 8, 10, 16, 22, 24, 27, 36
divorce 19, 20, 22, 25–7, 51, 78, 131, 156,
    195, 200, 207
Domitian 49–53, 222
dream 10, 16, 18, 21, 23, 26, 31, 34, 45, 87,
    102, 211

ecclesia 133, 136, 147
education 4, 72–4, 86, 94, 220
elder 45, 99, 146, 169, 172–3, 180, 198, 204,
    215–8
Eliam 152
Elijah 46, 64–6, 68
Emmanuel 31–3, 43, 58, 85, 95, 102
empire 183, 220
    Roman Empire 4, 49, 52, 65, 127, 183
empower 12, 128, 131, 171
enslave (see "slave")
enthrone 177, 184, 186
Epicurean 193
erotic 214, 219
eschatological 31, 55, 58, 66, 75–6, 143–4,
    146, 188
Essene 193
ethical action 71–2, 74–7, 79, 82, 45, 47
ethics 21, 200
ethnic 41–3, 125, 131, 153, 166, 177, 182,
    184, 187–8
ethos 198

eunuch 26
evil 66, 85, 93, 104, 106–7, 173, 176, 180,
    182, 207, 216–17
execution 8, 44–5, 47–8, 51, 197–8, 212–13,
    215, 218–20
    command-execution 21–2
exorcism 166, 184
extremist 193–4

fairy tale 5–6
faith 11, 63, 78, 91
faithful 7, 10, 12, 15–16, 18, 22–3, 27, 33,
    43–4, 49, 62–3, 90–2, 98, 104, 108,
    128, 130–1, 140, 150, 161–2, 175
false disciple 12, 134, 142, 145–8
father 5, 11, 15–18, 20–1, 24, 26, 33, 42, 49,
    66–7, 73, 88, 92, 100, 102, 104–12,
    115–17, 141, 155, 157, 193, 204, 206,
    212
feast 64
    (see also "banquet")
    parable of the wedding feast (see
    "parable")
feed 106, 166, 168, 171
feet 90, 99, 202
feminist 29, 39
fig tree 167
figured speech 220–2
filial 108–10, 116–17
final judgment 108, 187
fish 107, 139–40, 171
fisher 137, 139, 145
flashback 45, 51, 212
flat character (see "character")
flatten (of characters) 11, 120–1, 131
Flavian dynasty 48–9
focalize 2, 20, 137
folklore 46–9, 52
fool 77, 194, 214–18
forgive 32, 58, 62, 87, 107, 110, 145, 166, 185
Fourth Philosophy 193
fringes 206
fruit 12, 42, 57–8, 60, 76, 196, 198, 204
fulfillment 22, 26, 31, 57–9, 91, 139, 212

Gaius Caligula (see "Caligula")
Galilee 12, 15, 21, 23, 27, 60, 86, 125, 137,
    144–5, 159, 161, 165, 168–9, 175,
    194, 197, 203, 205, 212

garment 155, 206
Gehenna 67
genealogy 10, 12, 15–17, 19, 31–3, 35, 41, 43, 56–7, 64, 83–4, 88–96, 98–100, 102, 151–3, 157, 161–2, 189
generosity 41, 77, 86, 94, 100, 108, 188, 216
genre 1, 5, 7, 84, 199, 203
gentile 3, 15, 17, 27, 33, 41–3, 45–6, 52, 91–2, 96–7, 99, 107, 119–20, 125, 128, 130–1, 145, 165, 175, 177–90
Gethsemane 143, 159, 169, 172
girl 143, 214
glorification 167
glory 38, 107–8
Gracchi 84, 86
grammar 4, 19, 73
grief 144, 215
guest 214–15, 217

halakha 194–5, 199–200
Hasmonean 47
head 38, 47, 51, 85, 99, 160, 215
heal 8, 11, 12, 60, 63, 78, 99, 119, 126–9, 131, 153–4, 157–8, 166–7, 171, 184, 188, 199–200
Helvidius Priscus 51
Herod Agrippa I 125
Herod Agrippa II 48
Herod Antipas 10, 12–13, 45–8, 51–3, 60, 65, 68, 125–6, 197, 209, 212–15, 217–20, 222
Herod the Great 10–13, 18, 22–3, 34, 41–3, 45–9, 53, 57, 64–5, 83, 85, 91, 96–100, 125, 183, 196, 209–12, 218–20, 222
Herodian 48–9, 53, 214, 220, 222
  Herodian kings 45, 47, 49, 52
Herodias 46, 48, 51, 68, 156, 212–13
Hezekiah 95
hidden 31–2, 65–6, 85, 115, 220
high priest (see "priest")
Hillel 195
Hillelite 200
holiness 102, 107
holy 35, 37–8, 57, 101, 107, 116, 183, 213
Holy Spirit 18, 20, 25, 33, 59, 85, 95, 102
Hosanna 138
hostile 97, 169, 199
house 36, 38, 42, 49, 92–3, 95, 99, 105, 154, 160, 195, 198, 204

house of Israel 92–4, 139, 165–6, 168, 171
house of Judah 93–5
parable of the two houses (see "parable")
husband 10, 16–19, 33, 51, 90, 185

ideal reader (see "reader")
identity 5, 12, 38, 41, 51, 65–6, 68–9, 79, 82, 102, 108–11, 116–17, 119, 150–2, 155–8, 160–2, 165, 167–9, 173–4, 203, 208, 212, 215
illegal (see "legal")
illness 167
  (see also "sickness")
imitation 4, 102, 107, 117, 159, 160
immoral (see "moral")
implied audience (see "audience")
implied author (see "author")
implied reader (see "reader")
imprison (see "prison")
in-group 182, 184
incest 214, 219
injustice 213, 216–17
innocent 45–7, 87, 93–4, 98–9, 211, 216–18, 220
insider 180–1
intended audience (see "audience")
Isaac 17, 101

Jacob (of Genesis) 43, 90, 96–7, 99, 101
Jechoniah 93–4
Jericho 91, 97, 158
Jesse 65, 92
Jezebel 46, 68, 157
John the Baptist 10–12, 36, 45–6, 48, 51–2, 55–69, 86–7, 154, 156, 168, 196, 212–13, 215, 219
Jonah 109, 181
Jordan 11–12, 65, 86–7, 91, 165
Joseph (of Genesis) 18
Joseph, husband of Mary 10, 15–27, 29, 31, 33–4, 38, 56, 95, 105, 159, 161,
Joseph of Arimathea 207
Judah 16, 89–100
Judaism 72, 106, 108, 192, 195
Judas (brother of Jesus) 105
Judas Iscariot 134, 142, 144, 146–7, 160, 206, 215–16
Judea 23, 57–9, 165, 212

judgment 58–9, 63, 67, 89, 108–9, 139, 146, 177, 185–7
justice 79, 180, 185–6, 188, 190, 197, 217–20

keys 8, 11, 146
kill 23, 44, 46, 49–50, 61, 67–8, 83, 91–3, 97, 99, 160, 183, 185, 189, 201, 211–13, 215
Kingdom of Heaven 8, 11–12, 24–6, 57–8, 60, 65–6, 71, 73, 75–6, 107, 146, 171, 175–6, 181–2, 186, 188, 198, 202–4
kneel 96–7, 99, 127, 158

lament 73, 96, 98, 144, 205
lawful 86, 182–3, 198, 200
　unlawful 213
legal 15, 17, 19–20, 195, 198–201, 204, 208, 218
　illegal 213–14
legion 44, 48–9, 125, 130
literary-critical method (see "method")
Lollia Paulina 51
Lord's Prayer 111, 114–6
Lord's Virgin 35–40
love 37, 85, 104, 107, 134, 198, 201–2, 206
　beloved 116, 119
lovely 85, 88
lover 129
loyalty 49, 105, 175, 215
Lucius Lamia Aelianus 51

magi 15, 21, 23, 34, 41–3, 45, 49, 83, 85, 96–7, 99–100, 183–4, 219
manipulate 46, 51, 172–3, 218
margin 11, 44, 55, 64–6, 68–9, 76, 183–4
Mariamne 47
Markan 55, 58, 114, 137, 140, 142, 206, 213, 219
marriage 19–21, 23–6, 29, 38, 46–9, 51–2, 90, 213–14
Mary (mother of Jesus) 10–11, 15–25, 29–40, 89, 95, 105, 150–3, 159, 161
Mary Magdalene 159, 161
mercy 19–20, 25, 27, 98, 107–8, 152, 186
Messiah 15–16, 22–3, 27, 32–3, 36, 39, 56–7, 60, 62, 69, 80, 102, 104, 107–9, 111, 115–17, 152, 167, 171, 176–7, 181–7, 189–90, 202, 204, 206–7, 211–12, 218

messianic 17, 33, 56, 63, 65, 102, 109–10, 116, 149, 151–4, 156–7, 161, 168, 173–4, 177, 185, 187, 200, 202, 207–8, 215–6
method 2, 6, 33, 82, 111, 133, 135–6
　literary-critical method 2–3, 7, 9
ministry 1, 8, 26, 37, 55–6, 58–61, 63–4, 68, 76, 78, 81, 108, 125, 136, 149–55, 157–60, 162, 166, 171
minor character (see "character")
miracle 35, 63, 154, 166, 212
moon 50–1
moral 4, 19, 86, 100, 152, 200, 217
　immoral 215, 219
Mosaic law 43, 75, 78, 198, 207
Moses 18, 46, 72, 74, 76, 78–9, 81–2, 86–7, 91, 97, 193, 198–9, 206
mother 10, 15, 17–18, 26, 30, 32–4, 36, 38–9, 42, 47, 50–1, 73, 85–6, 91, 97–8, 104–5, 109, 155–6, 158–9, 161, 214
mother-in-law 104, 152–6
mountain 57, 78, 128, 171
murder 41–2, 46–7, 51, 67, 80, 105, 156, 183, 200–1, 207, 218–19
mute 154, 167

narrative analogy 150
narrative criticism 3, 6, 8, 74, 119, 135, 209
narratology 7, 69, 199
narrator 2–3, 9, 18, 20, 22, 24, 42, 77, 86–7, 89–90, 92–100, 124, 130, 136–7, 139, 146, 176–7, 181, 184, 187, 189, 204, 210
Nazareth 1, 11, 15, 22–3, 57, 60–1, 65, 87, 102, 136, 168, 212, 215
negative 8, 23, 102, 105, 123, 147–8, 155–8, 169–70, 173, 175–6, 182, 187, 193, 196, 200, 207, 213, 218, 220
Nero 50–1, 222
Nerva 50–1
Nicodemus 207
Niece 47, 51–3
Nineveh 181

oath 51, 143, 214–15
obedience 8, 10, 16, 19, 21–3, 26–7, 39, 60, 64, 77, 100, 102, 104, 107–9, 137, 140, 167, 198
　disobedience 91, 171

obeisance 96–7, 99, 175
offense 105, 199, 221
offensive 101, 184, 214
opponent 3, 46, 105, 109, 195, 204, 207, 215
outsider 77, 154, 180, 184, 186, 212

parable 67, 75, 150, 156, 166, 170, 203–4, 207
   parable of the bridesmaids 76
   parable of the scribe 207
   parable of the sheep and goats 74, 110
   parable of the sower 76, 108, 145
   parable of the two houses 75, 198, 204
   parable of the two sons 61
   parable of the wedding feast 67
   parable of the wicked tenants 61, 67, 204
parallel 3, 17–18, 36, 43, 55, 58–60, 62, 64, 78, 82, 108, 111–14, 126, 155, 157, 168, 213, 218
paralyze 128, 167
paranoia 41, 46–7, 50, 52, 211–12, 219
party 65, 214
passion (character trait) 94, 100
passion (of Jesus) 7, 22, 25, 141, 147, 158–60, 162, 164, 166, 169, 196–7
Paul 55, 187, 193
Pauline theology 109
Perez 92
Pericles 85, 88, 100
persecute 24–5, 64, 66–7, 107, 142, 147, 169, 189
Peter 8, 11–12, 109, 133–5, 137–48, 152–6, 199
Pharaoh (of Exodus) 23, 42–3, 46, 57, 91
Pharisaic 172, 194–5, 197, 199–201, 203–4, 206–8
Pharisee 12, 24–6, 44, 60, 66, 73–4, 76, 78–81, 105, 119, 154, 164, 167–8, 172–4, 181, 191–208
Philo 86–7, 221
philosopher 218–19
philosophy 2, 73, 85, 193, 219
phraseology 111, 195
phylactery 206
polemic 6, 133, 147, 192, 205, 207–8
pollution 45, 176, 185, 216
Pontius Pilate 12–13, 45, 87, 169, 172, 185, 209, 215–18, 220
Pontius Pilate's wife 45, 87, 185
Poppaea 86, 88

positive 4, 8, 23, 29, 39, 41–3, 64, 123, 126, 129–31, 137–8, 140, 148, 152, 156–60, 169–72, 176, 181–2, 184, 200, 202, 204, 216
power 11, 17, 31, 44–5, 47–8, 50, 55, 73, 80, 89, 105, 109, 121–4, 126–31, 149, 175, 182, 189, 194, 198, 211–12, 214, 219
   power dynamics 121, 123–4
powerless 126–9, 131, 220
predict 50, 58–9, 65, 104, 139, 143, 176, 191
prediction 50, 59, 66, 68, 144, 146, 160
priest 34, 37–8, 78, 192
   chief priest 45, 99, 169, 173, 180, 183, 185, 192, 196, 204–5, 207, 211, 215–8
   high priest 34, 38, 172, 196–7, 216
priestly 37–8, 193
prison 60, 64, 147, 213
   imprison 212–13, 219
prisoner 169, 216, 217
progymnasmata 4, 86
promise 31–2, 36, 53, 56, 61, 83, 88, 90–100, 108, 144, 146, 214, 217
prophet 11, 22, 31, 35–6, 44, 46, 57, 61–2, 64, 66–9, 80, 95, 97, 101, 105, 139, 168, 171, 173, 188, 202, 213, 215
proselyte 117, 187
prostitute 91
prostrate 183–4
protagonist 6, 10, 32, 34, 39–40, 82, 177, 181–3, 187, 189
public 4, 11, 19–20, 24, 45, 47–8, 51–2, 55, 59, 64, 80, 99, 136, 143, 155, 171, 203, 206, 220
purity 34–5, 38, 156, 193, 195, 199–201
Pythagoreans 193

rabbi 80, 194–5, 206, 213
   Rabbi Akiva 195
   Rabbi Ishmael 74
   Rabbi Yoshua 194
rabbinic 74, 79, 81, 90, 186, 194–5, 199–201, 203, 205–8
Rachel 11, 53, 83–4, 92, 95–100
Rahab 11, 32, 90–1, 94–5, 97, 99–100, 151–3, 157, 161
Ramah 96–8
reader 1–3, 5–6, 9, 12–13, 16–8, 20–1, 23–6, 30, 42, 53, 56–7, 62, 64, 68–9, 89, 91, 94–5, 97, 100–1, 108, 110,

117, 124, 127, 130, 134–9, 141,
    145–7, 174, 184, 191, 197, 198,
    202–3, 208, 210–16, 222
  ideal reader 19, 65
  implied reader 16, 20–1, 24, 26, 77, 99,
    135–7, 191, 202, 208
rebuke 65–6, 99, 141, 156, 158, 160, 202
Red Sea 57, 91
redact 112, 114, 116, 135, 213
reform 185, 187
repeat 12, 26, 63, 94, 116, 143, 155, 157,
    160, 163, 168, 174, 184, 199, 204
repent 55, 57–60, 62–3, 69, 87, 134, 137,
    142, 144–8, 181–2, 187, 196–7, 215
repetition 93, 136, 170, 191, 207
reputation 126, 166, 197, 210–11, 213, 215
resist 131, 192, 196, 217
resistance 91, 220
restoration 56, 59, 63, 144–5, 149–50,
    153–8, 162, 189
resurrect 1, 151, 159, 161–2
resurrection 134, 136, 149, 159, 161–2,
    176–7, 185–7, 193, 197, 202
rhetoric 2–4, 30, 73, 110, 116, 120, 176,
    181–3, 187, 195–7, 199, 200, 202–5,
    207–8, 220–1
right hand 110, 202
righteous 10–11, 15–6, 18–21, 24–5, 27,
    57, 61, 64, 67–8, 87, 107–8, 152, 181,
    185, 190, 198, 208, 213, 216, 219–20
rinse 199–200
risen (from the dead) 159, 169, 212
ritual 35, 38, 186–7
robes 60, 206
rock 45, 75, 134, 137, 143, 145
  rocky 134, 142–4
Roman Empire (see "empire")
Rome 11–12, 44–5, 48–50, 53, 65, 183, 212,
    214–15, 217
round character (see "character")
Rubellius Plautus 51
ruler 16, 22, 50, 90, 168, 177, 183, 186,
    209–10, 212–13, 218–22
Ruth 11, 32, 91–5, 97, 99–100, 151–3, 161

sabbath 195, 198–201, 204, 207
sacrifice 8, 37, 39, 62, 149–50, 158, 160,
    176, 185
Sadducee 12, 44, 60, 192–3, 196–8, 202–3, 207

sage 68, 194
Salman 90
salvation 36–7, 39, 55–9, 64, 66, 102, 140,
    144, 156, 184, 186
Sarah 89
Satan 8, 141–2
satire 4, 47, 52–3, 218
save 33, 56, 58, 62, 91, 102, 140, 155, 176
saying 30–1, 34, 50, 57, 68, 86–7, 97, 102,
    163, 167, 173, 196–9, 203–5
scribe 24–5, 65–6, 68, 73–4, 76, 79–81, 136,
    172–3, 180–1, 183, 192–3, 196–9,
    202, 204–8, 211
scripture 11, 26, 57, 59, 62–6, 76, 83–4, 89,
    94–6, 98, 100–1, 147, 151, 157, 181,
    183, 188, 194–5, 200, 202–3, 208,
    212
sea 140, 145, 167
  Sea of Galilee 137
  See also "Red Sea"
Second Temple (see "temple")
sectarian 202, 208
separatist 193–4
Sermon on the Mount 24, 30–1, 64, 66,
    74–6, 78, 109, 111–12, 114–16, 198,
    200, 204
servant 61, 67, 119, 126, 128–31, 143
sexual 21–2, 33, 35, 38, 48, 51, 129, 214, 219
shame 18–20, 24–5, 182, 187, 221
Shammai 74, 195, 200
sheep 139, 144, 165–6, 168, 171, 199
  parable of the sheep and goats (see
    'parable')
shepherd 16, 166, 168, 171, 174,
sickness 153–4, 166, 199
  (see also "illness")
Simon (the disciple) 105, 109, 137–8,
Simon the leper 99, 160
Sinai 57, 187
sinner 33, 85, 152, 163, 198–9
slave 67, 153–4
  enslave 42, 44
Sodom and Gomorrah 182
Solomon 42–3, 92, 152
son 10–11, 15, 17–18, 20–1, 23, 26, 31,
    33–4, 39, 47, 49, 51, 53, 61, 67–8,
    73, 89, 90–3, 95, 100, 102, 104–5,
    107, 109–11, 116, 129, 156, 158–9,
    172, 197, 202, 211–12, 220

son of Abraham 16–17, 83, 85, 88, 89, 92, 94, 98, 116
Son of David 16, 26, 42, 83, 85, 88–9, 91–6, 98–100, 116, 157, 167–8, 171, 174, 202
Son of God 11, 57, 117, 141, 167, 171
Son of Man 68, 108, 145, 154, 158
sonship 100, 110, 141
See also "Zebedee's sons"
sovereignty 91, 97, 99–100, 102
spatial 20, 111, 137, 162, 198–9
spiritual 102, 108, 111, 115, 117, 156
star 43, 49–50, 65, 96–7, 211
stepdaughter (see "daughter")
stone 107, 142–3, 197
structuralism 2, 6
structure 7, 23, 32–3, 56, 59, 96, 111–12, 114–16, 135, 153, 159–60, 175, 188–9, 205
submission 127, 182
submissive 34, 39
suffer 4, 18, 44, 57, 60, 68–9, 76, 87, 154, 177, 186, 189
suicide 142, 220
synagogue 68, 105, 153, 166, 204–6
synoptic 1, 3, 112–14, 154, 158, 192, 197, 203

tabernacle 38–9
Tamar 11, 32, 84, 89–98, 100, 151–3, 161
Tarquinius Superbus 218
tassel 206
tax collector 198, 199
teach 8, 10–11, 16, 21, 23–7, 55, 57, 60–7, 71–82, 105, 135, 153, 156, 166–7, 170, 172–3, 186, 192–3, 195–6, 198, 200–1, 203–7
teacher 4, 7, 11, 71–82, 193–4, 199, 202–3, 206–7
teeth 51, 144
temple 30, 34, 36–9, 42, 44–5, 48–9, 61, 169, 176, 185, 193–4, 197, 205, 221–2
Second Temple 72, 90, 193, 202, 208
tetrarch 212, 219
Titus 48–9, 222
tomb 67, 100, 134, 144–5, 159, 161, 173
Torah 15–16, 20, 27, 74, 173, 193, 213–14, 218

tragedy 4
trait 6–9, 16, 18–22, 25, 83, 87, 94, 120, 131, 137, 148, 152, 164, 175, 220
transfiguration 68, 109, 171
treasure 65, 82, 104
trial 8, 169, 172, 196, 215
triumphal entry 61, 156, 168–9
trope 46–8, 52, 121, 210, 214, 219–20
the Twelve (Disciples) 8, 60, 68, 143, 164
twelve tribes of Israel 93, 146, 165
tyrant 10, 210, 218–22

unlawful (see "lawful")
unparalleled 35, 38–40
unpredictable 148
Uriah 11, 32, 92–5, 97–8, 100, 151–2

Vespasian 48–50, 222
virgin 30–3, 35–40, 95
vocative 110–11, 114–16
voice 17, 34, 39, 57–9, 63, 95–7, 100, 109–10, 116, 136, 141, 159, 176, 213

warning 12, 23–4, 45, 57, 64, 108, 143, 172, 174–5, 181, 192, 196, 198, 211
wash 45, 198, 200, 216–18
water 12, 57, 59, 140, 145, 167, 186–7
wedding 64, 67, 91
weep 53, 83, 96–100, 144
wheat 59, 108, 145
wife 11, 17–20, 22, 25–6, 32–3, 38, 45, 47–8, 51, 87, 90, 92–5, 97, 100, 185, 200, 212–14, 216, 219
wilderness 11, 38, 43, 56–9, 65–6, 69
willingness 47, 77, 186, 203, 206, 211
wind 95, 140–1, 167
wisdom 17, 75, 77, 105, 181, 188
woe 205
woman 11–12, 29, 32–5, 37, 39, 46, 51, 64–5, 83–4, 86, 89–92, 94–6, 98–100, 127–8, 131, 149–62, 175, 184, 188, 194, 221
womb 33–4, 36, 38
worship 42, 101, 140–1, 167, 185, 188, 210

Zebedee's sons 102, 156, 158–9, 161